RALLY YEARBOOK
World Rally Championship
2008

CHRONOSPORTS
EDITEUR

DPPI Photographers
François Baudin, Jorge Cunha, Thierry Delaunay, François Flamand, Alexandre Guillaumot, Andre Lavadinho, Frédéric Le Floc'h and Claude Saulnier.

ISBN 978-2-84707-156-6

For the french edition "L'Année Rallyes 2008"
ISBN 978-2-84707-149-8

© December 2008, Chronosports S.A.
Le Vergnolet Parc, 8
CH-1070 Puidoux, Switzerland.
Tel.: +41 (0)21 694 24 44
Fax: +41 (0)21 694 24 46
E-mail: info@chronosports.com
Internet: www.chronosports.com

Printed by Imprimerie Clerc, 18206 St-Amand-Montrond, France
Bound by Reliures Brun, 45331 Malesherbes, France.
Clerc s.a.s. & Reliures Brun are both Qualibris companies.

All rights reserved. No part of this publication may be reproduced, stored in a retrieval system, or transmitted in any form or by any means, electronic, mechanical, photocopying, recording or otherwise, without the prior written permission of the publishers.

RALLY YEARBOOK
World Rally Championship

2008

Photos
DPPI

Authors
Jérôme Bourret - Philippe Joubin
"L'Equipe"

Translated from french by
Stuart Sykes

Artistic Director, coordination & Page Layout
Cyril Davillerd

Results
Loraine Lequint Elsig
& Sidonie Perrin

FOREWORDS

Sébastien Loeb

Once again it falls to me to write the Foreword to this book – for the fifth time in a row. It's a task I'm more than happy to undertake, since it means that's the number of world titles we have taken now.

Of course the first one will always have a special feeling about, simply because it was the first. But still I am very proud to have won a fifth this year. While I am not really one for figures, I am happy to own the two records which, to me, mean most: the number of victories and the number of titles.

It's often said that the hardest thing is not getting to the summit, it's staying there. So taking five titles is a performance to be proud of, and I owe it in large part to the whole Citroën team. Whether with the Xsara or the C4, with Guy Fréquelin or Olivier Quesnel, the guys at Citroën Sport have always given me reliable, efficient cars ever since I came into the World Championship, and that's something few drivers before me have ever enjoyed. It really is something to have achieved such consistent excellence, and of course we plan to keep the run going. Just like signing this Foreword, winning is a good habit and one I have no intention of giving up!

Daniel Elena

That's right, here we are again! I do hope you are not getting too tired of reading what we have to say, because we're certainly not getting tired of winning titles. And now we are out on our own in the rally world, at the very top of our sport. But it's simply not possible to draw comparisons with the Munaris, Kankkunens and Mäkinens: they weren't in the same cars, they didn't have the same opposition to contend with. All we can say is that we are the best of our generation, the generation of the 2000's, and that in itself is something we can take great pride in – because we have had some fierce rivals of our own.

This year's title wasn't any easier to win than the four before it. We handicapped ourselves from the start in Sweden and Jordan and we had to go flat out all year to make up that 20-point deficit. I can assure you that they were going fast out there: when it comes to sheer pace, Hirvonen and Latvala are in the Grönholm class and we really had to chase them hard.

I would like to take advantage of this Foreword to thank the whole Citroën team, all the people who helped give us our start in rallying a decade ago, and my wife for her unending patience, because we don't get to spend much time at home.

Now bring on 2009! We've finished counting on the fingers of one hand – and now it's time to start the other one!

CONTENTS

4	Forewords by Sébastien Loeb and Daniel Elena
8	Season Review
14	Teams and Drivers
27	Junior and Production Championships
28	The Young Ones
32	Loeb: the legend grows
38	Christian Loriaux: 'It'll pay off in the long run'
42	IRC: Getting some of their own back
46	Portfolios
52	2008 FIA World Rally Championship
54	01 Monte Carlo
62	02 Sweden
70	03 Mexico
78	04 Argentina
86	05 Jordan
94	06 Italy
102	07 Greece
110	08 Turkey
118	09 Finland
126	10 Germany
134	11 New Zealand
142	12 Spain
150	13 France
158	14 Japan
166	15 Great Britain
174	The 2008 FIA World Rally Championships
176	Statistics

2008 FIA WRC
Season Review

Loeb casts a giant shadow
Sébastien Loeb could write the book of rallying records all on his own – he owns virtually all of them, from most world titles to most World Championship rally wins, number of wins in a season, successive wins and podiums, wins on the same event and ratio of podiums to starts! End of discussion: the French driver really is the greatest there has ever been.

↗ Season Review

1 | Sébastien Loeb

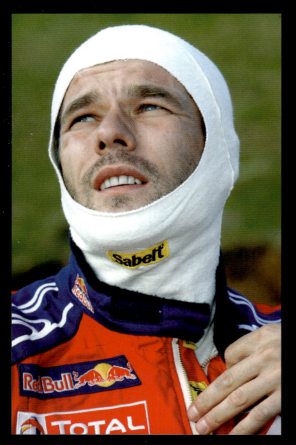

Sébastien Loeb is now out on his own: the only driver in the sport's history to have taken five world titles, and, what's more, five in a row. It's a feat that few sportsmen in any discipline have ever achieved. Like Michael Schumacher, Lance Armstrong, Michael Phelps, Pete Sampras, Valentino Rossi, Sergei Bubka, Carl Lewis and Michael Jordan before him, Loeb appears to be invincible. Unquestionably, he is the best driver of his generation; and there is little room for debate as to whether he is the most gifted of all time.

The figures speak for themselves. The Frenchman came onto the world scene with Citroën in 2002 and promptly put the rest of them to the sword: runner-up in 2003, title-winner in 2004, 2005, 2006, 2007 and 2008, 73 podiums including 47 World Championship wins in 101 starts, over 500 stage wins, the record for most wins (11) and podiums (13) in a season and the most consecutive wins (6).

In a seven-year period, Loeb has won as many rallies as Sainz and Auriol did between them in their own prolific careers. As many as Kankkunen and Mäkinen, too, and now he has gone past their number of world titles. Not much of a record, is it?

The facts also suggest Loeb really is the best of all time, quite simply because he has taken on and beaten a number of other men who might be candidates for that title. Before heading off into retirement, Mäkinen, Grönholm, Burns, McRae and Sainz all faced Loeb in cars that were as quick as his Citroën. He beat them all, the last two as early as 2003, in Xsaras that were identical to the Frenchman's.

And should there still be any doubters, Loeb's own toughest rivals acknowledge that he is the best, the crème de la crème, or, as the British put it, 'the best of the best', as they desperately cast around for a new star after the tragic loss of both Burns and McRae. "He is the greatest there has ever been," insists double World Champion Marcus Grönholm, a man whose 19-year World Championship career saw him come up against nine former champions. "I've competed against a lot of other drivers and Seb is the quickest of them all. There's never been such a quick driver who scored such good results: Tommi Mäkinen was very quick on a number of events, but he also tended to go off a lot. Colin had one very quick season, then wasn't as quick in the three that followed. Richard Burns was good, but not in the same class as Sébastien. Carlos Sainz and Juha Kankkunen were both very good but for me, no problem – Loeb's the best." And that says it all.

Like other great sportsmen who were dominant over a period of years, Loeb makes the extraordinary seem quite normal. And the fact that title number five came in a season where he was more dominant than ever, with 11 wins from 15 starts, simply underlines the impression that it all comes easily to the Frenchman – that it's no contest. But Sordo, Latvala and Hirvonen all showed they could, if the circumstances were right, give the Maestro a little nudge.

Sordo may not have a win on his own record yet, but he often brought the best out of Loeb on tarmac. In Sweden, Latvala became the youngest-ever winner of a World Championship rally, at just 22 and 10 months. He's neither the all-rounder nor the supremely consistent driver that Loeb is yet, but he's got the same kind of speed – even more, when the going is quick, as Loeb himself has acknowledged. Mikko Hirvonen is just the opposite: a winner in Jordan, Turkey and Japan, in the top five in every rally of the year, a podium finisher on 11 occasions, the man who finished 2008 as runner-up to Loeb goes off very rarely and he's quick everywhere. But when you're trying to keep up with a five-time World Champion, quick isn't enough: you need to be very, very quick, and that's where Hirvonen falls short.

2 | Mikko Hirvonen

Season Review

4 | Jari-Matti Latvala

6 | Petter Solberg

5 | Chris Atkinson

3 | Daniel Sordo

Against those three fast guys, and against Atkinson and Solberg too on the rare occasions when their Subarus allowed them to show what they could do, Loeb had to bring out the big guns, especially after a rather chaotic start to the season. He went off in the Swedish snow (the Frenchman's only bad habit), then had a collision on the road in Jordan, which put him five points adrift of Hirvonen despite his wins on the Monte, in Mexico and Argentina. But that's as far ahead as the Finn ever got. Wins in Sardinia and Greece put Loeb back in front, but the tit-for-tat continued in Turkey when a Ford 1-2 made it advantage Hirvonen again. Loeb promptly went into overdrive and took five wins on the trot, the first of them on his rival's home soil, over the Jyvaskyla bumps where only Auriol and Sainz had beaten the locals before he did. Another record fell to the Alsace driver when he took his seventh straight win in Germany, then took full advantage of a turn-around in New Zealand to open up a gap. On tarmac, Catalunya and Corsica were mere formalities for the Citroën star, the springboard to a Japanese event where his sole aim was to take the podium finish that would mean world title number five. And in Sapporo it was a case of mission (easily) accomplished. "Throughout the season Sébastien was at the same level he reached at the end of the year before," was how Grönholm saw it. "His biggest trump card is that he's just always there. There's never a problem with the car, it runs like clockwork. He's confident, he knows the car inside out and he knows he can beat anybody."

Hirvonen was gracious in defeat: "I'm disappointed, but Sébastien is an exceptional driver and he fully deserves his fifth world title. At least I know now what I can do – we were fighting for the title, that's the good news. And I was pretty much the only one who could do that. It was one of my best seasons so far. I was missing a bit of speed early on in the year, and I was relying on my consistency. Everything was going well enough but now I see that you need to take it up to another level. I feel stronger for next season, I'm quicker, I can get closer to the limit and I'm also more competitive on tarmac."

Not that there will be much of that in 2009: Loeb's three favourite events, Monte Carlo, Corsica and Germany, will all be missing from the schedule, so he will have his work cut out to keep that sequence going against more battle-hardened, mature opponents.

And, who knows? He might be usurped by the new star in his own camp, another Sébastien: Ogier, that is, the discovery of the year, Junior World Champion in his first season, who will be in a Citroën C4 next year and might well spring a surprise of his own.

7 | François Duval

9 | Gigi Galli

Sadly, 2008 was also marred by two dreadful accidents. The first of them, in Germany, ended Gigi Galli's season. For the first time in his career the Italian was guaranteed a full season thanks to Pirelli's support, but he was halted in his tracks by a big off that left him with a broken femur. The accident to François Duval's Ford in Japan could have had far more tragic consequences. The Belgian's co-driver Patrick Pivato received injuries to his pelvis and tibia in an incredibly severe collision with a fence-post and then suffered internal bleeding in a Sapporo hospital. Put into an induced coma, he came out of it after an unprecedented show of solidarity as people helped find blood for the Frenchman. Repatriated ten days later, Pivato started a long period of convalescence but said his navigating days were over. As the time for New

1 JWRC | Sébastien Ogier

10 | Matthew Wilson

8 | Henning Solberg

12 | Per-Gunnar Andersson
13 | Toni Gardemeister

Year wishes comes around again, let us send ours to Patrick Pivato and Gigi Galli and hope they are both back on their feet to follow the 2009 season one way or another. If the end of 2008 was anything to go by, it will be an absolute thriller. ∎

↗ Citroën Total World Rally Team

CITROËN Manufacturer
C4 WRC

Launching the 2008 season, Citroën MD Gilles Michel gave his troops the following marching orders: "We are aiming very high: we want the constructors' title – and the drivers'." His men obeyed them to the letter, Sébastien Loeb taking his own fifth title in a row in Japan, as Daniel Elena did among the co-drivers, the team winning the laurels in their own right after the final round in Great Britain.

But it wasn't all plain sailing, thanks to some major changes during the 2007-08 close season. A change at the top, to start with: the 'big daddy' of the set-up, Guy Fréquelin, had won the argument about being allowed to call it a day and was replaced by Olivier Quesnel. But 'Grizzly' had looked ahead and the new man in charge inherited an immaculately-prepared team. Fréquelin's desire to see the team keep winning after he was gone was well and truly fulfilled. We should also point out that Freddy Loix's former team-mate Sven Smeets came in for Yves Matton in another key position as team manager.

There was another possible stumbling-block, namely a switch of manufacturers. Having always previously worked with Michelin, then their other brand BF Goodrich, the chevroned team now had to learn all about Pirellis, the FIA having decided on a move to a single supplier. Of course, Ford and Subaru – the latter having spent just the one season on the BF Goodrich product – also had to adapt, but changes of that kind are never straightforward. To gauge just how sensitive the tyre-chassis package is on any race car, on the rally track or on the road, we need look no further than Renault in F1 when they lost their way after switching from Michelin to Bridgestone.

As for the car, that was an evolution version of the C4 WRC they had been running since the start of 2007. In the season just finished, the car not only underlined its superiority on tarmac, where Citroën hasn't been beaten since Markko Märtin's success in Catalunya, but had clearly made significant progress on gravel as well, consistently outrunning the Ford Focus, until then the benchmark in that area. The C4 WRC, then, was a car that started from a good base and was superbly developed by the end of 2008. The proof: of 15 rallies, it won no fewer than 11.

One point worth mentioning is that while the C4 was generally very reliable, it suffered more breakdowns of one kind or another than its direct Blue Oval rival, the majority of them afflicting the unlucky Sordo's car. And of course, Citroën built their success on a pair of immaculate drivers, Loeb and Sordo. While the Frenchman's ongoing presence is a given, that wasn't necessarily the case for Sordo; after an inconsistent 2007, he needed to show clear signs of progress in 2008. He duly did so, although that first victory still escaped him. This time around, however, as well as his superb turn of speed on tarmac, he also produced some very convincing times on gravel, notably when helping the team to a very nice 1-2 finish in New Zealand.

The French company also gave indirect backing this year to Aava and Rautenbach, whose Citroëns were entered by PH Sport, looking to them for some good performances to counter the Ford fleet. In 2007 Citroën returned to the world rally scene after an 'interim' year which was also a winning one thanks to Kronos. The C4 was too new that season, and Sordo too inexperienced, for them to lift the constructors' crown, but a year later they got the job done, and Citroën's stats are now getting close to those of Lancia, far and away the number one make in the annals of rallying. The Chevron has already gone past Peugeot in terms of events won, 53 to 48. There's still some work to do when it comes to titles, the Italian constructor having 10 to Citroën's four so far, but they only need 20 more wins to match Lancia's tally – and with a phenomenal talent like Loeb in the team, anything is possible. In keeping with new partners Red Bull, this was a year when Citroën had wings!

Identity

Citroën Sport
19, allée des Marronniers
78035 Versailles Cedex
France
- Tel.: +33 (0)1 30 70 23 00
- Fax: +33 (0)1 30 84 02 70
- Web: www.citroen-wrc.com

Team Members
- Sporting Director: Olivier Quesnel
- Team Manager: Sven Smeets
- Technical Director: Xavier Mestelan-Pinon

Records
- Manufacturers Titles: 4 (2003, 2004, 2005, 2008)
- Drivers Titles: 4 (2004, 2005, 2007, 2008)
- Wins: 45

- Team founded in: 1989
- Rally debut: 1973

Classifications
- 1973 - 6th
- 1974 - 15th
- 1975 - 12th
- 1976 - 13th
- 1977 - 13th
- 1982 - 11th
- 1983 - 12th
- 1984 - 13th
- 1985 - 18th
- 1986 - 10th
- 2001 - not classified
- 2002 - not classified
- 2003 - Champion
- 2004 - Champion
- 2005 - Champion
- 2007 - 2nd
- 2008 - Champion

Engine
- Type: Developed from the EW10J4S engine
- Disposition: front transverse 25°
- Number of cylinders: 4 in line
- Valve: 4 per cylinder
- Capacity: 1,998cc
- Camshaft: double overhead
- Bore x Stroke: 86 x 86 mm
- Power: 320 bhp @ 5,500 rpm
- Torque: 580 Nm @ 2,750 rpm
- Turbocharger: Garrett
- Engine management: Magnetti-Marelli ECB11
- Lubrification: carbon wet sump
- Lubrifiant / fuel: Total

Transmission
- Clutch: carbon triple-plate 140 mm
- Gearbox: X-trac longitudinal 6-speed sequential
- Differentials: active centre differentials

Steering
- Hydraulic power-assisted rack and pinion

Suspensions
- Front & Rear: McPherson strut with helicoidal spring

Shock absorbers
- Citroën / Exe-TC

Brakes
- Front: ventilated discs, 376 mm ø (asphalt), 310 mm ø (gravel) 6-pot calipers
- Rear: ventilated discs (318 mm ø), 4-pot calipers

Tyres Pirelli
(asphalt: Pirelli PO - gravel: Pirelli Scorpion)

Wheels O.Z. magnesium
(asphalt 8 x 18"; gravel 7 x 15")

Dimensions
- Wheelbase: 2,608 mm
- Overall length: 4,274 mm
- Overall width: 1,800 mm
- Overall height: 1,390 mm
- Front/rear track: 1,598 mm
- Car weight: 1,230 kg (minimum authorised)

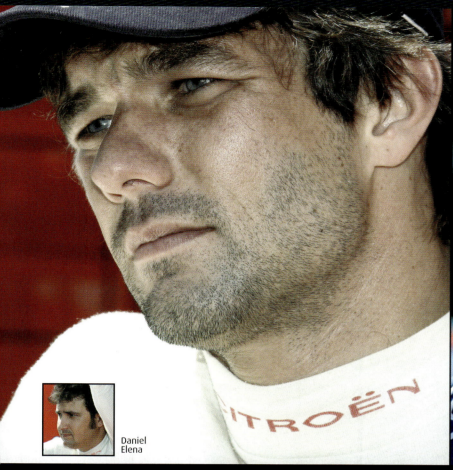

Sébastien LOEB #1

IDENTITY CARD
- Nationality: French
- Date of birth: February 26, 1974
- Place of birth: Haguenau (F)
- Resident: Bougy-Villars (CH)
- Marital status: Married to Séverine, a daughter (Valentine)
- Co-driver: Daniel Elena (MC)
- Web: www.sebastienloeb.com

CAREER
- Rally debut: 1995
- Nbr. of rallies in WRC: 113
- Number of wins: 47
- Podiums: 73

2001 - 15th in Championship; World Champion J-WRC (S1600)
2002 - 10th in Championship
2003 - 2nd in Championship
2004 - World Champion
2005 - World Champion
2006 - World Champion
2007 - World Champion
2008 - World Champion

Daniel "Dani" SORDO #2

IDENTITY CARD
- Nationality: Spanish
- Date of birth: May 2, 1983
- Place of birth: Torrelavega (E)
- Resident: Puente San Miguel (E)
- Marital status: Single
- Co-driver: Marc Marti (E)
- Web: www.danielsordo.com

CAREER
- Rally debut: 2003
- Nbr. of rallies in WRC: 59
- Best result: 8 x 2nd
- Podiums: 10

2005 – World Champion J-WRC
2006 – 5th in Championship
2007 – 4th in Championship
2008 – 3rd in Championship

Job done! A fifth title at the end of the 2008 season took Loeb past the previous benchmarks by the name of Tommi Mäkinen and Juha Kankkunen. The great Tommi himself was in Japan for the event that brought the French phenomenon his latest title, and he couldn't believe what he was seeing. He thought he'd set the bar pretty high with those four titles of his, four in a row from 1996 to 1999 what's more, and that it would be a long wait until someone took it up a notch. Then boom! Less than 10 years after his own last crowning, along comes a little guy from Alsace and goes one better. In sporting terms it's fun somet mes to imagine Fangio against Schumacher, Mark Spitz against Michael Phelps or Rossi versus Agostiri. Yes, Loeb did take on Mäkinen and beat him, but the latter was on the downhill slope by then and there were only flashes of his former brilliant self. A whole season of the two greatest drivers of all time at the peak of their powers, now that really would have been something to see. Tommi the Cat against Seb the Serial Killer: what a bill!

In his second full season at the wheel of the C4 WRC, now fully developed, the Frenchman didn't mess about, he set out his stall, marrying that incredible turn of speed of his to bullet-proof reliability, and made just one mistake on the Rally of Sweden. Loeb was simply untouchable: a mind-boggling tally of wins with more of them this season (11) than any other driver, a title wrapped up in the last but one rally in Japan – he might well have done it in Corsica but for Ford's team tactics – and a victory in Great Britain to end the year.

What put him so far out of reach was not just his own talent, but the relative feebleness of the opposition. It's no insult to Mikko Hirvonen to say that he isn't – at least not yet – as talented as Marcus Grönholm, the only man to have taken it up to the Frenchman these last few years. And the same applies to the rest of them: Sordo's taking his time to get to another level, Latvala's quick but he's not the finished product, Solberg hasn't got the car to enable him to shine...

In fact Loeb's utter dominance rather took the edge off the year: all those incredible stats, all those wins, podiums, stages won and so on... more convincing proof than any long discussion. And as he pointed out himself after the Tour of Corsica, after leaving the opposition for dead again: "What can I do about it? It's not for me to say what they have to do to get in front of us!" And that, in effect, summed up the season.

For the Championship's sake, let's hope someone comes up with the answer to Loeb's own question. It would be a pity if his achievements became commonplace, as they threatened to do at the end of the 2008 season. When Michael Schumacher was the dominant force in F1, even his own fans got sick and tired of it. Ah yes, Schumacher: there's a man who might not be sleeping quite so easy these days: if Loeb keeps this up, he might soon be the man with most titles in the whole history of motor sport!

Dani Sordo hasn't put all his youthful mistakes behind him just yet. As in previous seasons, he was once again too inconsistent to be the ideal foil for Loeb and take Citroën to a more comfortable constructors' win. Yes, there were times when he really was the perfect number two, helping the Chevron to those three successive 1-2 finishes from Germany to Spain by way of New Zealand, and at least once he showed he could step up when his team leader had problems, with that second place to Hirvonen in Jordan. He also stepped up a level on gravel with some outstanding performances, notably in Finland and New Zealand again. But still there were some blameworthy moments, one in Mexico, another more serious one in Corsica where he tried to get second place back too quickly and destroyed his C4, much to his team's dismay. To be absolutely fair, we should point out that Sordo wasn't spared his mechanical woes, such as those broken turbos in the Monte and Japan. He's still chasing his first win: he must make 2009 the year when he really kick-starts his career.

↗ BP Ford Abu Dhabi World Rally Team

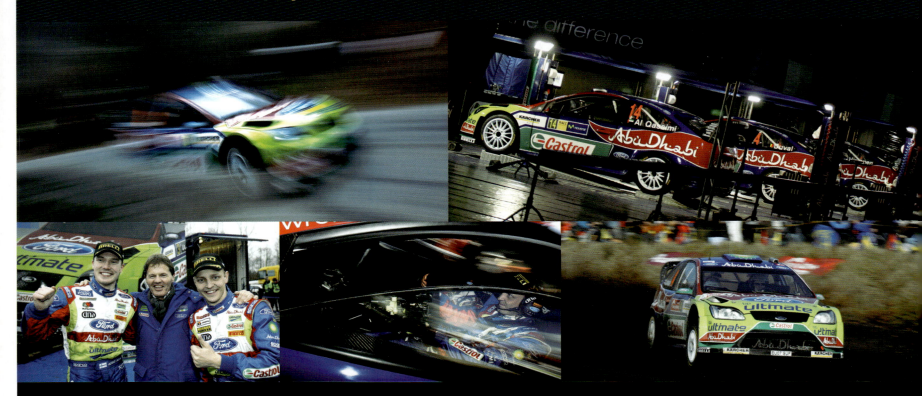

FORD Manufacturer
Focus RS WRC 07 & 08

It had to happen. After two world constructors' titles in as many years, Ford stumbled at the end of this last campaign and could not prove the truth of the old saying that good things come in threes. So 2008 was a lean year for the Anglo-American manufacturer whose cars are still built, developed and run by Malcolm Wilson's experienced M-Sport outfit. So what was the problem? In the next few pages (see pp.38-41), the team's Technical Director Christian Loriaux gives his own unequivocal analysis. While he is careful to defend his employers, the Belgian is probably right when he says the drivers have to shoulder a certain amount of blame. It's no disrespect to Mikko Hirvonen to say that he's no Marcus Grönholm, or at least not yet. The latter was capable of some monumental clangers himself, but his panache, his drive and his turn of speed not only made them forgivable, they also carried everyone else along on his coat-tails. Since 2006, adding Hirvonen and his knack of picking up points to their spectacular number one, Ford had just sat back and watched as it paid off handsomely. Putting it simply, Grönholm and his dash were the missing link between the 2007 title and the one that Hirvonen and Latvala should have won between them, as a close look at the results will tell you.

While the two front-running teams, Ford and Citroën, each had the same number of 1-2 finishes, thanks to Loeb the Chevron's number of victories weighed heavily in the final 2008 account, even though Hirvonen 103 of the 173 points achieved in the final tally. When Latvala, an unusually quick youngster, calms down and adds more experience, then he should start piling up the second places – something he didn't do often enough this year.

Still, we can't lay all the blame at the drivers' doorstep. In previous years the Ford Focus had been the best car on gravel, but this time Citroën's meticulously set-up C4 was every bit as good, as shown by Loeb's dominant wins in Mexico, Argentina and Sardinia. The only place where Malcolm Wilson's team reversed the trend was Turkey. And with the Focus and its drivers being no match for the C4 and Loeb or Sordo on tarmac, they had virtually no chance of winning on that surface.

We must, though, pay tribute to the 2007 Focus WRC's reliability. Like its predecessors, the Ford is bullet-proof: any breakdowns were usually not down to the car but to the drivers putting suspension, steering – or even roof -- to the test. Its excellent engine, developed by French specialists 'Pipo', made the sparks fly, and so did the chassis. You could count the serious failures, such as the turbos on Latvala's car in Mexico and again in Greece, on the fingers of one hand.

It was pretty well taken as read that Hirvonen wouldn't be able to beat Loeb in the drivers' stakes, so Ford made the constructors' title their priority, one of the reasons for Malcolm Wilson's push to give additional support to Stobart and Munchi's in his bid to block Citroën's path.

Ford's rallying future is not contingent on the 2008 results: barring any combination of circumstances due to the financial crisis, the team in its current guise will be there for the start of next season. But they are also doing the development work on a new Fiesta Super 2000 which will be available for sale from 2010. More irons in the fire...

Identity
Ford Motor Company, M-Sport Ltd
Dovenby Hall, Dovenby,
Cockermouth, Cumbria, CA13 0PN
Great Britain
· Tel.: +44 19 00 82 88 88
· Web: www.m-sport.co.uk
  www.wrcford.com

Team Members
· Director, Ford Motorsport: Mark Deans
· Team Principal: Malcolm Wilson
· Technical Director: Christian Loriaux

· Team founded in: 1986
· Rally debut: 1973

Records
· Manufacturers Titles:
  3 (1979, 2006, 2007)
· Drivers Titles: 2 (1979, 1981)
· Wins: 68

Classifications
· 1973 - 3rd
· 1974 - 3rd
· 1975 - 6th
· 1976 - 3rd
· 1977 - 2nd
· 1978 - 2nd
· 1979 - Champion
· 1980 - 3rd
· 1980 - 8th
· 1981 - 3rd
· 1982 - 4th
· 1983 - not classified
· 1984 - 12th
· 1985 - 11th
· 1986 - 5th
· 1987 - 5th
· 1988 - 2nd
· 1989 - 13th
· 1990 - 8th
· 1991 - 4th
· 1992 - 3rd
· 1993 - 2nd
· 1994 - 3rd
· 1995 - 3rd
· 1996 - 3rd
· 1997 - 2nd
· 1998 - 4th
· 1999 - 4th
· 2000 - 2nd
· 2001 - 2nd
· 2002 - 2nd
· 2003 - 4th
· 2004 - 2nd
· 2005 - 3rd
· 2006 - Champion
· 2007 - Champion
· 2008 - 2nd

Engine
· Type: Ford 1998cc Pipo I4 Duratec WRC
· Disposition: front transverse
· Number of cylinders: 4 in line
· Valve: 4 per cylinder
· Capacity: 1,998cc
· Camshaft: double overhead
· Bore x Stroke: 85 x 88 mm
· Power: 300 bhp @ 6,000 rpm
· Torque: 550 Nm @ 4,000 rpm
· Turbocharger: Garrett
· Engine management: Pi electronic
· Lubrification: carbon wet sump
· Exchanger: air-air
· Fuel tank capacity: 94 litre
· Lubrifiant / Fuel: Castrol / BP

Transmission
· Clutch: M-Sport / Sachs,
  multi disc carbon
· Gearbox: M-Sport / Ricardo
  5-speed sequential gearbox with electro-hydraulically controlled shift.
· Differentials: M-Sport, active centre differential

Steering
Power-assisted high-ratio (12:1) rack and pinion. One and a halfturns lock to lock.

Suspensions
· Front & Rear: MacPherson struts (front) and Trailing-Arm (rear)

Shock absorbers
Reiger

Brakes
Brembo
· Gravel (AV & AR): ventilated discs (300 mm ø) 4 piston monoblock calipers
· Asphalt (AV & AR): ventilated discs (370 mm ø) 8 piston monoblock calipers

Tyres
Pirelli
Wheels
Gravel: 7 x 15", Asphalt: 8 x 18"

Dimensions
· Wheelbase: 2,640 mm
· Overall length: 4,362 mm
· Overall width: 1,800 mm
· Overall height: 1,420 mm
· Car weight: 1,230 kg (minimum authorised)

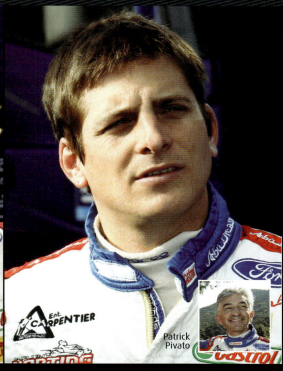

Mikko HIRVONEN #3

IDENTITY CARD
- Nationality: Finnish
- Date of birth: July 31, 1980
- Place of birth: Kannonkoski (FIN)
- Resident: Jyväskylä (FIN)
- Marital status: Engaged to Karoliina, one child
- Co-driver: Jarmo Lehtinen (FIN)
- Web: www.mikkohirvonen.com

CAREER
- Rally debut: 1998
- Nbr. of rallies in WRC: 86
- Number of wins: 7
- Podiums: 30

2003 - 15th in Championship
2004 - 7th in Championship
2005 - 10th in Championship
2006 - 3rd in Championship
2007 - 3rd in Championship
2008 - 2nd in Championship

As the 2008 Monte got under way, the big question-mark about the season ahead hung over Mikko Hirvonen. With Marcus Grönholm gone, could Ford's 2007 number two shoulder the burden of becoming Blue Oval team leader and trying to stop Loeb? Coming out of the 2003 campaign, the answer has to be... yes and no. Hirvonen was incredibly consistent – he was the driver most often in the points. He added to his own tally of victories, with some convincing performances in Jordan, Turkey and Japan. And he did look the man most likely to get in the French World Champion's way. But Hirvonen doesn't have what it takes to beat him fair and square. On tarmac he still can't do anything about Loeb, though he has progressed on that particular surface. In Corsica, for instance, it was team tactics that got him into second place, but his times were better than François Duval's in similar cars, and the Belgian's one of the benchmarks when it comes to tarmac. But between that and catching Loeb, there's quite a gap, and he hasn't got across it yet. Will he ever?

Gravel is the Finn's favourite surface, but there too he often played second fiddle to Loeb. And it was a real slap in the face when he was beaten by the Frenchman on home soil in Finland. Grönholm would never have stood for it. There was another one in Sweden – but there it was his own team-mate Jari-Matti Latvala who delivered it, beating him easily on an event that may not have had much snow but still seemed tailor-made for Hirvonen.

It was logical enough that he should lose any last hopes of the title in Japan. In fact it should have happened sooner had Loeb, like him, managed to finish every event up to that point, or had Ford not resorted to tactics that were effective if not exactly exemplary to get him into second place in Corsica.

Hirvonen knows his own limits and he is very honest with himself. His would have been a different career entirely if he hadn't found a creature by the name of Loeb in his way. That's the problem when it comes to good drivers and really good ones: if a good driver is around when there are no real geniuses out there, he looks like a star. But that still doesn't make him a really good driver... As things stand, Hirvonen is a banker when it comes to scoring points for his paymasters, and when you look around, there isn't really anyone else who could have done much better. So his future looks assured. But the rally world is obviously just waiting and hoping to see him take his game to the level where he really can be public enemy number one for Loeb and the worthy successor to Marcus Grönholm.

Jari-Matti LATVALA #4

IDENTITY CARD
- Nationality: Finnish
- Date of birth: April 3, 1985
- Place of birth: Töysä (FIN)
- Resident: Töysä (FIN)
- Marital status: Single
- Co-driver: Miikka Anttila (FIN)
- Web: www.latvalamotorsport.com

CAREER
- Rally debut: 2002
- Nbr. of rallies in WRC: 67
- Number of wins: 1
- Podiums: 7

2006 - 13th in Championship
2007 - 8th in Championship
2008 - 4th in Championship

Might this young fellow just be the one to follow in the footsteps of the Toivonens, Mikkolas, Salonens, Kankkunens, Mäkinens and Grönholms of this world? A look at what he's done so far suggests he will. Jari-Matti Latvala is from the Timo Joukhi stable that churns out champions, and he hasn't been hanging about. A test for Stobart in 2006 earned him a season in Ford's 'B' team last year, and he pulled off some real coups: first clean sheet in Norway, first time in the overall lead in Sardinia, first podium in Ireland. Moving to the works Ford team for 2008, he did even better: his first victory, in Sweden, made him the youngest-ever winner of a World Championship event at just 22 years and 10 months. Latvala's on the fast track, the great white hope for rallying's future. Apart from that win, where he finished in front of team leader Hirvonen, there were other convincing efforts – second places in Turkey and Japan, for instance, which clinched welcome 1-2 results for Ford on both events. But Latvala still needs to learn to rein himself in. His fiery temperament, as well as his occasionally inadequate note-taking, caused too many driver errors. The Monte, Argentina, Finland, to name but three, all came to a premature end after some classic clangers. At a stage of the season where Ford really needed results, his shortcomings on tarmac saw François Duval take over the works Focus WRC. But he did show a nice turn of speed on the bitumen at times. If he can keep himself in check in 2009 and really get to grips with tarmac, then maybe it's Latvala who will be the main challenger to Loeb next year.

François DUVAL #4

IDENTITY CARD
- Nationality: Belgian
- Date of birth: November 18, 1980
- Place of birth: Charleroi (B)
- Resident: Cul-des-Sarts (B)
- Marital status: Single
- Co-driver: Patrick Pivato (F)
- Web: www.fduval.com

CAREER
- Rally debut: 1999
- Nbr. of rallies in WRC: 83
- Number of wins: 1
- Podiums: 14

2002 - 30th in Championship
2003 - 9th in Championship
2004 - 6th in Championship
2005 - 6th in Championship
2006 - 19th in Championship
2007 - 10th in Championship
2008 - 7th in Championship

Ever since 2005 François Duval has kept appearing in the World Championship – and kept disappearing again: six rallies in 2006, four in 2007, and seven in 2008 in Ford 'B' team Stobart, then in the works outfit, with the emphasis on the tarmac events. His pace on that surface was what earned him a spot in the main Blue Oval line-up for Catalunya and then for Corsica, Ford seeing him as a safer bet for points than Latvala. The dynamic Obelix was among the front-runners every time and graciously bowed to team orders to hand over second place in Corsica to Hirvonen. But his season was marred by the terrible accident in Japan which almost cost co-driver Patrick Pivato his life. One of those who came to Pivato's aid was Denis Giraudet, the same Giraudet who then offered to sit at the Belgian's right elbow on the Rally of Great Britain, as much out of friendship for the injured Pivato as to help Duval get over the latest drama in a somewhat erratic career.

Khalid AL-QASSIMI

The contract between the works Ford team and Abu Dhabi included a clause giving Khalid Al-Qassimi a 10-event programme in 2008 in one of the front-running Ford Focuses. Malcolm Wilson honoured that commitment, but did the man from the Emirates? Did anyone see him in action this year? Not many, he was so low-key. Of course it's no easy task for a 36-year-old who's never shown any aptitude for competition outside the Middle East. It simply underlines the gulf between that region and world-class competition, since Al-Qassimi was the FIA Middle East champion of 2004.

Subaru World Rally Team

SUBARU Manufacturer
Impreza WRC 2007 & 2008

How far can Subaru fall? For years now, ever since Petter Solberg's 2003 title in fact, the team, with cars still developed and entered by Prodrive, have been on the slide. All right, they were third in the Championship – but they were light years away from Citroën and Ford. As each new year begins, management proclaims they are on the way back – and every year they fall just that little bit harder.

For 2008 the Japanese constructors were pinning their hopes on the new Impreza WRC, successor to the inconsistent, ill-balanced and sluggish S12. The new race car was built on the new road-car platform, with five doors instead of four, on sale since September 2007. This radical change in the Impreza lineage was accompanied by other major revisions: a longer wheelbase, shorter overhangs, a huge wing located on the tailgate rather than the boot. The engine was still a two-litre flat, boxer-style unit linked to the symmetrical integrated transmission. The livery also underwent an overhaul, though the traditional midnight blue remained.

After what the team called a long, searching set-up process, carried out with the help of the experienced Markko Märtin, Subaru's test driver since early 2008, the decision was taken to introduce the new car on the Acropolis Rally. It made a convincing start on this most demanding of events, with Petter Solberg taking second place. But it all turned pear-shaped after that as this new Impreza also proved uncompetitive against the C4's and Focuses. The Norwegian driver's morale took a knock – he was regularly beaten by team-mate Chris Atkinson, and the results just went to the dogs. Bringing Brice Tirabassi in for the late-season tarmac rallies in Catalunya and Corsica didn't help. The French driver did have an encouraging run in Spain, but then had to retire with mechanical problems in France.

There was much gnashing of teeth at the Japanese HQ of Fuji Heavy Industries, parent company of the cars with the stars. David Richards, the talismanic boss of Prodrive and the man responsible for past successes, threw himself into the project once more, but nothing changed. There are talented technical people working on the project, yet still nothing comes of it. There were worrying signs for the partnership between the British race preparation outfit and Japanese marque when a pair of Imprezas developed entirely in the Land of the Rising Sun was entered for the Rally of Japan. They were, admittedly, Group N cars, but was this the prelude to things being taken back in-house in the longer term?

The autumn 2008 announcement that the Subaru World Rally Team was setting up a satellite outfit could be taken as confirming the Prodrive-Subaru connection. The new team, to be known as Adapta World Rally Team, will run two cars in at least 10 2009 events. One will be driven by Norwegian rally champion Mads Ostberg. Rumour also had it that Marcus Grönholm, who tested the S14 in Great Britain in late October, would be back in one of the little blue beauties in 2009. Would that be enough to right the ship? Even a man as talented as Grönholm couldn't get them back on the right track all by himself. As the man with the permanent grin, David Richards, would say: "Wait and see..."

Identity
Subaru World Rally Team (Prodrive)
Banbury, Oxfordshire OX16 3ER
Great Britain
- Tel.: +44 12 95 273 335
- Fax: +44 12 95 271 188
- Web: www.swrt.com

Team Members
- Team Principal: David Richards
- Manufacturer Principal: Ichiro Kudoh
- Managing Director: Richard Taylor
- Technical Director: David Lapworth
- Operations Director and Team Manager: Paul Howarth
- Team Co-ordinator: Ken Rees
- Chief Engineer: Graham Moore
- Chief Designer: Christophe Chapelain

Records
- Manufacturers Titles: 3 (1995, 1996, 1997)
- Drivers Titles: 3 (1995, 2001, 2003)
- Wins: 47

- Rally debut: 1982
- Team founded in: 1990

Classifications
- 1983 - 7th
- 1984 - 9th
- 1985 - 12th
- 1986 - 8th
- 1987 - 10th
- 1988 - 9th
- 1989 - 12th
- 1990 - 4th
- 1991 - 6th
- 1992 - 4th
- 1993 - 3rd
- 1994 - 2nd
- 1995 - Champion
- 1996 - Champion
- 1997 - Champion
- 1998 - 3rd
- 1999 - 2nd
- 2000 - 3rd
- 2001 - 3rd
- 2002 - 3rd
- 2003 - 3rd
- 2004 - 3rd
- 2005 - 4th
- 2006 - 3rd
- 2007 - 3rd
- 2008 - 3rd

Engine
- Type: Flat four-cylinder
- Valve: 4 per cylinder
- Capacity: 1,994cc
- Camshaft: 2x double overhead
- Bore x Stroke: 92 x 75 mm
- Power: 300 bhp @ 5,500 rpm
- Torque: 650Nm @ 4,000 rpm
- Turbocharger: IHI
- Engine management: Subaru
- Spark plugs: DENSO
- Fuel tank capacity: 80 litres

Transmission
- Gearbox: 6-speed electro-hydraulic
- Differentials: electro-hydraulically controlled centre differential. Mechanical front and rear differentials

Steering
- Power assisted rack and pinion

Suspensions
- Front: MacPherson strut
- Rear: MacPherson strut with longitudinal and transverse link

Shock absorbers SWRT

Brakes AP Racing
- Front & Rear: ventilated discs (310 mm ø), 4-pot calipers
- Asphalt: ventilated discs (378 mm ø), 6-pot calipers

Tyres Pirelli

Wheels BBS

Dimensions
- Wheelbase: 2,635 mm
- Overall length: 4,415 mm
- Overall width: 1,800 mm
- Overall height: 1,475 mm
- Car weight: 1230 kg (minimum authorised)

Phil Mills

Stéphane Prévot

Petter SOLBERG #5

IDENTITY CARD
- Nationality: Norwegian
- Date of birth: November 18, 1974
- Place of birth: Askim (N)
- Resident: Monaco (MC)
- Marital status: Married to Pernilla, one son (Oliver)
- Co-driver: Phil Mills (GB)
- Web: www.pettersolberg.com

CAREER
- Rally debut: 1995
- Nbr. of rallies in WRC: 139
- Number of wins: 13
- Podiums: 35

1999 - 18th in Championship
2000 - 10th in Championship
2001 - 9th in Championship
2002 - 2nd in Championship
2003 - World Champion
2004 - 2nd in Championship
2006 - 6th in Championship
2007 - 5th in Championship
2008 - 6th in Championship

A season from hell, we wrote last time about Petter Solberg's 2007 year. Make that two. Wearisome it may be, but that's how it is: with Subaru unable to provide the Norwegian with a decent car, 'Hollywood' is simply tilting at windmills. In fact, has driving these dogs that just can't hack it against the Citroëns and Fords blunted the 2003 World Champion's edge? We won't have the answer to that question until he's got a car to provide it in. So what can we take out of 2008? A second place in Greece, that's what. In 2007 he was a two-time podium visitor; this year, just the once. What's worse, he was consistently outplayed by team-mate Chris Atkinson. Once again, then: is Petter Solberg still as quick as he was back in 2003 or not?

Chris ATKINSON #6

IDENTITY CARD
- Nationality: Australian
- Date of birth: November 30, 1979
- Place of birth: Bega (AUS)
- Resident: Gold Coast (AUS) & Monaco (MC)
- Marital status: Single
- Co-driver: Stéphane Prévot (B)
- Web: chrisatkinson.com.au

CAREER
- Rally debut: 2000
- Nbr. of rallies in WRC: 66
- Best result: 2 x 2nd
- Podiums: 6

2004 - 16th in Championship
2005 - 12th in Championship
2006 - 10th in Championship
2007 - 7th in Championship
2008 - 5th in Championship

There's been a changing of the guard at Subaru. Former number two Chris Atkinson is now number one. Just looking at results, and maybe the hunger and commitment as well, the Australian outclassed his former World Champion team-mate, taking a lot more podiums and second places than the Norwegian in the same car, and he was the quickest of the Subaru drivers. He showed that with a fine drive on the Monte, which is the antithesis of what he's supposed to be best at, and an event where he just keeps getting better. We might well wonder about Solberg's commitment in this late stage of his career, but there's no such question-mark over the Australian. Ever since Belgian Stéphane Prévot joined him as co-driver, Atkinson has kept going forward in what are very difficult times for Subaru.

Brice TIRABASSI

IDENTITY CARD
- Nationality: French
- Date of birth: June 15, 1977
- Co-driver: Fabrice Gordon (F)
- Web: www.bricetirabassi.com

CAREER
- Rally debut: 2001
- Nbr. of rallies in WRC: 23
- Best result: 1 x 10th

2000-2004 - not classified
2005 - 42nd in Championship
2006 - 53rd in Championship
2007 - 41st in Championship
2008 - 30th in Championship

Brice Tirabassi was Junior World Champion back in 2003, but his career hasn't reached the heights it was expected to. This year Subaru gave him an Impreza WRC on two occasions, for the Spanish and French rounds, to go along with his regular IRC drive. Despite a distinct lack of experience at the wheel of a WRC, and despite being unable to get his hands on the car before the Catalan event, the Frenchman still pulled off a fine 10th-place finish. He might have been in the points in Corsica but for an engine failure. Still, the driver seized both chances to remind the World Championship regulars that he's still here.

↗ Stobart VK M-Sport Ford Rally Team

FORD
Manufacturer Team

Focus RS WRC 07

There are three reasons for the ongoing presence of road haulage firm Stobart and the team created in 2006: to develop talented young drivers, to get pay-drivers into top-class Ford Focuses from the mother-ship, lining its coffers in the process, and to get as many cars as possible home in the points to frustrate Loeb's and Citroën's world title ambitions. With Latvala off to join the works team (though Malcolm Wilson heads up both), the full-time drive went to Gigi Galli. The spirited Italian, quick on all kinds of surface, scored a fair few points early in the season but trod water after that, then had to give up altogether after breaking his femur in Germany. The team's second car changed hands between François Duval, Henning Solberg and even Jari-Matti Latvala, when the Belgian replaced him for some tarmac events. The boss's son Matthew also spearheaded a full programme but the results were no more convincing than they had been the previous year. On some events, such as the German round, Stobart entered as many as four cars. One man to benefit was Barry Clarke, the stand-in for Pérez-Companc at Munchi's on the Tour of Corsica and again in Great Britain. In the end Stobart did what was asked of them, finishing fourth overall -- not that far behind Subaru when you take into account the resources used and the results achieved, and in front of the Suzuki works team.

Identity
Stobart Motorsport
Eddie Stobart Ltd,
Brunthill Road,
Kingstown Ind Est,
Carlisle, Cumbria, CA3 0EH
Great Britain
- Tel.: +44 1357 523188
- Fax: +44 1357 523188
- Web:
  www.stobartmotorsport.com

Team Members
- Director: Andrew Tinkler
- Team Manager: Malcolm Wilson

Drivers 2008
- Gigi Galli - Giovanni Bernacchini
- Henning Solberg - Cato Menkerud
- Matthew Wilson - Scott Martin
- Francois Duval - Eddy Chevaillier, Patrick Pivato, Denis Giraudet
- Barry Clark - Paul Nagel

- Team founded in: 1996

Records
- Manufacturers Titles: 0
- Drivers Titles: 0

Classifications
- 2006 - 5th
- 2007 - 4th
- 2008 - 4th

Engine
- Type: Ford 1998cc Pipo I4 Duratec WRC
- Disposition: front transverse
- Number of cylinders: 4 in line
- Valve: 4 per cylinder
- Capacity: 1,998cc
- Camshaft: double overhead
- Bore x Stroke: 85 x 88 mm
- Power: 300 bhp @ 6,000 rpm
- Torque: 550 Nm @ 4,000 rpm
- Turbocharger: Garrett
- Engine management: Pi electronic
- Lubrification: carbon wet sump
- Exchanger: air-air
- Fuel tank capacity: 94 litre
- Lubrifiant / Fuel: Castrol / BP

Transmission
- Clutch: M-Sport / Sachs, multi disc carbon
- Gearbox: M-Sport / Ricardo 5-speed sequential gearbox with electro-hydraulically controlled shift.
- Differentials: M-Sport, active centre differential

Steering
Power-assisted high-ratio (12:1) rack and pinion. One and a halfturns lock to lock.

Suspensions
- Front & Rear: MacPherson struts (front) and Trailing-Arm (rear)

Shock absorbers
Reiger

Brakes
Brembo
- Gravel (AV & AR): ventilated discs (300 mm ø), 4 piston monoblock calipers
- Asphalt (AV & AR): ventilated discs (370 mm ø), 8 piston monoblock calipers

Tyres
Pirelli
Wheels
Gravel: 7 x 15", Asphalt: 8 x 18"

Dimensions
- Wheelbase: 2,640 mm
- Overall length: 4,362 mm
- Overall width: 1,800 mm
- Overall height: 1,420 mm
- Car weight: 1,230 kg (minimum authorised)

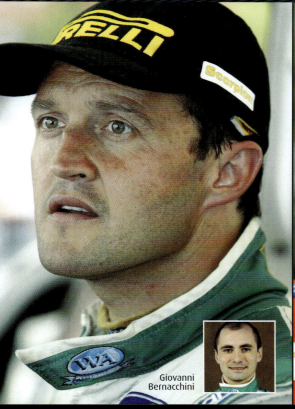

Gianluigi "Gigi" GALLI #7

IDENTITY CARD
- Nationality: Italian
- Date of birth: January 13, 1973
- Place of birth: Milan (I)
- Resident: Livigno (I)
- Marital status: Single
- Co-driver: Giovanni Bernacchini (I)
- Web: www.gigigalli.com

CAREER
- Rally debut: 1994
- Nbr. of rallies in WRC: 67
- Best result: 2 x 3rd
- Podiums: 2

2004 - 15th in Championship
2005 - 11th in Championship
2006 - 11th in Championship
2007 - 15th in Championship
2008 – 9th in Championship

With Latvala off to join the works Ford team, Stobart gave 'Gigi' Galli the use of one their Focuses. So keen were the team to have the Italian all-rounder, still backed by faithful sponsors Pirelli, on board that as the year began he was the one driver ear-marked to score points in every round. And his season got off to a great start with a sixth place in Monte Carlo followed by a podium finish in Sweden, which gave Ford a fine 1-2-3 result. After that, though, technical problems (Greece, where he was up with the leaders, then Turkey) and accidents marred his year. So heavy was the one in Germany that he broke his femur (his co-driver was unhurt), was taken to hospital in Trier and had to give the rest of the season away.

Henning SOLBERG #8

IDENTITY CARD
- Nationality: Norwegian
- Date of birth: January 8, 1973
- Place of birth: Spydeberg (N)
- Resident: Spydeberg (N)
- Marital status: Married to Maud, two children
- Co-driver: Cato Menkerud (N)
- Web: henningsolberg.com

CAREER
- Rally debut: 1997
- Nbr. of rallies in WRC: 71
- Best result: 3 x 3rd
- Podiums: 3

2004 - 19th in Championship
2005 - 14th in Championship
2006 - 8th in Championship
2007 - 6th in Championship
2008 - 8th in Championship

While Matthew Wilson hangs on to his father's dreams, Henning Solberg is well aware that he's no bright young thing any more and any career he wanted to carve out is now behind him. With the backing of a sponsor who has stayed loyal through it all, the elder of the Norwegian pair is having fun and probably doing quite nicely out of it in the process. He was better than Wilson without setting the world on fire. No problem: he racked up the points, finishing quite a few rallies in his Focus, but wasn't as successful as he had been in 2007, when he took two podiums. This year his best result was a fourth place in Jordan. Note: on occasion Solberg's entry came via Munchi's, Ford's other World Championship satellite team.

Matthew WILSON #7 #16

IDENTITY CARD
- Nationality: British
- Date of birth: January 29, 1987
- Place of birth: Cockermouth (GB)
- Resident: Cumbria (GB)
- Marital status: Single
- Co-driver: Michael Orr (GB)

CAREER
- Rally debut: 2004
- Nbr. of rallies in WRC: 49
- Best result: 1 x 4th

2006 - 28th in Championship
2007 - 11th in Championship
2008 - 10th in Championship

The only place where Matthew Wilson is seen as a world rallying prospect is in the dreams of his dad, Malcolm Wilson, the one-time driver now head of M-Sport, which prepares and runs the Ford Focus WRC cars. The 2008 season was his third full year and the best the young Brit could do was a fifth place in Jordan. The youngster is Britain's sole full-time representative at the moment, but maybe it's time he realised he's never going to be a Loeb: he may be only 21, but already there are a lot of young drivers a lot better than him around. He has an excellent car in the Focus, and there are some genuine prospects who are long overdue a crack at it. New co-driver Scott Martin, whom he competed with on Great Britain the previous year, didn't add much to the mixture either.

↗ Munchi's Ford World Rally Team

FORD
Manufacturer Team
Focus RS WRC 07

Malcolm Wilson saw his chance to turn Munchi's and the enthusiastic, well-heeled Pérez-Companc brothers from Argentina, good clients of M-Sport's, into a carbon copy of the Stobart operation. Financed by the South American ice cream kings and set up in 2007, this year the plan was to enter multiple national champion Federico Villagra, with Jorge Pérez-Companc as co-driver, in 10 events. But Luis Pérez-Companc, the boss, was also due to take part in three, and on an ad hoc basis they would also bring in one of the Stobart drivers when any of them was unable to take his place in the satellite team as they played musical chairs with the works outfit. That's how Henning Solberg ended up as team-mate to Villagra in several events. No lack of cash, but a lack of real talent at the wheel meant Munchi's never really did much and had to settle for last place in the Constructors' World Championship. Clearly Villagra wasn't up to World Championship standard, Solberg only just; and as for Luis Pérez-Companc, business took up too much of his time and he was only able to start in Argentina and Finland. In Jordan he handed over the drive to one of his mechanics, Barry Clarke, who also competed in Turkey. When we wrote these lines late last year there was a chance Munchi's would not be taking part in 2009. But when you're dealing with a (business)man like Malcolm Wilson, you can never really be sure of anything...

Identity
Ford Motor Company, M-Sport Ltd
Dovenby Hall, Dovenby,
Cockermouth, Cumbria, CA13 0PN
Great Britain
• Tel.: +44 19 00 82 88 88
• Web: www.m-sport.co.uk

Team Members
• Team Principal: Malcolm Wilson

Drivers 2008
• Luis Perez Companc - José Maria Volta
• Federico Villagra - Jorge Perez Companc
• Henning Solberg - Cato Menkerud
• Barry Clark - Paul Nagel

• Team founded in: 2007

Records
• Manufacturers Titles: 0
• Drivers Titles: 0

Classifications
• 2007 - 6th
• 2008 - 6th

Engine
• Type: Ford 1998cc Pipo I4 Duratec WRC
• Disposition: front transverse
• Number of cylinders: 4 in line
• Valve: 4 per cylinder
• Capacity: 1,998cc
• Camshaft: double overhead
• Bore x Stroke: 85 x 88 mm
• Power: 300 bhp @ 6,000 rpm
• Torque: 550 Nm @ 4,000 rpm
• Turbocharger: Garrett
• Engine management: Pi electronic
• Lubrification: carbon wet sump
• Exchanger: air-air
• Fuel tank capacity: 94 litre
• Lubrifiant / Fuel: Castrol / BP

Transmission
• Clutch: M-Sport / Sachs, multi disc carbon
• Gearbox: M-Sport / Ricardo 5-speed sequential gearbox with electro-hydraulically controlled shift.
• Differentials: M-Sport, active centre differential

Steering
Power-assisted high-ratio (12:1) rack and pinion. One and a halfturns lock to lock.

Suspensions
• Front & Rear: MacPherson struts (front) and Trailing-Arm (rear)

Shock absorbers
Reiger

Brakes
Brembo
• Gravel (AV & AR): ventilated discs (300 mm ø), 4 piston monoblock calipers
• Asphalt (AV & AR): ventilated discs (370 mm ø), 8 piston monoblock calipers

Tyres
Pirelli
Wheels
Gravel: 7 x 15", Asphalt: 8 x 18"

Dimensions
• Wheelbase: 2,640 mm
• Overall length: 4,362 mm
• Overall width: 1,800 mm
• Overall height: 1,420 mm
• Car weight: 1,230 kg (minimum authorised)

Luis PÉREZ-COMPANC #10

IDENTITY CARD
- Nationality: Argentinean
- Date of birth: January 2, 1972
- Place of birth: Buenos Aires (RA)
- Resident: Buenos Aires (RA)
- Marital status: Married, four children
- Co-driver: José Maria Volta (RA)

CAREER
- Rally debut: 2000
- Nbr. of rallies in WRC: 30
- Best result: 1 x 5th

2004 - 23rd in Championship
2005 - 54th in Championship
2006 - 26th in Championship
2007 - 16th in Championship
2008 - not classified

As business matters preoccupied him, the Argentine millionaire had to put the brake on his rally-driving ambitions. While he did six events in 2007, in 2008 there were just three on his schedule. One was his home event in Argentina, where he retired after an off, then another accident in Finland put an end to his 'career' in rallying. He was due to contest the Jordan round as well but his work prevented him from doing so. So the drive went at the eleventh hour to Scotsman Barry Clarke – who was in Jordan as a Pérez-Companc mechanic! It was a conclusive experience, too, as Clarke was offered the drive again in Turkey. Note: Greece's Aris Vovos drove this car on the Acropolis Rally. Luis Pérez-Companc has now decided to draw a line under his time in the World Championship.

Federico VILLAGRA #9

IDENTITY CARD
- Nationality: Argentinean
- Date of birth: May 1st, 1969
- Place of birth: Córdoba (RA)
- Resident: Córdoba (RA)
- Marital status: Single
- Co-driver: Jorge Pérez Companc (RA)
- Web: www.villagraracing.com.ar

CAREER
- Rally debut: 1997
- Nbr. of rallies in WRC: 19
- Best result: 2 x 6th

2006 - 45th in Championship
2007 - 20th in Championship
2008 - 14th in Championship

The oldest driver in the current field, the Argentine won't be leaving much of a mark on the World Championship. This year he headed up a schedule of 10 events in one of the Fords entered by his friends and fellow-countrymen the Pérez-Companc brothers – Jorge Pérez-Companc in fact co-drove with him in the World Championship. This programme was on top of his entry in the Argentine national series, where he won the title again in 2008. Villagra did get into the points in three early-season rallies before treading water as the year went on. If, as seemed likely at the end of '08, Munchi's are not there in 2009, the Argentine's absence will go largely unnoticed.

Suzuki World Rally Team

SUZUKI Manufacturer
SX4 WRC

After making their debut with just two rallies (Corsica and Great Britain) in 2007, Suzuki went into their first full season in the WRC category in 2008. And it didn't go all that well, despite everything the Japanese put into it. They reviewed their technical staff from top to bottom before the season got under way – the man behind the SX4, Michel Nandan, had bowed out – and brought in some Japanese brain power, including new Technical Director Shusuke Inagaki. The drivers they had signed, Toni Gardemeister and P.-G. Andersson, could be relied on for a reasonable level of performance and both had useful experience.

The SX4 gained a bit of weight; suspension and diffs were given a complete overhaul; the engine got more grunt – all to no avail. The car's all-round shortcomings meant neither Suzuki driver could put up much of a showing. In Corsica, a year exactly after the car came out, Toni Gardemeister let slip a telling comment: "I expected we would have a few problems this season, but not as many as this! And I was really, really hoping we would be quicker. At least things aren't too bad on the reliability front – we haven't had any major failures though there were just too many niggling little things at the start of the season. Those have been sorted out, and we've been heading in the right direction, but we still haven't picked up any speed."

So the results were nothing to write home about. Their best was Japan, where Andersson was fourth and Gardemeister fifth, and that result came at the right time as the firm's top brass turned out to watch them on home soil. Over the Championship Suzuki, a works team after all, were soundly beaten by privateer outfit Stobart.

What was lacking was the political will and, therefore, the resources to do the job properly. Suzuki didn't really tip in what was needed for a high-level category like the WRC, and they paid for that mistake. Their cars had worked wonders in the JWRC in previous years, but from there to the peak category was a step they found very difficult to make. And so, as 2008 ended, there were whispers of a complete pull-out, or at least a temporary departure from the scene. Would they miss the 2009 series and use the time instead to develop the SX4 further, returning in 2010 to coincide with the new regulations? Team management denied the rumours, but it was a pertinent question. Others have met disappointment in the WRC before, notable Seat and Skoda. Let's hope the worthy Japanese team doesn't go the same way.

Identity
Suzuki Sport Europe Ltd.
H-2500 Esztergom,
Schweidel Jozsef u.52
Hungary
- Tel.: +36 33 541 306
- Fax: +36 33 414 311
- Web: www.suzuki-wrc.com
  & www.suzukisport.com

Team members
- Team Principal: Nobuhiro Tajima
- Team Director: Yutaka Awazuhara
- Team Manager: Paul Wilding
- Technical Manager: Shusuke Inagaki

- Team founded in: 2007
- Rally debut: 2007

Classifications
- 2007 - n.c.
- 2008 - 5th

Engine
- Type: J20
- Disposition: front transverse
- Number of cylinders: 4 in line
- Valve: 4 per cylinder
- Capacity: 1,997cc
- Camshaft: double overhead
- Power: 320 bhp @ 4,000 - 4,500 rpm
- Torque: 590 Nm @ 3,500 rpm

Transmission
- Clutch: Carbon triple-plate
- Gearbox: 5-speed munual with sequential controls on steering wheel
- Differentials: Electronically controlled

Direction Power assisted rack and pinion

Suspensions
- Front & Rear: MacPherson strut with coil springs

Shock absorbers Reiger

Brakes
- Gravel (Front & Rear): ventilated discs (300 mm ø), 4-pot calipers
- Asphalt (Front & Rear): ventilated discs (370 mm ø/355 mm ø), 8-pot calipers

Tyres Pirelli (235/40 - 18 Asphalt, 205/65 - 15 Gravel, 145/85 - 16 Ice)

Wheels
Asphalt: 8 x 18", Gravel: 7 x 15", Ice 6 x 16"

Dimensions
- Wheelbase: 2,500 mm
- Overall length: 4,135 mm
- Overall width: 1,770 mm
- Overall height: 1,450 mm
- Car weight: 1,230 kg (minimum authorised)

Toni
GARDEMEISTER #11

IDENTITY CARD
- Nationality: Finnish
- Date of birth: March 31, 1975
- Place of birth: Kouvola (FIN)
- Resident: Monaco (MC)
- Marital status: Single
- Co-driver: Tomi Tuominen (FIN)
- Web: www.tonigardemeister.com

CAREER
- Rally debut: 1993
- Nbr. of rallies in WRC: 111
- Best result: 3 x 2nd
- Podiums: 6

1999 - 13th in Championship
2000 - 13th in Championship
2001 - 16th in Championship
2002 - 13th in Championship
2003 - 12th in Championship
2004 - 24th in Championship
2005 - 4th in Championship
2006 - 9th in Championship
2007 - 13th in Championship
2008 - 13th in Championship

Toni Gardemeister's has been an amazing career. Thanks mainly to Timo Joukhi and his circle of Finnish partners, Toni keeps bouncing back. Once a works driver for Seat and Skoda, in 2007 he drove a Mitsubishi Lancer WRC first of all, then a Xsara WRC. No-one would have believed he would ever find himself with a works drive but this year there he was, one of the two men given the new Suzuki SX4 WRC to play with. But neither he nor the car was brilliant. Gardemeister doesn't lack experience but when it comes to a new car that really needs to be properly set up, he's not necessarily the best man for the job. So he made the most of his own capacities and the equipment he was given, scoring the odd miraculous point or two. If Suzuki throw in the towel, will Gardemeister pull off another Phoenix act this time? We'll have to wait and see.

Per-Gunnar
ANDERSSON #12

IDENTITY CARD
- Nationality: Swedish
- Date of birth: March 10, 1980
- Place of birth: Årjäng (S)
- Resident: Årjäng (S)
- Marital status: Married to Marie-Louise
- Co-driver: Jonas Andersson (S)
- Web: www.pgandersson.se

CAREER
- Rally debut: 1999
- Nbr. of rallies in WRC: 59
- Best result: 2 x 5th

2004 - World Champion J-WRC / 36^{e}
2005 - 2nd J-WRC / 48th in Championship
2006 - 4th J-WRC / not classified
2007 - World Champion J-WRC / 50th
2008 - 12th in Championship

It would have been pretty surprising if Suzuki hadn't brought their star driver from the JWRC ranks into the WRC with them. And so, after two titles wins with them (2004, 2007), P.-G. Andersson duly formed part of the strike force that came into the top class this year. Alas, while his talent was not in question, his car most certainly was and the Swede was an also-ran, handicapped as Gardemeister was by technical troubles and the SX4's sheer lack of performance. Despite a disappointing season, he still came out of it as the Suzuki driver with the best result, a fifth place in Japan. As with Gardemeister's, his future hinges in part on whether or not Suzuki stay in the World Championship.

↗ **Spectacular stand-ins!**

Urmo AAVA

IDENTITY CARD
- Nationality: Estonian
- Date of birth: February 2, 1979
- Place of birth: Tallinn (EE)
- Resident: Lagedi (EE)
- Marital status: Married
- Co-driver: Kuldar Sikk (EE)
- Web: www.urmoaava.eu

CAREER
- Rally debut: 1997
- Nbr. of rallies in WRC: 48
- Best result: 1 x 4th

2003 - not classified
2004 - 56th in Championship
2005 - not classified
2006 - not classified
2007 - 19th in Championship
2008 - 11th in Championship

A leading light in the JWRC, where he was runner-up in 2006 and 2007, the Estonian was given a Citroën C4 WRC to drive in 10 events in the World Championship proper. It was entered by a team specially set up for the purpose, World Rally Team Estonia, and prepared by French outfit PH Sport with backing from Citroën Sports Technologies. After a difficult debut in Sweden, the quick Estonian got the hang of things in the car and claimed a fine fourth place in Greece, with some noteworthy clean sheets along the way. A convincing first season, one which Aava hoped to extend into 2009 if he could come up with the required finances.

Conrad RAUTENBACH

IDENTITY CARD
- Nationality: Zimbabwean
- Date of birth: November 12, 1984
- Place of birth: Harare (ZW)
- Resident: Harare (ZW)
- Marital status: Single
- Co-driver: David Senior (GB)
- Web: www.conradrautenbach.com

CAREER
- Rally debut: 2002
- Nbr. of rallies in WRC: 43
- Best result: 1 x 4th

2007 - 57th in Championship
2008 - 15th in Championship

Conrad Rautenbach's arrival on the WRC scene will forever be linked to the young Zimbabwean's spectacular accident with Sébastien Loeb on the Jordan Rally – the one that stopped them both in their tracks. African champion in 2007 and a prominent competitor in the JWRC in recent years, the young man from a comfortable background was, like Aava, in Citroëns prepared by PH Sport, a Xsara early in the year and then a C4. But his schedule was for the full Championship season. While Rautenbach showed a decent turn of speed here and there, he isn't mature enough yet to achieve any worthwhile results. His fourth place in Argentina owed a lot to luck; otherwise it was his slip-ups rather than his performances that caught the eye. But he was in touch with Citroën about continuing in the same car in 2009 with PH Sport as a member of the Citroën satellite team.

Andreas MIKKELSEN

IDENTITY CARD
- Nationality: Norwegian
- Date of birth: June 22, 1989
- Place of birth: (N)
- Marital status: Single
- Co-driver: Ola Fløene (N)
- Web: www.andreasmikkelsen.com

CAREER
- Rally debut: 2006
- Nbr. of rallies in WRC: 15
- Best result: 1 x 5th

2006 – not classified
2007 – 25th in Championship
2008 – 16th in Championship

With a driving instructor like Marcus Grönholm you're hardly likely to go unnoticed. The young Norwegian contested a number of rallies this year in a privateer Ford Focus WRC, finishing fifth in Sweden to become the youngest driver, at 18, ever to score points in a World Championship rally. The tall (1m 87) youngster impressed the rally world with his turn of speed in Finland, his times often among the top eight before he spoiled it all with an off. And the point he scored in Catalunya proved he also knew how to handle himself on tarmac. In late summer he had a test in a PH Sport C4 WRC with a view to perhaps joining the Citroën satellite outfit for 2009. It was a calling-card from the lad, whose father is neither poor nor unwilling to part with his money. He made no secret, either, of the fact that he was talking to Subaru about a third works Impreza – and that would almost certainly be a pay drive.

Junior Championship
Top of the class, Ogier

His name's Sébastien, he drives a Citroën and he's the World Champion. His name's not Loeb, though: it's Ogier, title-winner in his first season in the JWRC and only his third in motor sport. His meteoric rise is reminiscent of his older compatriot, who won the Super 1600 title, as the JWRC was then known, in 2001 in a Citroën Saxo.

Ogier is 24, 10 years younger than Loeb. Unlike his elder, the young ski monitor came to prominence with Peugeot. After winning the apprentice categories Rallye Jeunes in 2005 and Volant 206 in 2007, the driver from the Alps became part of the world elite this year, backed by the FFSA and Citroën and recommended by Loeb, who had been impressed by his namesake when spectating at a rally in France.

This year, as he took on drivers with a lot more experience, Ogier was helped by the fact that the season began with two events that had never been on the JWRC schedule previously, i.e. Mexico and Jordan. In Central America the Citroën man skipped away with it in his C2 Super 1600 to beat Suzuki pair Mölder and Kosciuszko.

Eighth overall on that event, he was also the first man in the Juniors to score a full World Championship point. Title contenders Sandell (Renault Clio) and Prokop (Citroën C2) were fifth and seventh respectively after hitting trouble of one kind or another.

In Jordan Ogier had a troubled start and fell down the order, but produced an incredible fightback drive in the next two legs and managed to win the event, again helped by Sandell's own problems. Burkart (Citroën C2) and Prokop had both opted to miss that round. Suzuki's Polish driver Kosciuszko won in Sardinia from Bettega (Renault Clio) and Burkart. There, Ogier was fifth after retiring from the opening leg.

Sandall and Prokop, seventh and 10th respectively in Italy, needed to take full advantage of Ogier's missing the Finnish round if they were to get back within reach of France's new diamond. The Czech did just that, beating the Swede and Kosciuszko, then second just two points behind Ogier.

But the Frenchman returned to winning ways in Germany, which the Pole missed. Just like Loeb among the big boys, Ogier ran away with it on this, his first tarmac event. Transmission failure put paid to Prokop's title hopes and Sandell, who missed the round, was also out of the running by then.

That missed opportunity will probably weigh on the Czech's mind for a while, because he went on to win both of the last two events in Catalunya and Corsica. In Spain Ogier made his first major mistake of the year, going off when victory seemed assured. So on his home soil in Corsica the Frenchman took it very steadily, settling for second place, enough to clinch the title – and a drive in a Citroën C4 WRC to play with in Great Britain, in the same playground as the other Seb!

Never out of the top five and on the podium three times, Aaron Burkart finished eight points adrift of Ogier while Prokop was third overall.

Sébastien Ogier

Production Championship
Aigner reborn

The WRC was one step too far for Andrea Aigner. Signed up by Red Bull as a member of the works Skoda team in 2006, the Austrian never hit the target, with a sixth place in Germany the best he had to show for it. But his sponsor stuck by him, maintaining that with a bit more experience the young man would show what he could really do. So Aigner stepped back a level, into the PWRC. Ninth in the 2007 campaign, the Red Bull protégé proved his backers right by winning this year's title. Mind you, his year got off to a bad start when he could only finish 14th in Sweden, won by Hänninen from Ketomaa and Sandell. But then Aigner strung three victories together. In Argentina he beat local driver Beltran, too strapped for cash to do the rest of the year, and Ketomaa, who was on the podium again and a surprise leader of the Championship at that stage – helped by Sandell's retirement and the fact that was this an event Hänninen missed. In Greece Aigner took over at the top, winning from Portuguese pair Arauho and Sousa as Hänninen could only manage seventh. The Austrian then drove his advantage home when he beat Sandell and Baldacci in Turkey. By then we thought he was pretty well home and dry. But while he gave Finland a miss, the local men ruled the roost, Hänninen getting the better of Valimaki and Ketomaa. In New Zealand, at last, Hänninen and Aigner were both in the same event – and for the first time this season one slipped through both men's fingers as Martin Prokop took it from Sandell and Raum. It was a good weekend's work for Hänninen, though, as he finished fifth while Aigner had to retire. A win in Japan, the second event Aigner skipped, put the Finn back in the Championship lead and he came to Great Britain six points to the good. Fourth place, then, would be enough for Hänninen. Sadly for him, his Mitsubishi would fail him on the first leg. Patrik Flodin gave the new Subaru Impreza its maiden win while second place gave Andrea Aigner the title by two points from Hänninen, 10 from Ketomaa and 16 from Sandell. "Fantastic!" said the 24-year-old Austrian, "I'm in heaven. It was a very diffiicult rally, you just need to count how many people retired to see that. We're happy just to be at the finish. After Juho retired a podium was enough for us, and we did it." It remains to be seen what Red Bull will do for their young protégé. The energy drink firm already sponsor Citroën, so will they look to make the logical next move?

Andreas Aigner

↗ The Young Ones

The Young Ones

At 34, Sébastien Loeb and Petter Solberg are the doyens of the world rallying scene, the last World Champions still in action. While Old Man Seb and Old Man Petter have no intention of letting go without a fight, it's time to ask ourselves who might be about to force them into retirement, or at least take over once they are gone. So let's look at the youngsters who want to be winners themselves. They're all under 25, they're quick, rich or handsome – or all three! These are the kids to watch in 2009.

↗ Jari-Matti Latvala

At 22, Jari-Matti Latvala looks like the man with the best chance of picking up the baton. In February he became the youngest World Championship rally winner with his victory in Sweden. Though this season brought the first works drive of his career, the Finn is a WRC veteran – he first arrived in 2002 for the Rally of Great Britain at just 17. With the help of manager Timo Jouhki he's been able to get into everything you can drive in rallying terms – Super 1600, Group A, Group N, WRC – and fine-tune his experience. Backed by rallying's most famous starmaker, Latvala's coming of age was low but steady: first point scored in 2006, first clean sheet 2007, first time in the lead of a rally, first podium and finally first win in 2008. Latvala, probably the quickest guy out there, needs a little more maturity to stop him going off quite as often as he did this year – something that cost him a temporary relegation from the Ford works team in Corsica and Catalunya. If he wants to become a title contender, he needs to channel his drive and concentration the way Grönholm did before him.

↗ Andreas Mikkelsen

No less a figure than double World Champion Marcus Grönholm has thrown his full weight behind Andrea Mikkelsen. It's hard to know if what convinced him was the Norwegian's own talent or his father's cash, but whatever it was, the young retiree became the driving instructor to the dashing young man of the WRC. They began their work together with thousands of kilometres on snow and ice, and the lessons bore fruit: in Sweden, at just 18, Mikkelsen became the youngest driver to score a World Championship point. Unlike Latvala, Mikkelsen was thrown straight in at the WRC deep end; all he has driven in his brief career is the Ford Focus. His mega-rich Dad thinks he doesn't have time to muck about in Group N's, Super 1600's or whatever... But the youngster and the Finn do have one thing in common: a nice turn of speed which they have yet to fully master, and that's an area to work on in 2009.

↗ The Young Ones

↗ Matthew Wilson

If you want to break into rallying it helps to have a rich father. Better still, a father who's not only well off but runs his own team as well. Matthew Wilson has been knocking around the rally scene since he was 17. Too young to race anywhere else in Europe, he made a promising enough start in the British series, notably in competition with Latvala. But 'The Child' has struggled to confirm that potential at world level. He was, until Mikkelsen came along, the youngest points-scorer in World Championship history, but that was because of his ability to get to the finish rather than his sheer speed. Maybe he's been told not to go breaking any cars when it's Dad – Malcolm, M-Sport boss and the man who runs Ford's world rally programme – who's paying for them. If he doesn't lift his game in 2009, it'll be hard to see him as the new star Britain has been desperately looking for since losing the much-missed Colin McRae and Richard Burns.

↗ Conrad Rautenbach

He's another one it's hard to see as the future star of the world rally scene. Now 23, the Zimbabwean is super-quick, thanks to the fortune his Dad is making out of diamonds. But the young heir to the business still needs a little polish himself. After several years in the JWRC and after winning the African title in 2007, Conrad was given a Citroën C4 WRC for 2008. While there was a lucky fourth-place finish in Argentina, he really hit the headlines with his head-on collision, on a road link, with Loeb in Jordan. But what could the Chevron say about that to one of their best clients?

↗ Dani Sordo

Maybe the man to take over from Loeb is already at Citroën. As he waits patiently in the great Frenchman's shadow, 25-year-old Dani Sordo must be learning plenty. The Spaniard is almost as good as his team-mate on tarmac, and the 2005 Junior World Champion has also gone up another level on gravel this year. He may find it hard to blossom while the five-time title-winner is still around, but when Loeb does eventually retire, that could be his chance. He will certainly be the most experienced of the lot by then. But there's another Sébastien who could carry on Loeb's winning ways, and that's Ogier, the young ski monitor who only made his rally debut in 2006 but was a clear-cut Junior title-winner this year. Citroën will throw him in among the WRC big boys next year in a satellite team. Is he on the same fast track Loeb followed?

↗ Evgeny Novikov

The star of tomorrow just might be someone coming in from the cold. At 17, Evgeny Novikov is the new name on many people's lips. He started his motor sport career at home in Russia with his Dad in the seat beside him. After winning the Russian Cup in 2006, he cut his teeth in the national series and Estonia in 2007 and caught the eye when the IRC visited his home country, leading that round before halted by mechanical failure. He finished the year with a promising first appearance in the World Championship in Great Britain – the only place he was allowed to compete while still under 18. This year he again showed up well in the IRC on the Russian round and was the youngest driver to enter the PWRC. He had an average year until Japan, where he only lost out on the class win in the final stage. This is the youngster to watch in 2009.

↗ Sébastien Loeb

The legend
Loeb
grows

Five world titles – on the trot, if you don't mind: the legend of Sébastien Loeb just grows and grows. At the end of yet another record-breaking season, it's time to look back on some of the landmark rallies in his WRC career.

2004 | Sweden

This was Loeb's first history-making win: heading home Petter Solberg's Subaru and the Peugeot of Marcus Grönholm, he became the first non-Nordic driver to win in the snows of Sweden, a fortnight after winning the season-opening Monte Carlo event. It was also the Frenchman's first win on a surface other than tarmac.

2004 | France

A decade after Didier Auriol and his Toyota, Loeb (aged 30) and his Citroën presented France with her second world title. After leading the Championship from its opening round, the Frenchman clinched the title on home soil on the French island of Corsica, where second behind Markko Märtin was enough to make him Champion in only his second full WRC season. To round off a dream Sunday for Citroën, they also took the constructors' crown.

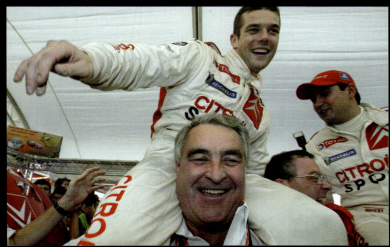

2004 | Australia

A first record for Loeb, ending the season in style with victory on Rally Australia. This was his sixth of the season, equaling the record number for a single season which had been the exclusive property of Didier Auriol since 1992. Loeb finished the season with a 36-point margin over Petter Solberg, who had beaten him by just one the previous year.

Sébastien Loeb

2005 | Argentina

He's from another planet! After winning in New Zealand, Sardinia, Cyprus, Turkey and on the Acropolis, Loeb took his Citroën Xsara to the first Argentine victory of his career. Six wins in a row: it had never been done before – the previous best was Timo Salonen's four back in 1985. The legend was growing…

2005 | Great Britain

Champions tend to want to win at all costs. Not Loeb: following Markko Märtin's accident and the death of his co-driver Michael Park, Peugeot withdrew Grönholm's Peugeot from the event, handing the title to comfortable leader Loeb. Loeb and Elena refused to take the title in such unhappy circumstances and deliberately incurred a penalty, which handed victory to Petter Solberg. Loeb's a class act.

2005 | Japan

Two weeks after that Cardiff tragedy, second pace in Japan brought Loeb his second straight title with three events still to be run. The Frenchman was the first driver since Tommi Mäkinen to retain his crown.

2005 | France

With the pressure of winning the title lifted, the Citroën driver starred once more in his home event, clean-sheeting 12 times on the Tour of Corsica. No driver had ever won every single stage on a World Championship rally. Loeb added yet another record a week later in Catalunya with his 10th win of the season.

2006 | Monte Carlo

With Citroën taking a year's sabbatical, Belgian team Kronos stepped in. Now in a blue Xsara, Loeb went off in the opening leg, restarted next day under SupeRally with five minutes' worth of penalties, set fastest time after fastest time and finished second behind Grönholm.

2006 | Japan

Loeb eclipsed Carlos Sainz's famous record, winning his 27th World Championship event in style. For three days he and Grönholm went at it hammer and tongs, Loeb eventually winning it by just 5.6 seconds – his sixth win of the season, putting him 33 points clear of the Finn.

2006 | Australia

Three months after Japan, just a solitary point separated Loeb and Grönholm at season's end. The Frenchman broke his arm falling off his bike in late September, missed the rest of the season and watched events unfold on TV from his home in Switzerland. Grönholm went off in the first leg, handing Loeb his third straight title on a plate.

Sébastien Loeb

2007 | Italy

Loeb can come up with the best – and, sometimes, the worst! In Sardinia and again in Japan he compromised his title chances by going off, both times while in the lead. On the island off Italy he had no-one to blame but himself, while in Hokkaido it was Daniel Elena who misread a pace note.

2007 | Monte Carlo

Citroën were back, complete with new car developed by Loeb during the 2006 season. The Alsace ace gave it a winning baptism on a new Monte Carlo lay-out taking in the Ardèche and the Vercors. Nothing, it seemed, could stop him...

2007 | New Zealand

A breathtaking, historic event as Loeb and Grönholm, both at the peak of their powers, fought out a classic duel that made headlines all round the world. After three days of intense competition, it was the Finn's Ford that came out on top, by just three-tenths of a second. We'd never seen the like...

2007 | Great Britain

Time to say good-bye: Loeb spent the season's final weekend in the company of his toughest rival, Grönholm, and the man who had been his mentor, Guy Fréquelin. The Finn was off-colour still after his off-road excursion in Ireland; the Frenchman settled for a third place that also meant a fourth world title, putting him on level pegging with Mäkinen and Kankkunen.

2008 | Jordan

Loeb made the front pages again as the World Championship went to this new venue, not by winning this time, but for retiring after a head-on with Rautenbach's C4 on a road link – not something you see very often in rallying.

2008 | Finland

He'd waited six years for this: six years playing second fiddle to Grönholm. With the Espoo giant in retirement, Loeb didn't pass up the chance to beat the Flying Finns at home at last, as Carlos Sainz and Didier Auriol had done before him. The Citroën star had his work cut out for him, though, as Mikko Hirvonen fought long and hard before going down by just nine seconds.

2008 | Germany

If Grönholm was invincible in Finland, Loeb just couldn't be beaten in Germany. An easy win in Trier made the Citroën man the first driver to win the same World Championship event seven times in a row – he'd never lost this particular rally since it came on to the calendar back in 2002!

2008 | Japan

The event that put Loeb in a place of his own: third on the Japanese round behind Hirvonen and Latvala, he became the first driver to win five titles – and five in a row at that, confirming the Frenchman as the greatest rally driver of all time.

Christian Loriaux

'It'll pay off in the long run'

Once again the Focus designed by Christian Loriaux's Belgian teams, with engines built by Jean-Pierre 'Pipo' Fleur and his men, was the only car to beat Loeb's Citroën C4 this year. But thanks mainly to mistakes by drivers Mikko Hirvonen and Jari-Matti Latvala, Ford couldn't hang on to their constructors' crown. No regrets, though, from the team's technical director – and he is adamant that, given a few years, the two Finns will wreak havoc. Provided Loeb retires – and rallying survives the current crisis. There were no holds barred when Christian Loriaux spoke to us.

How do you see the 2008 season? As Ford's TD, are you happy with how it went?
On the whole, yes. Our performance level was super, but unfortunately we were hamstrung by fragile suspension on the really tough rallies, and that was frustrating. We should have strengthened that componentry but we were caught out by the new Pirelli tyre: it's stiffer than we are used to, it feeds more back through the suspension and we didn't take full account of that. In competitive terms I think the Focus was the best car on gravel. Leaving aside Loeb, genius that he is, no-one was able to keep up with our drivers. Even our customers were quick, which shows what an easy car it is to use. On tarmac, on the other hand, we weren't as good as we were last year and Citroën were better than us. We didn't get to grips with the new Pirelli in terms of its driveability. It wasn't a tyre you could treat too roughly and Loeb grasped that very quickly, while our guys didn't. We got that one a bit wrong. We made some progress late in the season thanks to François Duval's contribution, but we never really caused Loeb any concern – unlike last year when Marcus took it up to him, especially in Ireland. Overall, I think it was a frustrating season for us. Sébastien Loeb thoroughly deserved his drivers' title, but I think we were good enough to take the constructors' – and we lost it in New Zealand.

What about the performance of your drivers, Hirvonen and Latvala?
Before the season began everybody said Loeb would win every rally. But straight away, in Sweden, Latvala surprised everyone by dominating the opposition. After that, though, Jari-Matti's lack of experience and his hot-headedness cost him dear. We paid dearly, too, for his apprenticeship year but he's a good long-term investment. Mikko was pretty good wherever we went. All right, he got beaten at home in Finland, but Loeb was just outstanding on that one. Mikko had a good, consistent season. His only problem is that he likes to drift the car a bit too much and that cost him quite a few punctures. New Zealand sums up our two drivers' performances, really: they were opening the road, yet Loeb couldn't catch them. But then Jari-Matti went off because of a mistake in his notes and Miko got another puncture. So what looked like a 1-2 for us went to Citroën instead, and the whole season hinged on that. You can't blame them, though – but for their speed we wouldn't have been able to think about winning. So we are very pleased these two young drivers are on long-term contracts with us, whereas over at Citroën Loeb is in the later stages of his career and Sordo can be good… and not so good. In the long run it will pay off.

Christian Loriaux

As early as 2009? Can Hirvonen or Latvala beat Loeb next year?
I don't know. This year they showed that on a good day they can go after Loeb, but I don't think they're as consistent as he is yet. Over the course of a whole year, he's really hard to beat. The sooner he retires, the better it will be for us!

Your boss, Malcolm Wilson, and a former driver of yours, Marcus Grönholm, think Loeb is the best ever. Would you agree?
In statistical terms, he's obviously the greatest. But I've never worked with him, I've followed his driving from afar, so I'm not as taken with him as some are, on top of which, he tends to keep himself to himself. And he never makes any real mistakes – he makes it all look so easy. If you're asking me about great drivers, then I'd say Colin McRae, and I did work with him. You'd watch him leave the service park with the suspension mangled – and he'd put 30 seconds on the rest of them in the next stage. The sort of stuff you can only dream about... For me, Colin was more charismatic than Seb as well, and those are the guys we don't have in rallying these days. Loeb, Hirvonen, Latvala: they're all a bit squeaky clean for me. But Sébastien is a fantastic driver and as long as he's here he's going to be hard to beat. The amazing thing is that he's still as motivated as ever even though he's won everything there is to win and he's got nothing left to prove.

What about Grönholm: do you think he was itching to get back into the cockpit this year?
He didn't come to many rallies. I thought he'd miss it more than he seems to have. But we certainly missed him. We'd obviously have been a lot stronger if he'd been with us.

What about the rest of the competition, aside from Citroën?
The trouble is that the Championship's all about us and Citroën. I don't know what's going on at Subaru! It must be something to do with the organization, the management – on the technical side they've got

everything it takes to make a good car. I know Christophe Chapelain, who designed the new Impreza, and he's good. On the other hand, Suzuki have really come on – they had a really good Japanese event, and now they need to keep that momentum going.

There's a lot of debate about the future World Championship regulations. What's the position there, and what do you think about it all?
We're in a bit of an impasse. Every time a decision is taken, the authorities go back on it at the next World Council meeting. The manufacturers aren't in particularly good financial health right now, and the uncertainty about where the sport's going isn't helping them. Rallying's in a bad way. The worst of it is that the manufacturers involved are quite happy with the regs as they are, and big efforts have been made to cut costs. Nobody's too sure where we're heading, but for our part we're working on the Fiesta Super 2000, which will go on sale in 2010. That's a nice project – and if the WRC falls over, we can always turn to the IRC.

Looking to the future, who will be the big star in rallying five years from now, in your view?
I'd say Latvala – he's very quick and he's very keen! But that remains to be seen: he can drop some real clangers, and that's a worry. Hirvonen needs to find a bit more speed. I thought he'd gone as far as he could last year but I've seen more progress from him this year, so maybe he can take it up another level. Ogier's obviously a good one, but I'm not sure about Mikkelsen: he's been competing for some time now and he's never really done much. The good ones – men like Delecour, McRae, Loeb – were winners as soon as they got their backsides in a WRC or Group A car. I think we should keep an eye on Novikov, the Russian – he really impressed me in Japan. He's obviously a talented guy. ■

↗ Intercontinental Rally Challenge

Freddy Loix, Nicolas Vouilloz, Valais (CH)

IRC
Getting some of their own back

After playing a big hand in Peugeot's constructors' title with some brilliant WRC performances, Kronos found themselves with nowhere to go in that series. But they bounced back in the IRC. Nicolas Vouilloz also got his own back on the drivers' front after a difficult 2007.

Luca Rossetti, Istanbul (TUR)

Anyone who thinks the points system introduced by the FIA is absurd will find further proof of that fact in the last two seasons of the Intercontinental Rally Challenge. With three wins, Nicolas Vouilloz was the stand-out performer in 2007, but lost out in the end to Peugeot Spain team-mate Garcia Odeja, who was consistently in the top places without ever winning an event. So this year the Frenchman went for consistency himself, and a good job he made of it: he won just the once but six second-place finishes put him ahead of Peugeot team-mate Freddy Loix (three wins, Abarth number one Giandomenico Basso (two) and another Italian, Luca Rossetti (also two).

It was the first international title on four wheels for the 32-year-old former cyclist, who was 10 times a mountain-bike World Champion, but not his first title in a car – Vouilloz was French tarmac champion in a Peugeot 307 WRC. That was back in 2006, two years after he made a difficult World Championship debut.

The man from Nice began his conversion from two wheels to four in 2003, and was soon just as much at home in special stages as he was on mountain slopes, easily winning Peugeot's promotional class, the Volant 206, run on gravel and asphalt. With Loeb coming through in the rival camp, Citroën, the top brass at Peugeot Sport thought they'd found a gem of their own. With the exception of Gilles Panizzi, they had never really given many opportunities to other drivers who had come through their own promotional series, men like Cédric Robert, for example. This time they threw everything behind Vouilloz, who was thrown into the World Championship after just 14 rallies in the amateur ranks. Given little chance to go testing either, the debutant duly got his wings singed. In a 206 WRC, he had a hard time of it in his six opportunities to show what he could do. He went off on the Monte, on the Acropolis and in Sardinia, broke down in Corsica, and his best result was ninth in Great Britain. "I really copped it!" Vouilloz recalls. "The top guys were putting at least a second a kilometre on me. I let people down, and I let

Giandomenico Basso, Faro (P)

IRC ↗ Intercontinental Rally Challenge

Giandomenico Basso, Ypres (B)

Freddy Loix, Valais (CH)

myself down. I never thought there would be such a big gap between a newcomer and the World Championship regulars. I didn't realize experience counted for so much in this sport. You can't just come in and expect to beat everyone – unless, of course, you're Loeb, but then he's from another planet! I put myself under a lot of pressure and I got it all wrong. I tried to tell myself that these guys were the best in the world and I wasn't doing as badly as all that, but it was really frustrating – I was used to winning everything there was to win on a mountain-bike."

Vouilloz thinks his IRC title is a better gauge of his talent than the French one.
"I'm proud to have won this one, because this is no minor series: my opposition may not be World Champions, but they're more experienced than I am and there are some good things on their CV's as well – Basso and Rossetti were both European Champions. This title shows the doubters that I belong in rallying. I'm not saying I can be World Champion, but I think I'm good enough to do well in the WRC, though I'm not obsessing about getting there."

Belgian team Kronos, which ran the Peugeot 207 Super 2000's of both Vouilloz and Loix in the colours of Peugeot Belgium/Luxembourg, played a big part in the French marque's constructors' title, with seven wins in nine rounds contested, three to Loix (Ypres, Barum, Valais), two to Rossetti (Turkey and Portugal) and one each to Vouilloz (Madeira) and Hanninen (Russia). It was sweet revenge, too, for Kronos, two years after taking the WRC title for Citroën with Loeb. "When we left the World Championship at the end of 2007 we were fed up with the part politics plays in it all,"

Nicolas Vouilloz, Istanbul (TUR)

Giandomenico Basso, San Remo (I)

Anton Alen, St Petersburg (RUS)

explained Marc Van Dalen, co-founder of the Namur outfit. "Ours was just a small team, and we did things from the heart and with a lot of passion. We got support when they needed us, and then they dumped us. I'm a real enthusiast, but even I was sick of rallying at that point. Some guys who had been with me for 10 years were on the brink of depression, and that's just not right. But the IRC has restored our spirits: there's still room for sport here, unlike the WRC, where business is all that matters. It's not all rosy in this series, we need more cars and well-known drivers, but it's a healthy atmosphere, and the regulations are fair enough and manageable enough to give everyone a chance of winning. And that makes for some good battles out there. It's a different mind-set, a refreshing one."
It may be a nice series, but its fate hangs in the balance. End-of-season rumours suggested that, given the dominance of the Peugeot 207's, Abarth, with just two wins, might be about to throw in the towel. But Skoda are in there now with their Fabia Super 2000, which will makes its Intercontinental Rally Challenge debut in 2009. ■

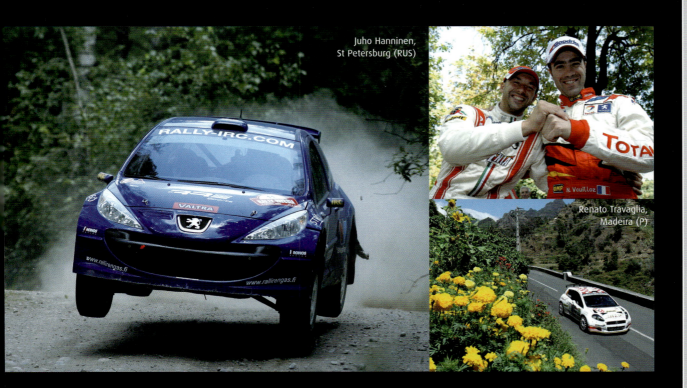

Juho Hanninen, St Petersburg (RUS)

Renato Travaglia, Madeira (P)

Championship

2008 Calendar
	Country	Date	Surface
1.	Turkey	4-6 April	Gravel
2.	Portugal	9-10 May	Gravel
3.	Belgium	27-28 June	Asphalt
4.	Russia	10-12 July	Gravel
5.	Madeira (P)	1-2 August	Asphalt
6.	Czech Rep.	22-24 August	Asphalt
7.	Spain	12-13 Sept.	Asphalt
8.	Italy	25-27 Sep.	Asphalt
9.	Switzerland	23-25 October	Asphalt
10.	China	5-7 December	Gravel

Drivers Standings*
1.	Nicolas Vouilloz (F)	1	58
2.	Freddy Loix (B)	3	48
3.	Giandomenico Basso (I)	2	46
4.	Luca Rossetti (I)	2	44
5.	Anton Alèn (FIN)		21
6.	Renato Travaglia (I)		19
7.	Jan Kopecky (CZ)		15
8.	Juho Hanninen (FIN)	1	14
9.	Bryan Bouffier (F)		11
10.	Alexandre Camacho (P)		6
11.	Pavel Valousek (CZ)		5
12.	Enrique Ojeda (E)		5
13.	Bernd Casier (B)		5
14.	Patrick Snijers (B)		4
15.	Bruno Magalhaes (P)		4
16.	Janos Toth (H)		4
17.	Miguel Fuster (E)		4
18.	Alessandro Perico (I)		3
19.	Dani Sola (E)		3
20.	Luca Cantamessa (I)		2
21.	Manfred Stohl (A)		2
22.	Jasper van den Heuvel (NL)		2
23.	Sergio Vallejo (E)		2
24.	Umberto Scandola (I)		2
25.	Gregoire Hotz (CH)		2
26.	Brice Tirabassi (F)		2
27.	Volkan Isik (TR)		2
28.	Paul Lietaer (B)		1
29.	Oleg Antropov (RUS)		1
30.	Andreas Aigner (A)		1
31.	Alberto Hevia (E)		1
32.	Josef Petak (CZ)		1

Constructors Standings*
1.	Peugeot	106
2.	Abarth	74
3.	Mitsubishi	10
4.	Volkswagen	5

* before the Rally of China

THERE'S NO DOUBT HE'S TALENTED

Just not talented enough to worry Sébastien Loeb. Mikko Hirvonen gave it everything he had in 2008, here in Central America for example, in his bid to take the title. But at least his year as Ford number one will have taught him a few good lessons. Will that be enough, though, to take him to another level in 2009?

Photographer François Baudin **Kit** Canon EOS-1D Mark II N; 300mm; 1/640 at F9

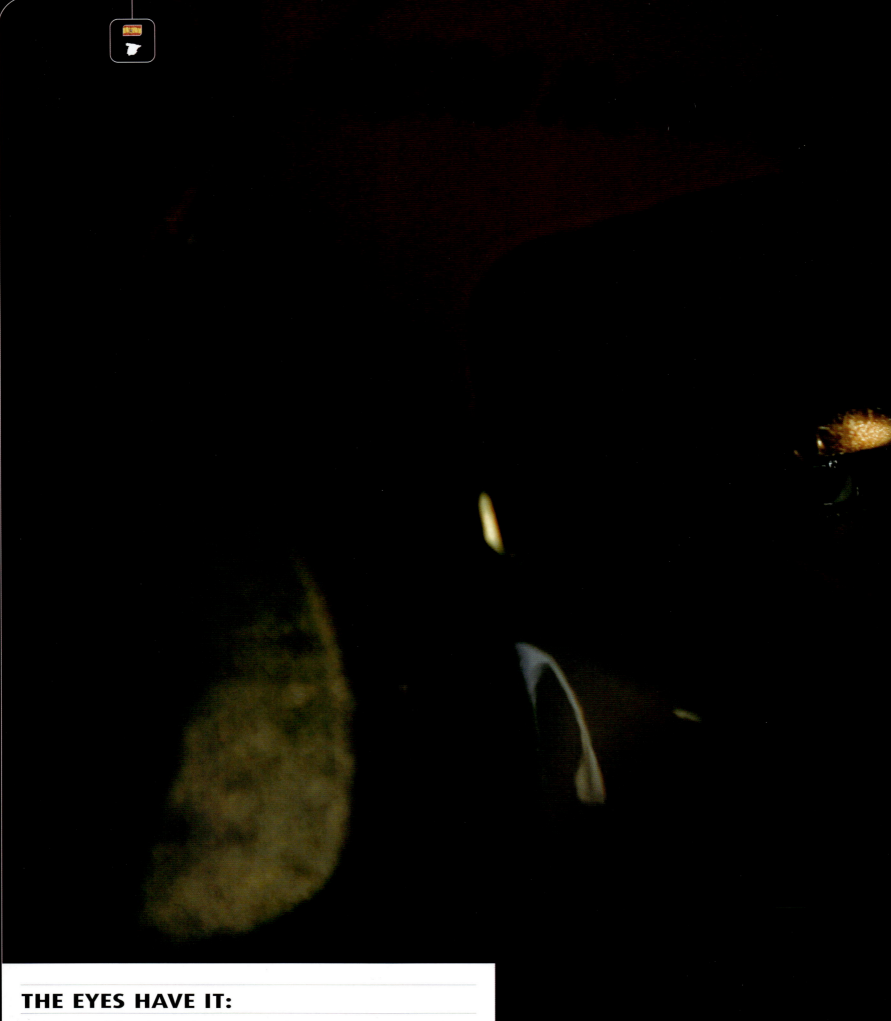

THE EYES HAVE IT:

all the focus, all the talent of the man now without question the greatest driver in rallying history. Wins, titles, points scored... he owns every record. For Sébastien Loeb, though, it's always possible to go a little bit higher – and the bad news for the opposition is that he has absolutely no intention of stopping. This is the look of a serial killer...

Photographer François Baudin **Kit** Canon EOS-1D Mark II N; 153mm; 1/250 at F4

COULD THE MAN

making light work of the Rally of Sweden in this Ford be the new face of rallying? On that event 18-year-old Andrea Mikkelsen became the youngest man in history to score points in a World Championship rally. Remember the name, and put it beside those of Latvala, Ogier and Novikov in a new generation full of promise.

Photographer François Baudin **Kit** Canon EOS-1D Mark II N; 35mm; 1/8 at F9

2009 FIA WRC

01	🇲🇨	Monte Carlo	54
02	🇸🇪	Sweden P-WRC	62
03	🇲🇽	Mexico J-WRC	70
04	🇦🇷	Argentina P-WRC	78
05	🇯🇴	Jordan J-WRC	86
06	🇮🇹	Italy J-WRC	94
07	🇬🇷	Greece P-WRC	102
08	🇹🇷	Turkey P-WRC	110
09	🇫🇮	Finland J-WRC P-WRC	118
10	🇩🇪	Germany J-WRC	126
11	🇳🇿	New Zealand P-WRC	134
12	🇪🇸	Spain J-WRC	142
13	🇫🇷	France J-WRC	150
14	🇯🇵	Japan P-WRC	158
15	🇬🇧	Great Britain P-WRC	166

01 MONTE-CARLO

🇲🇨 A flying start for Loeb

Sébastien Loeb had a new boss in Olivier Quesnel, new tyres from Pirelli and new rivals, with Hirvonen first among them – but it made no difference as he started his season in familiar fashion with a comfortable victory in Monte Carlo ahead of Hirvonen and Atkinson. Despite the turbo failure that brought Dani Sordo's rally to a premature end, it was the best possible start to the 2008 season for Citroën.

01 | Monte-Carlo

The year's first front-runner, and the only man to give Loeb a run for his money on the Monte, Dani Sordo was forced into retirement by a turbo failure midway through the second leg.

Back on World Championship duty, François Duval was hoping to set the Monte on fire. But the Belgian didn't have enough miles under his belt to fulfil that hope. Despite four stage wins he just missed out on a podium finish.

THE RALLY
Not quite what it seems?

Ten wins from 19 special stages, a 2m34s lead over his nearest pursuer in the Principality: Sébastien Loeb's crushing victory on the Monte seemed, on a January Sunday, to confirm what many people had been saying: in the absence of both Marcus Grönholm and Guy Fréquelin, Loeb would be head and shoulders above the rest of the field this season. But after setting a new record number of wins on the Monaco event the Citroën driver sounded a note of caution. "We mustn't get carried away," said Loeb, "because Monte Carlo isn't necessarily a true reflection of the rest of the season. It's my favourite hunting-ground, but not really my rivals'," he warned. "We saw what happened last year, when Dani (the other Citroën driver) and I were out in front here, but then things got a bit more complicated after that. Of course it's always good to get 10 points, it makes you feel good – but it doesn't tell you what's going to happen next. By the time we get to Sweden it'll be another story."

The 2007 finishing order: 1st Loeb, 2nd Sordo, 38 seconds down and 3rd Grönholm, 1m 22 back. So Hirvonen, second this year, 2:34 behind Loeb, couldn't match the pace of his older colleague, the great and newly-retired Marcus. But the scoreboard told a different, happier tale. "He drove a good rally," observed Loeb, "and that's no surprise. He showed he's not bad on tarmac, though maybe not at the same level as Sordo or me. But with nobody nipping in between us, he chalked up a lot of points, the way Grönholm used to do. He's obviously going to be the one I have to worry about over the Championship, because he will be my most consistent challenger. Last year he proved he could be quick without going off, so he's the man we should be looking at again this year."

A delighted Hirvonen said he had been hoping to get closer to Loeb's pace but just couldn't: "Still, second's a great way to start the season," he added. "That's the target I set myself for this year: to make sure I take the points for second place if I'm not able to win." That's a recipe that's already come in very handy for the man with four world titles to his name, Sébastien Loeb himself.

So while the Fords might have given cause for concern in terms of sheer performance, that wasn't reflected on the board, either on the driver front or the constructors', as Citroën came away from the Prncipality with 10 points to Ford's 8. Each team's second driver had kicked off his season with a no-score.

As in 2007 Sordo, who led after the first stage, was on Loeb's hammer until a diff problem dropped him back into the pack, and a turbo failure eliminated him on SS11. So the first task for Guy Fréquelin's successor as head of Citroën Sport, Olivier Quesnel, was to cheer up a downhearted young Spaniard after another dose of bad luck. "Pain in the backside," grumbled Sordo, "there aren't that many tarmac rallies on the calendar…"

Latvala, on the other hand, had only himself to blame. The man taking over from Grönholm at Ford made the worst possible start to his career as a works driver, losing over four minutes with a puncture on the opening stage. "It was about 13 kilometres from the end, on a right-hander," he explained after the opener, "and I

Always at home on the Monte Carlo stages, Chris Atkinson claimed his first tarmac podium, taking third place from François Duval on the very last test through the Monte Carlo streets.

Even without Guy Fréquelin's wise counsel, Sébastien Loeb was his usual calm self on his way to a fifth win in the Principality in six years – the perfect way to start the season.

went too far to the inside of the corner and hit a rock. I got a puncture and had to stop to change the wheel, but that took longer than I thought because the nuts had gripped up." You learn by your mistakes, as the saying goes. Not if you're Jari-Matti Latvala, it seems: he made a similar blunder on the Saturday, and this time he left his suspension behind. "Our intermediate time was good, but in the middle of the stage, on a very narrow stretch of road, I must have cut a corner too much and hit a lump of concrete," he confessed. "It took me another 500 metres to find a spot wide enough to stop. I made two mistakes that made it a very difficult weekend for me, but I learned a lot about the way to straight-line corners and, more generally, the driving style you need to get the best out of your tyres."

Ford's satellite Stobart team also scored 8 points thanks to the combined efforts of their two comeback men, Duval, who was 4th, and 6th-placed Galli. The Belgian hadn't been seen on the world stage since the 2007 Tour of Corsica, while Galli only did three events last year. There was one major difference between the two drivers as they returned: the effervescent Italian, backed by Pirelli, was guaranteed a start in every round for the fiirst time in his career, while the big Walloon had only the three tarmac rallies on his schedule. So while both adopted a cautious approach to the Monte Carlo Rally, it was for different reasons. "I don't want to rush things," said Galli, "I plan to use the first few rallies to get to grips with the car, then go on the attack a bit later in the season." For Duval there was one major worry: his new co-driver, one forced on him by his sponsor but not really up to the job. As he waited for the notes to come, the Belgian had to take things as he saw them and improvise. Nothing unusual there, some unkind souls might say. Left behind on the night stages, where his gravel crew had broken down and he had no notes for the icy roads, Duval fought back bit by bit. With four scratch times he came fourth, just a second off the podium, and that was his second-best result on the Monte. "At least I scored some points," said the Belgian drily, as much a reference to the Stobart haul as a reminder to Malcolm Wilson – and certainly better than nothing for a driver in search of a seat.

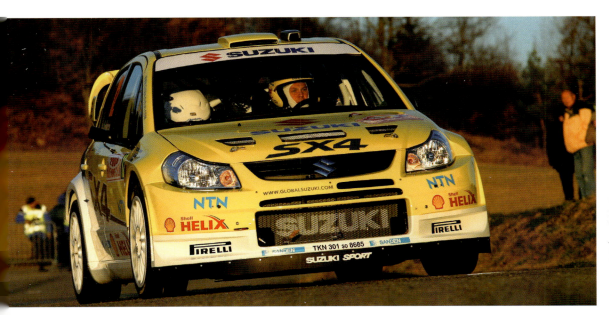

Per-Gunnar Andersson, Sweden's double Junior World Champion, did a good job on his debut among the big boys, bringing the Suzuki home in eighth place.

01 | Monte-Carlo

Marcus Grönholm used to like to have his say about the going on the Monte stages. His Ford successor Mikko Hirvonen wasn't entirely convincing but did some good damage limitation, yielding only two points to Loeb.

Subaru also got both cars home in the points. It was Chris Atkinson's third crack at the event, and he went one better again: 6th in 2006, 4th last year, and 3rd in 2008, snatching a podium place from Duval on the very last super-special through the Monaco streets. That's admirable consistency on such unpredictable terrain. "Last year on this stage I was fighting for a place with Mikko Hirvonen," recalled the Australian. "This year there was even more pressure because a podium finish was at stake. It's the perfect way to start the season." Petter Solberg would probably have loved a result like that, but he settled for fifth place, his best effort on the Monte in eight tries. Overall, then, a good result for the Blues as they wait for the new Impreza due later in the season. And here's a point worth noting just because it's so unusual: every constructor scored points on this event, with two-time Junior World Champion Per Gunnar Andersson's remarkable eighth place giving Suzuki a successful start to their official career on the world stage. Gardemeister, who is usually right at home here, had been forced into retirement with engine failure on the Staurday evening.

To round off on the people who came away from the season's first rally with something to smile about, let's not forget local man Jean-Marie Cuoq. The Ardèche driver, France's tarmac champion, lifted his Peugeot 307 WRC into seventh spot, finishing as the leading privateer and scoring his first World Championship points. Sadly his joy was short-lived: soon after, he was suspended by the FFSA over some sordid story of illegal reconnaissance in the 2007 national championship.

So he would be following the rest of the World Championship season from afar – a season that promised to be a thriller despite Loeb's easy win. "It's very satisfying to start my tenure with success on the Monte Carlo Rally," said new Citroën Sport boss Olivier Quesnel. "It gets us off to a solid start in both Championships, but I'm not getting carried away, and I know tarmac is often kind to us. The next event in Sweden presents us with a very different challenge straight away. On the slippery surface up there our rivals will be very strong and it will probably be a much more open race."

Fifth place isn't exactly the result a potential title contender's looking for, but after so many back-breaking years' work it was enough for Petter Solberg as he waited for the new Impreza, especially as it was also his best result on this particular event.

> Guaranteed a full season for the first time in his career, 'softly, softly' was Gigi Galli's approach to the Monte as he got his bearings in the Focus and settled for sixth place.

It's called a winter event, but even up at Mont-Gerbier-de-Jonc there was only a bit of snow left on the roadside this year. No matter what the conditions, though, the Principality is always King Seb's domain.

Ardèche driver Jean-Marie Cuoq was this year's local hero, bringing his privateer Peugeot 307 home seventh for his first World Championship points. But it all went wrong for the reigning French champion soon after: within weeks of the event he lost both his licence and his title for making illegal recces in the 2007 season.

Talk in the opposition camp was already of revenge. "There was a lot of pressure on Mikko's shoulders and I was impressed by the way he took it on," commented Malcolm Wilson, who was probably looking no futrther than Sweden at that stage. "I couldn't have asked for more from him in terms of the result. And Jari-Matti will be able to put his experience here to good use later in the season." ■

TALKING TECHNICAL
A clean, mistake-free start for Pirelli

There was some relief in the Pirelli camp on Sunday evening in Monaco. Their press officer was almost glad not to have seen the firm's name in the papers for the last four days. What about that? But that's how it goes when you are the sole supplier: when it all goes well, your name never comes up, but when something goes wrong it's open season on you. Well, the first event of the season produced just one puncture, Jari-Matti Latvala's on the opening stage. But Ford's Finn, overdoing it on an apex, shouldered the blame. No worries, then, for Pirelli, now the WRC's sole supplier in place of Michelin-BFGoodrich following the tender call by the FIA and a long court case.

There is now just one compound on offer, as opposed to five or six previously, and there are strict limits on the amount of re-cutting you can do. So this tyre will have to go for a whole season, dry or wet, hot or cold, and that's a major challenge for Pirelli. The occasional record set on the special stages showed the single tyre to be both tough and effective, contrary to what some of the drivers were anticipating. "Not many punctures, so no reason to complain," said Monte Carlo winner Sébastien Loeb, "in fact I was pleasantly surprised because in some conditions they worked very well – and we broke records to prove it. On the other hand we could have done with a harder compound when the conditions were warmer, as they were on Sunday. You couldn't let yourself go – that's not Pirelli's fault, it's down to the regulations insistng that we use a single compound." Still some unanswered questions, then, after the opening round... ■

01 | Monte-Carlo | Results

76th RALLY OF MONTE-CARLO

Organiser Details
ACM
B.P 464
23 Blvd Albert 1er
98012 MC Cedex, Monte-Carlo
Tel.: +377 9315 2600
Fax: +377 9315 8008

Rallye Automobile Monte-Carlo

1st leg of FIA 2008 World Championship for constructors and drivers.

Date January 24 - 27, 2008

Route
1481,25 km divised in four legs.
19 special stages on tarmac (365.09 km)

Ceremonial Start
Thursday, January 24 (17:30),
Champ de Mars, Valence
Leg 1
Thursday, January 24 (18:46/19:36),
Valence > Saint Jean en Royans > Valence,
169.31 km; 2 special stages (45.70 km)
Leg 2
Friday, January 25 (08:24/17:15),
Valence > Vals les Bains > Valence, 544.25 km;
6 special stages (116.96 km)
Leg 3
Saturday, January 26 (07:31/14:59),
Valence > Saint Bonnet le Froid > Valence,
443.26 km; 6 special stages (132.78 km)
Leg 4
Sunday, January 27 (09:50/15:10),
Monaco > Turini > Monaco, 324.43 km;
5 special stages (69.65 km)

Entry List (50) - 47 starters

N°	Driver (Nat.)	Co-Driver (Nat.)	Team	Car	Group & FIA Priority
1	SÉBASTIEN LOEB (F)	DANIEL ELENA (MC)	CITROEN TOTAL WRT	CITROEN C4 WRC	A8 1
2	DANIEL SORDO (E)	MARC MARTI (E)	CITROEN TOTAL WRT	CITROEN C4 WRC	A8 1
3	MIKKO HIRVONEN (FIN)	JARMO LEHTINEN (FIN)	BP FORD ABU DHABI WORLD RALLY TEAM	FORD FOCUS RS WRC 07	A8 1
4	JARI-MATTI LATVALA (FIN)	MIIKKA ANTTILA (FIN)	BP FORD ABU DHABI WORLD RALLY TEAM	FORD FOCUS RS WRC 07	A8 1
5	PETTER SOLBERG (N)	PHILIP MILLS (GB)	SUBARU WORLD RALLY TEAM	SUBARU IMPREZA WRC 2006	A8 1
6	CHRIS ATKINSON (AUS)	STÉPHANE PREVOT (B)	SUBARU WORLD RALLY TEAM	SUBARU IMPREZA WRC 2006	A8 1
7	GIGI GALLI (I)	GIOVANNI BERNACCHINI (I)	STOBART VK M-SPORT FORD RALLY TEAM	FORD FOCUS RS WRC 07	A8 1
8	FRANCOIS DUVAL (B)	EDDY CHEVAILLER (I)	STOBART VK M-SPORT FORD RALLY TEAM	FORD FOCUS RS WRC 07	A8 1
11	TONI GARDEMEISTER (FIN)	TOMI TUOMINEN (FIN)	SUZUKI WORLD RALLY TEAM	SUZUKI SX4	A8 1
12	PER-GUNNAR ANDERSSON (S)	JONAS ANDERSSON (S)	SUZUKI WORLD RALLY TEAM	SUZUKI SX4	A8 1
14	HENNING SOLBERG (N)	CATO MENKERUD (N)	STOBART VK M-SPORT FORD RALLY TEAM	FORD FOCUS RS WRC 07	A8 2
17	MATTHEW WILSON (GB)	SCOTT MARTIN (GB)	STOBART VK M-SPORT FORD RALLY TEAM	FORD FOCUS RS WRC 07	A8 2
18	JEAN MARIE CUOQ (F)	PHILIPPE JANVIER (F)	JEAN-MARIE CUOQ	PEUGEOT 307 WRC	A8 2
19	KHALID AL QASSIMI (UAE)	MICHAEL ORR (GB)	BP FORD ABU DHABI WORLD RALLY TEAM	FORD FOCUS RS WRC 07	A8 2
20	CONRAD RAUTENBACH (ZW)	DAVID SENIOR (GB)	CONRAD RAUTENBACH	CITROEN XSARA	A8 2
61	FRÉDÉRIC ROMEYER (F)	THOMAS FOURNEL (F)	FRÉDÉRIC ROMEYER	PEUGEOT 206 WRC	A8
64	RICCARDO ERRANI (I)	STEFANO CASADIO (I)	RICCARDO ERRANI	SKODA OCTAVIA WRC	A8
65	LAURENT CARBONARO (F)	MARC-EMILIEN CHOUDEY (F)	LAURENT CARBONARO	PEUGEOT 307 WRC	A8
66	FRÉDÉRIC COMBE (F)	HUBERT BRUN (F)	FRÉDÉRIC COMBE	RENAULT CLIO RS	A7
67	MARC DESSI (MC)	MICHEL FIESCHI (F)	LES CASINOS DE MONTE-CARLO	RENAULT CLIO RS	A7
68	LUCA BETTI (E)	GIOVANNI AGNESE (I)	LUCA BETTI	HONDA CIVIC TYPE-R	A7
69	DANIEL HOLCZER (H)	TIBOR JR. MARKO (H)	DANIEL HOLCZER	HONDA CIVIC	A7
70	EDDIE MERCIER (F)	JEAN-MICHEL VERET (F)	EDDIE MERCIER	RENAULT CLIO	A7
71	HENRI-MARC VENTURINI (F)	FRÉDÉRIC DART (F)	HENRI-MARC VENTURINI	RENAULT CLIO	A7
72	SILVANO PINTARELLI (I)	MAURO MARCHIORI (I)	SILVANO PINTARELLI	RENAULT CLIO	A7
73	LILIAN VIALLE (F)	PATRICE ROISSAC (F)	LILIAN VIALLE	RENAULT CLIO	A7
74	GERRI PRANZONI (I)	MAURA VACCARI (I)	GERRI PRANZONI	RENAULT CLIO	A7
75	ALESSANDRO BROCCOLI (RSM)	MONICA CICOGNINI (ITA)	ALESSANDRO BROCCOLI	RENAULT CLIO	A7
76	ANDREA PANICCO (I)	NICOLA RENNER (I)	ANDREA PANICCO	PEUGEOT 206 RC	A7
77	STEFANO MORETTI (I)	NICOLA DOGLIO (I)	STEFANO MORETTI	RENAULT CLIO	A6
78	ALEX RASCHI (RSM)	FABIO CADORE (ITA)	ALEX RASCHI	RENAULT CLIO	A7
79	OLIVIER BURRI (CH)	JEAN JAQUES FERRERO (F)	OLIVIER BURRI	SUBARU IMPREZA	N4
80	FRANCK AMAUDRU (F)	TBA TBA (TBA)	FRANCK AMAUDRU	SUBARU IMPREZA	N4
81	FLAVIO CASTEGNARO (I)	RENZO FRASCHIA (I)	FLAVIO CASTEGNARO	SUBARU IMPREZA	N4
82	ALAIN MACHARD (F)	ALAIN CONSTANT (F)	ALAIN MACHARD	SUBARU IMPREZA STI	N4
83	LAURENT NICOLAS (F)	CHRISTOPHE PREVE (F)	LAURENT NICOLAS	SUBARU IMPREZA	N4
84	RICHARD FRAU (F)	SERGE LE GARS (F)	RICHARD FRAU	MITSUBISHI LANCER EVO IX	N4
86	PATRICK ARTRU (F)	PATRICE VIRIEUX (F)	PATRICK ARTRU	MITSUBISHI LANCER EVO IX	N4
87	JÉRÔME AYMARD (F)	SANDRINE AYMARD (F)	JÉRÔME AYMARD	MITSUBISHI LANCER EVO IX	N4
88	LUDOVIC CLUZEL (F)	TEDDY DELMONICO (F)	LUDOVIC CLUZEL	MITSUBISHI LANCER EVO IX	N4
89	MIGUEL BAUDOUIN (F)	JEAN FRANCOIS GASTINEL (F)	MIGUEL BAUDOUIN	MITSUBISHI LANCER EVO	N4
90	FRÉDÉRIC SAUVAN (F)	PIERRE CAMPANA (F)	FRÉDÉRIC SAUVAN	MITSUBISHI LANCER EVO IX	N4
91	GIACOMO OGLIARI (F)	MARCO VERDELLI (I)	GIACOMO OGLIARI	MITSUBISHI LANCER EVO IX	N4
92	MILAN LISKA (CZ)	JAROSLAV JUGAS (CZ)	MILAN LISKA	MITSUBISHI LANCER EVO IX	N4
93	JOAN FONT (E)	ENRIQUE VELASCO ALONSO (E)	JOAN FONT	MITSUBISHI LANCER EVO IX	N4
94	GILBERT SAU (F)	ANNE DROUILEAU (F)	GILBERT SAU	MITSUBISHI LANCER EVO IX	N4
95	FRANCK DOVERI (F)	BENJAMIN VEILLAS (F)	FRANCK DOVERI	MITSUBISHI LANCER EVO VIII	N4
96	PHILIPPE ROUX (CH)	ERIC JORDAN (CH)	PHILIPPE ROUX	SUBARU IMPREZA	N4

M. Cuoq

C. Rautenbach

M. Wilson

H. Solberg

P.G. Andersson & T. Gardemeister

J. M. Latvala

Championship Classifications

FIA Drivers (1/15)
1. Loeb   1🏆   10
2. Hirvonen   8
3. Atkinson   6
4. Duval   5
5. P. Solberg   4
6. Galli   3
7. Cuoq   2
8. Andersson   1
9. H. Solberg   0
10. Wilson   0
11. Sordo   0
12. Latvala   0
13. Broccoli   0
14. Artru   0
15. Mercier   0

FIA Constructors (1/15)
1. Citroën Total World Rally Team   1🏆   11
2. Subaru World Rally Team   10
3. BP-Ford Abu Dhabi World Rally Team   8
4. Stobart VK M-Sport Ford Rally Team   8
5. Suzuki World Rally Team   2

Special Stages Times

www.acm.mc
www.wrc.com

SS1 St Jean En Royans - Col de la Chau 1 (28.12 km)
1.Sordo 14'08"9; 2.Loeb +3"8; 3.Hirvonen +20"1; 4.Atkinson +31"0; 5.Duval +38"7; 6.P.Solberg +41"2; 7.Galli +44"3; 8.Gardemeister +58"7...

SS2 La Cime Du Mas - Col de Gaudissart 1 (17.58 km)
1.Loeb 9'25"7; 2.Sordo +16"5; 3.Hirvonen +27"7; 4.Atkinson +31"4; 5.P.Solberg +37"1; 6.Duval +38"6; 7. Galli +45"6; 8.Latvala +48"0...

Classification Leg 1
1.Loeb 23'38"4; 2.Sordo +12"7; 3.Hirvonen +44"0; 4.Atkinson +58"6; 5.Duval +1'13"5; 6.P.Solberg +1'14"5; 7.Galli +1'26"1; 8.Gardemeister +1'53"1...

SS3 St Pierreville - Col de la Fayolle 1 (29.52 Km)
1.Loeb 18'54"4; 2.Sordo +8"3; 3.Hirvonen +10"1; 4.Duval +27"8; 5.Atkinson +39"8; 6.Latvala +40"0; 7.P.Solberg +42"8; 8.Galli +53"5...

SS4 Burzet - Lachamp Raphael 1 (16.30 km)
1.Sordo 9'37"1; 2.Loeb +2"7; 3.Hirvonen +7"5; 4.P.Solberg +13"3; 5.Atkinson +13"9; 6.Duval +16"4; 7.Latvala +16"6; 8.Galli +20"2...

SS5 St Martial - Le Chambon - Beleac 1 (12.66 km)
1.Loeb 8'06"2; 2.Sordo +5"2; 3.Hirvonen +5"8; 4.P.Solberg +11"7; 5.Atkinson +12"6; 6.Galli +13"6; 7.Duval +13"7; 8.Latvala +14"3...

SS6 St Pierreville - Col de la Fayolle 2 (29.52 Km)
1.Loeb 18'41"8; 2.Duval +9"3; 3.Hirvonen +10"1; 4.Sordo +10"8; 5.Atkinson +12"4; 6.Latvala +19"5; 7.P.Solberg +20"6; 8.Galli +27"3...

SS7 Burzet - Lachamp Raphael 2 (16.30 km)
1.Loeb 9'40"7; 2.Duval +2"3; 3.Atkinson +4"6; 4.Sordo +7"4; 5.Duval +10"1; 6.H.Solberg +13"6; 7.Latvala +13"7; 8.P.Solberg +14"0...

SS8 St Martial - Le Chambon - Beleac 2 (12.66 Km)
1.Loeb 8'03"6; 2.Hirvonen +5"7; 3.Atkinson +9"4; 4.Duval +14"5; 5.Sordo +14"9; 6.P.Solberg +16"1; 7.Latvala +20"0; 8.Cuoq +20"7...

Classification Leg 2
1.Loeb 1h36'44"9; 2.Sordo +56"6; 3.Hirvonen +1'22"8; 4.Atkinson +2'28"6; 5.Duval +2'42"6; 6.P.Solberg +3'09"6; 7.Galli +5'21"1; 8.Cuoq +5'27"9...

SS9 Labatie D'Andaure - Lalouvesc 1 (19.37 Km)
1.Sordo 11'18"1; 2.Loeb +2"0; 3.Atkinson +6"3; 4.Hirvonen +6"8; 5.Andersson +12"5; 6.P.Solberg +15"8; 7.Duval +19"9; 8.Gardemeister +21"7...

SS10 St Bonnet - St Bonnet 1 (25.36 Km)
1.Loeb 12'39"0; 2.Sordo +1"2; 3.Duval +6"0; 4.Hirvonen +7"8; 5.P.Solberg +9"3; 6.Atkinson +10"7; 7.Andersson +15"6; 8.Cuoq +23"0...

SS11 La Mastre - Gilhoc - Alboussiere 1 (21.66 Km)
1.Loeb 12'59"8; 2.Duval +8"9; 3.Hirvonen +18"1; 4.P.Solberg +21"2; 5.Atkinson +21"7; 6.Galli +24"1; 7.Andersson +34"1; 8.Cuoq +41"2...

SS12 Labatie D'Andaure - Lalouvesc 2 (19.37 Km)
1.Loeb 11'12"0; 2.Sordo +2"6; 3.Duval +6"1; 4.Hirvonen +6"6; 5.P.Solberg +7"3; 6.Galli +9"5; 7.Andersson +18"8; 8.Gardemeiser +19"3...

SS13 St Bonnet - St Bonnet 2 (25.36 Km)
1.Atkinson 12'23"9; 2.Duval +7"5; 3.Loeb +10"7; 4.P.Solberg +11"9; 5.Hirvonen +12"7; 6.Gardemeister +27"1; 7.Galli +28"4; 8.Andersson +30"2...

SS14 La Mastre - Gilhoc - Alboussiere 2 (21.66 Km)
1.Loeb 13'08"4; 2.Duval +4"4; 3.Atkinson +5"4; 4.Hirvonen +8"5; 5.P.Solberg +9"4; 6.Galli +19"0; 7.Andersson +27"2; 8.Cuoq +33"8...

Classification Leg 3
1.Loeb 3h06'35"8; 2.Hirvonen +2'20"8; 3.Atkinson +3'06"3; 4.Duval +3'14"3; 5.P.Solberg +4'27"2; 6.Galli +8'03"9; 7.Cuoq +9'00"2; 8.Andersson +9'56"0...

SS15 La Bollène Vesubie - Moulinet 1 (22.68 Km)
1.Duval 15'48"6; 2.Sordo +4"4; 3.Loeb +8"4; 4.Latvala +11"9; 5.Atkinson +12"1; 6.Hirvonen +18"6; 7.P.Solberg +23"8; 8.Galli +32"6...

SS16 Luceram - Loda (15.34 Km)
1.Sordo 10'51"7; 2.Duval +2"1; 3.Latvala +4"7; 4.Atkinson +6"1; 5.Loeb +6"6; 6.P.Solberg +7"4; 7.Hirvonen +11"8; 8.Andersson +20"4...

SS17 La Bollène Vesubie - Moulinet 2 (22.68 Km)
1.Duval 15'27"7; 2.Atkinson +0"5; 3.Sordo +1"3; 4.Loeb +5"9; 5.Hirvonen +14"8; 6.Latvala +19"3; 7.P.Solberg +20"1; 8.Galli + 25"8...

SS18 Lucéram - Col des Portes (6.25 Km)
1.Duval +4'24"4; 2.Latvala +0"2; 3.Loeb +1"2; 4.Hirvonen +1"7; 5.P.Solberg +2"3; 6.Atkinson +2"4; 7.H.Solberg +5"6; 8.Galli +7"9...

SS19 Monaco - Circuit (2.70 Km)
1.Atkinson / Duval 1'40"7; 3.Latvala +0"6; 4.P.Solberg +2"0; 5.Hirvonen +2"0; 6.Galli +2"7; 7.H.Solberg +2"9; 8.Loeb +3"0...

Results

	Driver - Co-Driver	Car	Gr.	Time
1.	Loeb - Elena	Citroën C4 WRC	A8	3h39'17"0
2.	Hirvonen - Lehtinen	Ford Focus RS WRC 07	A8	+2'34"4
3.	Atkinson - Prevot	Subaru Impreza WRC 06	A8	+2'58"6
4.	Duval - Chevailler	Ford Focus RS WRC 07	A8	+2'59"7
5.	P. Solberg - Mills	Subaru Impreza WRC 06	A8	+4'40"9
6.	Galli - Bernacchni	Citroën Xsara WRC	A8	+8'46"5
7.	Cuoq - Janvier	Peugeot 307 WRC	A8	+10'24"8
8.	Andersson - Andersson	SUZUKI SX4	A8	+11'19"5
9.	H. Solberg - Menkerud	Ford Focus RS WRC 07	A8	+12'43"6
10.	Wilson - Martin	Ford Focus RS WRC 07	A8	+14'00"1
14.	Artru - Virieux	Mitsubishi Lancer Evo. IX	N4	+31'20"2

Leading Retirements (13)

| Ctrl19 | Rautenbach - Senior | Citroën Xsara WRC | Off |
| Ctrl14C | Gardemeister -Tuominen | Suzuki SX4 WRC | Engine |

Performers

	1	2	3	4	5	6	C6	Nb SS
Loeb	10	3	3	1	1	-	18	19
Duval	4	5	2	2	2	2	17	19
Sordo	4	5	1	2	1	-	13	16
Atkinson	2	2	4	3	6	2	19	19
Hirvonen	-	2	7	5	3	1	18	19
Latvala	-	1	2	1	-	3	7	17
P. Solberg	-	-	-	5	5	4	14	19
Andersson	-	-	-	-	1	-	1	19
Galli	-	-	-	-	-	5	5	19
H.Solberg	-	-	-	-	-	1	1	19
Gardemeister	-	-	-	-	-	1	1	19

Leaders

| SS1 | Sordo |
| SS2 > SS19 | Loeb |

Previous Winners

1973	Andruet - "Biche" Alpine Renault A 110
1975	Munari - Mannucci Lancia Stratos
1976	Munari - Maiga Lancia Stratos
1977	Munari - Maiga Lancia Stratos
1978	Nicolas - Laverne Porsche 911 SC
1979	Darniche - Mahé Lancia Stratos
1980	Rohrl - Geistdorfer Fiat 131 Abarth
1981	Ragnotti - Andrié Renault 5 Turbo
1982	Rohrl - Geistdorfer Opel Ascona 400
1983	Rohrl - Geistdorfer Lancia rally 037
1984	Rohrl - Geistdorfer Audi Quattro
1985	Vatanen - Harryman Peugeot 205 T16
1986	Toivonen - Cresto Lancia Delta S4
1987	Biasion - Siviero Lancia Delta HF 4WD
1988	Saby - Fauchille Lancia Delta HF 4WD
1989	Biasion - Siviero Lancia Delta Integrale
1990	Auriol - Occelli Lancia Delta Integrale
1991	Sainz - Moya Toyota Celica GT-Four
1992	Auriol - Occelli Lancia Delta HF Integrale
1993	Auriol - Occelli Toyota Celica Turbo 4WD
1994	Delecour - Grataloup Ford Escort RS Cosworth
1995	Sainz - Moya Subaru Impreza 555
1996	Bernardini - Andrié Ford Escort Cosworth
1997	Liatti - Pons Subaru Impreza WRC
1998	Sainz - Moya Toyota Corolla WRC
1999	Mäkinen-Mannisenmäki Mitsubishi Lancer Evo VI
2000	Mäkinen-Mannisenmäki Mitsubishi Lancer Evo VI
2001	Mäkinen-Mannisenmäki Mitsubishi Lancer Evo VI
2002	Mäkinen - Lindström Subaru Impreza WRC
2003	Loeb - Elena Citroën Xsara WRC
2004	Loeb - Elena Citroën Xsara WRC
2005	Loeb - Elena Citroën Xsara WRC
2006	Grönholm - Rautiainen Ford Focus RS WRC 06
2007	Loeb - Elena Citroën C4 WRC

02 SWEDEN

🇸🇪 Latvala writes his name in the history books

Victory on a relatively snow-free Rally of Sweden, where he beat Mikko Hirvonen and Gigi Galli, made Jari-Matt Latvala the youngest winner of a World Championship event at just 22 years and 10 months. Sébastien Loeb lost the Championship lead to Hirvonen after an off in the very first stage, while a Ford 1-2-3 was a great confidence boost for the American company. Citroën had to make do with sixth place for Dani Sordo, who tried hard but was outclassed on this surface.

02 | Sweden

Sixth overall was Dani Sordo's best result in Sweden. But for that five-minute penalty for an engine change before the event got under way, the Spaniard's Citroën C4 would have taken a podium finish.

Petter Solberg was happier with fourth place than he was with the three-minute gap from him to the leader. But the Norwegian had warned us he would be happy to store up as many points as he could while waiting for his new Impreza.

THE RACE
Move over, the young guys are coming

Less than a year after the Norway Rally we saw visually the same scenario unfold. The works Fords scored a 1-2, as they did in Hamar in 2007, though not in the order we expected: Hirvonen, who had laid down the law to Grönholm in Norway, had to dance to Latvala's tune in Sweden. And, as had happened in the last snow rally to date – there may only have been a fine dusting, but Sweden's is still a winter event – the Citroëns got it all wrong. Sordo was a goner right from the start, incurring a five-minute penalty for his engine change after the Monte. He managed to climb back to sixth place in the end. Loeb, though, won't look back on his 100th World Championship rally with any great fondness. His campaign against the Northerners came to a halt at kilometre 19 in Mangen, the third special of the rally. "I turned in a little too soon for a quick left-hander," he explained. I wasn't on the right line and I clipped the snow bank on the apex. Pillock... The car got sideways and I couldn't correct it. We went up the bank, then a rock and that rolled us twice. We ended up on our wheels but across the road, and a clutch line had been damaged so I couldn't do anything with the car. We needed some help from the spectators to get going again, and we finished at a crawl because the turbo intercooler was broken as well. The whole thing cost us about four minutes. It didn't help when we had to stop on the road section because the water temperature light came on. We cobbled the clutch line together and got some water to top up the radiator."

Enough, at least, to get them to the mini-service park at Sunne, but the damage was too bad for the four mechanics allowed to work on the C4, minus its rear wing and sump guard, to do anything. Loeb was out, and this time for good. "The thing that gets me," he fumed, "is that if we'd had our full service help, as usual, we could have fixed it and got going again. But that's the rule... and it's the same for everybody. When you're on a day with no outside help, you know you can't afford to make a mistake. I've got this unfortunate habit of making a bad start to the season, so just like last year I'm going to be playing catch-up from the start. We need to get things back on track!"

With wins on six of the eight first-leg stages, Jari-Matti Latvala was, to use Malcolm Wilson's word, "sensational". The starting-order helped him but he was absolutely in his element – though he did have a few close shaves on his way to leading Mikko Hirvonen by 48.2 seconds. Put out by the young fellow's lack of respect for the rankings, Hirvonen was happier when he heard Loeb had been in the wars. "Jari-Matti drove superbly and I'm not surprised he's in the lead," he said on Friday evening. "Mind you, I didn't expect to see such a gap between us. Of course I'd love to win but with Loeb out, I'll be making sure I don't take any risks or make mistakes, but I'll be doing all I can to get back at Latvala."

At the end of day one Henning Solberg and Gigi Galli, third and fourth respectively, rounded out a triumphant provisional result for Ford. The Norwegian was out of the running at the start of day two. Delayed by a puncture in Horssjön 1, the Norwegian went after third spot but gave it a bit too much and was out for the count in SS11, Vargasen.

This picture is misleading, for Sébastien Loeb was in the Norsemen's shadow. The Frenchman's mistake right at the start cost him the event and the Championship lead.

<
Take-off for Jari-Matti Latvala: in only his second rally for Ford the Finn became the youngest winner of a World Championship event.

After Andersson's seventh-place finish on the Monte it was Gardemeister's turn to score some points – for seventh. But it seemed the SX4's engine woes had not been completely cured as the Swede had to retire.

A similar fate could have befallen Latvala as he walked the tightrope on one of the stages where there wasn't much snow about. "In comparison with yesterday I took it a bit easier and matched my pace to Mikko's, but I still gave myself one hell of a fright in SS13," he explained after getting his emotions under control. "There was a tarmac section and because the snow had melted there was just no grip on the studs. I ended up in a ditch but by some miracle there were no stumps or rocks and I got back on to the road. It gave me such a fright that I lost concentration – and missed my braking for the next chicane! I hit a straw bale on the passenger side, but luckily the car wasn't too badly damaged. It was a close call."

In fact Latvala really got out of jail on that one because he ended the second leg with a comfortable 49.8-second gap to a disenchanted Hirvonen. "This morning I was all set to close the gap," he said, "but I didn't feel right in the first two stages, though things got better after that. I'm a bit disappointed not to be leading but second place will do me nicely." With Galli third, Matthew Wilson fifth and Mikkelsen sixth, the Rally of Sweden was starting to look like a Ford Cup event, with Petter Solberg in fourth the only man spoiling the party. On the last leg, however, one Focus went missing – the one that belonged to the boss's son. Wilson's throttle stuck – maybe because he's not used to having it wide open – and he had to pull out in the penultimate stage, where he was having a ding-dong battle with Andreas Mikkelsen.

The Norwegian was delighted with a fifth place which made him, at 18, the youngest driver to score points in World Championship history. Those lessons with Marcus Grönholm may have cost a fortune but they were paying off. Our youngish Finnish retiree was suddenly made to feel a lot older as Latvala's victory made him the youngest winner in history at just 22 and 10 months. "I can't find the words to express the way I feel," said our hero. "It seems weird to beat my own hero Henri Toivonen's record – he was 24 when he won for the first time. It's a great honour and a very emotional one. Just like Marcus with Peugeot in 2000, I've started my career as a works driver with retirement on the Monte followed by a win in Sweden. He became World Champion at the end of that season. I don't know if I'll be able to do the same – talent may be enough to win you a rally but you need a touch of luck as well to take the title. Last year, with Stobart, helped me a lot, with my first podium and a move to the works team. This winter I did pre-season testing for the first time in my career. But for those 400 kilometres on snow before this event I'd never have been able to go all out from the start the way I did."

With his new recruit winning, and with four Focuses in the top five, Malcolm Wilson had good cause for celebration. "I was sure Jari-Matti would win a rally this year, but I never thought it would come on only the second event," said the boss man as his troops took over the lead in both Championships.

Gigi Galli hadn't expected to find himself on the podium this early in the season either. Petter Solberg, meanwhile, was happy with his fourth place as he stuck to the cautious approach he had decided on while waiting for the new Impreza. "We didn't really push," said 'Hollywood', "We just ran our own race, at our own pace, without worrying too much about anyone else."

Actually it was a rally that left practically everyone with something to smile about – even Sordo, who left Karlstad a happier man after fighting back to sixth place despite that pre-event penalty. "It was a below-par

02 | Sweden

The WRC is becoming a young man's game. Andrea Mikkelsen, just 18, became the youngest man ever to score World Championship points, in his privateer Focus. He had some help – his 'driving instructor' was none other than Marcus Grönholm.

Hirvonen shone in the powdery stuff in Norway last year but was much less decisive in the mud of this year's event, which came perilously close to being called off. But Ford's number one could console himself with the Championship lead.

start," the Spaniard explained, "so I changed my driving style and felt better straight away. I started enjoying myself and going faster, and that's something I'd never experienced on snow before." It was a nice surprise, but not enough to make Citroën forget the mishap that left Sébastien Loeb six points adrift of Hirvonen in the Championship. On the constructors' front the French firm were now fourth behind Ford, Stobart and Subaru – with Suzuki the only ones behind them.

While Gardemeister was seventh, a deeply disappointed Andersson was forced into retirement right at the start of his home event. So, one Swede smarting from defeat, one happy Finn: and it was the same state of affairs in the Production class, with a win for Hänninen's Mitsubishi, helped by an off for local man Patrik Sandell's Peugeot 207 Super 2000, which had seemed very happy in the conditions until that little faux pas. ■

A LITTLE HISTORY
Jouhki the star-maker

Timo Jouhki, who manages Latvala and Hirvonen, has no peer in the talent-spotting stakes. He was a modestly-gifted driver in the Seventies but decided, in 1979, to use the money he was making as an industrialist to give one of his friends a helping-hand. The beginner's name was Juha Kankkunen; within 14 years he had claimed four world titles. In fact Jouki was now in the business of collecting titles – his second try was another stroke of genius because Tommi Mäkinen went on to pick up four of them as well.

Buoyed by those two successes, the Finnish entrepreneur had earned his talent-spotting stripes and if his powers of persuasion fell short, team bosses could usually be swayed by his financial clout. Rovanperä going to Seat, then Peugeot, was his doing. So was Gardemeister's move to Seat, then Ford. And of course Loeb's two new rivals Hirvonen and Latvala are also his.

"I spotted Mikko and Jari-Matti in 2000," he told us. "The first one was starting out in the Finnish Junior Championship, the second didn't even have a driving licence at that stage! I called them in for a try-out along with two or three other drivers. We tested them on two events, then we put them through interviews, psychological tests, media sessions and note-taking with experienced co-drivers. We eventually went for Mikko, the most mature among them, and Jari-Matti, the most talented." Good choice...

Until the Swedish Rally, though, it was a long and sometimes winding road. Luckily, Jouhki has two trump cards – money and a passion for the sport – which mean his drivers can afford to mature slowly. The first allowed him to finance his two protégés' apprenticeship through national championships and on to the world scene. And the passion gave him confidence in his judgement, never hesitating to tip more money in when his drivers found themselves in a bit of a trough.

"I'd never have made it without him," says Hirvonen, whose career would have been over after a catastrophic 2004 with Subaru if Jouhki hadn't footed the bill for a privateer Ford campaign the following year. "He's the best manager you could possibly have," agrees Latvala. "He's got over 25 years' experience, and he's built up a huge network of contacts to help young Finnish drivers make it to the top. What makes him so strong is his passion for rallying. He really throws himself into it, he takes note of everything, comes to events to watch us drive, takes part-payments, analyses the way we all drive."

Sandell or Prokop was expected to come out on top but in the end it was Juho Hänninen who took the PWRC honours – and actually climbed to eighth place overall.

Jari-Matti Latvala's first trophy. The cabinet-maker back in his Finnish village Töysä had better take note – it's probably the first of many and the lad will soon be needing some shelves to put them all on!

In fact only one of Finland's recent star drivers hasn't been a product of the 'Jouhki Academy', of which Hirvonen and Latvala are the latest graduates. Back when Marcus Grönholm was winning national title after national title, the Finnish investor never took it into his head to help steer him into the World Championship. It left big Marcus to fend for himself on the outside of a very efficient system, and it left a painful mark. "I didn't pick Marcus because he kept going off the road," is how Jouhki remembers it. "Then when he started getting good results and being more consistent, I didn't have the scope to take on another driver because I already had contracts with four of them. In hindsight it's obvious he would have been a good choice – but I do get it wrong sometimes!" ∎

Who said you had to be neat to be quick in the WRC? Gigi Galli, who needs to get his bearings sorted out, didn't expect to snaffle such a good result so early in the season – the second podium of his career, and without compromising that flamboyant style!

02 | Sweden | Results

57th SWEDISH RALLY

Organiser Details
International Swedish Rally
BOX 594
651 13 Karlstad
Sweden
Tel.: +4654 102025
Fax: +4654 180530

Uddeholm Swedish Rally

2nd leg of FIA 2008 World Championship for constructors and drivers.
1st leg of FIA Production Car World Championship.

Date February 8 - 10, 2008

Route
1469.36 km divised in three legs.
20 special stages on snowy dirt roads (342.18 km), 18 raced

Starting Procedure
Thursday, February 7 (20:00)
Karlstad

Leg 1
Friday, February 8 (09:34/18:00),
Karlstad > Sunne > Karlstad, 513.40 km;
8 special stages (124.14 km)

Leg 2
Saturday, February 9 (08:25/15:20),
Karlstad > Hagfors > Karlstad, 523.78 km;
6 special stages (120.78 km); 5 raced

Leg 3
Sunday, February 10 (08:08/12:58),
Karlstad > Hagfors > Karlstad, 432.18 km;
6 special stages (97.26 km); 5 raced

Entry List (68) - 61 starters

N°	Driver (Nat.)	Co-driver (Nat.)	Team	Car	Group & FIA Priority
1	SÉBASTIEN LOEB (F)	DANIEL ELENA (MC)	CITROËN TOTAL WRT	CITROËN C4 WRC	A8 1
2	DANI SORDO (E)	MARC MARTI (E)	CITROËN TOTAL WRT	CITROËN C4 WRC	A8 1
3	MIKKO HIRVONEN (FIN)	JARMO LEHTINEN (FIN)	BP FORD ABU DHABI WORLD RALLY TEAM	FORD FOCUS RS WRC 07	A8 1
4	JARI-MATTI LATVALA (FIN)	MIIKKA ANTTILA (FIN)	BP FORD ABU DHABI WORLD RALLY TEAM	FORD FOCUS RS WRC 07	A8 1
5	PETTER SOLBERG (N)	PHILIP MILLS (GB)	SUBARU WORLD RALLY TEAM	SUBARU IMPREZA WRC 2006	A8 1
6	CHRIS ATKINSON (AUS)	STEPHANE PREVOT (B)	SUBARU WORLD RALLY TEAM	SUBARU IMPREZA WRC 2006	A8 1
7	GIGI GALLI (I)	GIOVANNI BERNACCHINI (I)	STOBART VK M-SPORT FORD RALLY TEAM	FORD FOCUS RS WRC 07	A8 1
8	HENNING SOLBERG (N)	CATO MENKERUD (N)	STOBART VK M-SPORT FORD RALLY TEAM	FORD FOCUS RS WRC 07	A8 1
11	TONI GARDEMEISTER (FIN)	TOMI TUOMINEN (FIN)	SUZUKI WORLD RALLY TEAM	SUZUKI SX4 WRC 08	A8 1
12	PER-GUNNAR ANDERSSON (S)	JONAS ANDERSSON (S)	SUZUKI WORLD RALLY TEAM	SUZUKI SX4 WRC 08	A8 1
16	MATTHEW WILSON (GB)	SCOTT MARTIN (GB)	STOBART VK M-SPORT FORD RALLY TEAM	FORD FOCUS RS WRC 07	A8 2
17	ANDREAS MIKKELSEN (N)	OLA FLOENE (N)	RAMSPORT	FORD FOCUS RS WRC 07	A8 2
19	MADS ØSTBERG (NOR)	OLE. K UNNERUD (NOR)	ADAPTA AS	SUBARU IMPREZA WRC	A8 2
20	URMO AAVA (EE)	KULDAR SIKK (EE)	WORLD RALLY TEAM ESTONIA	CITROËN C4 WRC	A8 2
21	CONRAD RAUTENBACH (ZW)	DAVID SENIOR (GB)	CONRAD RAUTENBACH	CITROËN C4 WRC	A8 2
22	PETER VAN MERKSTEIJN (NL)	HANS VAN BEEK (NL)	VAN MERKSTEIJN MOTORSPORT	FORD FOCUS RS WRC 06	A8 2
23	KHALID AL QASSIMI (UAE)	MICHAEL ORR (GB)	BP FORD ABU DHABI WORLD RALLY TEAM	FORD FOCUS RS WRC 07	A8 2
31	TOSHIHIRO ARAI (J)	GLENN MACNEALL (AUS)	SUBARU TEAM ARAI	SUBARU IMPREZA	N4 3
33	MARTIN PROKOP (CZ)	JAN TOMÁNEK (CZ)	MARTIN PROKOP	MITSUBISHI LANCER EVO IX	N4 3
34	GIANLUCA LINARI (I)	ROBERTO MOMETTI (I)	LINARI GIANLUGA	SUBARU IMPREZA STI	N4 3
36	EYVIND BRYNHILDSEN (NOR)	DENIS GIRAUDET (F)	EYVIND BRYNHILDSEN	MITSUBISHI LANCER EVO IX	N4 3
39	NASSER AL-ATTIYAH (QAT)	CHRIS PATTERSON (GB)	QMMF	SUBARU IMPREZA	N4 3
40	STEFANO MARRINI (I)	MATTEO BRAGA (ITA)	ERRANI TEAM GROUP SRL	MITSUBISHI LANCER EVO IX	N4 3
41	ANDREAS AIGNER (A)	KLAUS WICHA (D)	RED BULL RALLYE TEAM	MITSUBISHI LANCER EVO IX	N4 3
42	BERNARDO SOUSA (POR)	CARLOS MAGALHAES (P)	RED BULL RALLYE TEAM	MITSUBISHI LANCER EVO IX	N4 3
43	EVGENIY VERTUNOV (RUS)	GEORGY TROSHKIN (RUS)	SUBARU RALLY TEAM RUSSIA	SUBARU IMPREZA WRX STI	N4 3
45	JUSSI TIIPPANA (FIN)	MARKO SALMINEN (FIN)	MOTORING CLUB 2	SUBARU IMPREZA N12	N4 3
46	JARI KETOMAA (FIN)	MIIKA TEISKONEN (FIN)	MOTORING CLUB 1	SUBARU IMPREZA N14	N4 3
47	FABIO FRISIERO (I)	SIMONE SCATTOLIN (I)	MOTORING CLUB 3	MITSUBISHI LANCER EVO	N4 3
48	EVGENY AKSAKOV (RUS)	ALEXANDER KORNILOV (RUS)	RED WINGS MOSCOW REGION RALLY TEAM	MITSUBISHI LANCER EVO IX	N4 3
49	SIMONE CAMPEDELLI (I)	DANILO FAPPANI (I)	SCUDERIA RUBICONE CORSE	MITSUBISHI LANCER EVO IX	N4 3
50	ARMINDO ARAÚJO (P)	MIGUEL RAMALHO (P)	RALLIART ITALY	MITSUBISHI LANCER EVO IX	N4 3
51	SUBHAN AKSA (RI)	HENDRIK MBOI (RI)	INDONESIA RALLY TEAM	MITSUBISHI LANCER EVO VIII	N4 3
52	JUHO HÄNNINEN (FIN)	MIKKO MARKKULA (FIN)	RALLIART NEW ZEALAND	MITSUBISHI LANCER EVO IX	N4 3
53	UWE NITTEL (GER)	DETLEF RUF (D)	PRO RACE E C I	MITSUBISHI LANCER EVO IX	N4 3
55	PATRIK SANDELL (SWE)	EMIL AXELSSON (SWE)	PEUGEOT SPORT SWEDEN	PEUGEOT 207	N4 3
59	PATRIK FLODIN (SWE)	GÖRAN BERGSTEN (S)	SUBARU SWEDISH DEALER TEAM	SUBARU IMPREZA	N4 3
60	OSCAR SVEDLUND (S)	BJÖRN NILSSON (S)	SUBARU SWEDISH DEALER TEAM	SUBARU IMPREZA	N4 3
61	JARKKO KETOMÄKI (FIN)	JUKKA ALANEN (FIN)	JUKKA KETOMÄKI	SUBARU IMPREZA	N4
64	HASSE GUSTAFSSON (SWE)	NICKLAS EDVARDSSON (S)	SUBARU SWEDISH DEALER TEAM	SUBARU IMPREZA	N4
65	ARI LAIVOLA (FIN)	ANTTI VIRJULA (FIN)	ARI LAIVOLA	MITSUBISHI LANCER	N4
66	JOAKIM ROMAN (S)	ANDERS WALLBOM (S)	JOAKIM ROMAN	SUBARU IMPREZA WRX STI	N4
67	JOSEF SEMERA'D (CZE)	BOHUSLAV CEPLECHA (CZ)	JOSEF SEMERA'D	MTTSUBISHI LANCER EVO IX	N4
68	VYTAVTAS SVEDAS (LTU)	ZILVINAS SAKALAVSKA (LTU)	VYTAUTAS SVEDAS	MITSUBISHI LANCER EVO IX	N4
69	EGON KAUR (EE)	SIMO KOSKINEN (EST)	EGON KAUR	SUBARU IMPREZA WRX STI SPEC	N4
70	JASPER VAN DEN HEUVEL(NL)	MAETINE KOLMAN (NED)	JASPER VAN DEN HEUVEL	MITSUBISHI LANCER EVO IX	N4
72	BERNARD MUNSTER (B)	NICOLAS GRISOUL (BEL)	BERNARD MUNSTER	SUBARU IMPREZA N14	N4
73	P. JR VAN MERKSTEIJN (NL)	EDDY CHEVALLIER (B)	VAN MERKSTEIJN MOTORSPORT	MITSUBISHI LANCER EVO IX	N4
74	RAMONA KARLSSON (SWE)	MIRIAM WALFRIDSSON (SWE)	SUBARU SWEDISH DEALER TEAM	SUBARU IMPREZA	N4
75	LUCA HOELBLING (I)	TULLIO SIENA (I)	LUCA HOELBLING	SUBARU IMPREZA STI	N4
76	MARKUS BENES (AUT)	NORBERT WANNENACHER (AUT)	MARKUS BENES	SUBARU IMPREZA STI	N4
77	JAAP SINKE (NL)	PASCAL MEIJS (NL)	JAAP SINKE	MITSUBISHI LANCER EVO V	N4
78	KLAUS BODILSEN (DK)	THOMAS HENRIKSEN (DK)	KLAUS BODILSEN	MITSUBISHI LANCER EVO VII	N4
79	BERTRAND PIERRAT (FRA)	EUGENIE DECRE (SUI)	BERTRAND PIERRAT	SUBARU IMPREZA	N4
80	FRÉDRIC SAUVAN (FRA)	PIERRE CAMPANA (F)	FRÉDRIC SAUVAN	MITSUBISHI LANCER EVO IX	N4
81	LASSE STORM (S)	ULF STORM (S)	LASSE STORM	RENAULT CLIO RAGNOTTI	N3
82	ALEX RASCHI (RSM)	STEFANO DE BARBIERI (ITA)	ALEX RASCHI	RENAULT CLIO R3	A7
83	IREK DAUTOV (RUS)	MARINA DANILOVA (RUS)	USPENSKIY RALLY TECNICA	CITROEN C2	A6
84	TONY JARDINE (GB)	FRANCA DAVENPORT (GBR)	TONY JARDINE	FORD FIESTA ST 150	N3
85	ALESSANDRO BROCCOLI (RSM)	MONICA CICOGNINI (ITA)	ALESSANDRO BROCCOLI	RENAULT CLIO R3	A7
86	KARI HYTÖNEN (FIN)	MIKAEL LARSSON (SWE)	KARI HYTÖNEN	SUZUKI IGNIS SPORT	N2

M. Østberg

C. Rautenbach

T. Arai

M. Prokop

U. Aava

J. Ketomaa

P. Sandell

Championship Classifications

FIA Drivers (2/15)
1. Hirvonen — 16
2. Loeb — 1🏆 10
3. Latvala — 1🏆 10
4. P. Solberg — 9
5. Galli — 9
6. Atkinson — 6
7. Duval — 5
8. Mikkelsen — 4
9. Sordo — 3
10. Gardemeister — 2
11. Cuoq — 2
12. Andersson — 1
13. Hänninen — 1
14. Ketomaa — 0
15. Sandell — 0
16. Prokop — 0
17. Solberg — 0
18. Atkinson — 0

FIA Constructors (2/15)
1. BP-Ford Abu Dhabi World Rally Team — 1🏆 26
2. Subaru World Rally Team — 16
3. Stobart VK M-Sport Ford Rally Team — 16
4. Citroën Total World Rally Team — 1🏆 15
5. Suzuki World Rally Team — 5

FIA Production Car WRC (1/8)
1. Hänninen — 1🏆 10
2. Ketomaa — 8
3. Sandell — 6
4. Prokop — 5
5. Nittel — 4
6. Arai — 3
7. Araujo — 2
8. Sousa — 1
9. Campedelli — 0
10. Aksa — 0
11. Tiippana — 0
12. Frisiero — 0
13. Aksakov — 0
14. Aigner — 0
15. Bynidsen — 0
16. Flodin — 0
17. Marrini — 0

Special Stages Times

www.swedishrally.com
www.wrc.com

SS1 Karlstad 1 (1.90 km)
1.P.Solberg 1'28"9; 2.Latvala +0"5;
3.Hirvonen +0"9; 4.Loeb +1"1;
5.H.Solberg +1"5;
6.Galli/Andersson +2"0;
8.Sordo +3"2...
P-WRC > 16.Nittel 1'38"2

SS2 Stenjon 1 (15.50 km)
1.Latvala 7'24"0; 2.Hirvonen +3"3;
3.Østberg +4"3; 4.Loeb +6"7;
5.H.Solberg +7"0; 6.Galli +8"2;
7.P.Solberg/Atkinson +11"7...
P-WRC > 15.Ketomaa 7'58"5

SS3 Bjalverud 1 (21.58 km)
1.Latvala 10'33"7; 2.Hirvonen +1"9;
3.Loeb +4"6; 4.H.Solberg +7"9;
5.Galli +13"9; 6.P.Solberg +19"3;
7.Gardemeister +24"1;
8.Andersson +25"1...
P-WRC > 14.Sandell 11'29"5

SS4 Mangen 1 (22.09 km)
1.Latvala 12'20"27; 2.H.Solberg +16"7;
3.Hirvonen +17"4; 4.Galli +24"7;
5.P.Solberg +31"2; 6.Wilson +34"1;
7.Sordo +35"3; 8.Gardemeister +37"1...
P-WRC > 11.Sandell 13'12"1

SS5 Stensjon 2 (15.50 km)
1.Latvala 7'22"3; 2.Galli +4"2;
3.H.Solberg +4"4; 4.Hirvonen +6"1;
5.Østberg +7"2; 6.Sordo +9"2;
7.P.Solberg +10"14; 8.Aava +12"4...
P-WRC > 12.Sandell 7'57"8

SS6 Bjalverud 2 (21.58 km)
1.Latvala 10'32"4; 2.H.Solberg +7"5;
3.Galli +7"6; 4.Hirvonen +8"0;
5.P.Solberg +15"6; 6.Sordo +17"0
7.Aava +18"5; 8.Østberg +19"6...
P-WRC > 12.Hänninen 11'27"9

SS7 Mangen 2 (22.09 km)
1.Latvala 12'21"2; 2.Galli +3"3;
3.Sordo +7"1; 4.Østberg +9"5;
5.Hirvonen +10"9; 6.H.Solberg +12"3;
7.P.Solberg +18"2; 8.Wilson +25"8...
P-WRC > 11.Sandell 13'10"7

SS8 Karlstad 2 (1.90 km)
1.Galli 1'28"2; 2.P.Solberg +1"0;
3.H.Solberg +1"2; 4.Latvala +1"4;
5.Hirvonen +1"6; 6.Atkinson +2"1;
7.Sordo +3"9; 8.Østberg +4"4...
P-WRC > 13.Hänninen 1'39"1

Classification Leg 1
1.Latvala 1h03'33"3; 2.Hirvonen +48"2;
3.H.Solberg +56"3; 4.Galli +1'02"0;
5.P.Solberg +1'45"2; 6.Østberg +2'15"1
7.Wilson +2'59"6;
8.Gardemeister +3'21"6...
P-WRC > 12.Hänninen 9'41"1

SS9 Horrsjon 1 (14.89km)
1.Loeb 9'18"1; 2.Sordo +0"5;
3.Mikkelsen +5"3; 4.Latvala +6"9;
5.Hirvonen +11"8;
6.Gardemeister +13"2; 7.Galli +15"9;
8.Aava +17"4...
P-WRC > 12.Hänninen 9'41"1

SS10 Hagfors 1 (20.92 km)
1.Sordo 11'45"8;
2.Latvala/H.Solberg +1"6;
4.Loeb +4"6; 5.Mikkelsen +6"2;
6.Galli +6"3; 7.Hirvonen +10"6;
8.Aava +20"6...
P-WRC > 14.Sandell 12'25"0

SS11 Vargasen 1 (24.63 km)
1.Loeb 13'49"1; 2.Hirvonen +1"0;
3.Latvala +9"2; 4.Sordo +10"0;
5.Atkinson +13"5; 6.Galli +15"8;
7.Aava +21"6; 8.P.Solberg +23"5...
P-WRC > 12.14'36"2

SS12 Horrsjon 2 (14.89 km)
Cancelled

SS13 Hagfors 2 (20.92 km)
1.Sordo 11'30"1; 2.Latvala +1"7;
3.Hirvonen +3"0; 4.P.Solberg +5"2;
5.Galli +8"1; 6.Mikkelsen +9"6;
7.Østberg +13"4; 8.Atkinson +14"8...
P-WRC > 12.Sandell 12'15"4

SS14 Vargasen 2 (24.63 km)
1.Hirvonen 13'32"5; 2.Latvala +5"4;
3.Atkinson +5"6; 4.Sordo +6"0;
5.P.Solberg +9"0; 6.Galli +12"6;
7.Østberg +13"8; 8.Aava +19"0...
P-WRC > 12.Aigner 14'40"8

Classification Leg 2
1.Latvala 2h03'53"7; 2.Hirvonen +49"8;
3.Galli +1'35"9; 4.P.Solberg +2'40"9;
5.Wilson +4'37"6; 6.Mikkelsen +4'48"1;
7.Sordo +6'51"9;
8.Gardemeister +8'49"3...
P-WRC > 9.Hänninen 2h12'46"4

SS15 Ullen 1 (16.25 km)
1.H.Solberg 8'21"7; 2.P.Solberg +5"3;
3.Hirvonen +7"0; 4.Latvala +7"1;
5.Østberg +7"6; 6.Sordo +10"2;
7.Wilson +11"8; 8.Aava +13"0...
P-WRC > 14.Ketomaa 9'09"6

SS16 Lssjofors 1 (10.49 km)
1.H.Solberg 5'54"5; 2.Latvala +1"9;
3.Østberg +3"9; 4.Atkinson +5"4;
5.Aava +5"9; 6.Hirvonen +6"7;
7.Sordo +7"1; 8.Galli +7"4...
P-WRC > 12. Flodin 6'16"4

SS17 Rammen 1 (21.87 km)
1.H.Solberg 11'14"4; 2.Latvala +8"2;
3.Hirvonen +9"3; 4.Aava +12"3;
5.Sordo +12"6; 6.Østberg +12"7;
7.Mikkelsen +14"9; 8.P.Solberg +18"8...
P-WRC > 13.Sandell 12'07"2

SS18 Ullen 2 (16.25 km)
Cancelled

SS19 Lssjofors 2 (10.49 km)
1.H.Solberg 5'43"8; 2.P.Solberg +2"4;
3.Sordo +4"2; 4.Atkinson +4"4;
5.Latvala +4"5; 6.Østberg +5"2;
7.Hirvonen +7"1; 8.Aava +7"8...
P-WRC > 12.Sandell 6'11"1

SS20 Rammen 2 (21.87 km)
1.H.Solberg 11'07"1; 2.Latvala +4"3;
3.Hirvonen +4"4; 4.P.Solberg +8"0;
5.Aava +12"0; 6.Sordo +13"1;
7.Atkinson +15"2; 8.Galli +18"0...
P-WRC > 12.Sandell 11'56"1

Results

	Driver - Co-driver	Car	Gr.	Time
1.	**Latvala - Anttila**	**Ford Focus RS WRC 07**	A8	2h46'41"2
2.	Hirvonen - Lehtinen	Ford Focus RS WRC 07	A8	+58"3
3.	Galli - Bernachinni	Ford Focus RS WRC 07	A8	+2'23"2
4.	P. Solberg - Mills	Subaru Impreza WRC 07	A8	+2'59"4
5.	Mikkelsen - Floene	Ford Focus RS WRC 06	A8	+5'46"0
6.	Sordo - Marti	Citroën C4 WRC 08	A8	+7'13"1
7.	Gardemeister - Tuominen	Suzuki SX4 WRC 08	A8	+10'35"3
8.	**Hänninen - Markkula**	**Mitsubishi Lancer WRC IX**	N4/P	+12'27"5
9.	Østberg - Unnerud	Subaru Impreza WRC 07	A8	+13'28"5
10.	Ketomaa - Teiskonen	Subaru Impreza WRX STI	A8	+13'50"7
11.	Sandell - Axelsson	Peugeot 207 S 2000	N4/P	+14'19"3
12.	Prokop - Tomanek	Mitsubishi Lancer Evo. IX	N4/P	+14'30"5

Leading Retirements (14)

Ctrl19	Wilson - Martin	Ford Focus RS WRC 07	Accelerator
Ctrl11C	Loeb - Elena	Citroën C4 WRC 08	Engine
Ctrl4	Andersson - Andersson	Suzuki SX4 WRC	Engine

Performers

	1	2	3	4	5	6	C6	Nb SS
Latvala	6	7	1	3	1	-	18	18
H. Solberg	5	2	3	1	2	1	14	16
Sordo	2	1	2	2	1	4	12	18
Loeb	2	-	1	3	-	-	6	7
Hirvonen	1	3	6	2	3	1	16	18
P. Solberg	1	3	-	2	3	1	10	18
Galli	1	2	1	1	1	6	12	18
Østberg	-	-	2	1	2	2	7	18
Atkinson	-	1	2	1	1	-	5	18
Mikkelsen	-	-	1	-	1	1	3	18
Aava	-	-	-	1	2	-	3	17
Gardemeister	-	-	-	-	1	-	1	18
Wilson	-	-	-	1	1	1	1	18

Leaders

SS1	P. Solberg
SS2 > SS20	Latvala

Juho Hänninen

Previous Winners

1973	Blomqvist - Hertz Saab 96 V 4	1985	Vatanen - Harryman Peugeot 205 T16	1997	Eriksson - Parmander Subaru Impreza WRC
1975	Waldegaard - Thorszelius Lancia Stratos	1986	Kankkunen - Piironen Peugeot 205 T16	1998	Mäkinen - Mannisenmaki Mitsubishi Lancer Evo IV
1976	Eklund - Cederberg Saab 96 V 4	1987	Salonen - Harjanne Mazda 323 Turbo	1999	Mäkinen - Mannisenmaki Mitsubishi Lancer Evo VI
1977	Blomqvist - Sylvan Saab 99 ems	1988	Alen - Kivimaki Lancia Delta HF 4WD	2000	Grönholm - Rautiainen Peugeot 206 WRC
1978	Waldegaard - Thorszelius Ford Escort RS	1989	Carlsson - Carlsson Mazda 323 4WD	2001	Rovanperä - Pietilainen Peugeot 206 WRC
1979	Blomqvist - Cederberg Saab 99 Turbo	1991	Eriksson - Parmander Mitsubishii Galant VR-4	2002	Grönholm - Rautiainen Peugeot 206 WRC
1980	Kullang - Berglund Opel Ascona 400	1992	Jonsson - Backman Toyota Celica GT-Four	2003	Loeb - Elena Citroën Xsara WRC
1981	Mikkola - Hertz Audi Quattro	1993	Jonsson - Backman Toyota Celica Turbo 4WD	2004	Loeb - Elena Citroën Xsara WRC
1982	Blomqvist - Cederberg Audi Quattro	1994	Rådström - Backman Toyota Celica Turbo 4WD	2005	P. Solberg - Mills Subaru Impreza WRC 2004
1983	Mikkola - Hertz Audi Quattro	1995	Eriksson - Parmander Mitsubishi Lancer Evo II	2006	Grönholm - Rautiainen Ford Focus RS WRC 06
1984	Blomqvist - Cederberg Audi Quattro	1996	Mäkinen - Harjanne Mitsubishi Lancer Evo III	2007	Grönholm - Rautiainen Ford Focus RS WRC 06

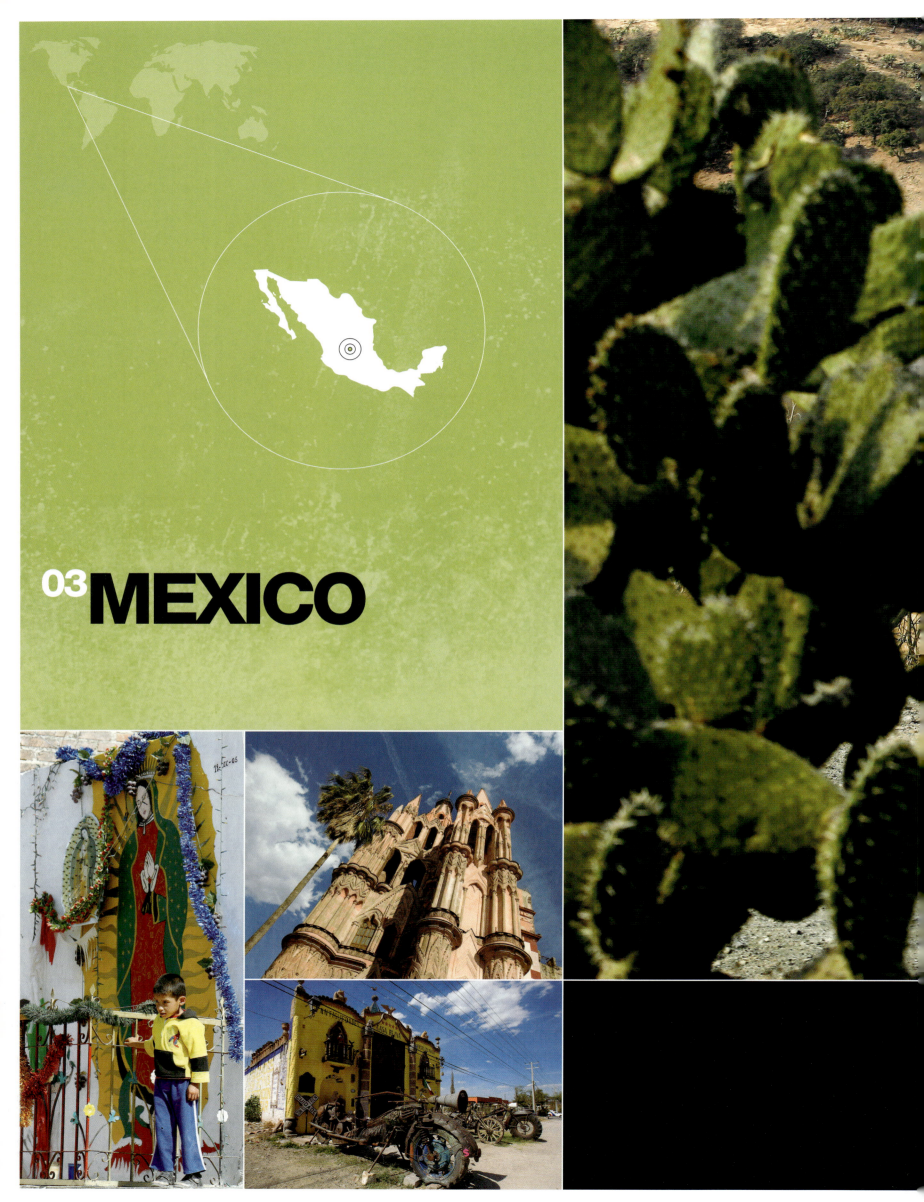

03 MEXICO

🇲🇽 Three in a row for Loeb
With his third straight win in Mexico, the Citroën driver not only made up for his Swedish slip-up but closed to within a point of Hirvonen, who finished fourth but with his confidence dented. Chris Atkinson scored a career-best result when he got the Subaru onto the second step of the podium, while Sébastien Ogier claimed a stunning win in the Junior category.

03 | Mexico

Chris Atkinson wrote his talented name all over this event with second place. There could have been double joy for Subaru if Petter Solberg hadn't been slowed by transmission problems after a good start.

It was hard to know what to make of Mikko Hirvonen this early in the season. Everyone expected him to be Loeb's number one challenger, but the Ford team leader had gone into defensive mode. With two punctures, he came fourth but retained his title lead.

THE RALLY
Blues for the Blues

It's not often you see a man leading the World Championship looking as downcast as Mikko Hirvonen did after the Rally of Mexico.

Not that the Finn had any real need to panic: fourth place meant he kept his Championship lead by a point from Loeb. But Grönholm's replacement in the Blue Oval camp was really down in the dumps as the rally finished.

"It just wasn't my weekend," grumbled a vexed Hirvonen. "Jari-Matti (Latvala) and Sébastien were very strong here. In future I'll need to be as quick as they are to have any hope of the drivers' title. Here's hoping this rally will turn out to be my worst for the year!" It was both a surprise and a worry, coming from the man even Sébastien Loeb himself had picked out as his strongest challenger before the season got under way. How could a supposed title candidate let himself get so down so early – just the third event of the year? Young Hirvonen, it seemed, hadn't quite got his mind around things yet.

In his defence he did take a lot of heavy punches during the Mexican weekend. As early as Friday afternoon, when he was still in touch with the front-runners, the Championship leader lost 40 seconds with a slow puncture. "I don't know what I hit but it sent me sliding into rocks on several corners," he told us. "The rim was cracked and the tyre slowly lost pressure." The same happened next day, only worse. After suffering two punctures the Finn had to stop and change a wheel – another three minutes gone. But these incidents apart, what really got to him was the way the other works Ford was going. Grönholm may have headed off into retirement but his former team-mate probably can't tell the difference, because since the season started Latvala has done a Marcus: a couple of blunders on the Monte, then a string of outstanding performances on the quick stages in Sweden and Mexico.

Our youngest-ever winner of a World Championship event took the lead in central America on the very first stage and kept it all day, helped by three clean sheets. "Winning in Sweden meant I was really confident coming into the Rally of Mexico," he explained. "Still, I'm surprised to be leading: my target before we came here was a podium finish. I kept up a good pace throughout the day and everything worked fine – driver, co-driver, car and tyres. We hit a few rocks quite hard this morning but the Pirellis stood up to it."

Entered by Munchi's, Henning Solberg thrilled the South American fans by bringing his Ford Focus home in fifth. That plus Villagra's two points put the Argentine outfit ahead of Suzuki overall.

The young Finnish prospect was in trouble with his position on the road from the first few kilometres of the second leg, however, and quickly lost the lead to France's reigning World Champion. But he wasn't about to let go – he was only 12.9 down when they came out of SS12. It wasn't till the next timed section and a turbo failure that his last chance flew out the window. "A kilometre after the start I suddenly lost power completely, with no warning. It was really bad luck," he said sadly. In the end Latvala came third, behind Loeb and surprise package Atkinson. "It's been a positive weekend," the Finn insisted, "no complaints. And the most encouraging thing is that I was able to challenge Sébastien Loeb. I hope I can do it again in future. My speed was really good this weekend."

No argument from the four-time World Champion: "We've lost Marcus but we've gained another class act – younger and just as tough. It looks as if we could have a few more fights on our hands, and I like that," said the Frenchman. He would probably have had a tough job on his hands with the Finn in a fair fight – given that he might not even have got past the start. On the Thursday before the event, on the way from the service park to the test session, the C4 WRC's brand-new engine broke down. Panic stations in the red camp – and some head-scratching over the rules. Top brass thought they could get away with changing the block, but changed their minds when the stewards said that would incur a five-minute penalty and opted to put the original engine back in – the one that had failed in the first place. It was, you might say, a loss of focus rarely seen in the Fréquelin days.

So it was with some relief that the Citroën team greeted victory three days later, the third in a row for Loeb – who had already gone through the Leon start gate on foot the previous two years because of technical problems! "It's a very satisfying result," proclaimed Seb as he left the podium. "After our no-score in Sweden it was vital to get back into it right away. And it wasn't easy. But it seems like we always get off to a bad start here in Mexico yet it all turns out all right in the end. It's the kind of victory I like, when you've really had to fight for it. On this hard going Pirelli opted to play it safe with very hard compounds to prevent punctures. We didn't have any of those, but it did mean we had to adjust the settings to get better traction. The team were able to cope, and the way our C4 performed here is very encouraging for what comes next."

The Subarus' pace was just as promising. He may not have been the quickest man out there but a reliable, consistent Chris Atkinson took second place and with

Leon looks like a bullring as the starting ceremony unfolds. The fun was short-lived for Spain's Dani Sordo, who hit a rock in the opening few kilometres and stopped, though he did fight back for seventh place.

03 | Mexico

Latvala had made an impressive start to the season and gave Loeb a hard time – the Finn was in the running for the win up until the halfway stage when a turbo failure ended his charge.

it the best result of his career. "Fantastic," beamed the Australian, now fourth overall. "It's a super start to the season. We've made a lot of progress and the car really behaved very well. We've been working on the dampers since Sweden and it paid off."

Fourth after the first leg, Petter Solberg was the big loser the following day when his transmission broke. Still, 11th place meant another point for Subaru. "It's a really encouraging start to the season, it puts us in a strong position for when we launch the new car," said head honcho David Richards, perhaps a trifle prematurely. "We've done some good work since Sweden and we need to keep the momentum going as we head for Argentina."

There was a fine performance, too, from Munchi's ahead of their home event. Consisting of Henning Solberg (5th) and Federico Villagra (7th), some 19 minutes behind Loeb) on this occasion, the team backed by the Perez-Companc brothers' ice-cream brand scored six points and thus leap-frogged Suzuki in the standings. The SX4s' first venture outside Europe was, in fact, a bit of a fiasco: Gardemeister and Andersson both retired in the fourth stage with engine trouble, a real Achilles heel for the Japanese cars.

The other big loser on the American trip was Dani Sordo, who was out after only a few kilometres. "I followed the line through the apex on a left-hander," explained the Spaniard. "There must have been a rock – we broke a wishbone. Very disappointing." Getting going again under the SupeRally rule, he finished an anonymous 16th – no use at all to Citroën as they slipped 12 points behind Ford.

Called up by Stobart for the first time this season, Matthew Wilson had a couple of close calls on his way to sixth. The first was down to a stray dog, the second came when some moron in the crowd decided to keep an unhappy Mexican tradition alive and hurled a stone through Wilson's windscreen. Stobart's other driver, Gigi Galli, posted his first non-finish of the season after hitting a rock on the first corner in SS4. ∎

JUNIORS
Ogier – Citroën's 'other' Seb

This year's Rally of Mexico saw the Junior Championship go there for the first time. Only nine of the Championship entrants made the costly trip: Prokop, Burkart, Fanari, Ogier and Gallagher in Citroën C2's, Mölder and Kosciusko in Suzuki Swifts, Sandell and Komljenovic in Renault Clios. The man who sprang the big surprise was rookie Sébastien Ogier, leading his first World Championship rally from start to finiish as others fell by the wayside, either through driver error (Prokop)

It wasn't the cactuses Matthew Wilson had to worry about, it was stray dogs and mindless Mexicans, but once he managed to avoid all of those he brought the Ford-Stobart home in sixth place.

or mechanical problems (Sandell). "We came here not really knowing what to expect," said the young driver. "It was my first time in the Citroën, in the PH-Sport team, in the World Championship – I had no idea where I really stood, and it was all a bit much! So of course I'm very happy to have won."

In the end Ogier finished well ahead of Mölder and Kosciusko. More than that, the young Frenchman finished eighth overall once Trivino was disqualified, thus becoming the first Junior ever to finish in the points on a World Championship event. At 24, and on his first WRC appearance, Ogier made a big impression. His feat was reminiscent of his famous senior, Sébastien Loeb, who had a brilliant first season of his own in the Juniors in 2000 in a Citroën Saxo.

While the two men compete in the same colours today, one in a C4 WRC and the other in a C2 Super 1600, the 'new' Seb is to Peugeot what the 'old' one is to Citroën. After winning a selection event for the Lion brand (Rallyes Jeunes) in 2005, the Savoy youngster won the Volant 206, a tarmac/gravel promotional series run in France, in 2007. Peugeot has quit the WRC and so had nothing to offer the young hopeful. But Loeb had been keeping a close watch on Ogier and recommended him to Guy Fréquelin. The FFSA, their minds turning to what comes after Loeb, came up with the financial contribution to give the young man his start in the JWRC. It was up to the driver to meet people's expectations, and his Mexican result was the perfect way to do it. "Sébastien and Julien (co-driver Ingrassia) were on such a steep learning-curve that it couldn't have been easy for them, but they drove the race everyone was looking for, fast at first then controlling it well. It's a very encouraging win," observed Sébastien Loeb, impressed like everyone else +by his namesake. ∎

Two careers about to take off? Chris Atinson took his second podium of the season and the best result of his career while Sébastien Ogier took his Citroën C2 to victory in the Juniors on his first World Championship outing.

Bravo, Gentlemen! Citroën's two Sebs both did the business in Mexico, the elder, Loeb, winning for the third time on the trot - and the younger version, Ogier, looks as if he's following in his wheelmarks.

03 | Mexico | Results

22nd RALLY OF MEXICO

Organiser Details
Reforma 2608
Piso 15
Lomas Atlas
Mexico DF 11950
Tel.: +441 483 459555
Fax: +447 887 508890

Corona Rally México

3rd leg of FIA 2008 World Championship for constructors and drivers.
1st leg of FIA WRC Junior Championship.

Date February 28 - March 2, 2008

Route
830.83 km divised in three legs.
20 special stages on dirt roads (353.75 km).

Ceremonial Start
Thursday, February 28 (20:00)
Guanajuato Ciudad
Leg 1
Friday, February 29 (08:28/16:38),
Leòn > Leòn, 347.38 km;
8 special stages (135.74 km)
Leg 2
Saturday, March 1st (08:24/16:46),
Leòn > Leòn, 340.32 km;
8 special stages (157.32 km)
Leg 3
Sunday, March 2 (08:28/11:34),
Leòn > Leòn, 143,13 km;
4 special stages (60.69 km); 3 roaded (38.39 km)

Entry List (42) - 39 starters

N°	Driver (Nat.)	Co-Driver (Nat.)	Team	Car	Group & FIA Priority
1	SÉBASTIEN LOEB (F)	DANIEL ELENA (MC)	CITROËN TOTAL WRT	CITROËN C4 WRC	A8 1
2	DANI SORDO (E)	MARC MARTI (E)	CITROËN TOTAL WRT	CITROËN C4 WRC	A8 1
3	MIKKO HIRVONEN (FIN)	JARMO LEHTINEN (FIN)	FORD ABU DHABI WORLD RALLY TEAM	FORD FOCUS RS WRC 07	A8 1
4	JARI-MATTI LATVALA (FIN)	MIIKKA ANTTILA (FIN)	BP FORD ABU DHABI WORLD RALLY TEAM	FORD FOCUS RS WRC 07	A8 1
5	PETTER SOLBERG (N)	PHILIP MILLS (GB)	SUBARU WORLD RALLY TEAM	SUBARU IMPREZA WRC 2006	A8 1
6	CHRIS ATKINSON (AUS)	STEPHANE PREVOT (B)	SUBARU WORLD RALLY TEAM	SUBARU IMPREZA WRC 2006	A8 1
7	GIGI GALLI (I)	GIOVANNI BERNACCHINI (I)	STOBART VK M-SPORT FORD RALLY TEAM	FORD FOCUS RS WRC 07	A8 1
8	MATTHEW WILSON (GB)	SCOTT MARTIN (GB)	STOBART VK M-SPORT FORD RALLY TEAM	FORD FOCUS RS WRC 07	A8 1
9	FEDERICO VILLAGRA (RA)	JORGE PÉREZ COMPANC (RA)	MUNCHI'S FORD WORLD RALLY TEAM	FORD FOCUS RS WRC 07	A8 1
10	HENNING SOLBERG (N)	CATO MENKERUD (N)	MUNCHI'S FORD WORLD RALLY TE	FORD FOCUS RS WRC 07	A8 1
11	TONI GARDEMEISTER (FIN)	TOMI TUOMINEN (FIN)	SUZUKI WORLD RALLY TEAM	SUZUKI SX4	A8 1
12	PER-GUNNAR ANDERSSON (S)	JONAS ANDERSSON (S)	SUZUKI WORLD RALLY TEAM	SUZUKI SX4	A8 1
14	CONRAD RAUTENBACH (ZW)	DAVID SENIOR (GB)	CONRAD RAUTENBAC	CITROËN C4 WRC	A8 2
15	RICARDO TRIVIÑO (MEX)	CHECO SALOM (E)	RICARDO TRIVIÑO	PEUGEOT 206 WRC	A8
31	MARTIN PROKOP (CZ)	JAN TOMÁNEK (CZ)	MARTIN PROKOP	CITROËN C2 S1600	A6 3
32	JAAN MÖLDER (EE)	FREDERIC MICLOTTE (B)	JAAN MÖLDER	SUZUKI SWIFT S1600	A6 3
33	AARON NICOLAI BURKART (D)	MICHAEL KOELBACH (D)	AARON NICOLAI BURKART	CITROËN C2 S1600	A6 3
35	MICHAL KOSCIUSZKO (PL)	MACIEK SZCZEPANIAK (PL)	MICHAL KOSCIUSZKO	SUZUKI SWIFT S1600	A6 3
38	FRANCESCO FANARI (I)	MASSIMILLIANO BOSI (I)	FRANCESCO FANARI	CITROËN C2 R2	R2 3
40	MILO? KOMLJENOVIC (SCG)	ALEKSANDAR JEREMIC (SCG)	INTERSPEED RACING TEAM	RENAULT CLIO R3	A7 3
41	PATRICK SANDELL (S)	EMIL AXELSSON (S)	INTERSPEED RACING TEAM	RENAULT CLIO S1600	A6 3
42	SÉBASTIEN OGIER (F)	JULIEN INGRASSIA (F)	FFSA	CITROËN C2 S1600	A6 3
46	SHAUN GALLAGHER (IRL)	MICHAEL MORRISSEY (IRL)	WORLD RALLY TEAM IRELAND	CITROËN C2 S1600	A6 3
61	JAN KOPECKY (CZ)	PETR STARY (CZ)	JAN KOPECKY	FIAT GRANDE PUNTO ABARTH S2000	N4
62	BENITO GUERRA (MEX)	SEGIO GONZALEZ (MEX)	BENITO GUERRA	MITSUBISHI LANCER EVO VIII	N4
63	SPYROS PAVLIDES (CY)	DENIS GIRAUDET (F)	SPYROS PAVLIDES	SUBARU IMPREZA	N4
64	CARLOS IZQUIERDO (MEX)	GUILLERMO IZQUIERDO (MEX)	CARLOS IZQUIERDO	MITSUBISHI LANCER EVO VI	N4
65	RODRIGO SALGADO (MEX)	DIÓDORO SALGADO (MEX)	RODRIGO SALGADO	MITSUBISHI LANCER EVO IX	N4
66	JOSÉ IGNACIO DE IZAURIETA (MEX)	MAURICIO PIMENTEL (MEX)	JOSÉ IGNACIÓ DE IZAURIETA	MITSUBISHI LANCER EVO IX	N4
67	OMAR CHÁVEZ (MEX)	AGUSTINA BASQUEZ (RA)	OMAR CHÁVEZ	PEUGEOT 206 XS	A6
68	JOS CORTÉS (MEX)	ADOLFO OLGUÍN (MEX)	JOSÉ CORTÉS	MITSUBISHI LANCER EVO IX	N4
69	JOSE FELIX PALACIOS (MEX)	MARCELINO SEGURA (MEX)	JOSE FELIX PALACIOS	MITSUBISHI LANCER EVO V	N4
70	JUAN CARLOS SARMIENTO (MEX)	ARMANDO ZAPATA (MEX)	JUAN CARLOS SARMIENTO	PEUGEOT 206 XS	A6
72	RAUL DE ALCAZAR (MEX)	EDGAR BADILLA (CR)	RAUL DE ALCAZAR	PEUGEOT 206 XS	A6
74	REMY ESPINOZA (CR)	ARTURO SUÁREZ (CR)	REMY ESPINOZA	RENAULT CLIO RS	N3
75	ALFREDO LORANCA (MEX)	MAURICIO YGLESIAS (MEX)	ALFREDO LORANCA	RENAULT CLIO RS	N3
76	LUIS ORDUÑA (MEX)	LUIS ORDUÑA JR. (MEX)	LUIS ORDUÑA	PEUGEOT 206 XS	A6
77	ARTURO TEJADA (MEX)	CEFERINO PAZ (E)	ARTURO TEJADA	PEUGEOT 206 XS	A6
78	CARLOS ALBERTO RAMÍREZ (MEX)	FRANCISCO XAVIER ESCALANTE (MEX)	CARLOS ALBERTO RAMÍREZ	PEUGEOT 206 XS	A6
79	JOSÉ MANUEL PONCE (MEX)	JUAN SEBASTI AVILA (MEX)	JOSÉ MANUEL PONCE	PEUGEOT 206 XS	A6

M. Prokop

P. Sandell

G. Galli

C. Rautenbach

P. Andersson

S. Ogier

Championship Classifications

•R•: Rookie

FIA Drivers (3/15)
1. Hirvonen — 21
2. Loeb — 2🏆 20
3. Latvala — 1🏆 16
4. Atkinson — 14
5. Galli — 9
6. P. Solberg — 9
7. Duval — 5
8. H. Solberg — 4
9. Mikkelsen — 4
10. Wilson — 3
11. Sordo — 3
12. Gardemeister — 2
13. Cuoq — 2
14. Villagra — 2
15. Andersson — 1
16. Hänninen — 1
17. Trivino — 1
18. Østberg, Ogier, Mölder, Ketomaa, Sandell, Kosciuszko, Prokop, Broccoli, Burkart, Artru, Nittel, Arai, Guerra, Mercier — 0

FIA Constructors (3/15)
1. BP-Ford Abu Dhabi World Rally Team — 1🏆 37
2. Citroën Total World Rally Team — 2🏆 25
3. Subaru World Rally Team — 25
4. Stobart VK M-Sport Ford Rally Team — 19
5. Munchi's Ford World Rally Team — 6
6. Suzuki World Rally Team — 5

FIA Production Car WRC (1/8)
1. Hänninen — 1🏆 10
2. Ketomaa — 8
3. Sandell — 6
4. Prokop — 5
5. Nittel — 4
6. Arai — 3
7. Araujo — 2
8. Sousa — 1
9. Campedelli — 0
10. Aksa — 0
11. Tiippana — 0
12. Frisiero — 0
13. Aksakov — 0
14. Aigner — 0
15. Brynildsen — 0
16. Flodin — 0
17. Marrini — 0

FIA Junior WRC (1/7)
1. Ogier — 1🏆 10
2. Mölder — 8
3. Kosciusko — 6
4. Burkart — 5
5. Sandell — 4
6. Gallagher — 3
7. Prokop — 2
8. Fanari •R• — 1

Special Stages Times

SS1 Alfaro 1 (22.96 km)
1.Latvala 14'14"6; 2.Atkinson +3"0;
3.Galli +7"3; 4.Loeb +7"4;
5.Hirvonen +9"8; 6.P.Solberg +10"4;
7.H.Solberg +13"1;
8.Andersson +18"4...
J-WRC > 13.Ogier 15'56"1

SS2 Ortega 1 (23.83 km)
1.Loeb 14'11"8; 2.Galli +1"6;
3.Latvala +2"5; 4.Atkinson +5"3;
5.Hirvonen +5"6; 6.P.Solberg +21"3;
7.Andersson +23"0; 8.Villagra +49"4...
J-WRC > 11.Ogier 15'48"9

SS3 El Cubilete 1 (18.87 km)
1.Loeb 11'51"5; 2.Latvala +0"5;
3.H.Solberg +4"7; 4.Atkinson +5"9;
5.Hirvonen +6"3; 6.Wilson +16"1;
7.Andersson +17"1; 8.P.Solberg +24"2...
J-WRC > 11.Ogier 12'59"2

SS4 Alfaro 2 (22.96 km)
1.P.Solberg 14'02"5; 2.Latvala +3"7;
3.Atkinson +5"8; 4.Loeb +6"3
5.Hirvonen +8"4; 6.H.Solberg +10"0;
7.Wilson +29"5; 8.Villagra +35"9...
J-WRC > 10.Ogier 15'45"5

SS5 Ortega 2 (23.83 km)
1.Latvala 14'00"0; 2.Loeb +2"3;
3.Atkinson +2"7; 4.P.Solberg +9"3;
5.H.Solberg +9"6; 6.Wilson +31"6.
7.Hirvonen +40"5; 8.Villagra +44"0...
J-WRC > 9.Ogier 15'33"3

SS6 El Cubilete 2 (18.87 km)
1.Latvala 11'45"5; 2.Loeb +1"9;
3.Atkinson +2"3; 4.H.Solberg +4"2;
5.P.Solberg/Hirvonen +5"3;
7.Wilson +14"1; 8.Villagra +25"7...
J-WRC > 10.Ogier 12'50"3

SS7 Super Special 1 (2.21 km)
1.P.Solberg 1'41"7; 2.Loeb +0"6;
3.Villagra/Atkinson +1"1;
5.Wilson/Latvala +1"9;
7.Hirvonen +2"2; 8.H.Solberg +2"6...
J-WRC > 10.Mölder 1'54"1

SS8 Super Special 2 (2.21 km)
1.Loeb 1'42"0;
2.Latvala/H.Solberg/P.Solberg +0"3;
5.Villagra +0"4. 6.Wilson +0"6;
7.Hirvonen +1"4; 8.Atkinson +5"2...
J-WRC > 10.Kosciusko 1'53"0

Classification Leg 1
1.Latvala 1h23'38"6; 2.Loeb +9"6;
3.Atkinson +22"4; 4.P.Solberg +1'01"9;
5.Hirvonen +1'10"6;
6.H.Solberg +2'4"6; 7.Wilson +2'52"9;
8.Villagra +5'30"0...
J-WRC >10.Ogier 1h23'38"6

SS9 Ibarrilla 1 (29.90 km)
1.Loeb 18'35"7; 2.Hirvonen +3"7;
3.Atkinson +6"7; 4.Sordo +8"3;
5.P.Solberg +9"0; 6.Latvala +9"5;
7.H.Solberg +24"2; 8.Wilson +41"0...
J-WRC > 12.Sandell 21'06"4

SS10 Duarte 1 (23.27 km)
1.Loeb 18'19"6; 2.Sordo +0"5;
3.Latvala +4"7; 4.Atkinson +6"4;
5.Hirvonen +6"8; 6.H.Solberg +27"1;
7.Wilson +29"2;
8.Rautenbach +1'07"4...
J-WRC > 9.Sandell 20'17"3

SS11 Derramadero 1 (23.28 km)
1.Sordo 14'04"6; 2.Loeb +0"5;
3.hirvonen +0"8; 4.Latvala +1"7;
5.Atkinson +2"8; 6.H.Solberg +10"2;
7.Wilson +36"4;
8.Rautenbach +1'00"9...
J-WRC > 10.Sandell 15'44"5

SS12 Ibarrilla 2 (29.90 km)
1.Loeb 18'21"0; 2.Latvala +7"1;
3.Atkinson +8"5; 4.Sordo +9"5;
5.H.Solberg +19"5; 6.Wilson +43"5;
7.Villagra +1'09"7;
8.Rautenbach +1'20"6...
J-WRC > 10.Mölder 20'50"6

SS13 Duarte 2 (23.27 km)
1.Sordo 17'56"2; 2.Loeb +8"2;
3.H.Solberg +14"6; 4.Hirvonen +16"7;
5.Atkinson +30"0; 6.Wilson +31"7;
7.Villagra +59"7; 8.Latvala +1'01"4...
J-WRC > 10.Sandell 19'47"3

SS14 Derramadero 2 (23.28 km)
1.H.Solberg 13'52"9; 2.Sordo +2"2;
3.Hirvonen +4"4; 4.Loeb +10"2;
5.Atkinson +12"4; 6.Wilson +35"6;
7.Rautenbach +51"5;
8.Villagra +53"6...
J-WRC > 11.Ogier 15'41"7

SS15 Super Special 3 (2.21 km)
1.H.Solberg/Loeb 1'41"9;
3.Hirvonen +0"5; 4.Atkinson +0"7;
5.Sordo +1"3;
6.Villagra +1"5; 7.Wilson +1"6;
8.Rautenbach +5"5...
J-WRC > 11.Ogier 1'55"4

SS16 Super Special 4 (2.21 km)
1.Atkinson/Loeb 1'40"8; 3.Sordo +0"6;
4.H.Solberg/Hirvonen +0"9;
6.Villagra +1"6; 7.Rautenbach +4"1;
8.Latvala +6"7...
J-WRC > 11.Sandell 1'53"5

Classification Leg 2
1.Loeb 3h08'39"8; 2.Atkinson +1'01"4;
3.Latvala +2'06"4; 4.H.Solberg +3'51"6;
5.Hirvonen +4'07"5; 6.Wilson +6'10"6;
7.Villagra +18'14"3;
8.Triviño +19'31"1...
J-WRC > 9.Ogier 3h30'40"6

SS17 León (16.09 km)
1.Latvala 10'43"3; 2.P.Solberg +0"2;
3.Hirvonen +2"9; 4.Sordo +3"4;
5.H.Solberg +9"6; 6.Loeb +10"5;
7.Atkinson +13"9; 8.Wilson +23"5...
J-WRC > 12.Mölder 12'14"5

SS18 Guanajuatto (22.30 km)
Cancelled

SS19 Comanjilla (17.88 km)
1.Hirvonen 12'12"7; 2.Latvala +1"0;
3.Sordo +1"5; 4.H.Solberg +11"7;
5.Loeb +19"2; 6.Wilson +23"2;
7.Atkinson +24"1;
8.Rautenbach +36"5...
J-WRC > 12.Sandell 11'32"3

SS20 Super Special 5 (4.42 km)
1.Sordo 3'19"3; 2.Atkinson +1"5;
3.Villagra/Hirvonen +3"1; 5.Loeb +5"1;
6.Wilson +6"4; 7.Latvala +7"1;
8.Rautenbach +8"9...
J-WRC > 11.Kosciuszko 3'44"8

Results

	Driver - Co-Driver	Car	Gr.	Time
1.	Loeb - Elena	Citroën C4 WRC 08	A8	3h33'29"9
2.	Atkinson - Prévot	Subaru Impreza WRC 07	A8	+1'06"1
3.	Latvala - Anttila	Ford Focus RS WRC 07	A8	+1'39"7
4.	Hirvonen - Lehtinen	Ford Focus RS WRC 07	A8	+3'38"7
5.	H. Solberg - Menkerud	Ford Focus RS WRC 07	A8	+4'57"9
6.	Wilson - Martin	Ford Focus RC WRC 07	A8	+6'28"9
7.	Villagra - Perez Companc	Ford Focus RC WRC 07	A8	+19'03"03
8.	Triviño - Salom	Peugeot 206 WRC	A8	+21'17"3
9.	**Ogier - Ingrassia**	**Citroën C2 S1600**	**A6/J**	**+25'24"9**
10.	Molder - Miclotte	Suzuki Swift S1600	A6/J	+26'56"8
11.	Kosciuszko - Szczepaniak	Suzuki Swift S1600	A6/J	+28'30"1
15.	**Guerra - Gonzalez**	**Mitsubishi Lancer Evo. VIII N4**		**+33'19"7**

Leading Retirements (11)

Ctrl4	Galli - Bernacchini	Ford Focus RS WRC 07	Off
Ctrl4	Gardemeister - Tuominen	Suzuki SX4 WRC	Engine
Ctrl3B	Andersson - Andersson	Suzuki SX4 WRC	Engine
Ctrl2	Kopecky - Stary	Fiat Grande Punto Abarth S2000	Oil pump

Performers

	1	2	3	4	5	6	C6	Nb SS
Loeb	8	5	-	3	2	1	19	19
Latvala	4	5	2	1	1	1	14	19
Sordo	3	2	2	3	1	-	11	12
P. Solberg	2	2	-	1	2	2	9	13
H. Solberg	2	1	2	3	3	3	14	19
Atkinson	1	2	6	4	3	-	16	19
Hirvonen	1	1	5	2	6	-	15	19
Galli	-	1	1	-	-	-	2	3
Villagra	-	-	3	-	1	2	5	19
Wilson	-	-	-	-	1	8	9	19

Leaders

SS1 > SS9	Latvala
SS10 > SS20	Loeb

Sébastien Ogier

Previous Winners

2004	Märtin - Park	2006	Loeb - Elena
	Ford Focus RS WRC 03		Citroën Xsara WRC
2005	P. Solberg - Mills	2007	Loeb - Elena
	Subaru Impreza WRC 2005		Citroën C4 WRC

www.rallymexico.com
www.wrc.com

04 ARGENTINA

No safe haven for Seb

Once the two works Fords were gone, especially Mikko Hirvonen's, so quick on the opening day, Sébastien Loeb cruised to a comfortable win. He regained the upper hand in the drivers' standings, while Citroën also closed the gap on Ford in the constructors'. But tyres that just couldn't get to grips with the tricky Argentine going left the World Champion feeling unsafe – and very angry.

04 | Argentina

One rally does not a summer make... Chris Atkinson took a well-earned second place but it didn't mean Subaru were back.

Sébastien Loeb produced an immaculate drive in terrible conditions, beating both the going and the rest of them on tyres that really weren't up to the task.

THE RALLY
No safe haven for Seb

It could – should – have been a wonderful event, one to put alongside some of the legendary Argentine Rallies: a race for real men, with no let-up, in a setting that borders on wilderness, with hordes of spectators, welcoming, wild about their rallying and very knowledgeable as well. The Argentine scenery, the Argentine fans throw the skill and talent of our hard-working heroes into sharp focus like nowhere else.

And the 2008 running was shaping up to be a beauty. Persistent rain, genuine cold, heavy, sticky ground, visibility so bad that the radio plane was late getting up... "a bit like Wales in December", as Sébastien Loeb said drily. In these particularly trying conditions, it didn't take long for the first drama to erupt as the roads got worse with every passing car. On just the second stage, La Cumbre 1, the fiery Latvala, blinded by the worsening conditions, had a violent off-road moment. A kilometre after the start he rolled it. "I made a mistake, but that's life," he said, apparently no more put out than that. "I came into a left-hander too fast and it tightened up on me. The impact with the bank rolled the car, and we stopped with Mikka's door (co-driver Anttila) up against a tree. Not too much damage – just a shattered windscreen. Thank goodness there were plenty of spectators on hand to get the car back on its wheels again." The slip-up meant nine minutes up in smoke, 29th place overall, and one potential winner out of the running.

While one Ford suffered another was doing very nicely thank you. As the young Finn went off to sample the local brew, his blue oval team-leader was having a ball. As witness his amazing time through the 18.7-km first stage, Agua de Oro 1: over that short distance he still managed to put 48.1 seconds on Latvala, 50.7 on Loeb and 1:14.8 on fourth-placed man Atkinson. It was unreal stuff in fog so dense you could have cut it with a knife, and with no info to go on. "We weren't getting any intermediates," said the man himself midway through the leg. "I had no idea if I was on the right pace, so I just kept doing the best I could. But the fog was terrible – in some places you couldn't see 10 metres past the bonnet of the car. When we got to the finish I really didn't think we'd done so well. I said to Jarno (co-driver Lehtinen) that we could just as easily be a minute down as a minute up! And it worked out in our favour." Hirvonen's exploit left his rivals speechless, especially when he increased his lead on SS2, albeit more modestly, taking another two seconds out of Loeb.

Munchi's were at home, and though head man and chief backer Perez-Companc went off, Argentine Champion Federico Villagra finished a fine sixth.

Mikko Hirvonen was dominant early on but tripped up and destroyed his Focus's steering, which dropped him down the order.

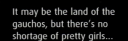

It may be the land of the gauchos, but there's no shortage of pretty girls...

Jari-Matti Latvala got carried away again; his roll in SS2 put him right back in the pack.

"At the end of SS1," said the latter, "I thought we had a 10-second lead over Mikko. It was only when we got to the start of SS3 that we realised we were 50 seconds behind. So Mikko's got a handy lead now, and it's hard to see how we can turn the tables because I was really pushing in those stages. Hirvonen's quicker than me and I'm not happy about it." The Frenchman, it seemed, was not only mystified but powerless to do anything about it. Could the Argentine Rally really have been played out through those first four timed sections, we wondered? At that stage Subaru duo Solberg and Atkinson, followed by Galli in the Stobart Ford, rounded out the top five.

But that's the way it is in gaucho country, as unforgiving as a classic Western. And speaking of classics, it was on the next timed section, one of the classic tests on this event (Ascochinga-La Cumbre, 23 km) that Mikko Hirvonen fell over his own feet. The Focus had a showdown with a rock, just to find out which was the tougher of the two. The car lost. And stayed put, eight kilometres from the end of the stage, with it steering shattered. Back in the service park the Finn told his sad story. "I hit a big rock in a tight left-hander. We were on full lock, and it just destroyed the track control arm. The rock was buried in the ground and just the top of it was sticking up after the first few cars had been through. I didn't have it in my notes because you couldn't see it on the recce. I was really out of luck, and it's demoralising because things had got off to such a fantastic start and I really needed to score some serious points to keep the Championship lead." That would be a little tricker now, though he started 25th next day under SuperRally... With the Fords gone, the first-leg lead was effectively handed to Sébastien Loeb. Steady enough, Loeb had endured the leg rather than dominating it, which was unlike him. "I prefer to be leading when I'm the quickest man out there," he noted, "and this morning I wasn't. Still, better that than being behind. But it just goes to show we still have some development work to do because in some conditions it's getting harder and harder to keep the Fords at bay."

Now the C4 was on easy street, if you can ever say that about the South American roads, as second-place man Chris Atkinson was 1m 30s down on the Frenchman. The Aussie was quick enough, but no match for the World Champion yet, as the Friday spin that cost him nearly 40 seconds showed. "I was pushing like crazy," he explained. "On the last stage I spun in a really slow corner and the engine cut out. No problem – but the car wouldn't start. It took 30 seconds before the engine turned over again. And then we had to get going with the car stuck in deep mud. But still, we're second and Petter (Solberg) third. So far so good for the Subarus. But we'll need to crank it up another level because we've got Galli behind us, and Petter of course, and they're very quick."

The second leg underlined his point. Solberg was indeed extremely rapid, with five clean sheets from a possible nine. "He must have taken some almighty risks," grumbled Atkinson, "especially putting 14 seconds on me through 10. I can't match that pace." No, said the Norwegian, he wasn't over-driving, it was just that the car was going well and he made the most of it. So much so that 'Hollywood' snaffled second place, though still 1m 19s down on the Citroën driver. And that was it as far as the front-runners were concerned. Behind them, though, chaos reigned. In SupeRally Hirvonen, champing at the bit in his Focus, was light-years down on the leaders, while Latvala had another off that morning. Gigi Galli got caught up

04 | Argentina

Gigi Galli at work: the spectacular Italian is never one to take it easy. Rallying's showman always lays it on for the fans.

in the blizzard of breakdowns, too, as exhaust damage triggered electrical problems and a small fire, and they couldn't fix it in the time alowed in the service park. Matthew Wilson, meanwhile, was running sixth when a suspension rod broke.

So the World Champion had no-one left to worry him – but you still didn't want to upset him on that second leg. He was upset enough already about the tyres from sole supplier Pirelli and the fact that they weren't coping with the conditions. Halfway through, he raised the alarm. The rain wasn't as bad as on the previous day, but there was an unbelievable amount of mud on the Saturday stages. And that's what had got Loeb's hackles up. "The tyres aren't working properly," he fumed. "The problem is we're using the same hard compound as in Greece, where it's 40 degrees in the shade, and here it's 10. And in some places the mud's 15 centimetres deep. It would make a tremendous difference in terms of safety if we were allowed to cut them." Yes, but... the current rules don't allow cutting, even in the interests of crew and spectator safety. Pirelli's competition manager registered the complaint and did go off and ask the other constructors if they would accept some re-cutting – only very minor, the same for everybody – but neither Ford nor Subaru would have it and Suzuki didn't offer an opinion one way or the other. With no unanimity forthcoming, things stayed as they were – which meant Loeb stayed very angry. "There have been plenty of decisions taken on safety grounds and this would be easy to do," he said. Nothing doing... good luck, everyone. Next day his anger was still there for all to see, even though it brought another victory. Though he claimed the win by 2m 33s from Atkinson, it had been a particularly difficult one to achieve. Yet again the hellish conditions, especially on the daunting Giulio Cesare and El Condor stages, meant they couldn't get the best out of the tyres. "I don't hate difficult conditions like these," protested the Frenchman, "but I felt today's were the hardest I've ever had to face. The grip was tricky from the start, but today it was really bad. With non-stop rain and fog and mud, it was a real ordeal. We had a comfortable lead but it was still a very challenging event. On hard tyres it was really tricky keeping the car on the road. We should be able to to have the right tyres for the conditions – I hope we can move forward and improve our options because right now they are too limited."

Petter Solberg thought second place was his until an electrical failure stopped his Subaru in the opening timed kilometres of the first day.

Dani Sordo, seen negotiating a ford, took third to confirm how comfortable he is on gravel.

No wonder Dani Sordo and Sébastien Loeb look happy up there on the podium: their collective efforts have brought Citroën back within striking distance of Ford in the constructors' standings.

Once he'd got that off his chest, the World Champion was quick to acknowledge that it had been a good weekend's work in Argentina. It was his fourth victory there, his third in four outings this season and the 39th of his World Championship career, but more than that, it meant he regained the Championship lead from Mikko Hirvonen, who finished fifth. On top of that, third place for Dani Sordo put Citroën back within three points of Ford in the constructors' standings. It was the second time in 2008 that the French firm had scored more points than their main rivals. Subaru should also have shown up well but Petter Solberg went missing in Sunday's action when there were really only two proper specials on the schedule. Electrical failure brought the Norwegian's Impreza to a standstill in the first few kilometres, depriving him of a well-earned second place that went instead to stablemate Chris Atkinson. ■

never able to force him into a costly mistake. "I just had to keep my concentration, and not rush things," expained the winner. "It was a long rally and a very technical one, right to the end – the final stages were very difficult. I hurt my hand when the wheel kicked back after we hit a stone and it was really painful driving right to the end. But after that disappointing off in Sweden, it's the perfect result to get back on target for the year." It was indeed, as Argentine driver Sebastian Baltran claimed second spot. Beltran is not going for the title this year, unlike the unfortunate Al-Attiyah. Determined to take the eight points for second and not tempt fate by chasing the leader through the closing leg, the Subaru driver was undone by his engine in the penultimate stage and didn't make it to the finish line. Aigner's victory was complete. ■

PRODUCTION CARS
Number one for Aigner

Youngster Andreas Aigner, now competing in the PWRC, took his first World Championship win in class in Argentina and with it eighth place in the overall classification. In the tricky South American conditions it was a fine effort by Mitsubishi's Austrian driver. Always in control, mistake-free but maintaining his pace, the man from the high pastures never put a foot wrong. He had to do it under constant threat from the very quick Nasser Al-Attoyah, too. But while the Subaru driver put pressure on his opponent, he was

Young Austrian Andrea Aigner took his first PWRC win and was installed as one of the favourites for the title.

04 | Argentina | Results

28th RALLY OF ARGENTINA

Organiser Details
Automovil Club Argentino
Avda del Libertador 1850
1425 Buenos Aires
Argentina
Tel.: +5435 14265252
Fax: +5435 14265300

Rally Argentina

4th leg of FIA 2008 World Championship for constructors and drivers.
2nd leg of FIA Production Car World Championship.

Date March 27 - 30, 2008

Route
1619.45 km divised in three legs.
21 special stages on dirt roads (347.91 km)

Ceremonial Start
Thursday, March 27 (20:00)
Córdoba
Leg 1
Friday, March 28 (07:45/18:45),
Villa Carlos Paz > Villa Carlos Paz, 605.59 km;
9 special stages (150.86 km)
Leg 2
Saturday, March 29 (08:05/18:45),
Villa Carlos Paz > Villa Carlos Paz, 708.72 km;
9 special stages (154.38 km)
Leg 3
Sunday, March 30 (09:13/11:50),
Villa Carlos Paz > Villa Carlos Paz, 305.14 km;
3 special stages (42.67 km)

Entry List (59) - 56 starters

N°	Driver (Nat.)	Co-Driver (Nat.)	Team	Car	Group & FIA Priority
1	SÉBASTIEN LOEB (F)	DANIEL ELENA (MC)	CITROËN TOTAL WRT	CITROËN C4 WRC 08	A8 1
2	DANIEL SORDO (E)	MARC MARTÍ (E)	CITROËN TOTAL WRT	CITROËN C4 WRC 08	A8 1
3	MIKKO HIRVONEN (FIN)	JARMO LEHTINEN (FIN)	BP-FORD ABU DHABI	FORD FOCUS WRC07	A8 1
4	JARI-MATTI LATVALA (FIN)	MIIKKA ANTTILA (FIN)	BP-FORD ABU DHABI	FORD FOCUS WRC07	A8 1
5	PETTER SOLBERG (N)	PHIL MILLS (GB)	SUBARU WRT	SUBARU IMPREZA WRC07	A8 1
6	CHRIS ATKINSON (AUS)	STEPHANE PREVOT (B)	SUBARU WRT	SUBARU IMPREZA WRC07	A8 1
7	GIGI GALLI (I)	GIOVANNI BERNACCHINI (I)	STOBART VK M-SPORT FORD RT	FORD FOCUS WRC07	A8 1
8	HENNING SOLBERG (N)	CATO MENKERUD (N)	STOBART VK M-SPORT FORD RT	FORD FOCUS WRC07	A8 1
9	FEDERICO VILLAGRA (RA)	JORGE PÉREZ COMPANC (RA)	MUNCHI'S FORD WRT	FORD FOCUS WRC07	A8 1
10	LUIS PÉREZ COMPANC (RA)	JOSÉ MARÍA VOLTA (RA)	MUNCHI'S FORD WRT	FORD FOCUS WRC07	A8 1
11	TONI GARDEMEISTER (FIN)	TIMO TUOMINEN (FIN)	SUZUKI WRT	SUZUKI SX4 WRC	A8 1
12	PER-GUNNAR ANDERSSON (S)	JONAS ANDERSSON (S)	SUZUKI WRT	SUZUKI SX4 WRC	A8 1
16	MATTHEW WILSON (GB)	SCOTT MARTIN (GB)	STOBART VK M-SPORT FORD RT	FORD FOCUS WRC07	A8 2
17	CONRAD RAUTENBACH (ZW)	DAVID SENIOR (GB)	RAUTENBACH CONRAD	CITROËN C4 WRC	A8 2
31	TOSHIHIRO ARAI (J)	GLENN MACNEALL (AUS)	SUBARU TEAM ARAI	SUBARU IMPREZA STI	N4 3
32	MIRCO BALDACCI (I)	GIOVANNI AGNESE (I)	MIRCO BALDACCI	MITSUBISHI LANCER EVO IX	N3
33	MARTIN PROKOP (CZ)	JAN TOMANEK (CZ)	MARTIN PROKOP	MITSUBISHI LANCER EVO IX	N4 3
34	GIANLUCA LINARI (I)	GIANNI MELANI (I)	GIANLUCA LINARI	SUBARU IMPREZA STI	N4 3
35	EVGENY NOVIKOV (RU)	DIMITRI CHUMAK (RU)	NOVIKOV EVGENY	SUBARU IMPREZA	N4 3
37	SPYROS PAVLIDES (CY)	DENIS GIRAUDET (F)	AUTOTEK	SUBARU IMPREZA	N4 3
38	AMJAD FARRAH (HKJ)	NICOLA ARENA (I)	ORION WRT	MITSUBISHI LANCER EVO IX	N4 3
39	NASSER AL-ATTIYAH (QAT)	CHRIS PATTERSON (GB)	QMMF	SUBARU IMPREZA	N4 3
40	STEFANO MARRINI (I)	MATTEO BRAGA (I)	ERRANI TEAM GROUP	MITSUBISHI LANCER EVO IX	N4 3
41	ANDREAS AIGNER (A)	KLAUS WICHA (D)	RED BULL RALLY TEAM I	MITSUBISHI LANCER EVO IX	N4 3
42	BERNARDO SOUSA (P)	CARLOS MAGALHAES (P)	RED BULL RALLY TEAM II	MITSUBISHI LANCER EVO IX	N4 3
44	GABOR MAYER (H)	ROBERT TAGAI (H)	GABOKO RACING	SUBARU IMPREZA N12	N4 3
45	ANDREJ JEREB (SLO)	MIRAN KACIN (SLO)	MOTORING CLUB I	SUBARU IMPREZA N12	N4 3
46	JARI KETOMAA (FIN)	MIIKA TEISKONEN (FIN)	MOTORING CLUB II	SUBARU IMPREZA N12	N4 3
47	GIORGIO BACCO (I)	SILVIO STEFANELI (I)	MOTORING CLUB	SUBARU IMPREZA N11	N4 3
48	EGVENY AKASAKOV (RU)	ALEXANDRE KORNILOV (EE)	RED WINGS	MITSUBISHI LANCER EVO IX	N4 3
50	SIMONE CAMPEDELLI (I)	DANILO FAPPANI (I)	SCUDERIA RUBINE CORSE	MITSUBISHI LANCER EVO IX	N4 3
51	SUBHAN AKSA (RI)	HENDRIK MBOI (RI)	INDONESIA RALLY TEAM	MITSUBISHI LANCER EVO IX	N4 3
53	UWE NITTEL (GER)	DETLEF RUF (GER)	PRO RACE RALLY	MITSUBISHI LANCER EVO IX	N4 3
54	TRAVIS PASTRANA (USA)	DEREK RINGER (GB)	SUBARU RALLY TEAM USA	SUBARU IMPREZA WRX STI	N4 3
55	PATRIK SANDELL (S)	EMIL AXELSSON (S)	PEUGEOT SPORT SWEDEN	PEUGEOT 207 S2000	N4 3
56	FUMIO NUTAHARA (J)	DANIEL BARRITT (GB)	ADVAN-PIAA RALLY TEAM	MITSUBISHI LANCER EVO IX	N4 3
57	MARTIN RAUAM (EE)	SILVER KÜTT (EE)	WORLD RALLY TEAM ESTONIA	MITSUBISHI LANCER EVO IX	N4 3
59	MARCOS LIGATO (RA)	RUBÉN GARCÍA (RA)	TANGO RALLY TEAM	MITSUBISHI LANCER EVO IX	N4 3
60	SEBASITÁN BELTRÁN (RA)	RICARDO ROJAS (RCH)	VRS RALLY TEAM	MITSUBISHI LANCER EVO IX	N4 3
61	GABRIEL POZZO (RA)	DANIEL STILLO (RA)	BARATERO	SUBARU IMPREZA STI 8	N4
62	NICOLÁS MADERO (RA)	GUILLERMO PIAZZANO (RA)	TANGO RALLY TEAM	MITSUBISHI LANCER EVO IX	N4
63	ALEJANDRO CANCIO (RA)	SANTIAGO GARCÍA (RA)	TANGO RALLY TEAM	MITSUBISHI LANCER EVO IX	N4
64	CLAUDIO MENZI (RA)	EDGARDO GALINDO (RA)	CLAUDIO MENZI	SUBARU IMPREZA	N4
65	RICARDO TRIVIÑO (MEX)	CHECO SALOM (E)	TRIVIÑO RICARDO	MITSUBISHI LANCER EVO IX	N4
66	WALTER RODRÍGUEZ (RA)	LAUREANO GRIGERA (RA)	TANGO RALLY TEAM	MITSUBISHI LANCER EVO IX	N4
67	YAZEED AL RAJHI (KSA)	STEVE LANCASTER (GB)	BARATEC MOTORSPORT	SUBARU IMPREZA WRX STI	N4
70	GASTÓN GENOVESE (RA)	GUSTAVO BECCARÍA (RA)	SCHROEDER COMPETICIÓN	MITSUBISHI LANCER EVO IX	N4
75	ALBERTO NICOLÁS (RA)	SERGIO PERUGINI (RA)	NICOLÁS COMPETICIÓN	MITSUBISHI LANCER EVO VIII	N4
76	GUILLERMO BOTTAZZINI (RA)	DIEGO DE LUCA (RA)	ZUNINO RALLY	RENAULT CLIO 1.6	A6
77	MANUEL MACHINEA (RA)	ENRIQUE MARONGIU (RA)	MILLÁN TRABAJOS ESPECIALES	PEUGEOT 206 RC 2	N3
78	ROBERTO JAUREGUI (RA)	FEDERICO SIRCH (RA)	TITO JAUREGUÍ RALLY GROUP	PEUGEOT 206 1.6	A6
79	JORGE DÍAZ (RA)	EDUARDO NOVELLI (RA)	ARIES AUTOMOTORES	FIAT PALIO 1.6	A6
80	ULISES MORALES (RA)	EZEQUIEL QUERALT (RA)	DS RACING	FIAT PALIO 1.6	A6
81	GUILLERMO CLEMENTE (RA)	FRANCO DONALICIO (RA)	BASAVILVASO	FIAT PALIO 1.6	A6
82	LUIS PÉREZ LOBO (RA)	GUSTAVO CARCIOTTO (RA)	ZUNINO RALLY	RENAULT CLIO 1.6	A6
83	MIGUEL ÁNGEL DURANTE (RA)	JUAN MANUEL CASAJÚS (RA)	ZUNINO RALLY	RENAULT CLIO	A6

S. Beltrán

J. Ketomaa

F. Nutahara

T. Pastrana

N. Al-Attiyah

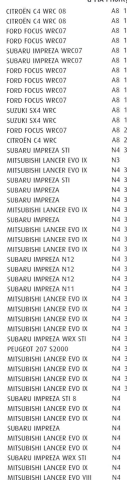

Championship Classifications

·R·: Rookie

FIA Drivers (4/15)
1. Loeb 3🏆 30
2. Hirvonen 25
3. Atkinson 22
4. Latvala 1🏆 16
5. Galli 11
6. Sordo 9
7. P. Solberg 9
8. Rautenbach 5
9. Duval 5
10. Villagra 5
11. H. Solberg 4
12. Mikkelsen 4
13. Wilson 3
14. Gardemeister 2
15. Cuoq 2
16. Andersson 1
17. Aigner 1
18. Hänninen 1
19. Ogier 1
20. Beltrán, Østberg, Mölder, Ketomaa, Kosciuszko, Sandell, Nutahara, Prokop, Burkart, Broccoli, Rauam, Farrah, Artru, Nittel, Guerra, Arai, Mercier 0

FIA Constructors (4/15)
1. BP-Ford Abu Dhabi World Rally Team 1🏆 44
2. Citroën Total World Rally Team 3🏆 41
3. Subaru World Rally Team 33
4. Stobart VK M-Sport Ford Rally Team 22
5. Munchi's Ford World Rally Team 10
6. Suzuki World Rally Team 5

FIA Production Car WRC (2/8)
1. Ketomaa 14
2. Aigner 1🏆 10
3. Hänninen 1🏆 10
4. Beltrán 8
5. Prokop 7
6. Sandell 6
7. Nutahara 5
8. Nittel 4
9. Rauam 4
10. Arai 3
11. Farrah 3
12. Araujo 2
13. Sousa 2
14. Campedelli 0
15. Aksa 0
16. Mayer 0
17. Tiippana 0
18. Pavlides 0
19. Aksakov 0
20. Frisiero 0
21. Bacco 0
22. Jereb 0
23. Brynildsen 0
24. Flodin 0
25. Marrini 0

FIA Junior WRC (1/7)
1. Ogier 1🏆 10
2. Mölder 8
3. Kosciusko 6
4. Burkart 5
5. Sandell 4
6. Gallagher 3
7. Prokop 2
8. Fanari ·R· 1

Special Stages Times

www.rallyargentina.com
www.wrc.com

SS1 La Cumbre - Agua De Oro I (18.70 km)
1.Hirvonen 16'29"3; 2.Latvala +48"1; 3.Loeb +50"7; 4.Atkinson +1'14"8 5.P.Solberg +1'33"8; 6.Galli +1'35"3; 7.Sordo +1'39"8; 8.Villagra +1'57"9... P-WRC > 12.Arai 19'15"2

SS2 Ascochinga - La Cumbre I (23.28 km)
1.Hirvonen 14'59"6; 2.Loeb +2"0; 3.Atkinson +11"6; 4.P.Solberg +13"6 5.Galli +36"0; 6.Sordo +37"8; 7.H.Solberg +1'05"1; 8.Wilson +1'25"3... P-WRC > 13.Aigner 17'41"6

SS3 Capilla Del Monte - San Marcos I (22.95 km)
1.Latvala 17'39"7; 2.Loeb +3"0; 3.Galli +6"5; 4.Hirvonen +7"2; 5.Sordo +8"0; 6.Atkinson +8"8; 7.H.Solberg +11"0; 8.Villagra +18"9... P-WRC > 14.Aigner 18'57"8

SS4 San Marcos - Charbonnier I (9.61 km)
1.Hirvonen 6'38"3; 2.Sordo +0"6; 3.H.Solberg +1"6; 4.Loeb +2"3; 5.P.Solberg 4"6; 6.Galli +5"2; 7.Atkinson +5"8; 8.Villagra +9"8... P-WRC > 14.Ligato 7'15"0

SS5 Ascochinga - La Cumbre I (23.28 km)
1.Loeb 14'51"3; 2.Galli +10"5; 3.Sordo +11"3; 4.Atkinson +11"7; 5.P.Solberg +13"7; 6.Latvala +16"9; 7.Pérez Companc +37"2; 8.Villagra +38"5... P-WRC > 12.Sandell 16'18"8

SS6 Capilla Del Monte - San Marcos II (22.95 km)
1.Hirvonen 17'23"1; 2.Galli +0"9; 3.Atkinson +5"9; 4.Sordo +6"0; 5.Loeb +7"1; 6.P.Solberg +13"8; 7.Villagra +24"6; 8.Pérez Companc +33"0... P-WRC > 13.Sousa 18'53"1

SS7 San Marcos - Charbonnier II (9.61 km)
1.Galli 6'33"5; 2.Atkinson +0"4; 3.Latvala +1"1; 4.Sordo +1"2; 5.Loeb +2"1; 6.P.Solberg +5"7; 7.Villagra +8"5; 8.Gardemeister +11"4... P-WRC > 12.Sandell 7'08"3

SS8 La Cumbre - Agua De Oro II (18.70 km)
1.Latvala 17'02"3; 2.Loeb +2"7; 3.Galli +3"0; 4.P.Solberg +5"8; 5.Sordo 30"3; 6.Atkinson +43"9; 7.Villagra +50"8; 8.Wilson +1'14"8... P-WRC > 10.Al-Attiyah 18'46"9

SS9 Cordoba Stadium I (1.78 km)
1.Atkinson 1'39"4; 2.P.Solberg +0"3; 3.Latvala +1"3; 4.Loeb +1"6; 5.Galli +1"8; 6.Sordo +3"4; 7.Villagra +4"4; 8.Wilson +5"2... P-WRC > 9.Al-Attiyah 1'49"1

Classification Leg 1
1.Loeb 1h54'28"0; 2.Atkinson +1'30"6; 3.P.Solberg +1'38"9; 4.Galli +1'47"7; 5.Sordo +2'06"9; 6.Villagra +4'48"3; 7.Wilson +6'18"3; 8.Latvala +9'27"5... P-WRC > 10.Aigner 2h06'49"0

SS10 Santica Monica - Amboy I (22.17 km)
1.P.Solberg 12'02"7; 2.Atkinson +14"0; 3.Loeb +15"5; 4.Hirvonen +19"9; 5.Latvala+21"3; 6.Sordo +22"1; 7.Galli +26"5; 8.Andersson +32"6... P-WRC > 12.Al-Attiyah 13'37"9

SS11 Villa Del Dique - Las Bajadas I (16.41 km)
1.Loeb 9'10"0; 2.P.Solberg +4"4; 3.Atkinson +7"8; 4.Sordo +9"3; 5.Galli +10"6; 6.Hirvonen +13"8; 7.Andersson +20"9; 8.H.Solberg +31"8... P-WRC > 12.Ketomaa 10'22"0

SS12 San Augustin - Villa General Belgrano I (16.31 km)
1.Loeb 11'26"5; 2.Atkinson +5"0; 3.P.Solberg +6"7; 4.Hirvonen +13"8; 5.Sordo +17"3; 6.Villagra +28"7; 7.Galli +28"8; 8.Andersson +31"0 P-WRC > 14. Sandell 12'53"6

SS13 Santa Rosa - San Augustin I (21.41 km)
1.Atkinson 13'37"3; 2.P.Solberg +3"3; 3.Hirvonen +3"5; 4.Loeb +5"4; 5.Galli +14"1; 6.Sordo +14"8; 7.Andersson +30"1; 8.H.Solberg +31"6... P-WRC > 13.Al-Attiyah 15'13"1

SS14 Santica Monica - Amboy II (22.17 km)
1.P.Solberg 11'37"2; 2.Loeb +7"6; 3.Hirvonen +8"6; 4.Atkinson +10"0; 5.Sordo +11"1; 6.Wilson +39"7; 7.Rautenbach +49"1; P-WRC > 8.Al-Attiyah +1'26"1 (13'03"3)...

SS15 Villa Del Dique - Las Bejadas II (16.41 km)
1.Loeb 8'57"8; 2.P.Solberg +0"5; 3.Hirvonen +8"2; 4.Atkinson +8"3; 5.Sordo +9"5; 6.Rautenbach +40"6; P-WRC > 7.Al-Attiyah +1'06"5 (10'04"3); 8.Mayer +1'07"2...

SS16 San Augustin - Villa General Belgrano II (16.31 km)
1.P.Solberg 11'18"8; 2.Loeb +0"4; 3.Hirvonen +9"6; 4.Sordo +13"7; 5.Atkinson +14"2; 6.Rautenbach +47"6; P-WRC > 7.Sandell +1'22"7 (12'41"5); 8.Beltràn +1'27"0...

SS17 Santa Rosa - San Augustin II (21.41 km)
1.P.Solberg 13'23"6; 2.Hirvonen +1"7; 3.Loeb +4"6; 4.Atkinson +10"6; 5.Sordo +16"2; 6.Rautenbach +1'14"5; P-WRC > 7.Al-Attiyah +1'14"5 (14'45"2); 8.Beltràn +1'21"6...

SS18 Cordoba Stadium II (1.78 km)
1.P.Solberg 1'40"6; 2.Loeb +0"5; 3.Atkinson +2"0; 4.Hirvonen +3"7; 5.Rautenbach +4"5; 6.Sordo +5"4; P-WRC > 7.Al-Attiyah +8"9 (1'49"5); 8.Campedelli +9"5...

Classification Leg 2
1.Loeb 3h28'16"5; 2.P.Solberg 1'19"6; 3.Atkinson +2'08"5; 4.Sordo +3'32"3; 5.Rautenbach +18'.00"1; 6.Hirvonen +24'44"5; P-WRC > 7.Aigner +25'27"2 (3h53'43"7); 8.Villagra +25'53"4...

SS19 Mina Clavero - Giulio Cssare (24.70 km)
1.Latvala 19'57"9; 2.Sordo +8"2; 3.Galli +8"6; 4.Hirvonen +9"9; 5.Loeb +10"7; 6.Villagra +12"4; 7.Atkinson +13"2; 8.Andersson +16"9... P-WRC > 11.Beltrán 21'27"4

SS20 El Condor - Copina (15.99 km)
1.Loeb 15'08"6; 2.Latvala +10"7; 3.Atkinson +19"3; 4.Galli +19"8; 5.Sordo +29"0; 6.Hirvonen 32"5; 7.Villagra 59"9; 8.Rautenbach +1'17"3... P-WRC > 10.Aigner 17'07"6

SS21 Cordoba Stadium (1.98 km)
1.Latvala 2'13"3; 2.Hirvonen +0"7; 3.Loeb +1"6; P-WRC > 4.Campedelli +1"8 (2'15"1); 5.Galli +2"0; 6.Akasakov +2"8; 7.Atkinson +4"5; 8.Nutahara +6"6...

Results

	Driver - Co-Driver	Car	Gr.	Time
1.	**Loeb - Elena**	**Citroën C4 WRC 08**	**A8**	**4h05'48"6**
2.	Atkinson - Prévot	Subaru Impreza WRC 07	A8	+2'33"2
3.	Sordo - Marti	Citroën C4 WRC 08	A8	+4'04"7
4.	Rautenbach - Senior	Citroën C4 WRC 08	A8	+20'03"5
5.	Hirvonen - Lehtinen	Ford Focus RS WRC 07	A8	+25'15"3
6.	Villagra - Perez Companc	Ford Focus RC WRC 07	A8	+27'42"0
7.	Galli - Bernacchini	Ford Focus RC WRC 07	A8	+27'51"8
8.	**Aigner - Wicha**	**Mitsubishi Lancer Evo IX**	**N4/P**	**+28'59"3**
9.	Beltràn - Rojas	Mitsubishi Lancer Evo IX	N4/P	+30'04"9
10.	Ketomaa - Teiskonen	Subaru Impreza	N4/P	+31'52"5

Leading Retirements (25)

Ctrl20	Gardemeister - Tuominen	Suzuki SX4 WRC	Engine
Ctrl20	Wilson - Martin	Ford Focus RS WRC 07	Suspension
Ctrl19	P. Solberg - Mills	Subaru Impreza WRC 07	Electrical
Ctrl19	H. Solberg - Menkerud	Ford Focus RS WRC 07	Suspension
Ctrl9D	Pérez Companc - Volta	Ford Focus RS WRC 07	Transmission

Conrad Rautenbach

Performers

	1	2	3	4	5	6	C6	NbSS
Loeb	5	6	4	3	3	-	21	21
P. Solberg	5	4	1	2	3	2	1	18
Latvala	5	2	2	-	2	2	13	16
Hirvonen	3	2	4	5	-	2	16	16
Atkinson	2	3	5	5	1	2	18	21
Galli	1	2	3	1	4	3	14	16
Sordo	-	2	1	4	7	4	18	21
H. Solberg	-	-	1	-	-	-	1	8
Campedelli	-	-	-	1	-	-	1	15
Rautenbach	-	-	-	-	1	3	4	21
Villagra	-	-	-	-	-	1	1	19
Wilson	-	-	-	-	-	1	1	15
Akasakov	-	-	-	-	-	1	1	14

Leaders

SS1 > SS4	Hirvonen
SS5 > SS21	Loeb

Previous Winners

1980	Röhrl - Geistdorfer Fiat 131 Abarth
1981	Fréquelin - Todt Talbot Sunbeam Lotus
1983	Mikkola - Hertz Audi Quattro
1984	Blomqvist - Cederberg Audi Quattro
1985	Salonen - Harjanne Peugeot 205 T16
1986	Biasion - Siviero Lancia Delta S4
1987	Biasion - Siviero Lancia Delta HF Turbo
1988	Recalde - Del Buono Lancia Delta Integrale
1989	Ericsson - Billstam Lancia Delta Integrale
1990	Biasion - Siviero Lancia Delta Integrale 16v
1991	Sainz - Moya Toyota Celica GT4
1992	Auriol - Occelli Lancia Delta HF Integrale
1993	Kankkunen - Grist Toyota Celica Turbo 4WD
1994	Auriol - Occelli Toyota Celica Turbo 4WD
1995	Recalde - Christie Lancia Delta HF Integrale
1996	Mäkinen - Harjanne Mitsubishi Lancer Evo III
1997	Mäkinen - Harjanne Mitsubishi Lancer Evo IV
1998	Mäkinen - Mannisenmäki Mitsubishi Lancer Evo V
1999	Kankkunen - Repo Subaru Impreza WRC
2000	Burns - Reid Subaru Impreza WRC 2000
2001	C. McRae - Grist Ford Focus RS WRC 01
2002	Sainz - Moya Ford Focus RS WRC 02
2003	Grönholm - Rautiainen Peugeot 206 WRC
2004	Sainz - Marti Citroën Xsara WRC
2005	Loeb - Elena Citroën Xsara WRC
2006	Loeb - Elena Citroën Xsara WRC
2007	Loeb - Elena Citroën C4 WRC

05 JORDAN

Mikko I, new king of Jordan
Ford's man did his confidence no harm with his first rally win of the season ahead of Dani Sordo, who just couldn't hang on to him, and the consistent Chris Atkinson. In so doing Mikko Hirvonen regained the Championship lead from Sébastien Loeb, victim of an unlikely accident with Conrad Rautenbach on the road section. The other big loser was Jari-Matti Latvala, who went off while leading the rally.

05 | Jordan

A ray of early-season sunshine for Mikko Hirvonen as he takes his first win through the Jordan mountains. The Finn won in Norway last year as well, so he obviously likes going to new places.

Dani Sordo took a superb second place on the Rally of Jordan. The Spaniard might have won it but for the Ford tactics that saw him having to open the road on the final leg.

THE RALLY
Crash of the season

Conrad Rautenbach is usually a discreet presence in the Junior WRC ranks, but this year he's in with the big boys thanks to his diamond magnate Dad, who has given him a new toy to play with: a Citroën C4 WRC. So ever since the Monte, the 23-year-old Zimbabwean has been riding high, more at his father's expense than on the strength of his own skills. And he's been making a name for himself: in Argentina, Rautenbach fluked fourth place, and as the Championship hit Jordan for the first time, he hit all the headlines. For rather less glorious reasons, this time: he was involved in the accident that forced Sébastien Loeb out of the rally.

Rewind: Saturday morning, at the finish of the 11th special stage, Shuna. Sébastien Loeb and Daniel Elena have just clean-sheeted for the third straight time, extending their lead over Dani Sordo to 34.1 seconds. As they start the road section, the crew are unwinding: the co-driver tidies the helmets away in the back, then does some figures as their opponents' times come through on the intercom. The driver is gathering his wits and thinking ahead to the next stage. As they come round a corner on the narrow road they run straight into another Citroën C4. It's Rautenbach's; he is using the same road link to get to the start of SS11. The South African youngster, a bit pushed for time maybe, has cut the corner. Both drivers jump on the brakes, but it's too late. On a slippery surface the wheels lock; the two Citroëns have a head-on. "The link road was very narrow, and there were a lot of places where you had no line of sight," said Loeb. "At one of them we just couldn't get out of Conrad's way as he came towards us. I think he was a bit late and was maybe going quite fast. I wasn't concentrating hard, because we had just come out of the stage. It was a big hit – we couldn't continue. I don't know whose fault it was. Maybe he was going too fast, but what can you do? All I know is that it's a great shame because we were looking good in both Championships and it's cost us a lot of points." A crestfallen Rautenbach said his door was broken, forcing him to hold it shut: "Maybe I wasn't concentrating hard enough on the road," he said. The Citroën camp was not happy about it – if the man at fault hadn't been one of the Chevron's backers, the tone of the conversation might well have been somewhat less polite.

While Loeb was able to restart under SupeRally next day, the disaster meant the French team were now pinning their hopes on Dani Sordo, who had inherited the lead. A fragile lead it was, though, with Latvala and Hirvonen up his chuff. Then a slow puncture through SS13 dropped him back to third where he stayed until the final stage of the day. Yet after Baptism 2 and its 13.13 kilometres, the closing stage of the second leg, Sordo was back in front – no thanks to him. Latvala and Hirvonen had

Petter Solberg started well enough, leading after SS6, but fragile suspension left his race in ruins. The Norwegian eventually went off in another rally to forget.

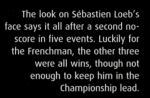

The look on Sébastien Loeb's face says it all after a second no-score in five events. Luckily for the Frenchman, the other three were all wins, though not enough to keep him in the Championship lead.

Gigi Galli was overshadowed by the other Ford drivers, finishing eighth. But the Italian looked set for another high-class showing on home ground in Sardinia next time out.

deliberately backed off near the end to allow the Spaniard to open the road next day and clean it for the stage to come. "I think it was the right decision," said Latvala, "even if it does feel a bit weird having to slow down deliberately." He went from first to second, aiming to take eight and a half seconds back from Sordo on the final day. "Loeb's retirement is a real thorn out of our side – he was doing unbelievable times and that gap was beyond us," Hirvonen acknowledged. "But now it's looking pretty good for us." Sordo, meanwhile, was livid. On Jordanian sand he knew he had no chance of fending off the Finns.

And so it turned out. Sunday's first timed section was enough for the Fords to regain the upper hand as Sordo lost 12.5 seconds to Hirvonen, now second overall, just three-tenths adrift of Latvala. Not knowing, at this early stage of the season, which driver he should favour, Malcolm Wilson hadn't issued any team orders or told them to go easy. And he had reason to regret it: on the next stage Latvala made yet another monumental blunder. "I hit a stone in the stage before, but I didn't feel any difference in the car's handling and I carried on," he said. "Then in the middle of the next stage a left rear suspension bracket just collapsed." Upshot: 10 minutes gone. Luckily for Latvala, the team worked wonders to change gearbox, diff and rear suspension in the service park and he was able to carry on and claim eighth place. "I've got to be more consistent and stop making these mistakes," acknowledged Latvala, with a rare gift for understatement...

So it was all between Hirvonen and Sordo, who were 5.7 apart halfway through the leg. The Spaniard had done some useful damage limitation and was still in the running for a win as they went into the second loop – which meant clean roads and a chance to take on Hirvonen on level terms. In the end, though, the latter was too strong for him and duly took his first win of the season. "I knew things weren't on our side at the start this morning, but I tried not to think about that and just go as fast as I could," said Sordo. "Sadly it wasn't enough."

Second time out in the PH Sport Citroën C4, Urmo Aava was in fifth place with just a few stages remaining and set for the best result of his career. Infuriatingly, the Estonian had to retire with mechanical problems.

05 | Jordan

No time for Henning Solberg to do the tourist bit and take in the spectacular scenery: fourth was the Norwegian's best effort since the season began.

Matthew Wilson was in the points for the second time this season. Sixth in Mexico, he went one better on this first running of the Jordan Rally.

Hirvonen meanwhile was just relieved to score 10 points in a oner at last – and to find himself back in the Championship lead. "I really needed a win to get me going again," he said. "Now I need to keep my feet on the ground, try to pick up my speed and win some more events – I know consistency is the thing, but there's nothing like a win!"

In third place, Chris Atkinson was on the podium for the fourth time out of five, his consistent front-running lifting him past Jari-Matti 'Lose-it' Latvala to third place overall. "Another bunch of points, which is good because it keeps us in touch with the others while we wait for the new car," was the way he summed it up. "But it was a tough rally for us – we were left behind at the start, then we had our share of problems, but this time it's worked out OK and we've been able to take advantage of others' misfortunes. But there's still a lot of work to be done if we want to start thinking about winning." On the dampers, for starters: they are the Impreza's Achilles heel, much to the chagrin of Petter Solberg.

Joint leader after the opener, the Norwegian saw his event fall apart on SS6. "I hit a little rock on the inside of a left-hander and the damper let go," he said, cursing the suspension's fragility after what had seemed like a harmless bump. Restarting under SupeRally next day, he had the same trouble in SS11, this time at the rear – and without hitting anything. Then, as his brakes went away, he had a heavy off in SS16. "Frustrating – a real pain in the arse," he said pointedly.

As for the Suzukis, they foundered as well. Gardemeister had an engine problem after hitting a rock in SS3, while P-G Andersson went off several times but was still given fourth-fastest time on the final leg. Behind Atkinson, the result looked like some kind of Focus Cup: fourth was Solberg, fifth Wilson, sixth Villagra, seventh Latvala, eighth Galli and ninth, ahead of Loeb, Al Qassimi! "That was a tough rally," said a delighted Malcolm Wilson. "Gigi showed how quick he can be with three clean sheets, and Matthew and Henning didn't put a foot wrong. Hats off to them all."

And to the organisers: the Jordan Rally had enjoyed a very successful World Championship baptism. ∎

Latvala was… Latvala. He was quick enough to have a chance of winning right up until the final few stages, but lost his head, made a mistake and slipped right back to seventh, denying Ford what looked like a certain 1-2 finish.

Chris Atkinson was one to watch in the early-season events. The Australian was a consistent front-runner, this being his fourth podium in five rallies. It was promising stuff as they waited for the new Impreza.

This is THE shot of the rally – and perhaps of the season so far. A head-on between Conrad Rautenbach (top) and Sébastien Loeb on the road link left their C4's in a sorry state as both men left Jordan feeling sorry for themselves.

JUNIORS
Ogier does it again

Frenchman Sébastien Ogier laid on another fine show in the second JWRC event, with a win that was very different from his previous success in Mexico. On his World Championship debut the young Citroën prospect had opened up a big lead early in the piece and managed the gap it from there. This time, in Jordan, he was the one who hit early trouble: after the first day he was down in sixth in the Junior standings, 4m 49s down on Patrick Sandell, who led from Mölder and Bettega. "We had fuel pressure problems in SS4, and it took a bit of work to fix it at midday service. So we were late out and copped a 3:20 penalty," said Ogier. "To crown it all we had a puncture in SS6 when we landed over a bump and lost more time. We'll be doing our utmost to get it all right on day two and make some of that lost time up."

Far from dowhearted, the Frenchman went straight on the attack next day in his Citroën C2, claiming seven stages out of eight and climbing back to second between Sandell and Mölder. And he wasn't done yet: on Sunday's first timed section Sandell, at that point two minutes in front, was out and the Ogier-Ingrassia Citroën was home free. "This time we were the hunters," said the French driver, "and it wasn't such a bad thing! It meant we had to go quickly to get back in touch, remembering we had to get to the finish. The win has really helped us in the Championship." His nine-point lead over Gallagher put a smile back on Citroën faces after Loeb's WRC misfortunes. ■

Points for Federico Villagra for the third time in a row! He took full advantage of other people's misfortunes to finish sixth, as he had in Argentina.

05 | Jordan | Results

25th JORDAN RALLY

Organiser Details
P. O. Box 143222
Bayader Wadi Seer
Amman 111814
Jordan
Tel.: +962 6 5850626
Fax: +962 6 5885999

Jordan Rally

5th leg of FIA 2008 World Championship for constructors and drivers.
2nd leg of FIA WRC Junior Championship.

Date April 24 - 27, 2008

Route
983.44 km divised in three legs.
22 special stages on dirt roads (359.26 km)

Ceremonial Start
Thursday, April 24 (18:00)
Emaar South Park / Dead Sea
Leg 1
Friday, April 25 (08:19/14:41),
Dead Sea > Dead Sea, 305.46 km;
8 special stages (115.18 km)
Leg 2
Saturday, April 26 (08:53/15:18),
Dead Sea > Dead Sea, 316.64 km;
8 special stages (109.84 km)
Leg 3
Sunday, April 27 (07:37/13:06),
Dead Sea > Dead Sea, 361.34 km;
6 special stages (134.24 km)

Entry List (55) - 54 starters

N°	Driver (Nat.)	Co-Driver (Nat.)	Team	Car	Group & FIA Priority
1	SEBASTIEN LOEB (F)	DANIEL ELENA (MC)	CITROEN TOTAL WRT	CITROEN C4	A8 1
2	DANI SORDO (E)	MARC MARTI (E)	CITROEN TOTAL WRT	CITROEN C4	A8 1
3	MIKKO HIRVONEN (FIN)	JARMO LEHTINEN (FIN)	BP FORD ABU DHABI WRT	FORD FOCUS RS WRC07	A8 1
4	JARI-MATTI LATVALA (FIN)	MIIKKA ANTTILA (FIN)	BP FORD ABU DHABI WRT	FORD FOCUS RS WRC07	A8 1
5	PETTER SOLBERG (N)	PHILIP MILLS (GB)	SUBARU WRT	SUBARU IMPREZA WRC06	A8 1
6	CHRIS ATKINSON (AUS)	STEPHANE PREVOT (B)	SUBARU WRT	SUBARU IMPREZA WRC06	A8 1
7	GIGI GALLI (I)	GIOVANI BERNACCHINI (I)	STOBART VK M-SPORT FRT	FORD FOCUS RS WRC07	A8 1
8	HENNING SOLBERG (N)	CATO MENKERUD (N)	STOBART VK M-SPORT FRT	FORD FOCUS RS WRC07	A8 1
9	FEDERICO VILLAGRA (AR)	JORGE PEREZ COMPANC (AR)	MUNCHI'S FORD WRT	FORD FOCUS RS WRC07	A8 1
10	BARRY CLARK (GB)	LUIS DIAZ (AR)	MUNCHI'S FORD WRT	FORD FOCUS RS WRC07	A8 1
11	TONI GARDEMEISTER (FIN)	TOMI TUOMINEN (FIN)	SUZUKI WRT	SUZUKI SX4	A8 1
12	PER-GUNNAR ANDERSSON (S)	JONAS ANDERSSON (S)	SUZUKI WRT	SUZUKI SX4	A8 1
14	KHALID AL-QASSIMI (UAE)	MICHAEL ORR (GB)	BP FORD ABU DHABI WRT	FORD FOCUS RS WRC07	A8 2
16	MATTHEW WILSON (GB)	SCOTT MARTIN (GB)	STOBART VK M-SPORT FRT	FORD FOCUS RS WRC07	A8 2
17	URMO AAVA (EE)	KULDAR SIKK (EE)	WORLD RALLY TEAM ESTONIA	CITROEN C4	A8 2
18	CONRAD RAUTENBACH (ZW)	DAVID SENIOR (GB)	CONRAD RAUTENBACH	CITROEN C4 WRC	A8 2
32	JAAN MOLDER (EE)	FREDERIC MICLOTTE (B)	JAAN MOLDER	SUZUKI SWIFT S1600	A6 3
34	ANDREA CORTINOVIS (I)	GIANCARLA GUZZI (I)	ANDREA CORTINOVIS	RENAULT CLIO S1600	A6 3
35	MICHAL KOSCIUSZKO (PL)	MACIEK SZCZEPANIAK (PL)	MICHAL KOSCIUSZKO	SUZUKI SWIFT S1600	A6 3
37	SIMONE BERTOLOTTI (I)	DANIELE VERNUCCIO (I)	SIMONE BERTOLOTTI	RENAULT CLIO R3	R3 3
38	FRANCESCO FANARI (I)	MASSIMILIANO BOSI (I)	FRANCESCO FANARI	CITROEN C2 S1600	R2 3
39	STEFANO ALBERTINI (I)	PIERCARLO CAPOLONGO (I)	STEFANO ALBERTINI	RENAULT CLIO R3	R3 3
40	MILOS KOMLJENOVIC (SCG)	ALEKSANDAR JEREMIC (SCG)	INTERSPEED RACING TEAM	RENAULT CLIO R3	R3 3
41	PATRIK SANDELL (S)	EMIL AXELSSON (S)	INTERSPEED RACING TEAM	RENAULT CLIO S1600	A6 3
42	SEBASTIEN OGIER (F)	JULIEN INGRASSIA (F)	FFSA	CITROEN C2 S1600	A6 3
43	FLORIAN NIEGEL (D)	ANDRE KACHEL (D)	SUZUKI RALLYE JUNIOR TEAM GERMANY	SUZUKI SWIFT S1600	A6 3
44	HANS WEIJS JR. (NL)	HANSVAN GOOR (NL)	KNAF TALENT FIRST TEAM	CITROEN C2 R2 MAX	R2 3
45	KEVIN ABBRING (NL)	ERWIN MOMBAERTS (B)	KNAF TALENT FIRST TEAM	RENAULT CLIO R3	R3 3
46	SHAUN GALLAGHER (IRL)	PAUL KIELY (IRL)	WORLD RALLY TEAM IRELAND	CITROEN C2 S1600	A6 3
47	GILLES SCHAMMEL (L)	RENAUD JAMOUL (B)	JPS JUNIOR TEAM LUXEMBOURG	RENAULT CLIO R3	R3 3
48	ALESSANDRO BETTEGA (I)	SIMONE SCATTOLIN (I)	TRT SRL	RENAULT CLIO R3	R3 3
61	AMJAD FARRAH (HKJ)	NICOLA ARENA (I)	AMJAD FARRAH	MITSUBISHI LANCER EVO. IX	N4
62	MICHAEL KAHLFUSS (D)	RONALD BAUER (D)	MICHAEL KAHLFUSS	MITSUBISHI LANCER EVO. VIII	N4
63	MICHEL SALEH (RL)	ZIAD CHEHAB (RL)	MICHEL SALEH	SUBARU IMPREZA N14	N4
64	ABDULLAH AL-QASSIMI (UAE)	DIETER GOCENTAS (LT)	ABDULLAH AL-QASSIMI	MITSUBISHI LANCER EVO. IX	N4
65	SUHAIL AL MAKTOUM (UAE)	AHMAD GHAZIRI (RL)	SUHAIL AL MAKTOUM	SUBARU IMPREZA	N4
66	AMEER NAJJAR (HKJ)	NICOLA FANOUS (HKJ)	AMEER NAJJAR	MITSUBISHI LANCER EVO. IX	N4
67	RICCARDO ERRANI (I)	STEFANO CASADIO (I)	ERRANI TEAM	MITSUBISHI LANCER EVO.	N4
68	FARIS BUSTAMI (HKJ)	BURHAN BAU QURA (HKJ)	FARIS BUSTAMI	SUBARU IMPREZA STI N10	N4
69	ALA' KHALIFEH (HKJ)	OTHMAN NASSIF (HKJ)	ALA' KHALIFEH	MITSUBISHI LANCER EVO. IX	N4
70	MUBARAK AL-HAJRI (QA)	ALLAN HARRYMAN (IRL)	MUBARAK AL-HAJRI	MITSUBISHI LANCER EVO. IX	N4
71	ANDREAS WIMMER (A)	MICHAEL KOELBACH (D)	ANDREAS WIMMER	SUBARU IMPREZA	N4
72	SALAH BIN EIDAN (KWT)	MJ MORRISSEY (IRL)	SALAH BIN EIDAN	SUBARU IMPREZA	N4
73	KHALID AL-SUWAIDI (QA)	ADEL HUSSEIN (QA)	KHALID AL-SUWAIDI	MITSUBISHI LANCER EVO. IX	N4
74	YAZEED AL-RAJHI (SA)	STEVE LANCASTER (GB)	YAZEED AL-RAJHI	SUBARU IMPREZA N14	N4
75	NICK GEORGIOU (RL)	JOSEPH MATAR (RL)	NICK GEOGIOU	MITSUBISHI LANCER EVO. IX	N4
76	FARIS HIJAZI (HKJ)	EMAD JUMA (HKJ)	FARIS HIJAZI	MITSUBISHI LANCER EVO. IX	N4
77	MAZEN TANTASH (HKJ)	ATA AL-HMOUD (HKJ)	MAZEN TANTASH	MITSUBISHI LANCER EVO. IX	N4
78	AMMAR HIJAZI (HKJ)	CALVIN COOLEDGE (HKJ)	AMMAR HIJAZI	SUBARU IMPREZA N14	N4
79	ISSA ABU JAMOUS (HKJ)	AKRAM OBIDAT (HKJ)	ISSA ABU JAMOUS	SUBARU IMPREZA STI N10	N4
80	TAMER TABBAA (HKJ)	SAED MUFLEH (HKJ)	TAMER TABBAA	SUBARU IMPREZA	N4
81	ABIR BATIKHI (HKJ)	MIKE HADDAD (HKJ)	ABIR BATIKHI	SUBARU IMPREZA	N4
82	AHMAD MIHYAR (HKJ)	ALA' HMOUD (HKJ)	AHMAD MIHYAR	SUBARU IMPREZA	N4
83	KAMERAN BESHADRY (IQ)	YOUSEF AL-ASMAR (HKJ)	KAMERAN BESHADRY	MITSUBISHI LANCER EVO. VIII	N4

K. Al-Qassimi

B. Clark

S. Gallagher

A. Al-Qassimi

M. Tantash

M. Al-Hajri

P. Sandell

Championship Classifications

•R•: Rookie

FIA Drivers (5/15)
1. Hirvonen 1🏆 35
2. Loeb 3🏆 30
3. Atkinson 28
4. Latvala 1🏆 18
5. Sordo 17
6. Galli 12
7. H. Solberg 9
8. P. Solberg 9
9. Villagra 8
10. Wilson 7
11. Rautenbach 5
12. Duval 5
13. Mikkelsen 4
14. Gardemeister 2
15. Cuoq 2
16. Andersson 1
17. Aigner 1
18. Hänninen 1
19. Ogier 1
20. K. Al-Qassimi, Beltrán, Østberg, Mölder, Ketomaa, Kosciuszko, Sandell, Nutahara, Prokop, Clark, Burkart, Broccoli, Gallagher, Rauam, Farrah, Artru, Nittel, Schammel, Guerra, A. Al-Qassimi, Arai, Mercier 0

FIA Constructors (5/15)
1. BP-Ford Abu Dhabi World Rally Team 2🏆 57
2. Citroën Total World Rally Team 3🏆 50
3. Subaru World Rally Team 39
4. Stobart VK M-Sport Ford Rally Team 29
5. Munchi's Ford World Rally Team 14
6. Suzuki World Rally Team 6

FIA Production Car WRC (2/8)
1. Ketomaa 14
2. Aigner 1🏆 10
3. Hänninen 1🏆 10
4. Beltrán 8
5. Prokop 7
6. Sandell 6
7. Nutahara 5
8. Nittel 4
9. Rauam 4
10. Arai 3
11. Farrah 3
12. Araujo 2
13. Sousa 2
14. Campedelli 0
15. Aksa 0
16. Mayer 0
17. Tiippana 0
18. Pavlides 0
19. Aksakov 0
20. Frisiero 0
21. Bacco 0
22. Jereb 0
23. Brynildsen 0
24. Flodin 0
25. Marrini 0

FIA Junior WRC (2/7)
1. Ogier 2🏆 20
2. Gallagher 11
3. Mölder 8
4. Kosciusko 6
5. Schammel 6
6. Burkart 5
7. Niegel 5
8. Sandell 4
9. Albertini 4
10. Bertolotti 3
11. Prokop 2
12. Cortinovis 2
13. Fanari •R• 1
14. Komljenovic 1

Special Stages Times

www.jordanrally.com
www.wrc.com

SS1 Suwayma 1 (13.03 km)
1.Sordo/P.Solberg 6'40"2;
3.Hirvonen +0"5; 4.Latvala +1"6;
5.Loeb +4"6; 6.Galli +13"0
7.Atkinson +13"9; 8.Aava +15"2...
J-WRC > 15.Sandell 7'23"7

SS2 Mahes 1 (20.00 km)
1.Sordo 13'54"8; 2.P.Solberg +'5"4;
3.Latvala +8"9; 4.Hirvonen +11"3;
5.Loeb +12"6; 6.Aava +12"7;
7.Atkinson +17"3; 8.Galli +22"2;
J-WRC > 15.Ogier 14'58"3

SS3 Mount Nebo 1 (11.10 km)
1.Sordo 8'02"9; 2.Loeb +4"7;
3.Latvala +5"7; 4.Hirvonen +6"5;
5.Atkinson +8"6; 6.P.Solberg +9"7;
7.Galli +10"4; 8.Wilson +10"4...
J-WRC > 14.Sandell 8'37"7

SS4 Mai'n 1 (13.46 km)
1.Loeb 9'55"4; 2.Latvala +5"0;
3.Hirvonen +5"8;
4.P.Solberg/Sordo +7"4;
6.Atkinson +19"1; 7.Aava +23"4;
8.Al-Qassimi +29"7...
J-WRC > 16.Sandell 10'58"4

SS5 Suwayma 2 (13.03 km)
1.Latvala 6'37"7; 2.Loeb +1"0;
3.Hirvonen +2"0; 4.Sordo +4"0;
5.Atkinson +4"4; 6.P.Solberg +5"8;
7.Galli +7"7; 8.H.Solberg +11"0...
J-WRC > 14.Ogier 7'20"0

SS6 Mahes 2 (20.00 km)
1.Loeb 13'38"5; 2.Sordo +1"1;
3.Latvala +2"6; 4.Hirvonen +7"1;
5.Atkinson +9"7; 6.Aava +19"4;
7.Galli +21"4; 8.Wilson +33"4...
J-WRC > 13.Sandell 14'51"4

SS7 Mount Nebo 2 (11.10 km)
1.Loeb 7'52"6; 2.Latvala +3"7;
3.Hirvonen +5"1; 4.Sordo +5"7;
5.Atkinson +10"6; 6.Aava +17"7;
7.H.Solberg +21"6; 8.Wilson +25"0...
J-WRC 12.Ogier 8'32"5

SS8 Mai'n 2 (13.46 km)
1.Hirvonen 9'46"2; 2.Loeb +3"1;
3.Latvala +5"9; 4.Sordo +6"7;
5.Atkinson +9"3; 6.Aava +17"2;
7.H.Solberg +17"3; 8.Wilson +23"9...
J-WRC > 11.Ogier 10'50"2

Classification Leg 1
1.Sordo 1h16'53"7; 2.Loeb +1"1;
3.Latvala +8"5; 4.Hirvonen +3"4;
5.Atkinson +1'08"0; 6.Aava +1'59"3;
7.Wilson +2'52"7; 8.H.Solberg +3'22"3
J-WRC > 11.Sandell 1h24'07"2

SS9 Turki 1 (14.13 km)
1.Loeb 8'18"1; 2.Latvala +5"1;
3.Hirvonen +8"0; 4.Sordo +9"2;
5.P.Solberg +11"2; 6.Galli +20"4;
7.Aava +20"9; 8.Andersson +23"4...
J-WRC > 14.Ogier 9'12"2

SS10 Erak Elamir 1 (12.47 km)
1.Loeb 8'40"9; 2.Hirvonen +6"7;
3.Sordo +8"2; 4.Latvala +10"7;
5.Galli +12"0; 6.P.Solberg +13"9;
7.Atkinson +18"9; 8.Aava +19"7...
J-WRC > 14.Ogier 9'32"1

SS11 Shuna 1 (15.19 km)
1.Loeb 11'54"9; 2.Latvala +11"3;
3.Hirvonen +11"4; 4.Sordo +17"8;
5.Galli +19"6; 6.Aava +23"2;
7.Atkinson +23"8; 8.Andersson +28"2...
J-WRC > 14.Kosciuszko 12'58"6

SS12 Baptism Site 1 (13.13 km)
1.Sordo 6'42"2; 2.Latvala +0"3;
3.Hirvonen 1"7; 4.Galli +5"2;
5.Aava +10"8; 6.Atkinson +12"0;
7.Wilson +15"9; 8.Al-Qassimi +17"3...
J-WRC > 12.Ogier 7'28"9

SS13 Turki 2 (14.13 km)
1.Hirvonen 8'15"7; 2.Latvala 1"8;
3.Sordo +6"4; 4.P.Solberg +8"3;
5.Galli +9"1; 6.Atkinson +10"5;
7.Aava +15"0; 8.Andersson +19"3...
J-WRC > 13.Ogier 9'01"4

SS14 Erak Elamir 2 (12.47 km)
1.Galli 8'40"8; 2.Hirvonen +1"5;
3.Latvala +3"0; 4.P.Solberg +5"4;
5.Sordo +5"5; 6.H.Solberg +7"3;
7.Atkinson +9"3;8.Aava +10"8...
J-WRC > 13.Ogier 9'23"1

SS15 Shuna 2 (15.19 km)
1.Galli 11'57"8; 2.Latvala +2"9;
3.Atkinson +4"9; 4.Hirvonen +5"5;
5.Sordo +7"6; 6.Andersson +11"9;
7.H.Solberg +16"9; 8.Aava +17"2...
J-WRC > 13.Ogier 12'42"7

SS16 Baptism Site 2 (13.13 km)
1Galli 6'41"2; 2.Sordo +2"9;
3.H.Solberg +7"2; 4.Atkinson +7"5;
5.Aava +7"9; 6.Wilson +9"2;
7.Atkinson +23"8; 8.Andersson +16"0...
J-WRC 12.Ogier 7'28"4

Classification Leg 2
1.Sordo 2h29'02"9; 2.Latvala +8"5;
3.Hirvonen +10"4; 4.Atkinson +2'02"5;
5.Aava +3'07"2; 6.Atkinson +4'56"5;
7.H.Solberg +5'10"9; 8.Villagra +6'56"3
J-WRC > 11.Sandell 2h44'50"0

SS17 Kafrain 1 (16.49 km)
1.Hirvonen 11'02"5; 2.Latvala 1"6;
3.Loeb +3"5; 4.Sordo 12"5;
5.Galli +14"0; 6.Villagra +24"4;
7.Atkinson +26"4; 8.Aava +26"9...
J-WRC > 14.Ogier 12'11"8

SS18 Wadi Shueib 1 (9.18 km)
1.Loeb 7'10"1; 2.Galli +6"4;
3.Hirvonen +9"3; 4.Andersson +11"8;
5.Sordo +12"6; 6.Wilson +19"0;
7.Atkinson +20"6; 8.Villagra +22"0...
J-WRC > 13.Gallagher 8'02"0

SS19 Jordan River 1 (41.45 km)
1.Loeb 28'32"8; 2.Hirvonen +4"0;
3.Sordo +6"3; 4.Galli +29"9;
5.H.Solberg 37"4; 6.Atkinson +53"0;
7.Villagra +1'31"3;
8.Rautenbach +1'49"3...
J-WRC > 10.Ogier 31'02"9

SS20 Kafrain 2 (16.49 km)
1.Latvala 11'00"4; 2.Loeb 6"0;
3.Hirvonen +8"5; 4.Galli +11"9;
5.Sordo 21"6; 6.H.Solberg +26"8;
7.Atkinson 30"0; 8.Villagra +31"7
J-WRC > 12.Ogier 12'22"9

SS21 Wadi Shueib 2 (9.18 km)
1.Loeb 7'04"8; 2.Galli +3"9;
3.Hirvonen +13"1; 4.Sordo +16"0;
5.H.Solberg +16"8; 6.Wilson +20"7;
7.Latvala +21"3; 8.Atkinson +24"6...
J-WRC > 13.Ogier 7'59"2

SS22 Jordan River 2 (41.45 km)
1.Hirvonen 28'09"1; 2.Loeb +10"4;
3.Latvala +21"1; 4.Galli 33"9";
5.H.Solberg +51"3; 6.Sordo +52"0;
7.Atkinson +1'07"7; 8.Wilson +1'23"8...
J-WRC > 12.Ogier 31'29"6

Results

	Driver - Co-Driver	Car	Gr.	Time
1.	Hirvonen - Lehtinen	Ford Focus RS WRC 07	A8	4h02'47"9
2.	Sordo - Marti	Citroën C4 WRC 08	A8	+1'15"7
3.	Atkinson - Prévot	Subaru Impreza WRC 07	A8	+4'59"5
4.	H.Solberg - Menkerud	Ford Focus RS WRC 07	A8	+7'35"8
5.	Wilson - Martin	Ford Focus RS WRC 07	A8	+10'41"7
6.	Villagra - Perez Companc	Ford Focus RS WRC 07	A8	+11'22"2
7.	Latvala - Antilla	Ford Focus RS WRC 07	A8	+12'15"6
8.	Galli - Bernacchini	Ford Focus RS WRC 07	A8	+12'24"4
9.	Al-Qassimi - Orr	Ford Focus RS WRC 07	A8	+19'05"7
10.	Loeb - Elena	Citroën C4 WRC 08	A8	+23'38"1
11.	Ogier - Ingrassia	Citroën C2 S1600	A6/J	+27'09"9
13.	Gallagher - Kiely	Citroën C2 S1600	A6/J	+32'10"0
15.	Al-Qassimi - Gocentas	Mitsubishi Lancer Evo. IX	N4	+34'45"4
22.	Niegel - Kachel	Suzuki Swift S1600	A6/J	+47'29"5

Leading Retirements (21)

Ctrl20	Mölder - Miclotte	Suzuki Swift S1600	Off
Ctrl19	Aava - Sikk	Citroën C4 WRC	Suspension
Ctrl19	Andersson - Andersson	Suzuki SX4 WRC	Off
Ctrl17	Sandell - Axelsson	Renault Clio S1600	Off
Ctrl16	P. Solberg - Mills	Subaru Impreza WRC 07	Off
Ctrl3	Gardemeister - Tuominen	Suzuki SX4 WRC	Oil pump

Performers

	1	2	3	4	5	6	C6	Nb SS
Loeb	10	5	-	-	2	-	17	17
Hirvonen	4	3	10	4	-	-	21	22
Sordo	4	2	3	8	4	1	22	22
Latvala	3	7	6	2	-	-	18	22
Galli	3	2	-	4	4	2	15	21
P. Solberg	1	1	-	3	1	3	9	18
Atkinson	-	-	1	1	5	4	11	22
H. Solberg	-	-	1	-	3	2	6	22
Andersson	-	-	-	1	-	1	2	12
Aava	-	-	-	-	2	5	7	19
Wilson	-	-	-	-	-	3	3	22
Villagra	-	-	-	-	-	1	1	22

Leaders

SS1	Sordo/P. Solberg
SS2 > SS8	Sordo
SS9 > SS11	Loeb
SS12	Sordo
SS13 > SS15	Latvala
SS16	Sordo
SS17	Latvala
SS18 > SS22	Hirvonen

Sébastien Ogier

06 ITALY

🇮🇹 **Under constant attack** from the Ford drivers and with the starting order working consistently against him, Sébastien Loeb fought them off brilliantly to take his 40th World Championship win. Second place saw Hirvonen keep the lead in the drivers' standings, while Ford retained the constructors' lead after they and Citroën finished the event on level pegging.

06 | Italy

THE RALLY
Defence with a capital D for Loeb

The FIA, in its infinite wisdom, changed one of rallying's basic rules for the 2008 season: the starting order for the second and third legs of each event. For some years, it had been based on reversing the finishing order of the previous day's, which meant the winners didn't have to open the road – something which, on gravel rallies, would handicap them by making them sweep the thin layer of dust and gravel off the route. It was all about rewarding excellence – you had to be quick right from the start. The other consequence, though, was that those who were quickest on the opening days were able to hold on to that advantage quite easily; those who were slower, whether in terms of sheer performance or as a result of something beyond their control, had to fight like hell to have any chance of making up ground.

It's a problem that fuelled many a debate in times gone by. So, as we said, the FIA in its wisdom decided to revert to the age-old format of sending the cars out on special stages on legs two and three in the actual order from the previous day. It was a ruling that used to cause heated argument in many a meeting between drivers and the governing body. Some will recall Carlos Sainz's outbursts against that state of affairs in the late 90s, or the Richard Burns got all het up when he was Tommi Mäkinen's Mitsubishi team-mate – he would blame that rule when his times didn't match his World Champion pal's. The same Mäkinen (and Colin McRae, for that matter) came off worst under the ruling by dint of being the quickest out there. But while he may have thought it, he never actually came out and said anything against it: he just went out, upped the ante and kept winning anyway.

Happy campers at Ford, where Mikko Hirvonen and Jari-Mati Latvala are good mates as well as fellow-countrymen.

One not to miss for Gigi Galli, who had one clean sheet to go with his fine fourth place.

Sébastien Loeb made light of regs that didn't help him, kept the pack of Fords at bay and claimed yet another win, his 40th.

Jari-Matti Latvala paid heavily for a first-leg mistake but rocketed back through the field to claim an outstanding podium finish.

Dani Sordo found his starting position much harder to cope with than Sébastien Loeb did his and was never able to lift his game enough to have a chance of a podium finish.

Jordan was the first 2008 gravel rally (see previous pages) to be run under this new-for-old ruling, but no-one tried anything tricky to get around it once Loeb's race was run early on in that head-on with Conrad Rautenbach's C4 WRC. So the Italian round, as ever run in Sardinia, was the first to put it to the test. The first leg went off without incident. Second on the road behind World Championship leader Hirvonen, Loeb didn't have to open the road, though that still didn't mean he went out there in ideal conditions. Still, he managed to finish the leg in first place, 35.7 seconds ahead of Dani Sordo and 53.8 in front of Solberg, who had brake problems, and almost a full minute clear of the day's big loser, who clearly was Hirvonen. "On this morning's first run through the stages," said the blue oval's first-leg standard-bearer, "the roads were very slippery and I wasn't able to really push. Sometimes I was just driving from one patch to the next, so every now and again I was backing off too much because I didn't want to go off."

The reigning World Champion had clean-sheeted three times out of a possible six, letting Galli have one and Latvala two. Latvala, in fact, started seventh – absolutely ideal, with six cars going before him – and should have made better use of it, but the spirited Finn had a puncture and damaged the suspension through the second section, Crastazza 1. Just one more mistake – and the lad didn't try to hide from it. "It's my fault entirely," he explained. "And all I could do was look in my mirrors and try to work out why. My notes weren't ideal, maybe I made them too quickly, but on a quick, downhill, narrow right 18 km after the start I hit a bank. The tyre was damaged and came off the rim. It was the right rear, so I decided to keep going because if I'd stopped to fix it that would have taken an enormous amount of time." The Ford driver did change it after that timed section, repaired a broken suspension strut and got going again. But he had indeed lost a huge chunk of time: by Friday evening he was already 1m 31.1 behind.

Next day, then, the man in the lead had to open the road. Loeb and Elena went to work aiming to give up as little ground as possible, keeping about 30 seconds in hand on their rivals. They hoped, briefly, to get some help from the rain, but the overnight showers hadn't been enough to lay the dust and put down a firm, stable layer on top. And that meant that from the very first loop, Loeb was more of a passenger than a driver able to rely on his reactions. Latvala was seevnth to start and he was really going for it, gobbling up clean sheet after clean sheet. All day long, no-one was faster. Loeb was cursing: "In conditions like these, even when the notes are good, with tight driving and a good car, you can't do a thing. No grip – you're just a passenger. It's nice to slip and slide but it's not a very efficient way to go." The second runs through the morning stages did nothing to alter the situation in the afternoon, either. "The Juniors and Group N cars don't take the same lines as we do in the WRC cars – but they do bring dust and stones back on to the road. I was in damage limitation mode again, trying to get the best out of the C4, but it's a frustrating position to be in."

Not over at Ford, it wasn't. Naturally Latvala and Hirvonen had rocketed back into the picture, both finishing exactly 29.4 seconds down on Loeb. "I was on the limit the whole day," Jari-Matti acknowledged. "When we set off this morning I had no idea I would be

06 | Italy

Henning Solberg goes quietly about his World Championship business, never bothering anyone and having a lot of fun in his excellent Ford Focus. This time it carried Munchi's livery and came home seventh.

Once again Chris Atkinson was the best of the Subaru drivers, with sixth place this time.

able to get a minute back on Seb! It was maximum attack, trying to recover some of the time I lost on Friday with that puncture. And with my road position, plus a fantastic Focus, I was able to do that. I was checking Loeb's splits, not Mikko's, because he's the one we need to go after."
Hirvonen, for his part, was relishing the fight through the final leg, sensing that the Frenchman might be about to crack.

The three of them certainly eclipsed everyone else. Petter Solberg had given it away, his irritation with the Impreza's dampers compounded by a puncture of his own that slowed him severely. Toni Gardemeister destroyed his Suzuki's suspension and was out, leaving Gigi Galli as the only one to keep his head above water on his home event. He hoisted the Stobart Focus up to fourth ahead of Dani Sordo, who was a lot more troubled by starting second than his team-leader had been by going first.

It looked like being an enjoyable fight for podium places, as Hirvonen underlined: "He may be 29 seconds ahead, but we're still in with a shout..."
And he was first to get down to business, taking the first Sunday stage and with it 10.3 seconds on Loeb. Back came the immediate response on the next stage – helped by Hirvonen's off. "I made a mistake a kilometre after the start," he explained. "I hit a rock and I slowed down because I thought I might have damaged the car. And it did feel a lot less precise."

So Latvala took over the Ford charge – he set fastest time through the third Sunday stage – until Hirvonen got back up to speed that afternoon, but Loeb fought them off with skill and style. "I went up another notch in the afternoon," said Hirvonen, "but I realised there was no way I could go after Seb, so I settled down, and finishing second is a great result for the Championship." So, despite being at the obvious disadvantage of opening the road for two days, the reigning champion controlled things superbly. "There was a good chance that the same thing would happen on Sunday as Saturday," he said with a sigh of relief, delighted to have taken his 40th World Championship success in such style. "I gave it everything – we really went for the win. It was frustrating at times, but we kept enough of a gap to win it. There wasn't much else we could have done: we didn't make a mistake and the C4 worked beautifully. It would have been disappointing not to win here."

The snapper who took this shot of a young spectator probably wanted to share some of the tricks of his trade, though maybe with some different equipment...

This was Petter Solberg's last event in the 2007 edition of the Impreza, and he was keen to get his hands on the new one.

The victory put the Frenchman just three points behind the remarkably consistent Hirvonen in the Drivers' Championship. The Finn had in fact scored in all five rallies so far, while his Citroën rival had no-scored in both Sweden and Jordan. The Championship's two leading manufacturers couldn't be separated, each scoring 14 points, which kept Ford three points ahead of Citroën overall. ■

Schoolboy stuff, seeing who can splash the furthest... They may be big boys now but there's still time for fun and games on the podium.

Urmo Aava took a big step forward in his privateer C4, finishing eighth on the Sardinian event for his first point of the season.

JUNIORS
A first for Poland

It had to happen... After winning both opening rounds of the 2008 Junior Championship, France's new discovery made his first faux pas of the season in Sardinia. Sébastien Ogier tripped up on the fourth stage of the first leg: briefly put off by the sight of Al Qassimi's Ford stopped on the side of the road, the crew signalling to him to keep over to the right, he hit a bush – and the boulder beneath it, causing a puncture on his C2. He kept going, but that only broke a steering arm and damaged a universal joint. That put the Frenchman out, though he restarted under SupeRally next day. Mind you, Ogier wasn't leading when disaster struck. There was a ding-dong struggle for top spot between Czech driver Prokop's Citroën C2 and Poland's Kosciuszko in the Suzuki Swift, both men clean-sheeting several times and regularly swapping the lead.

In the end victory went to the Suzuki man after the rival Citroën hit fuel injection problems in SS16, the last stage on the event. The 17th had been cancelled on safety grounds after the first 11 WRC cars went through. So Kosciuszko took his maiden World Championship win from Alessandro Bettega (Clio R3) and Aaron Burkart (Citroën C2). Despite a 15-minute penalty Ogier still salvaged fifth place and held on to the Championship lead, eight points clear of our Italian winner. ■

Mikko Hirvonen gave it everything he had to stop Loeb winning, but finished second. The Finn, though, was still leading the Drivers' Championship.

06 | Italy | Results

5th RALLY OF ITALY SARDINIA

Organisater Details
ACI - CSAI
Porto Industriale Cocciani (Località Cala Saccaia)
Settore 1 – Edificio B
07026 Olbia (OT) Italia
Tel.: +39 079 5551234
Fax: +39 079 5551244

Rally d'Italia-Sardegna

6th leg of FIA 2008 World Championship for constructors and drivers.
3rd leg of FIA WRC Junior Championship.

Date May 16 - 18, 2008

Route
1040.35 km divised in three legs.
17 special stages on dirt roads (344.73 km).

Ceremonial Start
Thursday, May 15 (20:00),
Porto Cervo
Leg 1
Friday, May 16 (10:23/17:02),
Olbia > Olbia, 371.02 km;
6 special stages (131.56 km)
Leg 2
Saturday, May 17 (09:39/16:33),
Olbia > Olbia, 410.68 km;
6 special stages (134.60 km)
Leg 3
Sunday, May 18 (08:10/14:10),
Olbia > Porto Cervo, 258.65 km;
5 special stages (78.57 km)

Entry List (59) - 57 starters

N°	Driver (Nat.)	Co-Driver (Nat.)	Team	Car	Group & FIA Priority
1	SÉBASTIEN LOEB (F)	DANIEL ELENA (MC)	CITROËN TOTAL WRT	CITROËN C4 WRC	A8 1
2	DANI SORDO (E)	MARC MARTI (E)	CITROËN TOTAL WRT	CITROËN C4 WRC	A8 1
3	MIKKO HIRVONEN (FIN)	JARMO LEHTINEN (FIN)	BP FORD ABU DHABI WRT	FORD FOCUS RS WRC	A8 1
4	JARI-MATTI LATVALA (FIN)	MIIKKA ANTTILA (FIN)	BP FORD ABU DHABI WRT	FORD FOCUS RS WRC	A8 1
5	PETTER SOLBERG (N)	PHILIP MILLS (GB)	SUBARU WORLD RALLY TEAM	SUBARU IMPREZA WRC	A8 1
6	CHRIS ATKINSON (AUS)	STEPHANE PREVOT (B)	SUBARU WORLD RALLY TEAM	SUBARU IMPREZA WRC	A8 1
7	GIGI GALLI (I)	GIOVANNI BERNACCHINI (I)	STOBART VK M-SPORT	FORD FOCUS RS WRC	A8 1
8	MATTHEW WILSON (GB)	SCOTT MARTIN (GB)	STOBART VK M-SPORT	FORD FOCUS RS WRC	A8 1
9	FEDERICO VILLAGRA (RA)	JORGE PEREZ COMPANC (RA)	MUNCHI'S FORD WRT	FORD FOCUS RS WRC	A8 1
10	HENNING SOLBERG (N)	CATO MENKERUD (N)	MUNCHI'S FORD WRT	FORD FOCUS RS WRC	A8 1
11	TONI GARDEMEISTER (FIN)	TOMI TUOMINEN (FIN)	SUZUKI WRT	SUZUKI SX4 WRC	A8 1
12	PER-GUNNAR ANDERSSON (S)	JONAS ANDERSSON (S)	SUZUKI WRT	SUZUKI SX4 WRC	A8 1
14	KHALID AL QASSIMI (UAE)	MICHAEL ORR (GB)	BP FORD ABU DHABI WRT	FORD FOCUS RS WRC	A8 2
15	CONRAD RAUTENBACH (ZW)	DAVID SENIOR (GB)	RAUTENBACH CONRAD	CITROËN C4 WRC	A8 2
16	URMO AAVA (EE)	KULDAR SIKK (EE)	WORLD RALLY TEAM ESTONIA	CITROËN C4 WRC	A8 2
18	ANDREAS MIKKELSEN (N)	MARIA ANDERSSON (N)	RAMSPORT	FORD FOCUS RS WRC	A8 2
19	MADS OSTBERG (N)	OLE KRISTIAN UNNERUD (N)	ADAPTA	SUBARU IMPREZA WRC	A8 2
20	PETER VAN MERKSTEYN (NL)	HANS VAN BEEK (NL)	VAN MERKSTEYN MOTORSPORT	FORD FOCUS RS WRC	A8 2
31	MARTIN PROKOP (CZ)	JAN TOMANEK (CZ)	PROKOP MARTIN	CITROËN C2 S1600	A6 3
32	JAAN MÖLDER (EE)	FREDERIC MICLOTTE (B)	MÖLDER JAAN	SUZUKI SWIFT S1600	A6 3
33	AARON NICOLAI BURKART (D)	MICHAEL KOELBACH (D)	BURKART AARON NICOLAI	CITROËN C2 S1600	A6 3
34	ANDREA CORTINOVIS (I)	GIANCARLA GUZZI (I)	CORTINOVIS ANDREA	RENAULT CLIO S1600	A6 3
35	MICHAL KOSCIUSZKO (PL)	MACIEK SZCZEPANIAK (PL)	KOSCIUSZKO MICHAL	SUZUKI SWIFT S1600	A6 3
37	SIMONE BERTOLOTTI (I)	DANIELE VERNUCCIO (I)	BERTOLOTTI SIMONE	RENAULT CLIO SPORT R3	A7 3
38	FRANCESCO FANARI (I)	MASSIMILIANO BOSI (I)	FANARI FRANCESCO	CITROËN C2 R2	A7 3
39	STEFANO ALBERTINI (I)	PIERCARLO CAPOLONGO (I)	ALBERTINI STEFANO	RENAULT CLIO R3	A7 3
40	MILOS KOMLJENOVIC (SCG)	ALEKSANDAR JEREMIC (SCG)	INTERSPEED RACING TEAM	RENAULT CLIO R3	A7 3
41	PATRIK SANDELL (S)	EMIL AXELSSON (S)	INTERSPEED RACING TEAM	RENAULT CLIO S1600	A6 3
42	SÉBASTIEN OGIER (F)	JULIEN INGRASSIA (F)	EQUIPE DE FRANCE FFSA	CITROËN C2 S1600	A6 3
43	FLORIAN NIEGEL (D)	ANDRÉ KACHEL (D)	SUZUKI RALLYE JUNIOR TEAM GERMANY	SUZUKI SWIFT S1600	A6 3
44	HANS WEIJS JR. (NL)	HANS VAN GOOR (NL)	KNAF TALENT FIRST TEAM HOLLAND	CITROËN C2 R2	A7 3
45	KEVIN ABBRING (NL)	BJORN DEGANDT (B)	KNAF TALENT FIRST TEAM HOLLAND	RENAULT CLIO RS R3	A7 3
46	SHAUN GALLAGHER (IRL)	CLAIRE SCHOTT MOLE (IRL)	WORLD RALLY TEAM IRELAND	CITROËN C2 S1600	A6 3
47	GILLES SCHAMMEL (LUX)	RENAUD JAMOUL (B)	JPS JUNIOR TEAM LUXEMBOURG	RENAULT CLIO R3	A7 3
48	ALESSANDRO BETTEGA (I)	SIMONE SCATTOLIN (I)	TRT SRL	RENAULT CLIO R3	A7 3
71	GIUSEPPE DETTORI (I)	MARCO CORDA (I)	DETTORI GIUSEPPE	MITSUBISHI LANCER EVO IX	N4
72	PETER VAN MERKSTEYN (NL)	EDDY CHEVAILLIER (B)	VAN MERKSTEYN MOTORSPORT	MITSUBISHI LANCER EVO IX	N4
73	GIANLUCA LINARI (I)	BARBARA PERUGINI (I)	LINARI GIANLUCA	SUBARU IMPREZA	N4
74	ADRIANO LOVISETTO (I)	MONICA FORTUNATO (I)	LOVISETTO ADRIANO	MITSUBISHI LANCER EVO IX	N4
75	FREDERIC SAUVAN (F)	THIBAUT GORCZYCA (F)	SAUVAN FREDERIC	MITSUBISHI LANCER EVO IX	N4
76	MORENO CENEDESE (I)	MARIKA ROSSETTO (I)	CENEDESE MORENO	MITSUBISHI LANCER EVO IX	N4
77	FABIO FRISIERO (I)	NICOLA VETTORETTI (I)	FRISIERO FABIO	MITSUBISHI LANCER EVO IX	N4
78	FABIO MONTANARI (I)	LIVIO CECI (RSM)	MONTANARI FABIO	MITSUBISHI LANCER EVO IX	N4
79	FRANCESCO MARRONE (I)	SEBASTIANO COLLA (I)	MARRONE FRANCESCO	MITSUBISHI LANCER EVO V	N4
80	BERNARDINO A. CARAGLIU (I)	MAURO ATZEI (I)	CARAGLIU BERNARDINO ANTONIO	MITSUBISHI LANCER EVO VI	N4
81	GIAMMARIA SERRA (I)	CHIARA SERRA (I)	SERRA GIAMMARIA	MITSUBISHI LANCER EVO VI	N4
83	ALEX RASCHI (RSM)	MASSIMO BIZZOCCHI (I)	RASCHI ALEX	RENAULT CLIO R3	A7
84	ALESSANDRO BROCCOLI (RSM)	EMANUELE INGLESI (I)	BROCCOLI ALESSANDRO	RENAULT CLIO R3	A7
85	GERRI PRANZONI (I)	MAURA VACCARI (I)	PRANZONI GERRI	RENAULT CLIO R3	A7
86	BOGDAN STANOIEV (RO)	DANUT HATIGAN (RO)	STANOIEV BOGDAN	CITROËN C2 R2	A6
87	VYTAUTAS BARANAUSKAS (LT)	GEDIMINAS CELIESIUS (LT)	BARANAUSKAS VYTAUTAS	FORD FIESTA ST	N3
88	EMRE YURDAKUL (TR)	CAN MUSTA FA ERKAL (TR)	CASTROL FORD TEAM TURKIYE	FORD FIESTA ST	N3
89	KORAY MURATOGLU (TR)	LEVENT OZOKUTUCU (TR)	CASTROL FORD TEAM TURKIYE	FORD FIESTA ST	N3
90	BURCU CETINKAYA (TR)	CICEK GUNEY (TR)	CASTROL FORD TEAM TURKIYE	FORD FIESTA ST	N3
91	DENIS GRODETSKIY (RUS)	SAFONIY LOTKO (RUS)	CUEKS RACING	FORD FIESTA ST	N3
92	MARKO JERAM (SLO)	SIMON LAPAJNE (SLO)	JERAM MARKO	FORD FIESTA ST	N3
93	RAFFAELE DONADIO (I)	ELIANA BRONDOLO (I)	DONADIO RAFFAELE	ROVER MG 105 ZR	N1

A. Bettega

T. Gardemeister

M. Prokop

C. Rautenbach

M. Wilson

Championship Classifications

•R•: Rookie

FIA Drivers (6/15)
1. Hirvonen 1🏆 43
2. Loeb 4🏆 40
3. Atkinson 31
4. Latvala 1🏆 24
5. Sordo 21
6. Galli 17
7. H. Solberg 11
8. P. Solberg 9
9. Villagra 8
10. Wilson 7
11. Rautenbach 5
12. Duval 5
13. Mikkelsen 4
14. Gardemeister 2
15. Cuoq 2
16. Andersson 1
17. Ogier 1
18. Aava 1
19. Aigner 1
20. Hänninen 1
21. K. Al-Qassimi, Østberg, Beltrán, Mölder, Ketomaa, Kosciuszko, Sandell, Nutahara, Prokop, Burkart, Clark, Gallagher, Broccoli, Rauam, Schammel, Farrah, Artru, Nittel, Guerra, A. Al-Qassimi, Arai, Mercier 0

FIA Constructors (6/15)
1. BP-Ford Abu Dhabi World Rally Team 2🏆 71
2. Citroën Total World Rally Team 4🏆 64
3. Subaru World Rally Team 42
4. Stobart VK M-Sport Ford Rally Team 34
5. Munchi's Ford World Rally Team 16
6. Suzuki World Rally Team 7

FIA Production Car WRC (2/8)
1. Ketomaa 14
2. Aigner 1🏆 10
3. Hänninen 1🏆 10
4. Beltrán 8
5. Prokop 7
6. Sandell 6
7. Nutahara 5
8. Nittel 4
9. Rauam 4
10. Arai 3
11. Farrah 3
12. Araujo 2
13. Sousa 2
14. Campedelli 0
15. Aksa 0
16. Mayer 0
17. Tiippana 0
18. Pavlides 0
19. Aksakov 0
20. Frisiero 0
21. Bacco 0
22. Jereb 0
23. Brynildsen 0
24. Flodin 0
25. Marrini 0

FIA Junior WRC (3/7)
1. Ogier 2🏆 24
2. Kosciusko 1🏆 16
3. Gallagher 16
4. Burkart 11
5. Mölder 8
6. Bettega 8
7. Albertini 7
8. Schammel 6
9. Sandell 6
10. Niegel 5
11. Bertolotti 3
12. Prokop 2
13. Cortinovis 2
14. Fanari •R• 1
15. Komljenovic 1
16. Weijs Jr. •R• 1

Special Stages Times

www.rallyitaliasardegna.com
www.wrc.com

SS1 Monte Corvos 1 (16.43 km)
1.Latvala 11″24″3; 2.Sordo +7″0;
3.Galli +7″4; 4.Loeb +7″8;
5.Mikkelsen +9″6; 6.P.Solberg +10″7;
7.Atkinson +13″0; 8.Hirvonen +13″0...
J-WRC > 19.Sandell 12′33″8

SS2 Crastazza 1 (33.96 km)
1.Loeb 23′56″1; 2.Sordo +18″2;
3.Hirvonen +20″9; 4.Atkinson +25″2
5.P.Solberg +29″1;
6.Gardemeister +36″9; 7.Aava +45″2;
8.H.Solberg +51″7...
J-WRC > 17.Prokop 26′17″6

SS3 Terranova 1 (15.39 km)
1.Loeb 10′48″3; 2.Latvala +4″4;
3.Galli +4″6; 4.Sordo +5″1;
5.Atkinson +8″4; 6.Hirvonen +9″7;
7.P.Solberg +9″7; 8.Aava +15″2...
J-WRC > 16.Kosciuszko 12′02″2

SS4 Monte Corvos 2 (16.43 km)
1.Galli 11′07″2; 2.Latvala +1″5;
3.P.Solberg +3″9; 4.Sordo +8″5;
5.Hirvonen +9″0; 6.Loeb +9″0;
7.H.Solberg +10″7; 8.Atkinson +11″1...
J-WRC > 16.Sandell 12′17″0

SS5 Crastazza 2 (33.96 km)
1.Loeb 23′21″4; 2.Latvala +3″5;
3.Galli +3″6; 4.Sordo +7″5;
5.P.Solberg +9″7; 6.Hirvonen +11″8;
7.Atkinson +17″1; 8.H.Solberg +24″5...
J-WRC > 16.Prokop 25′37″1

SS6 Terranova 2 (15.39 km)
1.Latvala 10′30″9; 2.Loeb +2″5;
3.Galli +3″6; 4.H.Solberg +6″9;
5.P.Solberg +4″3; 6.Sordo +8″7;
7.Hirvonen +10″8; 8.Atkinson +13″5...
J-WRC > 15.Kosciuszko 11′44″8

Classification Leg 1
1.Loeb 1h31′27″6; 2.Sordo +35″7;
3.P.Solberg +53″8; 4.Hirvonen +58″9;
5.Atkinson +1′09″0; 6.Galli +1′12″3;
7.Latvala +1′31″1; 8.H.Solberg +1′52″5...
J-WRC > 16.Prokop 1h40′48″5

SS7 Punta Pianedda 1 (18.53 km)
1.Latvala 11′27″8; 2.Hirvonen +8″4;
3.Galli +12″7; 4.Loeb +13″1;
5.Sordo +14″1; 6.Atkinson +18″7;
7.Ostberg +24″7;
8.Gardemeister +26″5...
J-WRC > 17.Prokop 12′47″9

SS8 Monte Lerno 1 (29.31 km)
1.Latvala 19′46″3; 2.Hirvonen +5″4;
3.Loeb +10″8; 4.Galli +18″8;
5.Sordo +22″0; 6.Atkinson +35″5;
7.Ostberg +39″5; 8.Andersson +40″9...
J-WRC > 16.Kosciuszko 21′52″2

SS9 Su Filigosu 1 (19.46 km)
1.Latvala 12′43″3; 2. Hirvonen +6″0;
3.Galli +8″1; 4.Loeb +12″8;
5.Sordo +20″7; 6.Aava +26″5;
7.Ostberg +28″7; 8.Andersson +28″8...
J-WRC > 17.Kosciuszko 13′57″7

SS10 Punta Pianedda 2 (18.53 km)
1.Latvala 11′09″3; 2.Hirvonen +5″3;
3.Loeb +9″1; 4.Galli +9″5;
5.Sordo +13″9; 6.Atkinson +24″4;
7.P.Solberg +25″9; 8.H.Solberg +26″5...
J-WRC > 17.Ogier 12′30″1

SS11 Monte Lerno 2 (29.31 km)
1.Latvala 19′19″9; 2.Hirvonen 4″3;
3.Galli +10″5; 4.Loeb +12″4;
5.Sordo +25″8; 6.Atkinson +27″5;
7.Aava +31″3; 8.P.Solberg +37″8...
J-WRC > 16.Prokop 21′25″1

SS12 Su Filigosu 2 (19.46 km)
1.Latvala 12′25″6; 2.Hirvonen 2″8;
3.Loeb +3″5; 4.Galli +7″5;
5.P.Solberg +17″6; 6.Atkinson +19″7;
7.Sordo +20″8; 8.H.Solberg +22″4...
J-WRC > 15.Kosciuszko 13′36″0

Classification Leg 2
1.Loeb 2h59′21″5; 2.Hirvonen +29″4;
3.Latvala +29″4; 4.Galli +1′17″7;
5.Sordo +1′31″1; 6.Atkinson +2′42″1;
7.H.Solberg +4′29″0; 8.Aava +4′34″5...
J-WRC > 16.Kosciuszko 3h17′32″5

SS13 Monte Olia 1 (19.28 km)
1.Hirvonen 14′03″2; 2.Latvala +5″1;
3.Loeb +10″3; 4.Galli +1823;
5.Sordo +19″8; 6.P.Solberg +25″1;
7.Andersson +35″6; 8.Ostberg +38″4...
J-WRC > 18.Kosciuszko 15′53″5

SS14 Sorilis 1 (18.66 Km)
1.Loeb 13′58″9; 2.Hirvonen +3″9;
3.Latvala +4″3; 4.Sordo +9″3;
5.Galli +11″2; 6.Rautenbach +26″4;
7.Aava +26″6; 8.H.Solberg +28″3...
J-WRC > 16.Prokop 15′37″4

SS15 Monte Olia 2 (19.28 Km)
1.Latvala 13′46″2; 2.Hirvonen +2″7;
3.Galli +9″3; 4.Loeb +9″5;
5.Sordo +16″4; 6.P.Solberg +17″5;
7.H.Solberg +28″1; 8.Ostberg +28″3...
J-WRC > 16.Kosciuszko 15′22″3

SS16 Sorilis 2 (18.66 Km)
1.Hirvonen 13′45″0; 2.Loeb +3″3;
3.Latvala +4″1; 4.Sordo +7″6;
5.Galli +11″3; 6.P.Solberg +11″4;
7.H.Solberg +16″9; 8.Ostberg +18″8...
J-WRC > 16.Mölder 15′15″5

SS17 Liscia Ruja (2.69 Km)
1.Latvala 1′54″8; 2.P.Solberg +1″9;
3.Hirvonen +2″2; 4.Galli +2″3;
5.Loeb +4″5; 6.Anderssson +6″3...
J-WRC > 15.Schammel 2′03″8

Results

	Driver - Co-Driver	Car	Gr.	Time
1.	**Loeb - Elena**	**Citroën C4 WRC 08**	A8	3h57′12″2
2.	Hirvonen - Lehtinen	Ford Focus RS WRC 07	A8	+10″6
3.	Latvala - Antilla	Ford Focus RS WRC 07	A8	+15″3
4.	Galli - Bernacchini	Ford Focus RS WRC 07	A8	+1′42″5
5.	Sordo - Marti	Citroën C4 WRC 08	A8	+2′05″6
6.	Atkinson - Prévot	Subaru Impreza WRC 07	A8	+5′08″6
7.	H.Solberg - Menkerud	Ford Focus RS WRC 07	A8	+6′01″0
8.	Aava - Sikk	Citroën C4 WRC 08	A8	+6′21″3
9.	Andersson - Andersson	Suzuki RWRT	A8	+7′48″7
10.	P. Solberg - Mills	Subaru Impreza WRC 07	A8	+9′41″0
15.	**Kosciuszko - Szczepaniak**	**Suzuki Swift**	A6/J	+24′35″7
17.	Bettega - Scattolin	Renault Clio R3	A6/J	+29′00″6
18.	**Cenedese - Rossetto**	**Mitsubishi Lancer Evo. IX**	N4	+33′30″7
19.	Burkart - Koelbach	Citroën C2 S1600	A6/J	+34′57″4

Leading Retirements (19)

Ctrl15	Gardemeister - Tuominen	Suzuki SX4 WRC	Electrical
Ctrl6C	Mikkelsen - Andersson	Ford Focus RS WRC 07	Off

Performers

	1	2	3	4	5	6	C6	Nb SS
Latvala	10	4	2	-	-	-	16	17
Loeb	4	2	4	5	2	-	17	17
Hirvonen	2	8	2	-	1	2	15	17
Galli	1	-	8	5	2	-	16	17
Sordo	-	2	-	5	7	1	15	17
P. Solberg	-	1	1	-	4	4	10	17
Atkinson	-	-	-	1	1	5	7	17
H. Solberg	-	-	-	2	-	-	1	17
Mikkelsen	-	-	-	-	1	-	1	2
Andersson	-	-	-	-	-	1	1	17
Aava	-	-	-	-	-	1	1	17
Gardemeister	-	-	-	-	-	1	1	14
Rautenbach	-	-	-	-	-	1	1	17

Leaders

SS1	Latvala
SS2 > SS17	Loeb

Previous Winners

2004	Solberg - Mills
	Subaru Impreza WRC 2004
2005	Loeb - Elena
	Citroën Xsara WRC
2006	Loeb - Elena
	Citroën Xsara WRC
2007	Grönholm - Rautiainen
	Ford Focus RS WRC 06

07 GREECE

🇬🇷 The rally from hell...

The 2008 Acropolis Rally will go down as one of the most unforgiving in the Greek classic's history. Some drivers just couldn't get the pace right, so there was often more haste than speed. But not Sébastien Loeb: he claimed victory number five from seven starts this season, and with Hirvonen unable to do better than third, that put the Frenchman in the Drivers' Championship lead..

07 | Greece

After being held up in the early stages, Latvala produced a splendid fightback drive before losing another chunk of time in the second leg when his Focus's turbo developed a problem.

THE RALLY
Loeb comes through the chaos

If we want to get a handle on just how difficult the 55th Acropolis Rally was, we need to pause for a moment and check out the list of incidents and accidents that punctuated the second leg, stage by stage:

Aghii Theodori 1, SS8, the longest timed section on the schedule: a puncture for Urmo Aava. The man in the PH Sport-prepared Citroën C4 WRC stops with the burst tyre, losing three minutes and with them the fine fifth place he occupied at the time. "That's sport," explains the disappointed driver. "We got the puncture soon after the start, and we had to stop to change the wheel."

Pissia 1, SS9: Chris Atkinson doesn't start because of electrical problems on his Subaru traced back to a wiring fault in the cockpit. Seventh at the time, the Australian is out. Six kilometres after the start, Loeb backs off with a puncture of his own. "We did 10 kilometres with no air in the tyre," the World Champion explains. "I tried to be as careful as I could. But we're still in it, and I hope not to lose any more time this afternoon." The upshot of this annoying hitch is that he loses the lead to team-mate Dani Sordo. Mikko Hirvonen makes a mistake, damages his rear suspension and is 30 seconds off the stage-winning time set by Galli, who does it with his right rear wheel virtually at right angles.

Subaru brought out the latest version of the Impreza, driven here by Petter Solberg, which was radically different from its predecessors.

Aghia Triada 1, SS10: Hirvonen's ordeal continues as he is forced to keep going in his crippled Focus, losing over two minutes and dropping from sixth to eighth. The Finn admits his mistake at midday service: "I slid on a slow corner and the car hit a low wall. The impact broke the right rear brake disc. We kept going with discs on the other three but after four kilometres of the final stage the suspension broke and I had no brakes left."

Aghii Theodori 2, SS11: the carnage among the front-runners goes from bad to worse. This time it's Dani Sordo's turn to swallow disappointment, as the Spaniard finishes the section with a front left puncture and another wheel badly damaged. He has to fit both his spare wheels to keep going, but manages to hang on to his lead. Jari-Matti Latvala produced a splendid morning comeback drive – he started 2m 57s down, but by the time this stage started he had cut that to 47s and gone from eighth to third – but he too saw all that effort go to waste when he was slowed by a turbo failure, losing 3:44.9 and dropping back to ninth. Same story, same result for Toni Gardemeister's Suzuki. Federico Villagra and P.G Andersson both retired as the Ford and Suzuki suspensions gave up the ghost. Another disappointed driver was Galli, who suffered hydrauic problems when he had set two fastest times since that morning.

A sigh of relief from Sébastien Loeb: Greece, its roads as merciless as its heat, is one of the toughest events on the calendar.

Nice look from Matthew Wilson – he gets more attention that way than when he's at the wheel.

Pissia 2, SS12: another puncture for Sordo, and with no spare wheel left, he has to slow right down, losing the overall lead to Loeb. Not only that, but the Spaniard has to get through the final stage with badly damaged tyres. Latvala's ordeal continues, still turbo-less, costing him 3:39.8.

Aghia Traida 2, SS13: as was to be expected, Sordo, no tread left on his tyres, loses huge chunks of time as well, now aiming just to get through the stage and into the service park. He lets 4m 24s slip away and is now seventh overall.

Let's stand back and see how that second leg from hell affected the overall picture in the Acropolis Rally. There had been astounding performances by both Solberg brothers: they were second and third, Petter ahead of Henning, after some careful driving which saw both looking after their tyres superbly. It brought this comment from the Subaru driver: "It's unbelievable to be in this position. We took it very carefully, and tomorrow I'll be doing all I can to consolidate. And Henning's on the podium too – not a bad effort by the brothers, eh?" The Ford man's view: "I've never been happier to be where I am now. I thought I had a problem in the last stage and went very slowly, but everything was fine. It was a difficult day, but I consolidated as well and here we are."

There was, too, an incredible fightback drive from Mikko Hirvonen. He thought all hope was gone in the morning, but eventually finished in fourth place, which left him still in with a chance of protecting his Championship position. "We've seen how quickly things can change," he said. "Who knows what might happen tomorrow?"

Last but not least, there was the man you just can't ignore, and he was back in control. "What a day!" said Loeb after those hellish 119 stage kilometres. "They threw everything at us. After a big road-sweeping job in SS8 (he was first off through the stages), we got a left rear puncture in the one after – while I was driving down the middle of the road! It was a downhill right and bang, a flat tyre! Last year's experience had taught me that I just had to get to the end on all four wheels, and we did it, but we had to be on our guard the whole time." Like his rivals, the World Champion pointed his finger in the direction of the tyres. Supplying just one tyre for a rally as unique as this one, with its appalling roads and intense heat, is clearly a cause for concern. The two factors make for quick and major degradation as chunks come off the carcasses. Loeb summed it up like this: "It was very hard on the tyres. We were losing chunks of rubber, but we managed to keep four good ones for the last stage."

If all the damage done on the first leg had started to sort them out, the second shook things up completely, with huge gaps between the leading runners. But while the third was another tricky one, the order didn't change all that much as the leaders chose to take it steady rather than tempting fate. There were still some tricky moments after the mechanical mayhem of the first two days. Henning Solberg's Ford engine, for instance, kept cutting out during the day's third stage, Aghia Sotira 1, and the Norwegian had to keep playing with the starter button. "It's as if there's some kind of ghost in the car," said the elder Solberg. "It's not over for us, but it's a pity. The team have changed all kinds of parts, and maybe it's fixed, but I'm not sure I can keep Mikko behind me. But it's not over yet." With third place now a distinct possibility for Hirvonen, the Ford team-leader upped his pace and, in the following stage, took over the final podium place as his rival's gremlin kept playing up. In fact Hirvonen got past Solberg in that 17th timed stretch.

The day's other big winner was Dani Sordo. The Spaniard's caution paid off as he moved forward one place thanks to Henning Solberg's fall from grace, and he also managed to deal with a lacklustre Matthew Wilson on the road. With Loeb winning and three cars in the top five (Aava 4th, Sordo 5th), though only two scored constructors' points, Citroën came out of the event best. "The C4 WRC has won the toughest event of the season," said a jubilant boss, Oliver Quesnel.

Urmo Aava was in a creditable fifth place early on in his C4 WRC before being slowed drastically by a puncture in the opening kilometres of the second leg.

07 | Greece

No luck for Henning Solberg: the Norwegian was third for a while and looking for a podium finish but his Focus engine kept cutting out through the final leg, dropping the Ford man to eighth.

David Richards and his men had every right to be proud of the new Impreza, which showed up very well first time out. It wouldn't last...

"Sébastien and Daniel are back in the lead in their Championship and Citroën are right back in the title hunt as well (now just two points behind Ford). How could we not be happy with that?"

Loeb, of course agreed: "It was a long, hard rally, but the circumstances worked in our favour," he explained when it was all over. "It was tricky driving in these conditions: it wasn't just a matter of going fast, sometimes you had to slow down as well. We got into a good rhythm and I'm happy with the way the C4 felt. In the past I've had trouble keeping up with the Fords on this rally, but not this year."

Ah yes, the Fords. Hirvonen on the podium, Latvala in seventh: a pretty mediocre result in an event where too many technical problems prevented them doing any better. "That was the hardest rally I've ever been in," Hirvonen insisted. "It was very hard on the machinery and we had so many problems that third is really an excellent outcome – quite a nice surprise, in fact. It would have been hard to beat Sébastien here anyway even without all the setbacks we encountered."

Many drivers fell victim to the single tyre supply rule in the Greek conditions – Dani Sordo had a nightmare of an event with his.

Happier still were Subaru after bringing out the latest version of their World Rally Car, the WRC 2008. Petter Solberg was thrilled with the new Impreza's potential: "It's perfect," he said. "I didn't have a single problem throughout the event. The team have done a wonderful job preparing this car and it's looking good for the next few events. The new Impreza showed it's on the pace and there's still more to come. Bravo!" Added to which there were some excellent times from Atkinson, though the Australian didn't make it to the end after breaking his car's suspension. "We've moved into a new development phase," trumpeted team principal David Richards. "We finished our first event and learned a lot from it, which will stand us in good stead for the second part of the season." Well might the blue team enjoy the moment: there were darker days ahead for the new Impreza. Same as every year, more or less... ∎

Mikko Hirvonen in action in what he called 'the toughest rally of his career'. The Finn felt lucky to have finished third.

Ford used to make light work of the hardest rallies, but this time they had to give best to Citroën.

Anyone would think they'd won: Phil Mills and Petter Solberg were thrilled with their hard-won second place on the demanding Greek event.

PRODUCTION CARS
Aigner hangs on

By the time the third leg started Andrea Aigner thought he'd done most of the hard work with a 2:10.3 lead over the man in second place. He had survived that far in the Mitsubishi Lancer, unlike some of his toughest opponents. Nasser Al-Attiyah and Juho Hänninen were very quick in the early stages but both went astray in the second leg, the first with a broken suspension, the second with his steering awry. The patient Aigner inherited the lead, and a substantial one at that. Sadly, Sunday morning brought a diff problem which meant he had to go through the first few stages in front-wheel-drive mode only. His lead evaporated but he hung in there and, his car restored halfway through, managed to win by some 35 seconds from another Mitsubishi man, Martin Rauam. "I'm really happy to have won," he said. "We needed these points because Juho (Hänninen) has done one event fewer than us and we had to build up a bit of a lead in the Championship. The fact that this is such a tough rally makes the win even better."

Soon after the finish, Estonian driver Rauam was disqualified: his team had put the wrong spec of front brakes on the car. They were lighter and had a different cooling system than the homologated parts. So second place, in the stewards' room, went instead to Aigner's team-mate Bernardo Sousa, a fine effort from the Portuguese in only his third World Championship rally.

The win put Aigner comfortably ahead of Subaru's Jari Ketomaa, who retired from the Acropolis, and Hänninen, who could only finish seventh. It should be pointed out that the Greek event underlined the healthy state of the Production Championship: there were a record 28 competitors at the start. ■

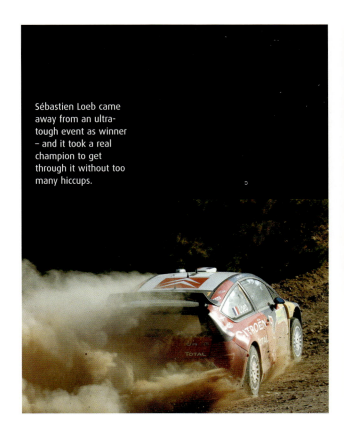

Sébastien Loeb came away from an ultra-tough event as winner – and it took a real champion to get through it without too many hiccups.

07 | Greece | Results

55th ACROPOLIS RALLY

Organiser Details
Automobile & Touring Club of Greece - ELPA,
395 Messogion Ave,
153 43 Agia Paraskevi,
Athens, Greece
Tel.: +39 079 5551234
Fax: +39 079 5551244

BP Ultimate Acropolis Rally

7th leg of FIA 2008 World Championship for constructors and drivers.
3rd leg of FIA Production Car World Championship.

Date May 29 - June 1st, 2008

Route
1311.32 km divised in three legs.
20 special stages on dirt roads (339.94 km)

Ceremonial Start
Thursday, May 29 (19:30),
Acropolis, Athens

Leg 1
Friday, May 30 (09:16/18:30),
Athens > Athens, 465.24 km;
7 special stages (110.08 km)

Leg 2
Saturday, May 31 (09:58/17:21),
Athens > Athens, 472.72 km;
6 special stages (119.12 km)

Leg 3
Sunday, June 1st (06:48/14:30),
Athens > Athens, 373.36 km;
7 special stages (110.74 km)

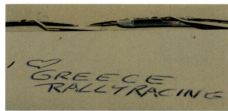

Entry List (60) - 60 starters

N°	Driver (Nat.)	Co-Driver (Nat.)	Team	Car	Group & FIA Priority
1	SÉBASTIEN LOEB (F)	DANIEL ELENA (MC)	CITROEN TOTAL WRT	CITROEN C4 WRC	A8 1
2	DANI SORDO (E)	MARC MARTI (E)	CITROEN TOTAL WRT	CITROEN C4 WRC	A8 1
3	MIKKO HIRVONEN (FIN)	JARMO LEHTINEN (FIN)	BP FORD ABU DHABI WORLD RALLY TEAM	FORD FOCUS RS WRC 07	A8 1
4	JARI-MATTI LATVALA (FIN)	MIIKKA ANTTILA (FIN)	BP FORD ABU DHABI WORLD RALLY TEAM	FORD FOCUS RS WRC 07	A8 1
5	PETTER SOLBERG (N)	PHILIP MILLS (GB)	SUBARU WORLD RALLY TEAM	SUBARU IMPREZA WRC 2008	A8 1
6	CHRIS ATKINSON (AUS)	STEPHANE PREVOT (B)	SUBARU WORLD RALLY TEAM	SUBARU IMPREZA WRC 2008	A8 1
7	GIGI GALLI (I)	GIOVANNI BERNACCHINI (I)	STOBART VK M-SPORT FORD RALLY TEAM	FORD FOCUS RS WRC 07	A8 1
8	HENNING SOLBERG (N)	CATO MENKERUD (N)	STOBART VK M-SPORT FORD RALLY TEAM	FORD FOCUS RS WRC 07	A8 1
9	FEDERICO VILLAGRA (RA)	JOSE MARIA VOLTA (RA)	MUNCHI'S FORD WORLD RALLY TEAM	FORD FOCUS RS WRC 07	A8 1
10	ARIS VOVOS (GR)	EL-EM (GR)	MUNCHI'S FORD WORLD RALLY TEAM	FORD FOCUS RS WRC 07	A8 1
11	TONI GARDEMEISTER (FIN)	TOMI TUOMINEN (FIN)	SUZUKI WORLD RALLY TEAM	SUZUKI SX4 WRC	A8 1
12	PER-GUNNAR ANDERSSON (S)	JONAS ANDERSSON (S)	SUZUKI WORLD RALLY TEAM	SUZUKI SX4 WRC	A8 1
14	KHALID AL QASSIMI (UAE)	MICHAEL ORR (GB)	BP FORD ABU DHABI WORLD RALLY TEAM	FORD FOCUS RS WRC 07	A8 2
15	URMO AAVA (EE)	KULDAR SIKK (EE)	WORLD RALLY TEAM ESTONIA	CITROEN C4	A8 2
16	MATTHEW WILSON (GB)	SCOTT MARTIN (GB)	STOBART VK M-SPORT FORD RALLY TEAM	FORD FOCUS RS WRC 07	A8 2
17	MADS OSTBERG (N)	OLE KRISTIAN UNNERUD (N)	ADAPTA AS	SUBARU IMPREZA WRC 07	A8 2
18	CONRAD RAUTENBACH (ZW)	DAVID SENIOR (GB)	RAUTENBACH CONRAD	CITROEN C4	A8 2
31	TOSHIHIRO ARAI (J)	GLENN MACNEALL (AUS)	SUBARU TEAM ARAI	SUBARU IMPREZA WRX STI	N4 3
32	MIRCO BALDACCI (RSM)	GIOVANNI AGNESE (I)	BALDACCI MIRCO	MITSUBISHI LANCER EVO 9	N4 3
33	MARTIN PROKOP (CZ)	JAN TOMANEK (CZ)	PROKOP MARTIN	MITSUBISHI LANCER EVO 9	N4 3
34	GIANLUCA LINARI (I)	PAOLO GREGORIANI (I)	LINARI GIANLUCA	SUBARU IMPREZA WRX STI	N4 3
35	EVGENY NOVIKOV (RUS)	DMITRY CHUMAK (RUS)	NOVIKOV EVGENY	MITSUBISHI LANCER EVO 9	N4 3
36	EYVIND BRYNILDSEN (N)	MARIA ANDERSSON (S)	BRYNILDSEN EYVIND	MITSUBISHI LANCER EVO 9	N4 3
37	SPYROS PAVLIDES (CY)	DENIS GIRAUDET (F)	AUTOTEK	SUBARU IMPREZA WRX STI	N4 3
38	AMJAD FARRAH (JO)	NICOLA ARENA (I)	ORION WORLD RALLY TEAM	MITSUBISHI LANCER EVO 9	N4 3
39	NASSER AL-ATTIYAH (QA)	CHRIS PATTERSON (GB)	QMMF	SUBARU IMPREZA WRX STI	N4 3
40	LORIS BALDACCI (RSM)	RUDY POLLET (I)	ERRANI TEAM GROUP	MITSUBISHI LANCER EVO 9	N4 3
41	ANDREAS AIGNER (A)	KLAUS WICHA (D)	RED BULL RALLYE TEAM	MITSUBISHI LANCER EVO 9	N4 3
42	BERNANDO SOUSA (P)	JORGE CARVALHO (P)	RED BULL RALLYE TEAM	MITSUBISHI LANCER EVO 9	N4 3
43	EVGENIY VERTUNOV (RUS)	GEORGY TROSHKIN (RUS)	SUBARU RALLY TEAM RUSSIA	SUBARU IMPREZA WRX STI	N4 3
45	ANDREJ JEREB (SLO)	MIRAN KACIN (SLO)	MOTORING CLUB 1	SUBARU IMPREZA WRX STI N12	N4 3
46	JARI KETOMAA (FIN)	MIIKA TEISKONEN (FIN)	MOTORING CLUB 2	SUBARU IMPREZA WRX STI N14	N4 3
48	EVGENY AKSAKOV (RUS)	ALEKSANDR KORNILOV (EE)	RED WINGS MOSCOW REGION RALLY TEAM	MITSUBISHI LANCER EVO 9	N4 3
49	SIMONE CAMPEDELLI (I)	DANILO FAPPANI (I)	SCUDERIA RUBICONE CORSE	MITSUBISHI LANCER EVO 9	N4 3
50	ARMINDO ARAUJO (P)	MIGUEL RAMALHO (P)	RALLIART ITALY	MITSUBISHI LANCER EVO 9	N4 3
51	SUBHAN AKSA (RI)	HENDRIK MBOI (RI)	INDONESIA RALLY TEAM	MITSUBISHI LANCER EVO 9	N4 3
52	JUHO HANNINEN (FIN)	MIKKO MARKKULA (FIN)	RALLIART NEW ZEALAND	MITSUBISHI LANCER EVO 9	N4 3
53	UWE NITTEL (D)	MICHAEL WENZEL (D)	PRO RACE RALLY	MITSUBISHI LANCER EVO 9	N4 3
54	TRAVIS PASTRANA (USA)	DEREK RINGER (GB)	SUBARU RALLY TEAM INTERNATIONAL	SUBARU IMPREZA WRX STI	N4 3
55	PATRIK SANDELL (S)	EMIL AXELSSON (S)	PEUGEOT SPORT SWEDEN	PEUGEOT 207 S2000	N4 3
56	FUMIO NUTAHARA (J)	DANIEL BARRITT (GB)	ADVAN-PIAA RALLY TEAM	MITSUBISHI LANCER EVO 9	N4 3
57	MARTIN RAUAM (EE)	SILVER KUTT (EE)	WORLD RALLY TEAM ESTONIA	MITSUBISHI LANCER EVO 9	N4 3
58	NAREN KUMAR (IND)	NICKY BEECH (GB)	TEAM SIDVIN INDIA	SUBARU IMPREZA WRX STI N14	N4 3
59	PAN. HATZITSOPANIS (GR)	ANDREAS ANDRIKOPOULOS (GR)	HATZITSOPANIS PANAYIOTIS	SUBARU IMPREZA WRX STI	N4 3
60	LABROS ATHANASSOULAS (GR)	NIKOLAOS ZAKHEOS (GR)	ATHANASSOULAS LABROS	SUBARU IMPREZA WRX STI	N4 3
61	DIMITRIS NASSOULAS (GR)	MIHALIS PATRIKOUSSIS (GR)	NASSOULAS DIMITRIS	MITSUBISHI LANCER EVO 9	N4
62	GRIGORIS NIORAS (GR)	ANASTASIOS GOUSSETIS (GR)	HELLENIC POLICE	SUBARU IMPREZA WRX STI N12	N4
63	EMM. PANAGIOTOPOULOS (GR)	HELEN MALAKTARI (GR)	PANAGIOTOPOULOS EMMANUEL	MITSUBISHI LANCER EVO 9	N4
64	KONSTANTINOS APOSTOLOU (GR)	STAVROS KIKIZAS (GR)	APOSTOLOU KONSTANTINOS	MITSUBISHI LANCER EVO 6	A8
66	ANDREAS WIMMER (A)	MICHAEL KOLBACH (D)	WIMMER ANDREAS	SUBARU IMPREZA WRX STI	N4
67	PANAYIOTIS ZISSIS (GR)	VASSILIS ZISSIS (GR)	ZISSIS PANAYIOTIS	MITSUBISHI LANCER EVO 9	N4
68	ATHANASIOS TSILILIS (GR)	EMMANOUEL AHTIDAS (GR)	TSILIS ATHANASIOS	MITSUBISHI LANCER EVO 7	A8
69	ELIAS ATHANASSIOU (GR)	PANTELIS IAKOVIDIS (GR)	ATHANASSIOU ELIAS	MITSUBISHI LANCER EVO 8	N4
70	MORENO CENEDESE (I)	CARLO PISANO (I)	CENEDESE MORENO	MITSUBISHI LANCER EVO 9	N4
71	DIONISSIOS GAZETAS (GR)	PANAYIOTIS TRIANDAFYLLOY (GR)	GAZETAS DIONISSIOS	MITSUBISHI LANCER EVO 7	A8
72	DIMITRIS VASSILIS (GR)	HARALAMBOS VARSOS (GR)	VASSILIS DIMITRIS	SUBARU IMPREZA 555	A8
73	HARIS KALTSOUNIS (GR)	ANDREAS PERIDIS (GR)	KALTSOUNIS HARIS	OPEL CORSA SUPER 1600	A6
74	IOANNIS ZOUNIS (GR)	SPYROS DEMERTZIS (GR)	PYROSVESTIKO SOMA	MG ROVER 25	A6
75	GRIGORIS LADOGIANNIS (GR)	NIKOLAOS LADOGIANNIS (GR)	LADOGIANNIS GRIGORIS	FIAT SEICENTO	A5
76	DIMITRIS ANGELETOS (GR)	ARIS LYBERIS (GR)	ANGELETOS DIMITRIS	TOYOTA YARIS	A5

B. Sousa

P. Andersson

Gardemeister

M. Rauam

C. Atkinson

Championship Classifications

•R•: Rookie

FIA Drivers (7/15)
1. Loeb — 5🏆 — 50
2. Hirvonen — 1🏆 — 49
3. Atkinson — 31
4. Latvala — 1🏆 — 26
5. Sordo — 25
6. P. Solberg — 17
7. Galli — 17
8. H. Solberg — 12
9. Wilson — 10
10. Villagra — 8
11. Aava — 6
12. Rautenbach — 5
13. Duval — 5
14. Mikkelsen — 4
15. Gardemeister — 2
16. Cuoq — 2
17. Andersson — 1
18. Ogier — 1
19. Aigner — 1
20. Hänninen — 1
21. K. Al-Qassimi, — 0
Østberg, — 0
Beltrán, Mölder, — 0
Ketomaa, Kosciuszko, — 0
Sandell, Nutahara, — 0
Prokop, Burkart, — 0
Clark, Rauam, — 0
Gallagher, Broccoli, — 0
Farrah, Schammel, — 0
Artru, Nittel, Guerra, — 0
A. Al-Qassimi, Arai, — 0
Mercier — 0

FIA Constructors (7/15)
1. BP-Ford Abu Dhabi World Rally Team — 2🏆 — 81
2. Citroën Total World Rally Team — 5🏆 — 79
3. Subaru World Rally Team — 50
4. Stobart VK M-Sport Ford Rally Team — 37
5. Munchi's Ford World Rally Team — 16
6. Suzuki World Rally Team — 10

FIA Production Car WRC (3/8)
1. Aigner — 2🏆 — 20
2. Ketomaa — 14
3. Rauam — 12
4. Hänninen — 1🏆 — 11
5. Nutahara — 9
6. Beltrán — 8
7. Sousa — 8
8. Prokop — 7
9. Araujo — 7
10. Sandell — 6
11. Nittel — 4
12. Farrah — 3
13. Aksakov — 3
14. Arai — 3
15. Vertunov — 2
16. Campedelli — 0
17. Baldacci — 0
18. Aksa — 0
19. Mayer — 0
20. Tiippaana — 0
21. Pavlides — 0
20. Frisiero — 0
22. Kumar — 0
23. Frisiero — 0
24. Linari — 0
25. Bacco — 0
26. Athanassoulas — 0
27. Jereb — 0
28. Pastrana — 0
29. Brynildsen — 0
30. Novikov — 0
31. Flodin — 0
32. Marrini — 0

FIA Junior WRC (3/7)
1. Ogier — 2🏆 — 24
2. Kosciusko — 1🏆 — 16
3. Gallagher — 16
4. Burkart — 11
5. Mölder — 8
6. Bettega — 8
7. Albertini — 7
8. Schammel — 6
9. Sandell — 6
10. Niegel — 5
11. Bertolotti — 3
12. Prokop — 2
13. Cortinovis — 2
14. Fanari •R• — 1
15. Komljenovic — 1
16. Weijs Jr. •R• — 1

Special Stages Times

www.acropolisrally.gr
www.wrc.com

SS1 Shimatari 1 (11.57 km)
1.Latvala 10'34"3; 2. Sordo +5"2;
3.Hirvonen +5"8; 4.Loeb +5"8;
5.P.Solberg +9"3; 6.Atkinson +12"1;
7.Wilson +13"9; 8.Ostberg +14"0...
P-WRC > 18.Baldacci 11'09"0

SS2 Thiva 1 (23.76 km)
1.Loeb 17'15"2; 2.Sordo +0"3;
3.Latvala +4"3; 4.Aava +8"3
5.H.Solberg +10"9; 6.P.Solberg +11"6;
7.Hirvonen +13"3; 8.Wilson +17"3...
P-WRC > 16.Hanninen 18'14"4...

SS3 Psatha 1 (17.41 km)
1.Latvala 11'28"7; 2.Loeb +2"7;
3.Sordo +5"0; 4.P.Solberg 10"8;
5.Hirvonen +11"4; 6.H.Solberg +13"4;
7.Aava +19"8; 8.Atkinson +20"1...
P-WRC > 16.Hanninen 12'36"3

SS4 Shimatari 2 (11.57 km)
1.Loeb 10'26"7; 2.Sordo +1"3;
3.Hirvonen +4"6; 4.H.Solberg +5"9;
5.P.Solberg +10"0; 6.Wilson +10"8;
7.Latvala +10"8; 8.Aava +11"3...
P-WRC > 14.Aigner 10'56"2

SS5 Thiva 2 (23.76 km)
1.Loeb 16'53"8; 2.Sordo +3"9;
3.Latvala +4"5; 4.H.Solberg +11"3;
5.Atkinson +13"1; 6.Hirvonen +14"5;
7.Aava +15"8; 8.P.Solberg +18"1...
P-WRC > 16.Hanninen 18'05"8

SS6 Psatha 2 (17.41 km)
1.Loeb 11'12"5; 2.Latvala +1"7;
3.Sordo +8"3; 4.Hirvonen +8"6;
5.P.Solberg +9"2; 6.Atkinson +14"0;
7.Aava +16"8; 8.H.Solberg +18"2...
P-WRC > 16.Al-Attiyah 12'27"1

SS7 SSS Tatoi 1 (4.60 km)
1.Aava 3'31"3; 2.P.Solberg +2"4;
3.Loeb +3"8; 4.Sordo +4"0;
5.Rautenbach +4"0; 6.H.Solberg +4"2;
7.Andersson +4"7;
8.Gardemeister +5"2;
P-WRC > 12.Hanninen 3'42"1

Classification Leg 1
1.Loeb 1h21'34"8; 2.Sordo +15"7;
3.P.Solberg +59"1; 4.H.Solberg +1'06"0;
5.Aava +1'15"5; 6.Latvala +1'18"9;
7.Hirvonen +1'36"4;
8.Atkinson +1'56"8...
P-WRC > 15.Al-Attiyah 1h27'44"0

SS8 Aghii Theodori 1 (32.16 km)
1.Hirvonen 22'42"1; 2.Latvala +1"8;
3.P.Solberg +4"6; 4.Atkinson +5"9;
5.Sordo +9"1; 6.Loeb +16"1;
7.H.Solberg +20"1;
8.Gardemeister +33"6...
P-WRC > 15.Hanninen 24'12"6

SS9 Pissia 1 (16.60 km)
1.Galli 12'17"2; 2.Latvala +0"3;
3.Aava +4"4; 4.P.Solberg +5"6;
5.H.Solberg +6"0; 6.Sordo +6"2;
7.Wilson +10"9; 8.Ostberg +13"7...
P-WRC > 16.Hanninen 12'53"1

SS10 Aghia Triada 1 (10.80 km)
1.Galli 7'46"1; 2.Loeb +0"4;
3.Latvala +0"8; 4.H.Solberg +2"9;
5.Sordo +3"4; 6.Aava +7"9;
7.P.Solberg +11"0; 8.Hirvonen +17"8...
P-WRC > 12.Hanninen 8'16"9

SS11 Aghii Theodori 2 (32.16 km)
1.Hirvonen 22'36"1; 2.P.Solberg +3"2;
3.H.Solberg +4"6; 4.Sordo +6"8;
5.Aava +17"7; 6.Loeb +17"9;
7.Wilson +46"0; 8.Ostberg +47"8...
P-WRC > 12.Aigner 24'31"7

SS12 Pissia 2 (16.60 km)
1.Aava 12'13"9; 2.Loeb +2"4;
3.Hirvonen +6"2; 4.P.Solberg +13"2;
5.Wilson +17"2; 6.H.Solberg +18"3;
7.Rautenbach +19"6; 8.Ostberg +21"5...
P-WRC > 11.Athanassoulas 13'02"5

SS13 Aghia Triada 2 (10.80 km)
1.Hirvonen 7'45"4; 2.Loeb +4"4;
3.P.Solberg +7"5; 4.Rautenbach +14"4;
5.Al Qassimi +20"5; 6.Wilson +21"0;
7.H.Solberg +22"9;
P-WRC > 8.Prokop +35"8 (8'21"2)

Classification Leg 2
1.Loeb 2h48'11"1; 2.P.Solberg +28"7;
3.H.Solberg +1'05"3;
4.Hirvonen +3'01"2; 5.Aava +4'11"6;
6.Wilson +4'22"8; 7.Sordo +5'33"6;
8.Latvala +8'51"3...
P-WRC > 12.Aigner 3h01'06"4

SS14 Avlonas 1 (20.00 km)
1.Atkinson 9'09"6; 2.Latvala +6"4;
3.Loeb +7"3; 4.Hirvonen +11"9;
5.Galli +12"7; 6.Sordo +20"1;
7.Aava +32"4; 8.P.Solberg +32"6...
P-WRC > 15.Hanninen 10'00"6

SS15 Assopia 1 (17.87 km)
1.Latvala 11'39"9; 2.Galli +6"9;
3.Hirvonen +8"7; 4.Sordo +14"1;
5.Loeb +20"6; 6.Andersson +25"8;
7.H.Solberg +26"7; 8.Ostberg +29"7...
P-WRC > 15.Hanninen 12'30"8

SS16 Aghia Sotira 1 (15.20 km)
1.Galli 9'47"2; 2.Latvala +1"5;
3.Hirvonen +5"3; 4.Sordo +17"9;
5.Aava +22"9; 6.P.Solberg +24"6;
7.Andersson +27"2; 8.Villagra +27"8...
P-WRC > 14.Hanninen 10'38"1

SS17 Avlonas 2 (20.00 km)
1.Galli 9'00"9; 2.Latvala +0"6;
3.Sordo +9"3; 4.Aava +12"4;
5.Hirvonen +15"0; 6.Andersson +17"8;
7.Loeb +18"6; 8.Gardemeister +20"7...
P-WRC > 15.Hanninen 9'47"1

SS18 Assopia 2 (17.87 km)
1.Latvala 11'26"6; 2.Sordo +10"3;
3.Hirvonen +19"4; 4.Loeb +22"8;
5.Ostberg +23"2; 6.Villagra +23"3;
7.Andersson +24"4; 8.Aava +28"3...
P-WRC > 13.Hanninen 12'19"2

SS19 Aghia Sotira 2 (15.20 km)
1.Latvala 9'52"2; 2.Aava +9"3;
3.Sordo +13"3; 4.Hirvonen +15"4;
5.Andersson +19"8; 6.P.Solberg +24"5;
7.Rautenbach +29"9; 8.Wilson +31"6...
P-WRC > 14.Hanninen 10'47"0

SS20 SSS Tatoi 2 (4.60 km)
1.Sordo 3'33"0; 2.Hirvonen +0"2;
3.Ostberg +1"1; 4.Gardemeister +1"4;
5.Latvala +1"9; 6.Aava +2"3;
7.Rautenbach +2"4; 8.Wilson +2"5...
P-WRC > 15.Novikov 3'48"7

Results

	Driver - Co-Driver	Car	Gr.	Time
1.	Loeb - Elena	Citroën C4 WRC 08	A8	3h54'54"7
2.	P. Solberg - Mills	Subaru Impreza WRC 2008	A8	+1'09"5
3.	Hirvonen - Lehtinen	Ford Focus RS WRC 07	A8	+1'56"1
4.	Aava - Sikk	Citroën C4 WRC 08	A8	+4'19"7
5.	Sordo - Marti	Citroën C4 WRC 08	A8	+4'49"4
6.	Wilson - Orr	Ford Focus RS WRC 06	A8	+6'11"3
7.	Latvala - Antilla	Ford Focus RS WRC 07	A8	+6'47"5
8.	H. Solberg - Menkerud	Ford Focus RS WRC 07	A8	+9'14"0
9.	Gardemeister - Tuominen	Suzuki SX4 WRC	A8	+10'13"8
10.	Rautenbach - Senior	Citroën C4 WRC 08	A8	+13'29"1
14.	Aigner - Wicha	Mitsubishi Lancer Evo IX	N4/P	+21'12"0
15.	Sousa - Carvalho	Mistubishi Lancer Evo IX	N4/P	+22'10"1
16.	Araujo - Ramalho	Mistubishi Lancer Evo IX	N4/P	+22'39"7

Leading Retirements (18)

Ctrl18	Galli - Bernacchini	Ford Focus RS WRC 07	Transmission
Ctrl16A	Sandell - Axelsson	Peugeot 207 S2000	Suspension
Ctrl16	Atkinson - Prevot	Subaru Impreza WRC 2008	Suspension
Ctrl10	Arai - McNeall	Subaru Impreza WRX Sti	Suspension

Andreas Aigner

Performers

	1	2	3	4	5	6	C6	NbSS
Latvala	-	5	6	3	1	1	16	20
Loeb	4	4	3	1	1	2	15	20
Hirvonen	3	1	6	3	1	1	15	20
Sordo	1	5	4	4	2	2	18	20
Atkinson	1	-	-	1	1	2	5	10
Aava	2	1	1	2	2	2	10	20
P. Solberg	-	2	2	3	3	3	13	20
H. Solberg	-	-	1	3	2	3	9	20
Wilson	-	-	-	1	1	-	2	20
Gardemeister	-	-	-	1	-	-	1	20
Rautenbach	-	-	-	1	-	-	1	20
Andersson	-	-	-	-	1	2	3	18

Leaders

SS1 > SS3	Latvala
SS4 > SS8	Loeb
SS9 > SS11	Sordo
SS12 > SS20	Loeb

Previous Winners

1973	Thérier - Delferrier / Alpine Renault A110	1986	Kankkunen - Piironen / Peugeot 205 T16	1998	McRae - Grist / Subaru Impreza WRC
1975	Rohrl - Berger / Opel Ascona	1987	Alen - Kivimaki / Lancia Delta HF Turbo	1999	Burns - Reid / Subaru Impreza WRC
1976	Kallstrom - Andersson / Datsun 160J	1988	Biasion - Siviero / Lancia Delta Integrale	2000	C. McRae - Grist / Ford Focus WRC
1977	Waldegaard - Thorszelius / Ford Escort RS	1989	Biasion - Siviero / Lancia Delta Integrale	2001	C. McRae - Grist / Ford Focus RS WRC 01
1978	Rohrl - Geistdorfer / Fiat 131 Abarth	1990	Sainz - Moya / Toyota Celica GT4	2002	C. McRae - Grist / Ford Focus RS WRC 02
1979	Waldegaard - Thorszelius / Ford escort RS	1991	Kankkunen - Piironen / Lancia Delta Integrale 16v	2003	Märtin - Park / Ford Focus RS WRC 03
1980	Vatanen - Richards / Ford Escort RS	1992	Auriol - Occelli / Lancia Delta Integrale	2004	P. Solberg - Mills / Subaru Impreza WRC 2004
1981	Vatanen - Richards / Ford Escort RS	1993	Biasion - Siviero / Ford Escort RS Cosworth	2005	Loeb - Elena / Citroën Xsara WRC
1982	Mouton - Pons / Audi Quattro	1994	Sainz - Moya / Subaru Impreza	2006	Grönholm - Rautiainen / Ford Focus RS WRC 06
1983	Rohrl - Geistdorfer / Lancia Rally 037	1995	Vovos - Stefanis / Lancia Delta Integrale	2007	Grönholm - Rautiainen / Ford Focus RS WRC 06
1984	Blomqvist - Cederberg / Audi Quattro	1996	McRae - Ringer / Subaru Impreza		
1985	Salonen - Harjanne / Peugeot 205 T16	1997	Sainz - Moya / Ford Escort WRC		

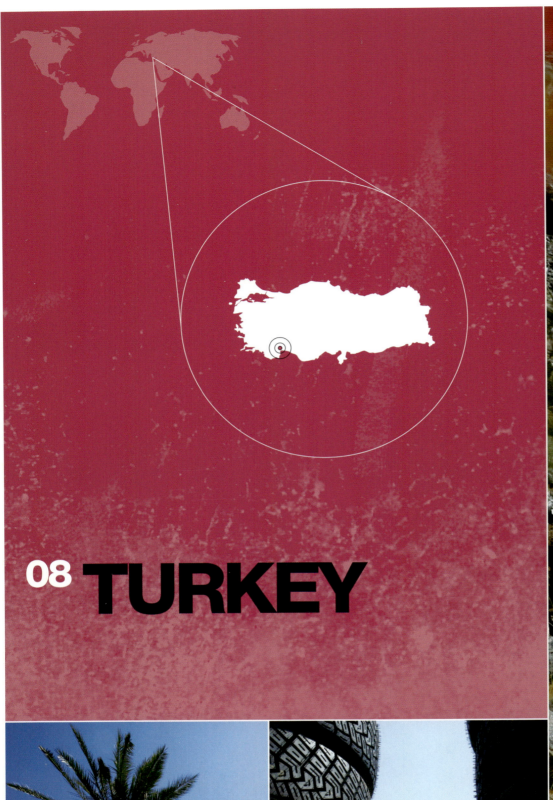

08 TURKEY

Hirvonen back on track

After a couple of difficult events, the Ford driver got back to winning ways, regaining the Championship lead from Sébastien Loeb, who was third behind Jari-Matti Latvala. It meant Ford could go off on the summer break on a high. But the way they exploited the rules to get their drivers into a winning position left a bad taste in Citroën mouths.

08 | Turkey

Sébastien Loeb spent two days sweeping the roads for the Ford drivers. The Citroën man's a bonny fighter, but even he couldn't do much about it and had to settle for third.

So it was a bit of a false dawn for Petter Solberg, who could manage only sixth. That second place in Greece is a distant memory already…

THE RALLY
One up the chuff...

Mikko Hirvonen had already tasted victory five times and enjoyed it – but never had he shown it as exuberantly as he did in Turkey. The Finn, more 'Hollywood' than Solberg himself, came into the service park like a rallycross driver, door open, perched on the roll bar, leapt from the Focus in to his team's waiting arms then climbed up on the bonnet, punching the air as a big grin lit up his face. A few metres away, Loeb was looking black. He'd had worse results than the third place he'd just managed, but Citroën's man felt thwarted and frustrated. The victim of Ford's questionable tactics, he'd been unable to take Hirvonen and Latvala on fair and square. While they enjoyed two days of favourable starting positions, he had to go out and open the road.

So what was it all about? On Wednesday evening after the recces, Loeb wasn't exactly optimistic. "As Championship leader I'll be first on the road on Friday," he reminded us. "That's going to cost me, because there's quite a layer of surface gravel. I have to open the road all day long, and we could get hammered from the start – maybe as much as a minute, then we'll have to try and get that back in the other two legs."

Over at the customary Ford 'happy hour' that happens every Wednesday in the World Championship service park, the Finnish cronies knew things were looking good. "In Sardinia and Greece I was the one who did the road-sweeping for everybody else," said Hirvonen. "Seb took advantage of that and high-tailed it. This weekend it's the other way round: it's my turn to open up a gap from the first stage." As for Latvala, he knew his current fourth place overall meant he would have a nice, wide, billiard-table smooth road in front of him after the guys in front had cleaned it up.

But this was one Finn who would let his chance go begging. In the very first Friday stage, after the Antalya showcase special won by Loeb the day before, he gave up 30 seconds or so. "Ten kilometres from the finish I hit a rock on a tight right-hander on a crest and got a puncture," he explained. "My fault, I cut the corner too much." Latvala had gone off like a rocket, desperate to get away, then paid the price for being over-hasty – as is his wont. Remember the Monte? To make up for his blunder, he piled on the pace, regained the lead – and got another puncture in the next timed section. The upshot: going into the day's last stage he was second, 2.1s down on Hirvonen. Loeb, fourth and 15.2 behind the leader, had done some useful damage limitation. "Thank goodness Latvala had some trouble," he said, "otherwise we'd have been left for dead as we expected. But that's not too bad: we pushed hard and didn't make any mistakes."

Matthew Wilson was in the points for the fourth time in eight starts, this time in seventh. His cause was helped when a spent, unwell Galli had to retire at the end of the second leg.

This time Jari-Matti Latvala really got the job done, holding off Loeb and letting team leader Mikko Hirvonen take the win to put more points in the bag.

Henning Solberg made the absolute most of his position on the road, just missing fourth place.

So, just a few lengths from the end of the first leg, that left the Frenchman ideally placed for the remainder of the event, with the Ford drivers taking over road-sweeping duties and a relatively small gap to make up. Blue oval boss Malcolm Wilson knew that if things stayed the way they were his men had little hope of the win. So he told Hirvonen, Latvala and Galli to slow down in the last few hundred metres of the day's closing stage. "As soon as Loeb crossed the line and we knew his time we got on the radio to our crews and told them the times they needed to set to finish the leg just behind him, so they wouldn't have to open the road on the second leg," Christian Loriaux explained shamelessly. So as the first leg ended Loeb was leader despite himself, from Henning Solberg, Latvala, Galli and Hirvonen. Ford owed their numbers guys a vote of thanks – the whole bunch were covered by just 6.9 seconds.

The new state of affairs didn't exactly go down well at Citroën and there was tension in the air at the end-of-day get-together. A few names were hurled at Hirvonen's engineer when, camera in hand, he got a little too close to Loeb's C4 for some people's comfort. In fact the man who replaced Guy Fréquelin in charge of the Red camp, Olivier Quesnel, even got a bit carried away with the British press, threatening a WRC pull-out – which he had to deny next day as the press in turn got a little excited about this little cry from the heart. "It's a bit annoying, but what can you do about it?" asked a resigned Loeb. "The Fords couldn't match us and that was the only thing they could come up with. Maybe we'd have

done the same thing in their position, but it's not how we like to do things. Rallying, when it comes down to it, is about speed, not going slow. But they did well to get three cars between me and Hirvonen. It won't be easy to hang on tomorrow, but we'll try and lift our game another notch – if we can, because we've been going pretty hard so far!"

There wasn't much bragging coming from the Ford camp. Hirvonen and Latvala knew they were the main reasons for the questionable strategy after failing to build a big enough lead over Loeb, one through driver errors, the other through sheer lack of pace; they'd left their team principal no option in his eagerness to manufacture a win somehow. Especially when there's nothing in the rules to stop you...

"We adopted these tactics because I was never able to get far enough ahead of Sébastien," said a rather disenchanted Mikko. "But it's not all done and dusted yet. It's always risky to deliberately give up 20 seconds like we have."

But nothing had been left to chance, especially given that Hirvonen can be a lot more light-footed than Latvala when he has to. Putting the youngest member of his flock second and the most experienced a long way behind him, Malcolm Wilson was making sure Hirvonen had the best possible starting position next day – a clear indication of the pecking order among his drivers. "Yes, Malcolm gave Mikko preferential treatment," said Latvala, "because he's best placed to go for the drivers' title. I let my chance slip on rallies like the Monte and Argentina."

The Championship lead changed hands again as Mikko Hirvonen's Turkish win put him back in front ahead of his home rally.

08 | Turquie

Dani Sordo was a long way off the pace in the early stages but worked like hell to haul himself up to fourth, taking the place from Henning Solberg right at the death.

Mikko Hirvonen managed his rally and his equipment superbly, and followed team orders to the letter – he couldn't have shaken Loeb off in normal circumstances.

Things really didn't go well for Suzuki, with Gardemeister and Andersson both forced out by mechanical problems in the same stage. Still some work to do for Team Yellow!

The second leg went very much as expected. Loeb paid a heavy penalty for opening the road, giving up 19.2 seconds to Latvala and 41.1 to Hirvonen over the day. "And we've done well to keep it to that," he said, "because with Hirvonen fifth on the road the gap should have been about a second for every kilometre, and it's nowhere near that. I'm really pushing hard – no choice, I have to go flat out to keep the gap down. It's a bit frustrating to give it all you've got and still come up with such pathetic times, but that's the way it is. The rules are unfair, but we can't blame Ford for exploiting them. I'm 35 seconds down at the end of the day. All isn't lost yet, but it's going to be tough."

"Now it's my turn to sweep the road on the last leg, and you can't say I did much of a job of it in Sardinia or Greece," said Hirvonen anxiously. "But those 30 seconds we've got on Seb should be enough. I'm more worried about Jari-Matti!" Ford's number two was in fact just 16.2 behind his team leader and wasn't expecting team orders to come into play. "With Seb so close, we can't just control the situation," said Latvala. "We're team-mates, but we're also competitive and we both want to win. With Mikko first to go, I'll have the advantage over him, and of course Seb will be pushing like hell. And when you see what he managed to do today when he had to open the road, you can imagine what he'll do when he goes third!" True enough, the bare stats don't tell you just what a feat Loeb pulled off on day two. It takes some driver to sweep roads the way he did...

On Sunday morning, as they got ready to head off into the last three stages, Hirvonen seemed the edgiest of the three men still in the hunt. He got really hot under the collar at the Olympos start-line – he stalled the Focus. "I hadn't even gone a metre and I'd lost six seconds. I was beside myself – and yet somehow it released me. I couldn't let the rally win slip away like that, I thought, and I gave it everything I had. I drove perfectly through the rest of the stage and matched Seb and Jari-Matti." Going into the final timed section, Hirvonen still had 12.7 in hand over Latvala and 25.5 on Loeb. But within 11 kilometres – just one-third of the way through – the Frenchman had already clawed back half of that. Nervous times for Ford, hope renewed at Citroën. "If he wins this I'm going to kiss him on the mouth!" said Polo, Loeb's car crew chief, glued to the splits screen like all the other mechanics. But Polo wouldn't have the chance to taste his driver's lips, as Loeb flagged towards the end of the stage. "We went for it," said Loeb. "We went off like a rocket and we were coming back really well, but I pushed a bit too hard and the tyres gave up the ghost. We had to slow down towards the end. We tried as hard as we could, so no regrets – except about those rules!" A big, satisfied 'Yes!' from the Ford tent greeted the end of the stage as the team sealed a second 1-2 finish of the season to go with the one in Sweden.

"That was a wonderful team win," said a happy Malcolm Wilson. "It was a risky tactic – you're always playing with fire when you let 20 seconds go – but it worked beautifully and the drivers did a great job. I can't really believe we're leading both Championships at the halfway mark with two young drivers. There are three tarmac rallies in the second half of the season, so it's not going to be easy, but I'm sure Mikko and Jari-Matti have some more tricks up their sleeves."

No joy for Federico Villagra when the front-runners all make it to the finish: this time the Argentine was just outside the points.

Olivier Quesnel, meanwhile, still hadn't got over it. "Hirvonen and Latvala showed in that last leg that they could take Seb on fair and square," he complained, "and they didn't need to resort to the kind of farce we've witnessed this weekend."

Dani Sordo, on the other hand, showed he couldn't match the Ford men on gravel. The Spaniard was too cautiously away, then broke a steering arm on a rock. He was 2m 30s down on Hirvonen but snatched fourth when he got past Henning Solberg in the final stage – though he did give himself a bit of a fright with a late spin.

PRODUCTION CARS
Another one to Aigner

Is Austria's Andrea Aigner following in Mikko Hirvonen's weheel tracks? The Red Bull prospect was as anonymous with Skoda in 2006 as the Finn was at Subaru back in 2003, but he seemed to have lifted his game to a new level early in this 2008 season – Turkey was his third win in a row, and no-one had done that in the category since Araï in 2003. Baldacci, who eventually finished third, made a flying start but the fourth round of the PWRC

Got to look after the horse if you want to get far: Rautenbach avoided all the pitfalls on a difficult event to take the point for eighth place, some 3m 30s down on Matthew Wilson.

The strain of the last three days is gone as Hirvonen enjoys the podium. He had to win – and he did, getting his Championship charge back on track.

Gigi Galli, meanwhile, had thoroughly deserved that fourth place himself. The Italian ran third for quite a while with a flawless drive, until his turbo let him down around midday on Friday. Dehydrated, dizzy and sick, he retired that very evening and followed the remainder of the rally from his hospital bed. The retirement handed sixth to Petter Solberg after a very low-key event. "In the quick stuff it's OK, but when it's twisty and slow, no grip," the Norwegian explained. "But we know what the problem is so we'll get it fixed quickly." Matthew Wilson was in the points for the fourth time this year after finishing seventh, one place ahead of Rautenbach. Both Suzuki drivers retired in the same stage, SS12, with mechanical problems. Gardemeister had suffered personal damage as well, dislocating his shoulder on the first leg and putting it back like Mel Gibson in 'Lethal Weapon'. ∎

soon came down to an all-out battle between Aigner's Mitsubishi Lancer Evo IX and Sandell's Peugeot 207 Super 2000. The Swede showed he could be quick on surfaces other than gravel, too. Just nine-tenths behind the Austrian at the end of day one, the 2006 title-winner saw his chances slip away at the end of the second leg when transmission damage cost him a full minute. "I'm glad to be here because we had warning signs on the engine temperature," said a relieved Aigner. "We had a lot of trouble over the weekend, like most people, but we just didn't have as much as our rivals. Now we've got a good lead in the Championship, but Juho Hänninen has done two rallies fewer than I have, so I had to open up a gap while he wasn't here. We'll be keeping a close eye on what he does in Finland when it's our turn to skip one." ∎

08 | Turkey | Results

5th RALLY OF TURKEY

Organiser Details
Turkish Automobile Sports Federation (TOSFED),
Göksuevleri, Kartopu Caddesi No B168/A,
Anadoluhisari,
Istanbul, Turkey
Tel.: +90 (216) 465 11 55
Fax: +90 (216) 465 11 57

Rally of Turkey

8th leg of FIA 2008 World Championship for constructors and drivers.
4th leg of FIA Production Car World Championship.

Date June 12 - 15, 2008

Route
1263.74 km divised in three legs.
19 special stages on dirt roads (360.12 km)

Ceremonial Start
Thursday, June 12 (17:25), Antalya
1 super special stage
Leg 1
Friday, June 13 (08:38/17:47),
Kemer > Kemer, 569.18 km;
8 special stages (154.90 km)
Leg 2
Saturday, June 14 (09:28/19:01),
Kemer > Kemer, 463.57 km;
7 special stages (137.66 km)
Leg 3
Sunday, June 15 (09:38/13:07),
Kemer > Kemer, 230.99 km;
3 special stages (67.56 km)

Entry List (60) - 60 starters

N°	Driver (Nat.)	Co-Driver (Nat.)	Team	Car	Group & FIA Priority
1	SEBASTIEN LOEB (F)	DANIEL ELENA (MC)	CITROEN TOTAL WORLD RALLY TEAM	CITROEN C4 WRC	A8 1
2	DANI SORDO (E)	MARC MARTI (E)	CITROEN TOTAL WORLD RALLY TEAM	CITROEN C4 WRC	A8 1
3	MIKKO HIRVONEN (FIN)	JARMO LEHTINEN (FIN)	BP FORD ABU DHABI WORLD RALLY TEAM	FORD FOCUS RS WRC 07	A8 1
4	JARI MATTI LATVALA (FIN)	MIIKKA ANTTILA (FIN)	BP FORD ABU DHABI WORLD RALLY TEAM	FORD FOCUS RS WRC 07	A8 1
5	PETTER SOLBERG (N)	PHILIP MILLS (GB)	SUBARU WORLD RALLY TEAM	SUBARU IMPREZA WRC 2008	A8 1
6	CHRIS ATKINSON (AUS)	STEPHANE PREVOT (B)	SUBARU WORLD RALLY TEAM	SUBARU IMPREZA WRC 2008	A8 1
7	GIGI GALLI (I)	GIOVANNI BERNACCHINI (I)	STOBART-VK-M-SPORT FORD RALLY TEAM	FORD FOCUS RS WRC 07	A8 1
8	HENNING SOLBERG (N)	CATO MENKERUD (N)	STOBART-VK-M-SPORT FORD RALLY TEAM	FORD FOCUS RS WRC 07	A8 1
9	FEDERICO VILLAGRA (RA)	JORGE PEREZ COMPANC (RA)	MUNCHI'S FORD WORLD RALLY TEAM	FORD FOCUS RS WRC 07	A8 1
10	BARRY CLARK (GB)	PAUL NAGLE (GB)	MUNCHI'S FORD WORLD RALLY TEAM	FORD FOCUS RS WRC 07	A8 1
11	TONI GARDEMEISTER (FIN)	TOMI TUOMINEN (FIN)	SUZUKI WORLD RALLY TEAM	SUZUKI SX4 WRC	A8 1
12	PER GUNNAR ANDERSSON (S)	JONAS ANDERSSON (S)	SUZUKI WORLD RALLY TEAM	SUZUKI SX4 WRC	A8 1
14	CONRAD RAUTENBACH (ZW)	DAVID SENIOR (GB)	CONRAD RAUTENBACH	CITROEN C4 WRC	A8 2
15	ANDREAS MIKKELSEN (N)	OLA FLOENE (N)	RAMSPORT	FORD FOCUS RS WRC 06	A8 2
16	MATTHEW WILSON (GB)	SCOTT MARTIN (GB)	STOBART-VK-M-SPORT FORD RALLY TEAM	FORD FOCUS RS WRC 07	A8 2
17	URMO AAVA (EE)	KULDAR SIKK (EE)	WORLD RALLY TEAM ESTONIAN	CITROEN C4 WRC	A8 2
31	TOSHI ARAI (J)	GLEN MACNEALL (AUS)	SUBARU TEAM ARAI	SUBARU IMPREZA	N4 3
32	MIRCO BALDACCI (I)	GIOVANNI AGNESE (I)	MIRCO BALDACCI	MITSUBISHI LANCER EVO 9	N4 3
33	MARTIN PROKOP (CZ)	JAN TOMANEK (CZ)	MARTIN PROKOP	MITSUBISHI LANCER EVO 9	N4 3
34	GIANLUCA LINARI (I)	GUADAGNI LORENZO (I)	GIANLUCA LUNARI	SUBARU IMPREZA	N4 3
35	EVGENY NOVIKOV (RUS)	EVGENY KALACHEV (RUS)	EVGENY NOVIKOV	MITSUBISHI LANCER EVO 9	N4 3
36	EYVIND BRYNILDSEN (N)	DENIS GIRAUDET (F)	EYVIND BRYNILDSEN	MITSUBISHI LANCER EVO 9	N4 3
38	AMJAD FARRAH (JO)	NICOLA ARENA (I)	ORION WORLD RALLY TEAM	MITSUBISHI LANCER EVO 9	N4 3
39	NASSER AL-ATTIYAH (Q)	CHRIS PATTERSON (GB)	QMMF	SUBARU IMPREZA	N4 3
40	RICCARDO ERRANI (I)	STEFANO CASADIO (I)	ERRANI TEAM GROUP	MITSUBISHI LANCER EVO 9	N4 3
41	ANDREAS AIGNER (A)	KLAUS WICHA (D)	RED BULL RALLYE TEAM	MITSUBISHI LANCER EVO 9	N4 3
42	BERNARDO SOUSA (P)	JORGE CAVALHO (P)	RED BULL RALLYE TEAM	MITSUBISHI LANCER EVO 9	N4 3
43	EVGENIY VERTUNOV (RUS)	GEORGY TROSHKIN (RUS)	SUBARU RALLY TEAM RUSSIA	SUBARU IMPREZA	N4 3
45	FRANCESCO TREVISIN (I)	ALESSANDRO BIORDI (SM)	MOTORING CLUB 1	SUBARU IMPREZA	N4 3
47	GIORGIO BACCO (I)	SILVIO STEFANELLI (SM)	MOTORING CLUB 3	SUBARU IMPREZA	N4 3
48	EVGENY AKSAKOV (RUS)	ALEKSANDR KORNILOV (EE)	RED WINGS MOSCOW REGION RT	MITSUBISHI LANCER EVO 9	N4 3
49	SIMONE CAMPEDELLI (I)	DANILO FAPPANI (I)	SCUDERIA RUBICONE CORSE	MITSUBISHI LANCER EVO 9	N4 3
50	ARMINDO ARAUJO (I)	MIGUEL RAMALHO (I)	RALLIART ITALY	MITSUBISHI LANCER EVO 9	N4 3
53	UWE NITTEL (D)	MICHAEL WENZEL (D)	PRO RACE RALLY	MITSUBISHI LANCER EVO 9	N4 3
55	PATRIK SANDELL (S)	EMIL AXELSSON (S)	PEUGEOT SPORT SWEDEN	PEUGEOT 207 S2000	N4 3
57	MARTIN RAUAM (EE)	SILVER KUTT (EE)	WORLD RALLY TEAM ESTONIAN	MITSUBISHI LANCER EVO 9	N4 3
58	NAREN KUMAR (IND)	NICKY BEECH (GB)	TEAM SIDVIN INDIA	SUBARU IMPREZA	N4 3
64	CENEDESE MORENO (I)	CARLO PISANO (I)	CENEDESE MORENO	MITSUBISHI LANCER EVO 9	N4
65	HAMDI ÜNAL (TR)	BAHADIR GÜCENMEZ (TR)	HAMDI ÜNAL	FIAT PUNTO S1600	A6
67	ÖMER ERDEM (TR)	ERHAN AKPINAR (TR)	ÖMER ERDEM	MITSUBISHI LANCER EVO 8	N4
68	ÖZEN ÖZER (TR)	ONUR VATANSEVER (TR)	ÖZEN ÖZER	OPEL CORSA S1600	A6
70	EMRE YURDAKUL (TR)	CAN ERKAL (TR)	CASTROL FORD TEAM TÜRKIYE	FORD FIESTA ST	N3
71	MUSTAFA SÖYLEMEZ (TR)	BORA ARABACI (TR)	MUSTAFA SÖYLEMEZ	MITSUBISHI LANCER EVO 9	N4
72	VYTAUTAS BARANAUSKAS (LT)	GEDIMINAS CELIESUS (LT)	VYTAUTAS BARANAUSKAS	FORD FIESTA ST	N3
73	ADIL KÜÇÜKSARI (TR)	FERDI OZCANAN (TR)	ADIL KÜÇÜKSARI	FORD FIESTA ST	A7
74	KORAY MURATOGLU (TR)	LEVENT ÖZOKUTUCU (TR)	CASTROL FORD TEAM TÜRKIYE	FORD FIESTA ST	N3
75	TARIK ÖKTEM (TR)	AHMET YORUK (TR)	TARIK ÖKTEM	FORD FIESTA ST	N3
76	BURCU ÇETINKAYA (TR)	ÇIÇEK GÜNEY (TR)	CASTROL FORD TEAM TÜRKIYE	FORD FIESTA ST	N3
77	DENIS GRODETSKIY (RUS)	SAFONIY LOTKO (RUS)	CUEKS RACING	FORD FIESTA ST	N3
78	JOACHIM MULLER WENDE (D)	RICHARD WARDLE (GB)	JOACHIM MULLER WENDE	FORD FIESTA ST	N3
79	BERKAY SAVKAY (TR)	TOLGA SANSAL (TR)	BERKAY SAVKAY	FORD FIESTA ST	N3
80	BERNA AKSOY (TR)	BELMA ÇELIK (TR)	BERNA AKSOY	FORD FIESTA ST	N3
83	ZOHREH VATANKHAH (IR)	FATIMA AHMADI (IR)	ZOHREH VATANKHAH	FORD FIESTA ST	A7
84	MENDERES OKUR (TR)	NEHIR YILMAZ (TR)	MENDERES OKUR	FORD FIESTA ST	N3
85	ÜNAL SENBAHAR (TR)	FATIH YALÇINKAYA (TR)	ÜNAL SENBAHAR	FORD FIESTA ST	N3
86	MURAT BOSTANCI (TR)	AFSIN BAYDAR (TR)	MURAT BOSTANCI	FORD KA KIT CAR	A5
87	MITHAT DIKER (TR)	ERDAL ORAL (TR)	DELTA SPORT	FIAT PALIO	N2
92	SELAY KAYA (TR)	DILEK EYLI (TR)	SELAY KAYA	FORD FIESTA ST	N3
94	SÜLEYMAN DERICI (TR)	YÜCEL GOÇMEN (TR)	SÜLEYMAN DERICI	FIAT PALIO	N2
95	ALI ONKÖK (TR)	GÖKHAN SERIM (TR)	DELTA SPORT	FIAT PALIO	N2

Championship Classifications

•R•: Rookie

FIA Drivers (8/15)

1. Hirvonen 2🏆 59
2. Loeb 5🏆 56
3. Latvala 1🏆 34
4. Atkinson 31
5. Sordo 30
6. P. Solberg 20
7. Galli 17
8. H. Solberg 16
9. Wilson 12
10. Villagra 8
11. Rautenbach 6
12. Aava 6
13. Duval 5
14. Mikkelsen 4
15. Gardemeister 2
16. Cuoq 2
17. Andersson 1
18. Aigner 1
19. Ogier 1
20. Hänninen 1
21. Østberg, 0
    K. Al-Qassimi, 0
    Beltrán, Mölder, 0
    Ketomaa, Clark, 0
    Kosciuszko, Sandell, 0
    Nutahara, Prokop, 0
    Burkart, Rauam, 0
    Gallagher, Broccoli, 0
    Farrah, Schammel, 0
    Nittel, Baldacci, 0
    Artru, Guerra, Arai, 0
    A. Al-Qassimi, 0
    Mercier 0

FIA Constructors (8/15)

1. BP-Ford Abu Dhabi World Rally Team 3🏆 99
2. Citroën Total World Rally Team 5🏆 90
3. Subaru World Rally Team 53
4. Stobart VK M-Sport Ford Rally Team 41
5. Munchi's Ford World Rally Team 19
6. Suzuki World Rally Team 10

FIA Production Car WRC (4/8)

1. Aigner 3🏆 30
2. Ketomaa 14
3. Sandell 14
4. Hänninen 1🏆 12
5. Araujo 12
6. Sousa 10
7. Nutahara 10
8. Rauam 9
9. Beltrán 8
10. Prokop 7
11. M. Baldacci 6
12. Vertunov 6
13. Aksakov 4
14. Nittel 4
15. Farrah 3
16. Arai 3
17. Campedelli 2
18. Bacco 1
19. L. Baldacci 1
20. Linari 0
21. Aksa 0
22. Al-Attiyah 0
23. Mayer 0
24. Kumar 0
25. Tiippaana 0
26. Pavlides 0
27. Frisiero 0
28. Athanassoulas 0
29. Errani 0
30. Pastrana 0
31. Jereb 0
32. Brynildsen 0
33. Novikov 0
34. Flodin 0
35. Marrini 0

FIA Junior WRC (3/7)

1. Ogier 2🏆 24
2. Kosciusko 1🏆 16
3. Gallagher 16
4. Burkart 11
5. Mölder 8
6. Bettega 8
7. Albertini 7
8. Schammel 6
9. Sandell 6
10. Niegel 5
11. Bertolotti 3
12. Prokop 2
13. Cortinovis 2
14. Fanari •R• 1
15. Komljenovic 1
16. Weijs Jr. •R• 1

Special Stages Times

www.wrcturkey.com
www.wrc.com

SS1 Antalya SSS 1 (2.60 km)
1.Loeb 2'07"6; 2.P.Solberg +0"7; 3.Hirvonen +1"1; 4.Latvala +2"2; 5.Sordo +2"9; 6.Atkinson +3"7; 7.P.Solberg +4"0; 8.Villagra +4"0...
P-WRC > 12.Baldacci 2'13"0

SS2 Perge 1 (22.43 km)
1.Aava 16'03"6; 2.Galli +1"6; 3.Mikkelsen +2"2; 4.Hirvonen +2"3; 5.Sordo +6"9; 6.Andersson +8"; 7.H.Solberg +10"6; 8.Wilson +10"9...
P-WRC > 16.Aigner 16'56"7

SS3 Myra 1 (24.15 km)
1.Latvala 21'05"3; 2.Sordo +15"2; 3.Galli +16"7; 4.H.Solberg +17"6; 5.Hirvonen +18"8; 6.Loeb +1925; 7.Wilson +27"4; 8.P.Solberg +34"1...
P-WRC > 16.Nittel 22'26"9

SS4 Kumluca 1 (9.90 km)
1.Galli 7'47"4; 2.Latvala +0"9; 3.H.Solberg +1"0; 4.Loeb +3"0; 5.Atkinson +3"5; 6.Hirvonen +3"5; 7.P.Solberg +3"8; 8.Andersson +5"3...
P-WRC > 16.Nittel 8'11"5

SS5 Perge 2 (22.43 km)
1.Galli 15'42"8; 2.Latvala +0"9; 3.Hirvonen +1"7; 4.H.Solberg +1"9; 5.Sordo +4"4; 6.Loeb +5"6; 7.P.Solberg +7"1; 8.Atkinson +10"4...
P-WRC > 16.Aigner 16'46"5

SS6 Myra 2 (24.15 km)
1.Latvala 20'46"0; 2.Hirvonen +10"4; 3.Loeb +11"2; 4.Sordo +11"7; 5.Galli +15"0; 6.Andersson +23"3; 7.P.Solberg +28"1; 8.H.Solberg +31"0...
P-WRC > 15.Sandell 22'10"9

SS7 Kumluca 2 (9.90 km)
1.Loeb 7'38"9; 2.Hirvonen +1"3; 3.Galli +5"5; 4.H.Solberg +6"7; 5.P.Solberg +12"0; 6.Wilson +12"8; 7.Villagra +13"5; 8.Gardemeister +14"0...
P-WRC > 11.Aigner 8'09"2

SS8 Chimera 1 (16.94 km)
1.Galli 12'21"5; 2.H.Solberg +0"1; 3.Latvala +2"4; 4.Andersson +8"9; 5.Hirvonen +9"7; 6.P.Solberg +10"0; 7.Loeb +11"3; 8.Sordo +15"6...
P-WRC > 14.Aigner 13'16"0

SS9 Phaselis 1 (22.40 km)
1.H.Solberg 17'49"3; 2.Sordo +4"2; 3.Wilson +6"8; 4.Loeb +8"8; 5.Gardemeister +10"7; 6.P.Solberg +14"6; 7.Mikkelsen +17"3; 8.Rautenbach +19"5...
P-WRC > 14.Nittel 18'44"4

Classification Leg 1
1.Loeb 2h02'35"2; 2.H.Solberg +1"0; 3.Latvala +1"1; 4.Galli +2"2; 5.Hirvonen +6"8; 6.P.Solberg +49"1; 7.Wilson +1'05"9; 8.Sordo +1'06"8...
P-WRC > 14.Aigner 2h09'49"9

SS10 Chimera 2 (16.94 km)
1.Hirvonen 11'57"3; 2.Latvala +2"9; 3.Loeb +3"9; 4.Galli +4"2; 5.Sordo +6"1; 6.P.Solberg +14"0; 7.Mikkelsen +17"7; 8.Aava +19"7...
P-WRC > 17.Aigner 13'01"4

SS11 Silyon 1 (27.36 km)
1.Hirvonen 21'53"5; 2.Galli +5"6; 3.Latvala +5"7; 4.Aava +9"3; 5.Loeb +16"6; 6.Atkinson +22"5; 7.Mikkelsen +23"8; 8.H.Solberg +37"3...
P-WRC > 15.Al-Attiyah 23'30"2

SS12 Kemer 1 (20.50 km)
1.Aava 15'06"9; 2.Atkinson +0"9; 3.Hirvonen +3"5; 4.Sordo +4"9; 5.Loeb +8"8; 6.P.Solberg +8"8; 7.Latvala +9"2; 8.Wilson +12"3...
P-WRC > 15.Nittel 16'10"0

SS13 Silyon 2 (27.36 km)
1.Hirvonen 21'36"8; 2.Latvala +3"5; 3.Sordo 10"1; 4.Loeb +15"8; 5.Atkinson +16"7; 6.H.Solberg +17"3; 7.P.Solberg +20"7; 8.Wilson +35"8...
P-WRC > 14.Al-Attiyah 23'10"9

SS14 Kemer 2 (20.50 km)
1.Latvala 14'49"4; 2.Hirvonen +0"6; 3.Sordo +1"3; 4.Loeb +2"3; 5.Aava +229; 6.P.Solberg +7"5; 7.Wilson +15"1; 8.H.Solberg +15"1...
P-WRC > 14.Baldacci 15'53"3

SS15 Phaselis 2 (22.40 km)
1.Loeb 17'19"2; 2.Hirvonen +0"0; 3.Latvala +3"9; 4.Sordo +10"2; 5.Aava +19"1; 6.P.Solberg +26"6; 7.Rautenbach +28"2; 8.H.Solberg +28"8...
P-WRC > 14.Baldacci 1'14"8

SS16 Antalya SSS 2 (2.60 km)
1.Loeb 2'06"3; 2.H.Solberg +1"5; 3.Hirvonen +2"2; 4.P.Solberg +2"8; 5.Galli +3"0; 6.Latvala +3"0; 7.Sordo +3"5; 8.Aava +4"9...
P-WRC > 14.Baldacci 2'15"8

Classification Leg 2
1.Hirvonen 3h47'37"7; 2.Latvala +16"2; 3.Loeb +34"3; 4.H.Solberg +2'08"5; 5.Sordo +2'15"1; 6.P.Solberg +2'33"7; 7.Wilson +3'41"2; 8.Galli +5'40"1...
P-WRC > 12.Aigner 4h03'16"8

SS17 Olympos 1 (31.03 km)
1.Aava 25'07"5; 2.Mikkelson +3"9; 3.Sordo +5"8; 4.Latvala +7"4; 5.Loeb +8"2; 6.P.Solberg +14"8; 7.Hirvonen +16"1; 8.H.Solberg +14"8...
P-WRC > 13.Campedelli 26'28"0

SS18 Çamyuva 1 (5.50 km)
1.Loeb 4'11"2; 2.Hirvonen +0"9; 3.Aktinson +3"9; 4.Latvala +6"9; 5.Mikkelsen +6"8; 6.Aava +7"9; 7.H.Solberg +9"4; 8.Sordo +10"4...
P-WRC > 14.Campedelli 4'38"8

SS19 Olympos 2 (31.03 km)
1.Latvala 24'48"9; 2.Hirvonen 4"8; 3.Loeb +5"0; 4.P.Solberg +10"9; 5.Atkinson +14"9; 6.Sordo +16"1; 7.H.Solberg +17"1; 8.Wilson +19"1...
P-WRC > 12.Campedelli 26'18"8

Results 🇹🇷

	Driver - Co-Driver	Car	Gr.	Time
1.	Hirvonen - Lehtinen	Ford Focus WRC 07	A8	4h42'07"1
2.	Latvala - Antilla	Ford Focus RS WRC 07	A8	+7"9
3.	Loeb - Elena	Citroën C4 WRC 08	A8	+25"7
4.	Sordo - Marti	Citroën C4 WRC 08	A8	+2'25"6
5.	H.Solberg - Menkerud	Ford Focus WRC 07	A8	+2'33"7
6.	P.Solberg - Mills	Subaru Impreza WRC 07	A8	+2'48"2
7.	Wilson - Orr	Ford Focus WRC 06	A8	+4'24"2
8.	Rautenbach - Senior	Citroën C4 WRC 08	A8	+7'46"7
9.	Villagra - Perez Companc	Ford Focus RS WRC 07	A8	+9'34"1
10.	Clark - Nagle	Ford Focus RS WRC 07	A8	+14'48"8
11.	**Aigner - Wicha**	**Mitsubishi Lancer Evo IX**	**N4/P**	**+20'14"5**
12.	Sandell - Axelsson	Peugeot 207 S2000	N4/P	+21'03"2
14.	Baldacci - Agnese	Mitsubishi Lancer Evo IX	N4/P	+23'15"5

Leading Retirements (22)

Ctrl19C	Aava - Sikk	Citroën C4 WRC	Puncture
Ctrl16D	Arai - McNeall	Subaru Impreza WRX Sti	Engine
Ctrl16D	Galli - Bernacchini	Ford Focus WRC 07	Driver ill
Ctrl15	Gardemeister - Tuominen	Suzuki SX4 WRC	Radiator and Engine
Ctrl15	Andersson - Andersson	Suzuki SX4 WRC	Electrical
Ctrl11A	Prokop - Tomanek	Mitsubishi Lancer Evo IX	Excluded

Performers

	1	2	3	4	5	6	C6	NbSS
Hirvonen	5	5	3	1	2	-	16	19
Loeb	5	-	4	4	2	2	17	19
Latvala	3	6	3	3	-	1	16	19
Galli	3	2	2	2	2	-	11	19
Aava	2	-	-	1	2	1	6	19
H.Solberg	1	2	1	3	2	1	10	19
Sordo	-	1	4	2	4	1	12	19
Mikkelsen	-	1	1	-	1	-	3	19
P.Solberg	-	1	-	2	1	7	11	19
Atkinson	-	-	1	-	2	3	6	19
Wilson	-	-	1	-	-	1	2	19
Andersson	-	-	-	1	-	2	3	11
Gardemeister	-	-	-	-	1	-	1	11

Leaders

SS1	Loeb
SS2 > SS5	Hirvonen
SS6	Latvala
SS7 > SS8	Hirvonen
SS9 > SS10	Loeb
SS11 > SS19	Hirvonen

Andreas Aigner

Previous Winners

2003	Sainz - Marti Citroën Xsara WRC	2005	Loeb - Elena Citroën Xsara WRC
2004	Loeb - Elena Citroën Xsara WRC	2006	Grönholm - Rautiainen Ford Focus RS WRC 06

09 FINLAND

Another coup for Loeb
This time there was nothing the Finns could do about it. Since Marcus Grönholm's retirement, not one of them can match Sébastien Loeb. The French ace added another great achievement to his record, winning on Finnish soil – something only Carlos Sainz and Didier Auriol among the non-Nordic drivers had ever done before.

09 | Finland

For all his fire, Mikko Hirvonen will always be the known as the Finn who threw in the towel against Sébastien Loeb on his home ground. He needs to get his revenge – and fast!

Rallying is Finland's national sport and there are always huge numbers of fans and connoisseurs – all there to cheer on every one the drivers, Dani Sordo included.

Henning Solberg briefly occupied third place but dropped back as the rally went on, eventually finishing fifth ahead of brother Petter.

THE RALLY
Finns left floundering in Frenchman's wake

Well, it wasn't one of those races where, if you get lucky and everyone else falls off, you can knock off a win without really trying. Nor was it an easy victory: just nine seconds separated Sébastien Loeb and Mikko Hirvonen after three days and 340 stage kilometres. That was the second-narrowest winning margin in the history of this famous rally, beaten only back in 1997 when Tommi Mäkinen finished seven seconds ahead of Juha Kankkunen. No, this was a high-class rally, full of suspense, the outcome always in doubt even though the World Champion did lead from start to finish, from the first to the 24th and last special stage.

Coming away from the 58th Rally of Finland with the winners' trophy in their hands was a significant achievement by Loeb and Daniel Elena in the context of the sport. They are, in fact, only the third non-Nordic crew to win the event other than Carlos Sainz's in 1990 and Didier Auriol's in 1992. Theirs may even be the slightly superior performance, given that recces were much less restricted back then than they are nowadays. So the drivers of the day had much more time for learning the route, and they were able to get that much more out of it. Which meant they could, to a degree, overcome the difference in local knowledge between North and South – only to a degree, though, because it still took some doing to beat the Norsemen on their own terrain!

So it was a beaming World Champion who greeted the finish of the ninth round in the 2008 season. "I'm really thrilled with this win," said Loeb. "And especially the way we won it. Through the three legs, it was as intense as the battles I used to have with Marcus Grönholm last year. It was full-on, we couldn't relax for a moment." Daniel Elena agreed: beating the Finns in their own backyard was something to relish. "For me, this is a dream come true. Reading the notes out isn't any different from any other event but in the C4 you have to churn them out that bit faster. And what a feeling it is on tracks like these when you go into a four-wheel drift at 200 km/h!"

No strangers to winning and setting new records, the Franco-Monegasque pairing duly chalked up victory number 42 together. The only thing missing from their CV now is the Rally of Great Britain, and if they add that they will be the first men ever to win every World Championship round at least once.

It was also a first for the Chevron, one that helped Loeb narrow the gap to Hirvonen by another two points, the Finn now just one tiny point ahead of his French nemesis. It was also a great weekend's work for Citroën in terms of the constructors' standings: with Loeb first and Sordo fourth they scored 15 points, six more than Ford, who had been counting on their Finnish duo to show the French the way home. No wonder Reds boss Olivier Quesnel was such a happy man. "Today the enormous amount of work the tech team have put into the C4 since last year has really paid off," he said. "Our car worked amazingly well here. It was a good result for the Constructors' Championship, and very encouraging for the rest of the season. A wonderful win, excellent efforts by the drivers, fantastic reliability, lots of points: this was a perfect weekend for Citroën..."
What more could you ask for?

It was a bitter pill for Ford to swallow. "This wasn't the result (nine points, eight of them to Hirvonen) we were looking for. Mikko had not only to think about winning the rally but also about not compromising his Championship chances. He put in a superb effort and he also learned a lot from his three-day fight with Loeb. He will be all the stronger for it. In the end they were both half a kilometre quicker than everybody else, and I think Mikko drove even better than he did last year, which is really saying something. On the other hand, losing Jari-Matti so early in the piece didn't help."

Jari-Matti as in Latvala, of course: the promising but inconsistent Finn made another one of his trademark howlers. In SS3 (Mokkipera 1), a hot head and sheer lack of experience caught him out. A young man's mistake, maybe – but maybe one too many as well. "I was going into a left-right-left section over some jumps and I decided to keep the car as straight as I could, but I hit a rock – one that wasn't in my notes – with the front right of the car. The steering felt very funny after the impact and I was pitched off the road and half-rolled into a ditch. The data showed I was doing 117 when I went off." Happily neither he nor his co-driver was injured, but the impact broke the right steering arm and scuppered their chances of finishing on the podium. That was the primary objective, maybe even the win, as the master of all things Rally of Finland himself, Marcus Grönholm, had suggested. Blue Oval boss Malcolm Wilson was, naturally, not happy with his headstrong Finn. "I'm very disappointed with Jari-Matti," he grumbled. "Not including that rock in his notes was a fundamental mistake, and it puts even more pressure on Mikko after the sensational job he did today."

Latvala did restart in SupeRally next day but it was a big thorn out of Loeb and Elena's side, easing the tension and pressure on them.

As Wilson had pointed out, Hirvonen tried manfully to take up the gauntlet. The man from Jyvaskala, who had his 28th birthday on the Thursday of the first evening special, did his damnedest to keep Loeb in his sights. "It's so close between us that I'm not keen to take any silly risks," said the Ford number one after the first leg. "This fight is almost as intense as the one with Marcus last year."

The two front-runners played cat and mouse throughout the rally, the Frenchman never relaxing his grip on the lead. The World Champion took full advantage of his starting position to give himself a bit of a margin from the opening leg. On the Friday, in fact, a long day with

Ogier the learner consults maestro Loeb. Handling, set-up, how to get over the infamous bumps: the youngster knows the older man will give him good advice.

Petter Solberg was never comfortable on the event, complaining endlessly about his Subaru's handling.

09 | Finland

Toni Gardemeister hoisted his Suzuki into eighth place in his own backyard.

Isn't rallying a beautiful thing? Magnificent scenery, summer in the countryside, a fantastic show – and a champion without equal. Sébastien Loeb slides gracefully to one of the best wins of his prolific career.

10 special stages scheduled, he clean-sheeted no fewer than nine times and came back to Jyvaskyla 14.4s clear of Hirvonen. Mikko was able to have more of a go in the two closing legs but ended up knocking just 5.4 seconds off the gap. It was quite a duel, the French driver always just ahead but never able to ease up for a second. And when they got to the finish, Hirvonen couldn't hide his disappointment: "I'm happy with the way I drove," he said, "but I came here to win in front of my home fans and Loeb has found a few seconds on me. We went at it all weekend and if I won a stage, then usually he won the next one. And here we are with just those nine little seconds between us at the finish. The pace was unbelievable. There were places where we might as well have chucked our notes out, we seemed to be going so much faster. It's taught me that I need to up the pace in my notes. I think what cost me time was not being brave enough through the narrow sections. Still, I'm delighted to be still in the Championship lead, though a point is nothing, really."

Behind that wonderful scrap, third place on the podium went to Chris Atkinson – an incredible 3m 17s behind the winner. But the Australian had done well to keep the Impreza on track in the early stages when it was at its least sure-footed. The changes they made meant he could go faster after that. In contrast, Subaru number one Petter Solberg's sixth place in an Impreza as ill-handling as Atkinson's was a pretty low-key effort. A convincing fourth showed Dani Sordo was making progress and getting to grips with it all, much to Citroën's satisfaction.

If there were some flops (Galli, Aava, Villagra, Perez-Companc. P.G. Andersson all had offs), there were also some top efforts, especially from some of the promising youngsters such as Finland's Matti Rantanen, who finished seventh first time at the wheel of a WRC in earnest, and Norway's Andrea Mikkelsen. Just 19 and being schooled by Marcus Grönholm, he put up some very interesting times and clearly has what it takes.

The Finnish event was also a round of the PWRC, and two sharp young Finns gave us another head-to-head on this hallowed rallying ground. Juha Salo was the early leader but went off in the second leg, leaving Juho Hänninen to come home first once his biggest threat, Jari Ketooma, slipped up. It was a handy win for Hanninen in Championship terms, bringing him to within eight points of Austria's Aigner, who was also guilty of a costly mistake. ■

JUNIORS
Prokop – just

By a quirk of the 2008 calendar the Rally of Finland embraced not only the Junior Championship but also the PWRC. Though they are both entered in this season's PWRC, Patrik Sandell and Martin Prokop

Age doesn't count for anything in Finland: kids are initiated into the religion of motor sport from their earliest days.

Matti Rantanen may have come late to rallying – he's 27 – but he's still a hot prospect. First time out in a WRC, he finished seventh.

decided to try their hand among the Juniors this time. Good thinking, with Championship leader Sébastien Ogier not involved. The Frenchman was on the event in his Citroën C2 R2 but not counting it towards the Championship. He was there to get the hang of the Rally of Finland, which is such a one-off, for future years. He came out of it pretty well, too, setting some good times on his way to 36th place. Prokop in his Citroën C2 S1600 took his first win of the season after an excellent dice with the Suzuki Swift of Polish driver Kosciuszko, who made life easier for him in the closing stages by going off in SS20. The slip-up let Sandell through into second place although his Renault Clio R3 had never been able to match the two other youngsters. "It was vital to win here," said Prokop, "because I haven't had much chance since the season began – and I had a big off in 2007. We didn't make any mistakes and it was a brilliant fight with Kosciuszko." Now just two points behind Ogier, Prokop had given his Championship chances a real boost. ■

Chris Atkinson's podium, his first in the latest-generation Impreza WRC, was a fine effort.

It takes more than a camera flash in his rear mirror to light up Matthew Wilson. Once again he was completely anonymous.

09 | Finland | Results

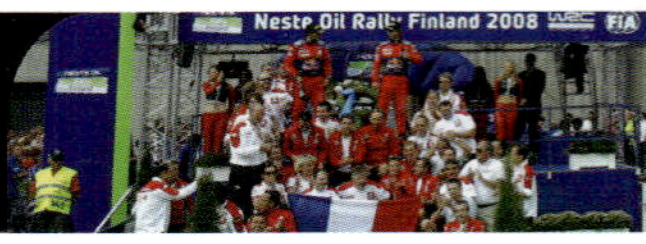

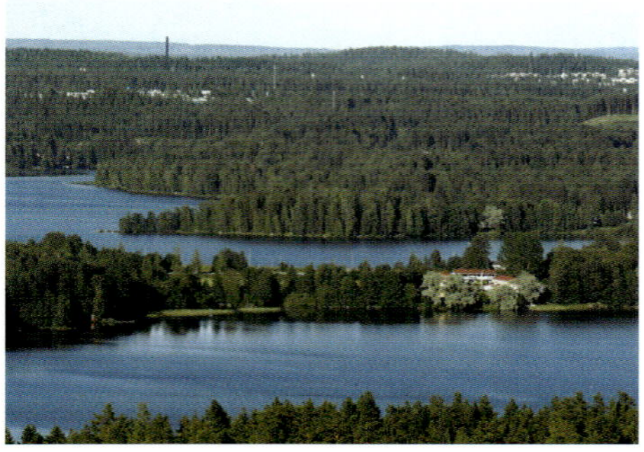

58th RALLY OF FINLAND

Organiser Details
AKK Sports Ltd,
Box 54, FIN-00551 Helsinki,
Finland
Tel.: +3589 725 822 39
Fax: +3589 725 822 40

Neste Oil Rally Finland

9th leg of FIA 2008 World Championship for constructors and drivers.
4th leg of FIA WRC Junior Championship.
5th leg of FIA Production Car World Championship.

Date July 31 juillet - August 3, 2008

Route
1466.68 km divised in three legs.
24 special stages on dirt roads (342.08 km)

Ceremonial Start
Thursday, July 31 (19:25),
Jyväskylä Paviljonki
1 super special stage (2.06 km)

Leg 1
Friday, August 1st (07:40/20:05),
Jyväskylä > Jyväskylä, 595.01 km;
11 special stages (130.69 km)

Leg 2
Saturday, August 2 (07:13/17:56),
Jyväskylä > Jyväskylä, 662.23 km;
10 special stages (169.95 km)

Leg 3
Sunday, August 3 (09:58/12:12),
Jyväskylä > Jyväskylä, 209.44 km;
3 special stages (41.44 km)

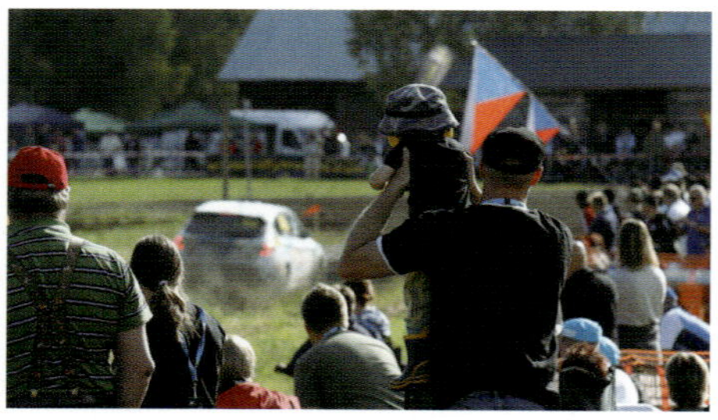

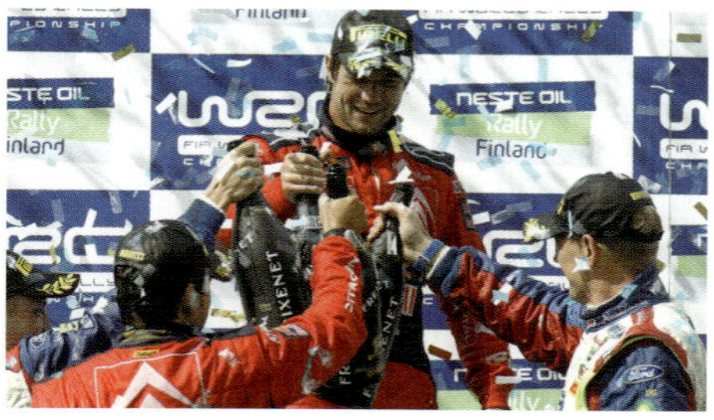

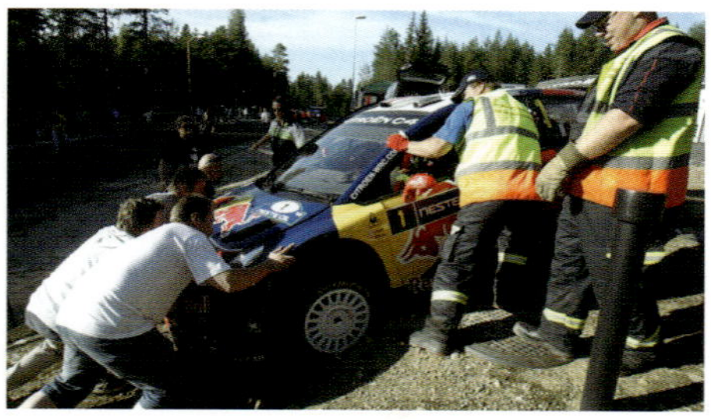

Entry List (109) - 99 starters

N°	Driver (Nat.)	Co-Driver (Nat.)	Team	Car	Group & FIA Priority
1	SÉBASTIEN LOEB (F)	DANIEL ELENA (MC)	CITROËN TOTAL WORLD RALLY TEAM	CITROËN C4 WRC	A8 1
2	DANI SORDO (E)	MARC MARTI (E)	CITROËN TOTAL WORLD RALLY TEAM	CITROËN C4 WRC	A8 1
3	MIKKO HIRVONEN (FIN)	JARMO LEHTINEN (FIN)	BP FORD ABU DHABI WORLD RALLY TEAM	FORD FOCUS RS WRC 07	A8 1
4	JARI-MATTI LATVALA (FIN)	MIIKKA ANTTILA (FIN)	BP FORD ABU DHABI WORLD RALLY TEAM	FORD FOCUS RS WRC 07	A8 1
5	PETTER SOLBERG (N)	PHILIP MILLS (GB)	SUBARU WORLD RALLY TEAM	SUBARU IMPREZA WRC 2008	A8 1
6	CHRIS ATKINSON (AUS)	STEPHANE PREVOT (B)	SUBARU WORLD RALLY TEAM	SUBARU IMPREZA WRC 2008	A8 1
7	GIGI GALLI (I)	GIOVANNI BERNACCHINI (I)	STOBART VK M-SPORT FORD RALLY TEAM	FORD FOCUS RS WRC 07	A8 1
8	HENNING SOLBERG (N)	CATO MENKERUD (N)	STOBART VK M-SPORT FORD RALLY TEAM	FORD FOCUS RS WRC 07	A8 1
9	FEDERICO VILLAGRA (ARG)	JORGE PEREZ COMPANC (ARG)	MUNCHI'S FORD WORLD RALLY TEAM	FORD FOCUS RS WRC 07	A8 1
10	LUIS PEREZ COMPANC (ARG)	JOSE MARIA VOLTA (ARG)	MUNCHI'S FORD WORLD RALLY TEAM	FORD FOCUS RS WRC 07	A8 1
11	TONI GARDEMEISTER (FIN)	TOMI TUOMINEN (FIN)	SUZUKI WORLD RALLY TEAM	SUZUKI SX4 WRC	A8 1
12	PER-GUNNAR ANDERSSON (S)	JONAS ANDERSSON (S)	SUZUKI WORLD RALLY TEAM	SUZUKI SX4 WRC	A8 1
14	CONRAD RAUTENBACH (ZWE)	DAVID SENIOR (GB)	CONRAD RAUTENBACH	CITROËN C4 WRC	A8 2
15	URMO AAVA (EE)	KULDAR SIKK (EE)	WORLD RALLY TEAM ESTONIA	CITROËN C4 WRC	A8 2
16	MATTHEW WILSON (GB)	SCOTT MARTIN (GB)	STOBART VK M-SPORT FORD RALLY TEAM	FORD FOCUS RS WRC 07	A8 2
17	MADS ÖSTBERG (N)	OLE KRISTIAN UNNERUD (N)	ADAPTA AS	SUBARU IMPREZA WRC	A8 2
18	KHALID AL QASSIMI (UAE)	MICHAEL ORR (GB)	BP FORD ABU DHABI WORLD RALLY TEAM	FORD FOCUS RS WRC 07	A8 2
19	ANDREAS MIKKELSEN (N)	OLA FLOENE (N)	RAMSPORT	FORD FOCUS RS WRC 06	A8 2
20	MATTI RANTANEN (FIN)	JAN LÖNEGREN (FIN)	MATTI RANTANEN	FORD FOCUS RS WRC 06	A8 2
31	MARTIN PROKOP (CZE)	JAN TOMÁNEK (CZE)	MARTIN PROKOP	CITROËN C2 S1600	A6 3
32	JAAN MÖLDER (EE)	FREDRIC MICLOTTE (B)	JAAN MÖLDER	SUZUKI SWIFT S1600	A6 3
33	AARON NIKOLAI BURKART (D)	MICHAEL KOELBACH (D)	AARON NIKOLAI BURKART	CITROËN C2 S1600	A6 3
35	MICHAL KOSCIUSZKO (PL)	MACIEK SZCZEPANIAK (PL)	MICHAL KOSCIUSZKO	SUZUKI SWIFT S1600	A6 3
37	SIMONE BERTOLOTTI (I)	DANIELE VERNUCCIO (I)	SIMONE BERTOLOTTI	RENAULT CLIO R3	A7 3
38	FRANSESCO FANARI (I)	DANIELE BENEDETTI (I)	FRANSESCO FANARI	CITROËN C2 R2	A6 3
39	STEFANO ALBERTINI (I)	PIERCARLO CAPOLONGO (I)	STEFANO ALBERTINI	RENAULT CLIO R3	A7 3
40	MILOS KOMLJENOVIC (SRB)	ALEKSANDER JEREMIC (SRB)	INTERSPEED RACING TEAM	RENAULT CLIO R3	A7 3
41	PATRIK SANDELL (S)	EMIL AXELSSON (S)	INTERSPEED RACING TEAM	RENAULT CLIO S1600	A6 3
43	FLORIAN NIEGEL (D)	ANDRÉ KAHEL (D)	SUZUKI RALLYE JUNIOR TEAM GERMANY	SUZUKI SWIFT SPORT	N2 3
44	HANS WEIJS JR. (NL)	HANS VAN GOOR (NL)	KNAF TALENT FIRST TEAM HOLLAND	CITROËN C2 R2	A6 3
45	KEVIN ABBRING (NL)	ERWIN MOMBAERTS (B)	KNAF TALENT FIRST TEAM HOLLAND	RENAULT CLIO R3	A7 3
46	SHAUN GALLAGHER (IRL)	PAUL KIELY (IRL)	WORLD RALLY TEAM IRELAND	CITROËN C2 S1600	A6 3
47	GILLES SCHAMMEL (L)	RENAUD JAMOUL (B)	JPS JUNIOR TEAM LUXEMBURG	RENAULT CLIO R3	A7 3
48	ALESSANDRO BETTEGA (I)	SIMONE SCATTOLIN (I)	TRT SRL	RENAULT CLIO R3	A7 3
59	KALLE PINOMÄKI (FIN)	MATTI KASKINEN (FIN)	KALLE PINOMÄKI	SUZUKI SWIFT S1600	A6 3
61	ANDREAS AIGNER (A)	KLAUS WICHA (D)	ANDREAS AIGNER	MITSUBISHI LANCER EVOLUTION 9	N4
63	JOUNI AROLAINEN (FIN)	RISTO PIETILÄINEN (FIN)	CLO RACING	FORD FOCUS RS WRC 05	A8
64	JUHA SIPILÄ (FIN)	JUHA LUMMAA (FIN)	JUHA SIPILÄ	MITSUBISHI LANCER EVOLUTION 9	N4
66	KARRI MARTTILA (FIN)	ARI HAIPUS (FIN)	KARRI MARTTILA	SUBARU IMPREZA WRX STI	N4
69	GUY WILKS (GB)	DAVID MOYNIHAN (IRL)	JAS MOTORSPORT	HONDA CIVIC TYPE-R R3	A7
70	SEBASTIÉN OGIER (F)	JULIEN INGRASSIA (F)	SEBASTIÉN OGIER	CITROËN C2 R2	A6
71	LAURI RIIPINEN (FIN)	MIKKO JOKINEN (FIN)	LAURI RIIPINEN	SUBARU IMPREZA WRX STI	N4
72	JUKKA HARA (FIN)	PETTERI LUOSTARINEN (FIN)	JUKKA HARA	SUBARU IMPREZA 555	A8
73	PETRI LEHTOVIRTA (FIN)	JUHA KANERVA (FIN)	PETRI LEHTOVIRTA	SUBARU IMPREZA WRX STI	A8
74	VILLE SILVASTI (FIN)	JARI SCHUURMAN (FIN)	VILLE SILVASTI	SUBARU IMPREZA WRX STI	N4
75	MARCO TEMPESTINI (I)	DORIN PULPEA (RO)	MARCO TEMPESTINI	SUBARU IMPREZA WRX STI	N4
76	JUKKA METSÄLÄ (FIN)	SARI OHRA-AHO (FIN)	JUKKA METSÄLÄ	SKODA OCTAVIA WRC	A8
77	RADIK SHAYMIEV (RUS)	TIMUR KAFAROV (RUS)	RADIK SHAYMIEV	PEUGEOT 207 S2000	N4
78	ERKKI KAIKKONEN (FIN)	TAKAYO HAYASI (FIN)	ERKKI KAIKKONEN	SUBARU IMPREZA WRX STI	N4
79	ANDIS NEIKSANS (LV)	PETERIS DZIRKALS (LV)	ANDIS NEIKSANS	MITSUBISHI LANCER EVOLUTION 9	N4
80	VYTAUTAS SVEDAS (LT)	ZILVINAS SAKALAUSKAS (LT)	VYTAUTAS SVEDAS	MITSUBISHI LANCER EVOLUTION 9	N4
81	ANSSI MUSTONEN (FIN)	KARI KALLIO (FIN)	ANSSI MUSTONEN	MITSUBISHI LANCER EVOLUTION 6	A8
82	JUKKA KIHLMAN (FIN)	HARRI KIHLMAN (FIN)	JUKKA KIHLMAN	MITSUBISHI LANCER EVOLUTION 8	A8
83	JARMO KOMSI (FIN)	TIMO HANTUNEN (FIN)	JARMO KOMSI	MITSUBISHI LANCER EVOLUTION 9	N4
84	PEKKA SAVELA (FIN)	JARI KIHLMAN (FIN)	PEKKA SAVELA	MITSUBISHI LANCER EVOLUTION 9	N4
85	DANIEL UNGUR (RO)	SEBASTIAN ITU (RO)	DANIEL UNGUR	SUBARU IMPREZA WRX STI	N4
86	ALESSANDRO BRUSCHETTA (I)	EDOARDO CIVIERO (I)	ALESSANDRO BRUSHETTA	SUBARU IMPREZA WRX STI	N4
87	VITTORIO CANEVA (I)	BARBARA PERUGINI (I)	VITTORIO CANEVA	MITSUBISHI LANCER EVOLUTION 7	N4
88	DANIELE CECCOLI (SM)	CRISTIANA BIONDI (SM)	DANIELE CECCOLI	MITSUBISHI LANCER EVOLUTION 9	N4
89	FABRIZIO DE SANCTIS (I)	IURI ROSIGNOLI (I)	FABRIZIO DE SANCTIS	MITSUBISHI LANCER EVOLUTION 6	A8
90	LUCA GRIOTTI (I)	MASSIMILIANO BOSI (I)	LUCA GRIOTTI	RENAULT CLIO R3	A7
92	BOGDAN STANOIEV (RO)	DANUT HATIGAN (RO)	BOGDAN STANOIEV	CITROËN C2 R2	A6
93	KASPAR KOITLA (EE)	REIN JÕESSAR (EE)	KASPAR KOITLA	HONDA CIVIC TYPE-R	A7
94	JARKKO NIKARA (FIN)	PETRI NIKARA (FIN)	JARKKO NIKARA	FORD FIESTA ST	N3
96	EMRE YURDAKUL (TR)	CAN ERKAL (TR)	CASTROL FORD TEAM TURKIEY	FORD FIESTA ST	N3
97	KORAY MURATOGLU (TR)	LEVENT OZOKUTUCU (TR)	CASTROL FORD TEAM TURKIEY	FORD FIESTA ST	N3
98	BURCU CETINKAYA (TR)	CICEK GUNEY (TR)	CASTROL FORD TEAM TURKIEY	FORD FIESTA ST	N3
99	DENIS GRODETSKIY (RUS)	SAFONIY LOTKO (RUS)	CUEKS RACING	FORD FIESTA ST	N3
100	ATTE ALANEN (FIN)	TOMMI ALKULA (FIN)	ATTE ALANEN	FORD FIESTA ST	N3
101	TEEMU HORKAMA (FIN)	VESA HAKOLA (FIN)	TEEMU HORKAMA	FORD FIESTA ST	N3
104	SERGEY GERASIMOV (RUS)	MIKHAIL SOSKIN (RUS)	SERGEY GERASIMOV	FORD FIESTA ST	N3
105	JARI LAAKSO (FIN)	JARI TARVAINEN (FIN)	JARI LAAKSO	VOLKSWAGEN POLO 1.4	A5
106	ANTERO SAARI (FIN)	PEKKA LEPPÄLÄ (FIN)	ANTERO SAARI	VOLKSWAGEN POLO 1.4	A5
107	VILLE RUOKANEN (FIN)	TIMO PALLARI (FIN)	VILLE RUOKANEN	VOLKSWAGEN POLO 1.4	A5
108	JAAKKO TAPPER (FIN)	JARI RAJALA (FIN)	JAAKKO TAPPER	VOLKSWAGEN POLO 1.4	A5
109	TOMI VILENIUS (FIN)	MIKA AALTONEN (FIN)	TOMI VILENIUS	VOLKSWAGEN POLO 1.4	A5
110	ILKKA PASTILA (FIN)	HEIKKI HELENIUS (FIN)	ILKKA PASTILA	SKODA FELICIA	A5
111	RAIMO KAISANLAHTI (FIN)	TAPANI PULKKINEN (FIN)	RAIMO KAISANLAHTI	VOLKSWAGEN POLO 1.4	A5
112	KARI HYTÖNEN (FIN)	ISMO PIETILÄINEN (FIN)	KARI HYTÖNEN	SUZUKI SWIFT SPORT	N2
113	CHRISTOFFER DAHLSTRÖM (FIN)	PASI HAATAJA (FIN)	CHRISTOFFER DAHLSTRÖM	SUZUKI IGNIS SPORT	N2
114	SAMI TUOMINEN (FIN)	ARTO RÄMÄNEN (FIN)	ARTO RÄMÄNEN	SUZUKI IGNIS SPORT	N2
136	EYVIND BRYNILDSEN (N)	DENIS GIRAUDET (F)	EYVIND BRYNILDSEN	MITSUBISHI LANCER EVOLUTION 9	N4 3
137	OSCAR SVEDLUND (S)	BJÖRN NILSON (S)	AUTOTEK	SUBARU IMPREZA WRX STI	N4 3
138	PATRIK FLODIN (S)	GÖRAN BERGSTEN (S)	ORION HOLDING WORLD RALLY TEAM	MITSUBISHI LANCER EVOLUTION 9	N4 3
143	EVGENIY VERTUNOV (RUS)	GEORGY TROSHKIN (RUS)	SUBARU RALLY TEAM RUSSIA	SUBARU IMPREZA WRX STI	N4 3
144	TAPIO SUOMINEN (FIN)	PASI HEDMAN (FIN)	GABOKO RALLY TEAM	MITSUBISHI LANCER EVOLUTION 9	N4 3
145	TEEMU ARMINEN (FIN)	SEPPO VARMAVUO (FIN)	MOTORING CLUB 1	SUBARU IMPREZA WRX STI	N4 3
146	JARI KETOMAA (FIN)	MIIKA TEISKONEN (FIN)	MOTORING CLUB 2	SUBARU IMPREZA WRX STI	N4 3
147	FABIO FRISIERO (I)	NICOLA VETTORETTI (I)	MOTORING CLUB	MITSUBISHI LANCER EVOLUTION 9	N4 3
148	EVGENY AKSAKOV (RUS)	ALEKSANDER KORNILOV (EE)	RED WINGS MOSCOW REGION RALLY TEAM	MITSUBISHI LANCER EVOLUTION 9	N4 3
149	SIMONE CAMPEDELLI (I)	DANILO FAPPANI (I)	SCUDERIA RUBICONE CORSE	MITSUBISHI LANCER EVOLUTION 9	N4 3
151	SUBHAN AKSA (RI)	HENDERIK MBOI (RI)	INDONESIA RALLY TEAM	MITSUBISHI LANCER EVOLUTION 9	N4 3
152	JUHO HÄNNINEN (FIN)	MIKKO MARKKULA (FIN)	RALLIART NEW ZEALAND	MITSUBISHI LANCER EVOLUTION 9	N4 3
153	GIOVANNI MANFRINATO (I)	CARLO PISANO (I)	PRO RACE SAS	MITSUBISHI LANCER EVOLUTION 9	N4 3
154	JUSSI TIIPPANA (FIN)	MARKO SALMINEN (FIN)	SUBARU RALLY TEAM USA	SUBARU IMPREZA WRX STI	N4 3
156	FUMIO NUTAHARA (J)	DANIEL BARRITT (GB)	ADVAN-PIAA RALLY TEAM	MITSUBISHI LANCER EVOLUTION 9	N4 3
158	NAREN KUMAR (ID)	NICKY BEECH (GB)	TEAM SIDVIN INDIA	SUBARU IMPREZA WRX STI	N4 3
159	JUHA SALO (FIN)	MIKA STENBERG (FIN)	MITSUBISHI RALLIART FINLAND	MITSUBISHI LANCER EVOLUTION 9	N4 3
160	JUSSI VÄLIMÄKI (FIN)	JARKKO KALLIOLEPO (FIN)	STC-MEAT RALLY TEAM	MITSUBISHI LANCER EVOLUTION 9	N4 3

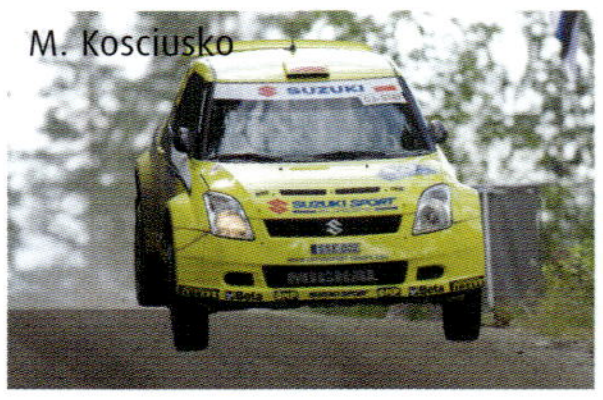
M. Kosciusko

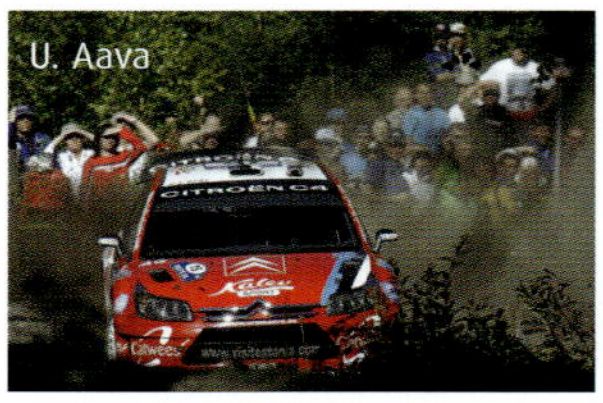
U. Aava

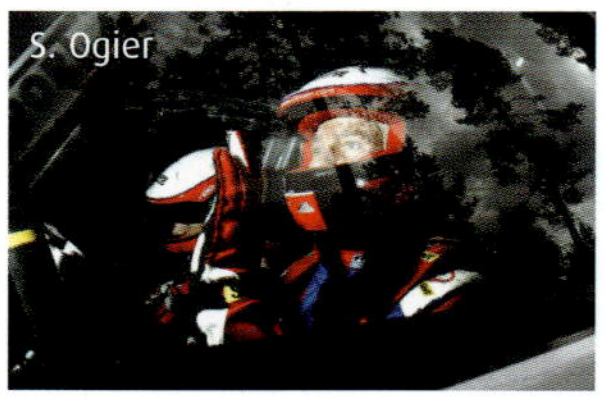
S. Ogier

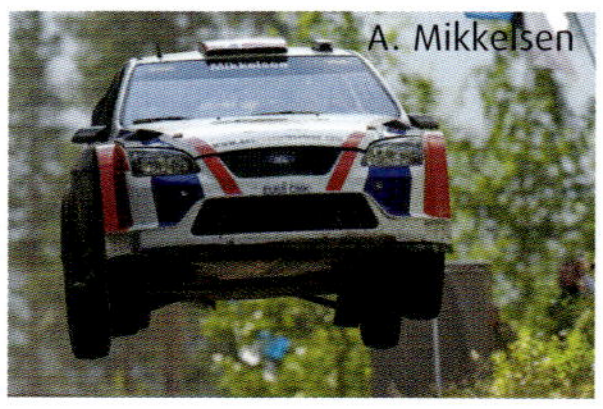
A. Mikkelsen

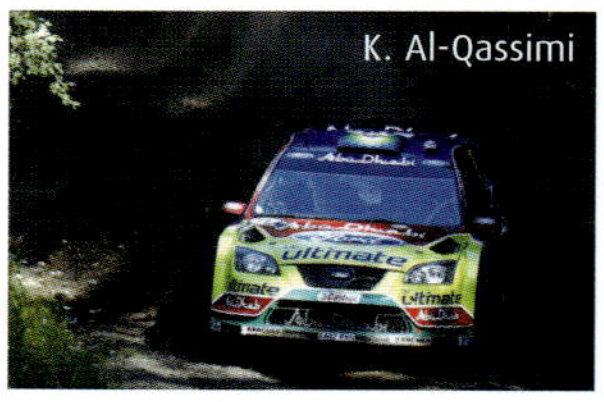
K. Al-Qassimi

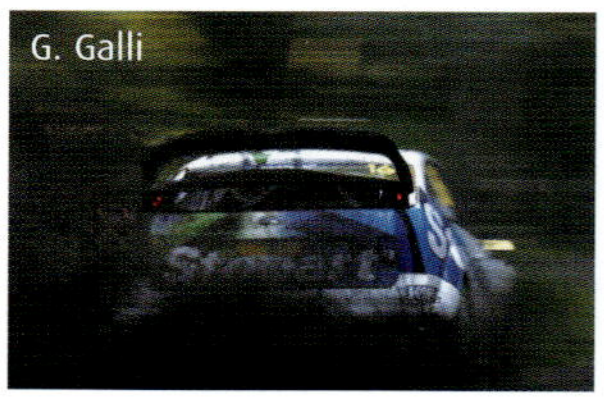
G. Galli

Championship Classifications

•R•: Rookie

FIA Drivers (9/15)

1.	Hirvonen	2🏆	67
2.	Loeb	6🏆	66
3.	Atkinson		37
4.	Sordo		35
5.	Latvala	1🏆	34
6.	P. Solberg		23
7.	H. Solberg		20
8.	Galli		17
9.	Wilson		12
10.	Villagra		8
11.	Rautenbach		6
12.	Aava		6
13.	Duval		5
14.	Mikkelsen		4
15.	Gardemeister		3
16.	Rantanen		2
17.	Cuoq		2
18.	Andersson		1
19.	Aigner		1
20.	Ogier		1
21.	Hänninen		1
22.	Østberg,		0
	K. Al-Qassimi,		0
	Beltrán, Mölder,		0
	Ketomaa, Clark,		0
	Kosciuszko, Sandell,		0
	Nutahara, Prokop,		0
	Burkart, Rauam,		0
	Gallagher, Broccoli,		0
	Farrah, Schammel,		0
	Nittel, Baldacci,		0
	Valimaki, Artru,		0
	Guerra, Arai,		0
	A. Al-Qassimi,		0
	Mercier		0

FIA Constructors (9/15)

1.	BP-Ford Abu Dhabi World Rally Team	3🏆	108
2.	Citroën Total World Rally Team	6🏆	105
3.	Subaru World Rally Team		62
4.	Stobart VK M-Sport Ford Rally Team		45
5.	Munchi's Ford World Rally Team		19
6.	Suzuki World Rally Team		12

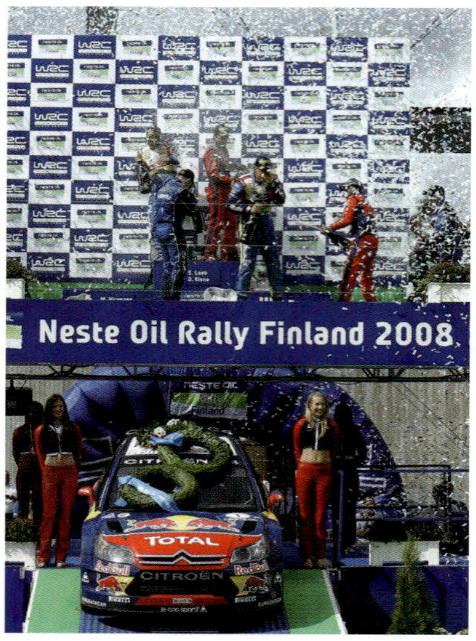

FIA Production Car WRC (5/8)

1.	Aigner	3🏆	30
2.	Hänninen	2🏆	22
3.	Ketomaa		20
4.	Sandell		14
5.	Nutahara		14
6.	Araujo		12
7.	Sousa		10
8.	Rauam		9
9.	Beltrán		8
10.	Valimaki		8
11.	Prokop		7
12.	M. Baldacci		6
13.	Aksakov		6
14.	Vertunov		6
15.	Svedlund		5
16.	Nittel		4
17.	Farrah		3
18.	Tiippana		3
19.	Arai		3
20.	Campedelli		3
21.	Bacco		1
22.	L. Baldacci		1
23.	Linari, Frisiero,		0
	Brynildsen, Aksa,		0
	Al-Attiyah, Kumar,		0
	Mayer, Pavlides,		0
	Manfrinato,		0
	Athanassoulas,		0
	Errani, Pastrana,		0
	Jereb, Novikov,		0
	Flodin, Marrini		0

FIA Junior WRC (4/7)

1.	Ogier	2🏆	24
2.	Kosciusko	1🏆	22
3.	Gallagher		20
4.	Burkart		16
5.	Sandell		14
6.	Prokop	1🏆	12
7.	Mölder		8
8.	Bettega		8
9.	Schammel		8
10.	Albertini		7
11.	Niegel •R•		5
12.	Bertolotti		3
13.	Abbring		3
14.	Cortinovis		2
15.	Weijs Jr. •R•		2
16.	Fanari •R•		1
17.	Komljenovic		1
18.	Pinomaki		0

Rookie

1.	Fanari	34
2.	Weijs Jr.	20
3.	Niegel	8

Special Stages Times

www.nesteoilrallyfinland.fi
www.wrc.com

SS1 SSS Killeri 1 (2.06 km)
1.Loeb 1'20"5; 2.Sordo +0"3;
3.Atkinson +0"4; 4.Hirvonen +0"4;
5.P.Solberg +0"6; 6.Latvala +0"8;
7.Aava +0"9; 8.Mikkelsen +1"0...
P-WRC > 20.Hänninen 1'26"1
J-WRC > 43.Prokop 1'30"0

SS2 Vellipohja 1 (17.20 km)
1.Loeb 8'16"9; 2.Hirvonen +0"0;
3.Latvala +3"2; 4.Sordo +4"8;
5.Mikkelsen +5"4; 6.Atkinson +5"5;
7.Aava +5"9; 8.P.Solberg +9"7...
P-WRC > 20.Hänninen 8'59"9
J-WRC > 29.Prokop 9'21"9

SS3 Mökkiperä 1 (11.50 km)
1.Loeb 5'30"5; 2.Hirvonen +1"1;
3.Galli +4"0; 4.Aava +5"8;
5.Sordo +6"2; 6.P.Solberg +7"0;
7.H.Solberg +7"2; 8.Atkinson +7"5...
P-WRC > 19.Salo 5'59"5
J-WRC > 30.Kosciuszko 6'14"5

SS4 Palsankylä 1 (13.31 km)
1.Loeb 7'12"7; 2.Hirvonen +2"4
3.Aava +4"3; 4.H.Solberg +5"5;
5.Mikkelsen +6"2; 6.Galli +6";
7.Sordo +7"3; 8.P.Solberg 11"3...
P-WRC > 19.Salo 7'46"4
J-WRC > 37.Mölder 8'17"5

SS5 Vellipohja 2 (17.20 km)
1.Loeb 8'09"9; 2.Hirvonen +2"7;
3.Sordo +3"8; 4.Galli +6"0;
5.H.Solberg +8"7; 6.Mikkelsen +9"1;
7.P.Solberg +10"2; 8.Aava 11"3...
P-WRC > 19.Salo 8'55"1
J-WRC > 30.Kosciuszko 9'16"9

SS6 Mökkiperä 2 (11.50 km)
1.Loeb 5'2828; 2.Hirvonen +0"0;
3.Sordo +3"1; 4.Galli +3"6;
5.H.Solberg +3"8; 6.Aava +7"6;
7.P.Solberg +7"9; 8.Mikkelsen +8"9...
P-WRC > 18.Salo 6'00"6
J-WRC > 26.Kosciuszko 6'16"1

SS7 Palsankylä 2 (13.31 km)
1.Loeb 7'07"8; 2.Hirvonen +2"5;
3.H.Solberg +4"1; 4.Galli +4"2;
5.Sordo +6"7; 6.Aava +9"0
7.P.Solberg +9"8; 8.Mikkelsen +12"3...
P-WRC > 17.Salo 7'43"8
J-WRC > 30.Kosciuszko 8'11"5

SS8 Urria (12.10 km)
1.Hirvonen 6'0025; 2.Loeb +0"7;
3.H.Solberg +1"4; 4.Galli +2"8;
5.Aava +6"1; 6.Mikkelsen +7"1;
7.Atkinson +7"1; 8.Rantanen +9"1...
P-WRC > 16.Salo 6'27"0
J-WRC > 30.Kosciuszko 6'43"5

SS9 Lautaperä (8.20 km)
1.Loeb 3'52"4; 2.Hirvonen +0"7;
3.H.Solberg +3"1; 4.Galli +5"8;
5.Mikkelsen +6"0; 6.Andersson +6"1;
7.Atkinson +6"7; 8.Rantanen +6"9...
P-WRC > 15.Salo 4'08"9
J-WRC > 30.Sandell 4'23"1

SS10 Jukojärvi (22.25 km)
1.Loeb 10'37"2; 2.Hirvonen +4"0;
3.H.Solberg +6"2; 4.Galli +9"6;
5.Sordo +15"4; 6.Atkinson +15"9;
7.Rantanen +16"2;
8.Andersson +19"2...
P-WRC > 14.Hänninen 11'26"0
J-WRC > 25.Sandell 11'59"2

SS11 SSS Killeri 2 (2.06 km)
1.Loeb 1'20"0; 2.Atkinson +0"6;
3.Sordo +0"6; 4.P.Solberg +1"1;
5.H.Solberg +1"1; 6.Hirvonen +1"3;
7.Galli +2"2; 8.Villagra +2"2...
P-WRC > 15.Hänninen 1'25"0
J-WRC > 36.Prokop 1'30"0

Classification Leg 1
1.Loeb 1h04'57"9; 2.Hirvonen +14"4;
3.H.Solberg +53"1; 4.Galli +56"2;
5.Sordo +1'05"4; 6.P.Solberg +1'37"8;
7.Atkinson +1'41"1;
8.Andersson +2'20"4...
P-WRC > 16.Salo 1h10'26"4
J-WRC > 28.Kosciuszko 1h14'01"4

SS12 Himos (14.95 km)
1.Hirvonen 8'37"3; 2.Loeb +3"0;
3.Atkinson +12"2; 4.Galli +13"2;
5.P.Solberg +14"5; 6.Rantanen +15"1;
7.Sordo +16"6; 8.Mikkelsen +17"6...
P-WRC > 15.Hänninen 9'16"4
J-WRC > 31.Prokop 9'55"4

SS13 Hirvimäki (11.00 km)
1.Loeb 5'47"7; 2.Hirvonen +3"7;
3.Latvala +9"4; 4.Sordo +10"7;
5.Atkinson +10"8; 6.P.Solberg +12"9
7.Galli +13"7; 8.H.Solberg +13"7...
P-WRC > 18.Salo 6'17"5
J-WRC > 31.Kosciuszko 6'47"6

SS14 Surkee 1 (14.89 km)
1.Loeb 8'03"4; 2.Hirvonen +0"6;
3.Latvala +5"4; 4.Atkinson +8"5;
5.Sordo +11"1; 6.Galli +11"1;
7.Aava +14"2; 8.H.Solberg +16"0...
P-WRC > 14.Hänninen 8'32"0
J-WRC > 29.Kosciuszko 9'02"8

SS15 Leustu (21.27 km)
1.Hirvonen 10'12"4; 2.Loeb +4"6;
3.Latvala +10"0; 4.Sordo +13"7;
5.P.Solberg +14"2; 6.Atkinson +14"3;
7.Galli +15"9; 8.H.Solberg +17"5
P-WRC > 17.Salo 11'01"3
J-WRC > 28.Prokop 11'43"4

SS16 Kakaristo 1 (20.50 km)
1.Latvala 10'43"2; 2.Loeb +5"1;
3.Hirvonen +8"3; 4.Atkinson +18"9;
5.Sordo +21"7; 6.H.Solberg +23"8;
7.Aava +23"9; 8.Mikkelsen +25"7...
P-WRC > 17.Hänninen 11'26"2
J-WRC > 22.Sandell 11'58"2

SS17 Kaipolanvuori (14.10 km)
1.Latvala 7'06"6; 2.Hirvonen +0"3;
3.Loeb +1"7; 4.Atkinson +4"5;
5.Mikkelsen +5"8; 6.Sordo +6"1;
7.Aava +7"8; 8.P.Solberg +11"4...
P-WRC > 17.Hänninen 7'43"4
J-WRC > 23.Sandell 7'55"6

SS18 Surkee 2 (14.89 km)
1.Loeb 7'55"9; 2.Hirvonen 1"9;
3.Atkinson +6"8; 4.Latvala +7"8;
5.H.Solberg +8"6; 6.P.Solberg +11"5;
7.Sordo +11"9; 8.Aava +12"4...
P-WRC > 17.Campedelli 8'44"8
J-WRC > 22.Kosciuszko 8'52"7...

SS19 Kakaristo 2 (20.50 km)
1.Hirvonen 10'34"7; 2.Latvala +1"2;
3.Loeb +3"3; 4.P.Solberg +11"4;
5.Atkinson +12"5; 6.Sordo +15"6
7.H.Solberg +17"1; 8.Aava +18"2...
P-WRC > 17.Hänninen 11'35"8
J-WRC > 21.Kosciuszko 11'51"2

SS20 Juupajoki (21.40 km)
1.Latvala 10'57"4; 2.Loeb +6"8;
3.Hirvonen +9"4; 4.Atkinson +19"2;
5.Mikkelsen +20"2; 6.Sordo +20"3;
7.P.Solberg +21"2; 8.Aava +25"2...
P-WRC > 15.Ketomaa 11'52"6
J-WRC > 25.Prokop 12'27"7

SS21 Väärinmaja (16.45 km)
1.Loeb 8'22"5; 2.Hirvonen +4"1;
3.Latvala +7"3; 4.Atkinson +8"9;
5.Aava +15"2; 6.Sordo +16"0;
7.H.Solberg +16"0; 8.P.Solberg +16"0...
P-WRC > 15.Hänninen 9'07"7
J-WRC > 25.Kosciuszko 9'35"0

Classification Leg 2
1.Loeb 2h33'43"5; 2.Hirvonen +18"2;
3.Atkinson +3'03"6; 4.Sordo +3'04"6;
5.H.Solberg +3'31"6;
6.P.Solberg +3'58"7;
7.Rantanen +5'55"2;
8.Gardemeister +7'28"6...
P-WRC > 12.Hänninen 2h46'25"7
J-WRC > 21.Prokop 2h54'37"6

SS22 Lankamaa (23.00 km)
1.Loeb 11'11"0; 2.Hirvonen +0"0;
3.Latvala +0"9; 4.Aava +9"7;
5.Atkinson +9"8; 6.P.Solberg +10"6;
7.Rantanen +11"0; 8.H.Solberg +16"0...
P-WRC > 14.Ketomaa 12'05"9
J-WRC > 21.Sandell 12'38"8

SS23 Hannula (10.90 km)
1.Latvala 5'43"8; 2.Hirvonen +4"9;
3.Mikkelsen +5"5; 4.Wilson +8"3;
5.P.Solberg +9"1; 6.Loeb +11"3;
7.Aava +12"2; 8.Sordo +12"5...
P-WRC > 15.Ketomaa 6'13"3
J-WRC > 25.Sandell 6'28"0

SS24 Ruuhimäki (7.54 km)
1.P.Solberg 3'12"9; 2.Hirvonen +0"2;
3.Aava +0"3; 4.Latvala +0"6;
5.Loeb +3"0; 6.Rantanen +3"1;
7.Wilson +3"5; 8.Mikkelsen +3"8...
P-WRC > 15.Hänninen 3'29"2
J-WRC > 25.Sandell 3'36"9

Results

	Driver - Co-Driver	Car	Gr.	Time
1.	**Loeb - Elena**	**Citroën C4 WRC**	**A8**	**2h54'05"5**
2.	Hirvonen - Lehtinen	Ford Focus RS WRC 07	A8	+9"0
3.	Atkinson - Prevot	Subaru Impreza WRC 2008	A8	+3'17"0
4.	Sordo - Marti	Citroën C4 WRC 08	A8	+3'30"9
5.	H. Solberg - Menkerud	Ford Focus RS WRC 07	A8	+3'57"7
6.	P. Solberg - Mills	Subaru Impreza WRC 2008	A8	+4'04"1
7.	Rantanen - Lönengren	Ford Focus RS WRC 06	A8	+6'11"1
8.	Gardemeister - Tuominen	Suzuki SX4 WRC	A8	+8'18"7
9.	Wilson - Martin	Ford Focus RS WRC 07	A8	+8'37"3
10.	Rautenbach - Senior	Citroën C4 WRC	A8	+10'30"9
13.	**Hänninen - Markkula**	**Mitsubishi Lancer Evo IX**	**N4/P**	**+14'32"6**
14.	Välimäki - Kallioleppo	Mitsubishi Lancer Evo IX	N4/P	+17'46"2
16.	Ketomaa - Teiskonen	Subaru Impreza Sti	N4/P	+19'48"1
20.	**Prokop - Tomanek**	**Citroën C2 S1600**	**A6/J**	**+23'46"7**
21.	Sandell - Axellson	Renault Clio S1600	A6/J	+24'04"2
22.	Kosciuszko - Szczepaniak	Suzuki Swift	A6/J	+25'21"4

Leading Retirements (26)

Ctrl20	Villagra - Perez Companc	Ford Focus RS WRC 07	Off
Ctrl16	Salo - Stenberg	Mitsubishi Lancer Evo IX	Off
Ctrl16	Galli - Bernacchini	Ford Focus RS WRC 07	Off
Ctrl16	Andersson - Andersson	Suzuki SX4 WRC	Off
Ctrl7	Aigner - Wicha	Mitsubishi Lancer Evo IX	Off
Ctrl6	Östberg - Unne	Subaru Impreza WRC	Off

Performers

	1	2	3	4	5	6	C6	Nb SS
Loeb	14	6	2	-	1	1	24	24
Hirvonen	7	13	2	1	-	1	24	24
Latvala	4	1	6	2	-	1	16	19
P. Solberg	1	-	-	2	4	4	11	24
Sordo	-	2	2	3	4	4	15	24
Atkinson	-	-	5	4	3	4	16	24
H. Solberg	-	-	4	1	4	2	11	24
Aava	-	-	2	2	2	2	8	22
Galli	-	-	1	-	1	1	10	16
Mikkelsen	-	-	1	-	5	1	7	23
Wilson	-	-	-	1	-	-	1	24
Rantanen	-	-	-	-	-	2	2	24
Andersson	-	-	-	-	-	1	1	16

Leaders

SS1 > SS24	Loeb

Previous Winners

1973	Mäkinen - Liddon Ford Escort RS 1600
1974	Mikkola - Davenport Ford Escort RS 1600
1975	Mikkola - Aho Toyota Corolla
1976	Alen - Kivimaki Fiat 131 Abarth
1977	Hamalaiinen - Tiukkanen Ford Escort RS
1978	Alen - Kivimaki Fiat 131 Abarth
1979	Alen - Kivimaki Fiat 131 Abarth
1980	Alen - Kivimaki Fiat 131 Abarth
1981	Vatanen - Richards Ford Escort RS
1982	Mikkola - Hertz Audi Quattro
1983	Mikkola - Hertz Audi Quattro
1984	Vatanen - Harryman Peugeot 205 T16
1985	Salonen - Harjanne Peugeot 205 T16
1986	Salonen - Harjanne Peugeot 205 T16
1987	Alen - Harjanne Lancia Delta HF Turbo
1988	Alen - Kivimaki Lancia Delta Integrale
1989	Ericsson - Billstam Mitsubishi Galant VR4
1990	Sainz - Moya Toyota Celica GT-Four
1991	Kankkunen - Piironen Lancia Delta Integrale 16v
1992	Auriol - Occelli Lancia Delta Integrale
1993	Kankkunen - Giraudet Toyota Celica Turbo 4WD
1994	Mäkinen - Harjanne Ford Escort RS Cosworth
1995	Mäkinen - Harjanne Mitsubishi Lancer Evo 3
1996	Mäkinen - Harjanne Mitsubishi Lancer Evo 3
1997	Mäkinen - Harjanne Mitsubishi Lancer Evo 4
1998	Mäkinen - Mannisenmäki Mitsubishi Lancer Evo 5
1999	Kankkunen - Repo Subaru Impreza WRC
2000	Grönholm - Rautiainen Peugeot 206 WRC
2001	Grönholm - Rautiainen Peugeot 206 WRC
2002	Grönholm - Rautiainen Peugeot 206 WRC
2003	Märtin - Park Ford Focus RS WRC 03
2004	Grönholm - Rautiainen Peugeot 307 WRC
2005	Grönholm - Rautiainen Peugeot 307 WRC
2006	Grönholm - Rautiainen Ford Focus RS WRC 06
2007	Grönholm - Rautiainen Ford Focus RS WRC 06

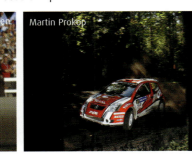

Juho Hänninen — Martin Prokop

10 GERMANY

🇩🇪 Loeb in seventh heaven

A seventh successive victory on the German round of the calendar meant the Frenchman was still unbeaten in that country – and back in the Championship lead. It was a good weekend for Citroën too, with Dani Sordo finishing second – and François Duval did Ford no favours by taking third place in a privateer Focus ahead of Mikko Hirvonen, who looked more dynamic than ever on tarmac.

10 | Germany

After four straight podiums, Mikko Hirvonen was back among the also-rans. On a surface – tarmac – he doesn't like, in front of all those Loeb-Citroën fans, fourth was the best he could manage.

THE RALLY
Duval spoils Ford's fun

It was Ford versus the Rest, with a record number of Focuses – no fewer than 13 of them out of M-Sport's British workshops – taking the start for the 10th rally of the year. Lined up against them in the WRC event were four Citroën C4's, the same number of Subaru Imprezas, two Suzuki SX4's and an elderly Skoda Fabia. Clearly Malcolm Wilson was doing nicely thank you, at least in financial terms, since he had either sold or leased every one of those 13 Fords. But what if sheer weight of numbers were to prove his downfall?

So it turned out: François Duval, getting his hands on one of the dual world title-winning cars with a sponsor's help, dealt the M-Sport boss's title hopes a serious blow in Germany. Third overall and first Ford driver home in Trier, the Belgian may have added a few Euros to the Stobart coffers but in return he stole some precious points from the works team and its leader, Mikko Hirvonen. Duval had been nominated by the satellite Ford outfit but actually took part in a car carrying his personal sponsors' colours, as Henning Solberg normally does. So, unlike a Gigi Galli or a Matthew Wilson, he was under no obligation to Malcolm Wilson. And he put that freedom to full use with his 13th World Championship podium and his fourth in Germany. "It's a brilliant result after so little testing," said a delighted Obelix. "But it will be hard to go for a win against drivers who spend all year either racing or testing. Still, the experience will come in handy on the two tarmac rallies left on my schedule." That was probably his way of telling Malcolm Wilson that with a little more running – i.e. with a works team behind him – he felt he had the beating of the Citroëns. It was a nice reminder...

Fourth, 10 seconds behind the cross-border raider, Hirvonen dropped a point to be just four clear of Loeb in the Championship. No fault of his, as he piloted the newly-homologated version of his Ford Focus and the latest evolution of the engine from the Blue Oval engineers in France. After the opening leg the Finn was lying second between Loeb and Sordo but lost two places the following day with a puncture, and push as he might on Sunday he couldn't get a podium place back.

"It was maximum attack this morning," he said, "in fact I gave myself quite a fright when I cut a corner too close and was up on two wheels for an eternity. That was a close call. In the third stage, when I heard my split was three seconds up on Duval's, I decided to lift off and settle for the points for fourth. I drove well on Friday and with a little more consistency I could have got a better result, but I just couldn't match the front two's pace."

Things were even bleaker for Ford in constructors's terms. While Duval was nicking six points for Stobart, Latvala could only manage two for the works team. Even with Hirvonen's haul in fourth, it was a poor return in comparison with Citroën's for that 1-2 finish as they opened up a commanding 123 to 115-point lead in the provisional standings.

Contrary to appearances, Henning Solberg came away from this event with head held high, seventh overall and first privateer on only his second German outing. But there's still a way to go before he makes his first podium in a tarmac event – he was 5m. 30s down on Loeb.

Second place behind his lordship Loeb was exactly what Citroën needed from Dani Sordo. But the Spaniard may have to wait a while for his own first World Championship win – the Alsatian's not one to share them around.

Sébastien Loeb is right at home here: this was his seventh straight win in Germany. No driver had ever managed such a streak – just one more record to the Frenchman's name!

Mind the bumps! Petter Solberg jumps for joy after finishing fifth on a rally that's never been particularly good to him. He had beaten his team-mate for the fourth time in 10 rallies this season.

Yet again, Latvala hadn't managed to keep himself in check. He was fifth after the opening leg but rolled it on the second and had a puncture after hitting a kerb on Sunday. "I was feeling good on Friday, but the next two days were a bit of a nightmare," he confessed. "It was very frustrating. This is the hardest tarmac rally of them all: the surface changes all the time. I was quite at home when it was rough, but a lot less so both in myself and in my car's set-up when it was smoother. This rally also taught me just how important your mental preparation can be, and that's something I need to work on. I'll be doing just that this week, before New Zealand, so as to get back on track and start going forward again. I also want to do some more tarmac training before the Catalunya Rally in October."

With or without Duval on board, Ford couldn't have done anything about the Citroëns on a rally the Chevron has made its own since 2001. There was an initial non-title victory for Philippe Bugalski back in 2001, and since it became a World Championship event in 2002, Loeb has reigned supreme. Once again the Frenchman had no equal, leading from start to finish and winning 14 of the 19 stages. Imperious in changing conditions, like on the Monte, he is right at home on the German event. His home territory's not all that far away, and once again the people of Alsace turned up in their thousands to support their hero's quest for title number five. "It's a super result and a super time to keep my unbeaten record in Germany," said Loeb. "Seven wins: they're starting to add up! It's pretty hard to believe, really – even we can't quite take it in. I really like this event: all my fans are here, all my mates, my family... At the start and again at the podium there were loads of people and a fantastic atmosphere. It's great when the fans sing the Marseillaise and wave French flags, I really enjoyed it. It was all down to Friday, we went all out from the start. It was touch-and-go at times, but at that pace you expect that, and we were on the limit all the time. We had to be, because Hirvonen was quick as well – he's really starting to come good on tarmac. It was a great 1-2 with Sordo and that puts Citroën top in the constructors' standings and me in the drivers'. So with Duval getting in there and relegating Hirvonen to fourth, it really was a very positive weekend. It's great to be going to the next round with a four-point lead, because Hirvonen will bounce back in New Zealand and we'll have to be up for the fight."

Finishing second, 47.7 behind Loeb, Sordo gave Citroën their first 1-2 finish of the season – but it left the Spaniard, who clean-sheeted just the once, still looking for the first victory of his career. "Germany's not my favourite rally, it's too stop-start, but I was very happy to be back on tarmac," he said. "We were feeling our way a bit on the set-up, but working with the tech team we got the car perfect by Saturday morning." With the Chevron back on top in the Constructors' Championship, Citroën Sport boss Olivier Quesnel was a happy man. "Everybody said we were the favourites, there was a lot of pressure. It's a superb outcome for us. But we mustn't relax, we have to get back to work tomorrow because it's all happening very quickly now." Ford and their Finns were planning to hit back in New Zealand and get back on top before the back-to-back Catalunya-Corsica events that were expected to favour the French.

It never rains but it pours, and sure enough Ford would now have to get through the latter part of the season without their best performer on tarmac, Gigi Galli. The fiery Italian had a major off in the fifth stage and got a fractured femur for his trouble, though co-driver Bernacchini was unhurt. Galli was taken to hospital in Trier; the rest of his season was a write-off.

10 | Germany

> Armin Schwarz, now a consultant to a German TV network, enjoyed acting as a tour guide to young autograph-hunters on his home event.

A stand-out on this rally: in a privateer Ford after a long lay-off, François Duval showed why this is his favourite event, enjoying the heady heights of another World Championship podium. It was also one in the eye for Ford as he nicked a point from Hirvonen.

Once again Jari-Matti Latvala paid the price for being too headstrong. After a decent opening leg, he rolled it during the second. The Finn was about to have some serious thinking time: Malcolm Wilson sent him back to school with the Stobart team for the upcoming tarmac rallies.

Germany is an unforgiving round, as Petter Solberg well knows after the biggest accident of his career here in 2005. The Norwegian has always taken this event very cannily since then and settled for fifth place ahead of team-mate Chris Atkinson, who dropped behind Sordo in the drivers' standings. So there were no miracles from the new Impreza on its tarmac debut, but then, with just two days' testing on the surface before the event, what else could they expect? Henning Solberg and Urmo Aava rounded out the top eight, the Norwegian finishing in the points for the sixth time this year, the Estonian for only the third time. Gardemeister's 10th place brought Suzuki a point, which could have been Andersson's if he hadn't lost so much time with a little tap in the second leg. ■

Dani Sordo, second to Loeb for the sixth time in three years, has his eye on a bigger prize. But will he need to wait till his team-mate calls it a day?

JUNIORS
Ogier mimics the maestro

Here too a Sébastien and a Citroën lorded it over everyone else. Ogier didn't let himself down on his World Championship debut on tarmac, bringing his Citroën C2 home well ahead of rivals with much more experience on this difficult route. Winning 11 stages out of 16, he was over three and a half minutes ahead of local man Aaron Burkart! Fresh from his Finnish exploits, Martin Prokop was the only man to challenge the French driver. The Czech led out of the first leg but had to give best as the French debutant attacked early on Saturday, then broke the transmission on the next

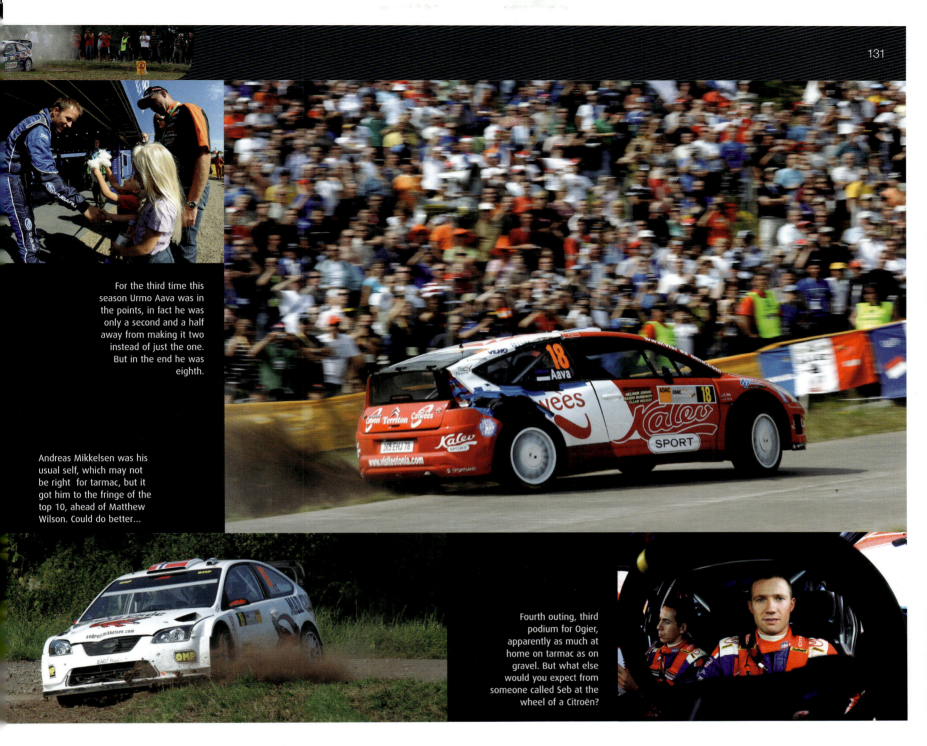

For the third time this season Urmo Aava was in the points, in fact he was only a second and a half away from making it two instead of just the one. But in the end he was eighth.

Andreas Mikkelsen was his usual self, which may not be right for tarmac, but it got him to the fringe of the top 10, ahead of Matthew Wilson. Could do better...

Fourth outing, third podium for Ogier, apparently as much at home on tarmac as on gravel. But what else would you expect from someone called Seb at the wheel of a Citroën?

stage. That put Prokop in fifth place and ended his title hopes. "Early on I realised I was doing the same times as Prokop, who won here last year, and that gave me a lot of confidence," said Ogier after. "And than I really got into the rhythm of things in the quick stages. Once Martin was out it was another race altogether, and it was not as straightforward as you might think. We had to keep our concentration, not make any mistakes and look after the equipment. It's not always easy to find the right pace, but we managed it and I'm very pleased to have won."

Aaron Burkart's second place, his own best finish of the season, made him the likeliest man to challenge Ogier for the title, thanks to his consistency rather than out-and-out speed. "I couldn't get into it early in the event," the German explained, "and on Saturday I brushed a little tree and got a puncture. Then I had steering problems that cost me a lot of time. It's disappointing – I'd hoped to put in a good performance here at home." Italian Alessandro Bettega took the last podium place, his second of the year, in the Renault Clio R3. Shaun Gallagher made hay as Kosciuszko gave this event a miss, fourth place taking him back to second place overall, nine points behind Ogier. ■

Atkinson struggled on this, the least typical of the tarmac events. No doubt about it, the Australian is much more at home with a good Shiraz than the local vintage.

10 | Germany | Results

27th RALLY OF GERMANY

Organisater Details
ADAK Motorsport Ltd,
Garmischer Strasse19 - 21
81377 Munchen,
Germany,
Tel.: +4922 195743434
Fax: +4922 195743444

ADAC Rallye Deutschland

10th leg of FIA 2008 World Championship for constructors and drivers.
5th leg of FIA WRC Junior Championship.

Date August 14 - 17, 2008

Route
1174.91 km divised in three legs.
19 special stages on tarmac (352,63 km)

Ceremonial Start
Thursday, August 14 (20h00),
Trier, Porta Nigra
Leg 1
Friday, August 15 (09:13/16:58),
Trier > Trier, 366.82 km;
6 special stages (108.16 km)
Leg 2
Saturday, August 16 (08:18/17:23),
Trier > Trier, 574.90 km;
8 special stages (159.76 km)
Leg 3
Sunday, August 17 (07:28/13:08),
Trier > Trier, 233.19 km;
5 special stages (84.97 km)

Entry List (84) - 81 starters

N°	Driver (Nat.)	Co-Driver (Nat.)	Team	Car	Group & FIA Priority	
1	SÉBASTIEN LOEB (F)	DANIEL ELENA (MC)	CITROËN TOTAL WORLD RALLY TEAM	CITROËN C4 WRC	A8	1
2	DANIEL SORDO (E)	MARC MARTI (E)	CITROËN TOTAL WORLD RALLY TEAM	CITROËN C4 WRC	A8	1
3	MIKKO HIRVONEN (FIN)	JARMO LEHTINEN (FIN)	BP FORD ABU DHABI WORLD RALLY TEAM	FORD FOCUS RS WRC 07	A8	1
4	JARI-MATTI LATVALA (FIN)	MIIKKA ANTTILA (FIN)	BP FORD ABU DHABI WORLD RALLY TEAM	FORD FOCUS RS WRC 07	A8	1
5	PETTER SOLBERG (N)	PHILIP MILLS (GB)	SUBARU WORLD RALLY TEAM	SUBARU IMPREZA WRC 2008	A8	1
6	CHRISTOPHER ATKINSON (AUS)	STÉPHANE PRÉVOT (B)	SUBARU WORLD RALLY TEAM	SUBARU IMPREZA WRC 2008	A8	1
7	GIGI GALLI (I)	GIOVANNI BERNACCHINI (I)	STOBART VK M-SPORT FORD RALLY TEAM	FORD FOCUS RS WRC 07	A8	1
8	FRANÇOIS DUVAL (B)	PATRICK PIVATO (F)	STOBART VK M-SPORT FORD RALLY TEAM	FORD FOCUS RS WRC 07	A8	1
11	TONI GARDEMEISTER (FIN)	TOMI TUOMINEN (FIN)	SUZUKI WORLD RALLY TEAM	SUZUKI SX4 WRC	A8	1
12	PER-GUNNAR ANDERSSON (S)	JONAS ANDERSSON (S)	SUZUKI WORLD RALLY TEAM	SUZUKI SX4 WRC	A8	1
15	HENNING SOLBERG (N)	CATO MENKERUD (N)	STOBART VK M-SPORT FORD RALLY TEAM	FORD FOCUS RS WRC 07	A8	2
16	MATTHEW WILSON (GB)	SCOTT MARTIN (GB)	STOBART VK M-SPORT FORD RALLY TEAM	FORD FOCUS RS WRC 07	A8	2
17	CONRAD RAUTENBACH (ZW)	DAVID SENIOR (GB)	CONRAD RAUTENBACH	CITROËN C4 WRC	A8	2
18	URMO AAVA (EE)	KULDAR SIKK (EE)	WORLD RALLY TEAM ESTONIA	CITROËN C4 WRC	A8	2
19	ANDREAS MIKKELSEN (N)	OLA FLOENE (N)	RAMSPORT	FORD FOCUS RS WRC 07	A8	2
21	KHALID AL QASSIMI (UAE)	MICHAEL ORR (GB)	BP FORD ABU DHABI WORLD RALLY TEAM	FORD FOCUS RS WRC 07	A8	2
22	MARK VAN ELDIK (NL)	MICHEL GROENEWOUD (NL)	MARK VAN ELDIK	SUBARU IMPREZA WRC 07	A8	2
23	ERIK WEVERS (NL)	JALMAR VAN WEEREN (NL)	ERIK WEVERS	FORD FOCUS RS WRC 06	A8	2
24	PETER VAN MERKSTEIJN (NL)	HANS VAN BEEK (NL)	VAN MERKSTEIJN MOTORSPORT	FORD FOCUS RS WRC 07	A8	2
25	GARETH JONES (GB)	DAVID MOYNIHAN (IRL)	GARETH JONES	SUBARU IMPREZA WRC 07	A8	2
31	MARTIN PROKOP (CZ)	JAN TOMÁNEK (CZ)	MARTIN PROKOP	CITROËN C2 SUPER 1600	A6	3
33	AARON NICOLAI BURKART (D)	MICHAEL KÖLBACH (D)	AARON NICOLAI BURKART	CITROËN C2 SUPER 1600	A6	3
34	ANDREA CORTINOVIS (I)	GIANCARLA GUZZI (I)	ANDREA CORTINOVIS	RENAULT CLIO SUPER 1600	A6	3
37	SIMONE BERTOLOTTI (I)	DANIELE VERNUCCIO (I)	SIMONE BERTOLOTTI	RENAULT CLIO SUPER 1600	A6	3
38	FRANCESCO FANARI (I)	MASSIMILIANO BOSI (I)	FRANCESCO FANARI	CITROËN C2 R2	A6	3
39	STEFANO ALBERTINI (I)	PIERCARLO CAPOLONGO (I)	STEFANO ALBERTINI	RENAULT CLIO SPORT R3	A7	3
42	SÉBASTIEN OGIER (F)	JULIEN INGRASSIA (F)	EQUIPE DE FRANCE	CITROËN C2 SUPER 1600	A6	3
43	FLORIAN NIEGEL (D)	ANDRÉ KACHEL (D)	SUZUKI RALLYE JUNIOR TEAM GERMANY	SUZUKI SWIFT SUPER 1600	A6	3
44	HANS WEIJS JR. (NL)	HANS VAN GOOR (NL)	KNAF TALENT FIRST TEAM HOLLAND	CITROËN C2 R2	A6	3
45	KEVIN ABBRING (NL)	BJORN DEGANDT (B)	KNAF TALENT FIRST TEAM HOLLAND	RENAULT CLIO SPORT R3	A7	3
46	SHAUN GALLAGHER (IRL)	PAUL KIELY (IRL)	WORLD RALLY TEAM IRELAND	CITROËN C2 SUPER 1600	A6	3
47	GILLES SCHAMMEL (L)	RENAUD JAMOUL (B)	JPS JUNIOR TEAM LUXEMBOURG	RENAULT CLIO SPORT R3	A7	3
48	ALESSANDRO BETTEGA (I)	SIMONE SCATTOLIN (I)	TRT SRL	RENAULT CLIO SPORT R3	A7	3
61	RENE KUIPERS (NL)	ERWIN MOMBAERTS (NL)	RENE KUIPERS	FORD FOCUS RS WRC 06	A8	
62	HARRY KLEINJAN (NL)	ANNEMIEKE HULZEBOS (NL)	HARRY KLEINJAN	SKODA FABIA WRC 05	A8	
63	PETER VAN MERKSTEIJN JUN. (NL)	EDDY CHEVAILLIER (B)	VAN MERKSTEIJN MOTORSPORT	FORD FOCUS RS WRC 06	A8	
64	DENNIS KUIPERS (NL)	KEES HAGMAN (NL)	DENNIS KUIPERS	FORD FOCUS RS WRC 06	A8	
65	JASPER VAN DEN HEUVEL (NL)	MARTINE KOLMAN (NL)	JASPER VAN DEN HEUVEL	MITSUBISHI LANCER EVO 9	N4	
66	HERMANN GASSNER (D)	KARIN THANNHÄUSER (D)	HERMANN GASSNER	MITSUBISHI LANCER EVO 9	N4	
67	KRIS MEEKE (GB)	PAUL NAGLE (IRL)	KRIS MEEKE	RENAULT CLIO SUPER 1600	A6	
68	EDDIE MERCIER (F)	JEAN MICHEL VERET (F)	EDDIE MERCIER	RENAULT CLIO SPORT R3	A7	
69	KARL FRIEDRICH BECK (D)	JÖRG STIERLE (D)	KARL FRIEDRICH BECK	RENAULT CLIO SPORT R3	A7	
70	MARTIN JOHANSEN (DK)	FINN THOMSEN (DK)	FINN THOMSEN	SUZUKI SWIFT SUPER 1600	A6	
71	JEAN-NICOLAS HOT (F)	XAVIER PANSERI (F)	JEAN-NICOLAS HOT	SUBARU IMPREZA WRX STI	N4	
72	HERMANN GASSNER JUN. (D)	KATHI WÜSTENHAGEN (D)	HERMANN GASSNER JUN.	MITSUBISHI LANCER EVO 9	N4	
73	HENK VOSSEN (NL)	JOHAN FINDHAMMER (NL)	HENK VOSSEN	MITSUBISHI LANCER EVO 9	N4	
74	VACLAV ARAZIM (CZ)	ONDREJ BENES (CZ)	ONDREJ BENES	MITSUBISHI LANCER EVO 8	N4	
75	KLAUS BODILSEN (DK)	OLE FREDERIKSEN (DK)	KLAUS BODILSEN	MITSUBISHI LANCER EVO 7	N4	
76	LUDVIK OTTO (CZ)	RENATA OTTOVA (CZ)	LUDVIK OTTO	SUBARU IMPREZA WRX STI	N4	
77	BRIAN O'MAHONY (IRL)	JOHN HIGGINS (IRL)	BRIAN O'MAHONY	RENAULT CLIO SUPER 1600	A6	
78	TOMÁS PLETKA (CZ)	PETR NOVAK (CZ)	TOMAS PLETKA	CITROËN C2 R2	A6	
79	MICHAEL ABENDROTH (D)	FRANK OSCHMANN (D)	SCUDERIA BLAU-WEISS KAMP-LINTFORT E.V.	HONDA CIVIC TYPE R	N3	
83	ERIK MOREE (NL)	SANDER RÖLING (NL)	ERIK MOREE	MITSUBISHI LANCER EVO 8	N4	
84	ANDREAS KONRATH (D)	ISABELLE BRACK (D)	ANDREAS KONRATH	SUBARU IMPREZA GT	N4	
85	THORSTEN KUHLMANN (D)	DETLEF RUF (D)	ADAC TEAM HANSA	MITSUBISHI LANCER EVO 7	N4	
86	MILAN LISKA (CZ)	JAROSLAV JUGAS (CZ)	MILAN LISKA	MITSUBISHI LANCER EVO 9	N4	
87	JAROMIR TOMASTIK (CZ)	JAROSLAV VRECKA (CZ)	JAROMIR TOMASTIK	SUBARU IMPREZA WRX STI	N4	
88	HAN HOENDERVANGERS (NL)	GEERT GROOTEN (B)	HESBAYE	MITSUBISHI LANCER EVO 7	N4	
89	GERT VAN DEN HEUVEL (NL)	BERT BLOEMENDAAL (NL)	GERT VAN DEN HEUVEL	MITSUBISHI LANCER EVO 9	N4	
90	MARTIN VAN IERSEL (NL)	SYLVIA BOS (NL)	SYLVIA BOS	MITSUBISHI LANCER EVO 9	N4	
91	PATRICK ANGLADE (D)	BJÖRN RÖHM (D)	ADAC SAARLAND E.V.	OPEL ASTRA GTC TDI	N4	
92	ARMIN HOLZ (D)	SEBASTIAN GEIPEL (D)	FUNMOTORSPORTS E.V.	VW GOLF IV TDI	N4	
93	JOSEF WECKER (D)	MARTIN BRACK (D)	JOSEF WECKER	OPEL ASTRA GTC TDI	N4	
95	FRANK LAUER (D)	INGOLF MERGEN (D)	FUNMOTORSPORTS E.V.	CITROËN SAXO VTS	A6	
96	VYTAUTAS BARANAUSKAS (LT)	GEDIMINAS CELIESIUS (LT)	VYTAUTAS BARANAUSKAS	FORD FIESTA ST	N3	
97	EMRE YURDAKUL (TR)	CAN ERKAL (TR)	CASTROL FORD TEAM TURKIYE	FORD FIESTA ST	N3	
98	BURCU CETINKAYA (TR)	CICEK GUNEY (TR)	CASTROL FORD TEAM TURKIYE	FORD FIESTA ST	N3	
99	KORAY MURATOGLU (TR)	LEVENT OZOKUTUCU (TR)	CASTROL FORD TEAM TURKIYE	FORD FIESTA ST	N3	
100	ANTHONY MARTIN (B)	ERIC BORGUET (B)	ANTHONY MARTIN	FORD FIESTA ST	N3	
101	TIMOTHY VAN PARIJS (B)	KURT HEYNDRICKX (B)	TIMOTHY VAN PARIJS	FORD FIESTA ST	N3	
103	JOACHIM MÜLLER-WENDE (D)	UMBERTO CALAMIDA (CH)	JOACHIM MÜLLER-WENDE	FORD FIESTA ST	N3	
104	PHILIPPE MAERTENS (B)	TONY LEFEBVRE (B)	DUINDISTEL	FORD FIESTA ST	N3	
105	RICHARD MOORE (GB)	SEBASTIAN MARSHALL (GB)	RICHARD MOORE	FORD FIESTA ST	N3	
106	CHARLES-ANTOINE HASTIR (B)	ETIENNE COLLIN (B)	CHARLES-ANTOINE HASTIR	FORD FIESTA ST	N3	
107	SEBASTIAN SCHWINN (D)	MICHAEL RIGA (D)	SEBASTIAN SCHWINN	PEUGEOT 206 RC	N3	
108	JAN TIMO VAN DER MAREL (NL)	RUUD STROOPER (NL)	JAN TIMO VAN DER MAREL	RENAULT CLIO RAGNOTTI	N3	
109	FRANK SCHRÖDER (B)	VINCENT JUSTIN (B)	E.B.R.T.	OPEL ASTRA OPC	N3	
110	HUGO ARELLANO (L)	KENDRA STOCKMAR (D)	KENDRA STOCKMAR	SUZUKI SWIFT SPORT	N2	
111	JÜRGEN HOHLHEIMER (D)	WILFRIED KIPPE (D)	JÜRGEN HOHLHEIMER	FIAT SEICENTO SPORTING	A5	
112	TIM JONES (GB)	STEVE JONES (GB)	TIM JONES	FORD KA	A5	
113	ANDREAS WERNER (D)	JENS LEMBKE (D)	ADAC MITTELRHEIN E.V.	OPEL CORSA B 1.6I	N2	

C. Atkinson

A. N. Burkart

P. Andersson

G. Galli

F. Niegel

C. Rautenbach

Championship Classifications

•R•: Rookie

FIA Drivers (10/15)

1.	Loeb	7🏆	76
2.	Hirvonen	2🏆	72
3.	Sordo		43
4.	Atkinson		40
5.	Latvala	1🏆	34
6.	P. Solberg		27
7.	H. Solberg		22
8.	Galli		17
9.	Wilson		12
10.	Duval		11
11.	Villagra		8
12.	Aava		7
13.	Rautenbach		6
14.	Mikkelsen		4
15.	Gardemeister		3
16.	Rantanen		2
17.	Cuoq		2
18.	Andersson		1
19.	Aigner		1
20.	Ogier		1
21.	Hänninen		1
22.	Østberg,		0
	K. Al-Qassimi,		0
	Beltrán, Mölder,		0
	Ketomaa, Clark,		0
	Kosciuszko, Sandell,		0
	Nutahara, Prokop,		0
	Burkart, Rauam,		0
	Gallagher, Broccoli,		0
	Farrah, Schammel,		0
	Nittel, Baldacci,		0
	Valimaki, Artru,		0
	Guerra, Arai,		0
	A. Al-Qassimi,		0
	Mercier		0

FIA Constructors (10/15)

1.	Citroën Total World Rally Team	7🏆	123
1.	BP-Ford Abu Dhabi World Rally Team	3🏆	115
3.	Subaru World Rally Team		69
4.	Stobart VK M-Sport Ford Rally Team		51
5.	Munchi's Ford World Rally Team		19
6.	Suzuki World Rally Team		13

FIA Production Car WRC (5/8)

1.	Aigner	3🏆	30
2.	Hänninen	2🏆	22
3.	Ketomaa		20
4.	Sandell		14
5.	Nutahara		14
6.	Araujo		12
7.	Sousa		10
8.	Rauam		9
9.	Beltrán		8
10.	Valimaki		8
11.	Prokop		7
12.	M. Baldacci		6
13.	Aksakov		6
14.	Vertunov		6
15.	Svedlund		5
16.	Nittel		4
17.	Farrah		3
18.	Tiippana		3
19.	Arai		3
20.	Campedelli		3
21.	Bacco		1
22.	L. Baldacci		1
23.	Linari, Frisiero,		0
	Brynildsen, Aksa,		0
	Al-Attiyah, Kumar,		0
	Mayer, Pavlides,		0
	Manfrinato,		0
	Athanassoulas,		0
	Errani, Pastrana,		0
	Jereb, Novikov,		0
	Flodin, Marrini		0

FIA Junior WRC (5/7)

1.	Ogier	3🏆	34
2.	Gallagher		25
3.	Burkart		24
4.	Kosciusko	1🏆	22
5.	Bettega		14
6.	Sandell		14
7.	Prokop	1🏆	12
8.	Mölder		8
9.	Schammel		8
10.	Albertini		7
11.	Bertolotti		7
12.	Niegel •R•		6
13.	Abbring		6
14.	Cortinovis		4
15.	Weijs Jr. •R•		2
16.	Fanari •R•		1
17.	Komljenovic		1
18.	Pinomaki		0

Rookie

1.	Fanari	44
2.	Weijs Jr.	20
3.	Niegel	8

Special Stages Times

www.rallye-deutschland.de
www.wrc.com

SS1 Ruwertal/Fell 1 (21.22 km)
1.Loeb 11'31"6; 2.Sordo +5"8;
3.Hirvonen +5"9; 4.Duval +6"3;
5.Atkinson +9"3; 6.P.Solberg +9"6;
7.Latvala +15"0; 8.Galli +17"2...
J-WRC > 22.Ogier 12'39"9

SS2 Grafschaft Veldenz 1 (23.04 km)
1.Loeb 13'14"4; 2.Sordo +5"5;
3.Hirvonen +6"7; 4.Latvala +13"4
5.P.Solberg +15"7; 6.Atkinson +16"4;
7.Duvla +17"9; 8.H.Solberg +19"7...
J-WRC > 23.Prokop 14'37"1

SS3 Moselland 1 (9.82 km)
1.Loeb 5'29"3; 2.Hirvonen +2"7;
3.Duval +3"7; 4.Sordo +4"0;
5.Atkinson +5"3; 6.P.Solberg +7"1;
7.Latvala +7"4; 8.Aava +7"9...
J-WRC > 19.Prokop 5'57"3

SS4 Ruwertal/Fell 2 (21.22 km)
1.Loeb 11'28"7; 2.Duval +2"2;
3.Sordo +2"4; 4.Hirvonen +3"4;
6.Galli +4"6; 7.Latvala +10"2;
8.P.Solberg +11"8...
J-WRC > 23.Ogier 12'30"5

SS5 Grafschaft Veldenz 2 (23.04 km)
1.Loeb 13'12"36; 2.Hirvonen +0"1;
3.Sordo +6"8; 4.Duval +7"5;
5.Latvala +8"6; 6.Atkinson +18"1;
7.P.Solberg +18"6; 8.Aava +19"3...
J-WRC > 44.Niegel 13'44"8

SS6 Moselland 2 (9.82 km)
1.Loeb 5'26"2; 2.Abendroth +1"1;
3.Pletka +1"1; 4.Bodilsen +1"1;
5.Kuhlmann +1"1; 6.Liska +1"1;
7.van den Heuvel +1"1...
J-WRC > 42.Prokop 5'27"3

Classification Leg 1
1.Loeb 1h00'22"5;
2.Hirvonen +19"9; 3.Sordo +25"6;
4.Duval +38"7; 5.Latvala +55"7;
6.P.Solberg +1'03"9; 7.Atkinson 1'34"0;
8.H.Solberg +1'36"2...
J-WRC > 20.Prokop 1h04'59"6

SS7 Bosenberg 1 (19.12 km)
1.Loeb 10'50"1; 2.Sordo +0"3;
3.Duval +4"1; 4.Hirvonen +7"5;
5.Latvala +11"4; 6.Atkinson +15"8;
7.P.Solberg +17"4; 8.Andersson +27"1...
J-WRC > 21.Ogier 12'05"5

SS8 Freisen/Westrich 1 (16.16 km)
1.Loeb 9'26"9; 2.Sordo +3"5;
3.Duval +6"7; 4.Hirvonen +7"7;
5.Atkinson +16"7; 6.P.Solberg +17"5;
7.Latvala +17"9; 8.Aava +24"0...
J-WRC > 25.Ogier 10'40"2

SS9 Birkenfelder Land 1 (14.22 km)
1.Loeb 7'57"1; 2.Duval +0"5;
3.Sordo +2"8; 4.Hirvonen +3"6;
5.Aava +9"2; 6.P.Solberg +9"4;
7.Atkinson +11"1; 8.H.Solberg +14"1...
J-WRC > 20.Ogier 8'52"6

SS10 Arena Panzerplatte 1 (30.38 km)
1.Loeb 17'44"5; 2.Sordo +3"7;
3.Hirvonen +11"6; 4.P.Solberg +13"9;
5.Atkinson +20"8; 6.Duval +27"7;
7.Latvala +30"8; 8.H.Solberg +38"3...
J-WRC > 21.Ogier 19'42"4

SS11 Bosenberg 2 (19.12 km)
1.Loeb 10'50"6; 2.Sordo +3"9;
3.Hirvonen +5"5; 4.Duval +5"6;
5.P.Solberg +6"6; 6.Atkinson +18"0;
7.Latvala +20"4; 8.Atkinson +21"8
J-WRC > 23.Ogier 12'09"5

SS12 Freisen/Westrich 2 (16.16 km)
1.Loeb 9'30"4; 2.Sordo +2"9;
3.Hirvonen +4"6; 4.Duval +4"7;
5.Atkinson +8"4; 6.P.Solberg +9"3;
7.Latvala +13"2; 8.H.Solberg +18"2...
J-WRC > 24.Ogier 10'38"1

SS13 Birkenfelder Land 2 (14.22 km)
1.Loeb 7'56"3; 2.Sordo +0"3;
3.Hirvonen +2"5; 4.Duval +5"0;
5.P.Solberg +5"2; 6.Atkinson +6"0;
7.Latvala +9"4; 8.Aava +10"0
J-WRC > 22.Burkart 8'46"5

SS14 Arena Panzerplatte 2 (30.38 km)
1.Sordo 17'41"5; 2.Loeb +2"7;
3.P.Solberg +8"2; 4.Latvala +12"5;
5.Duval +14"0; 6.Atkinson +20"2;
7.H.Solberg +24"5; 8.Aava +27"3...
J-WRC > 21.Ogier 19'26"6

Classification Leg 2
1.Loeb 2h32'22"6; 2.Sordo +40"3;
3.Duval +1'44"3; 4.Hirvonen +1'48"2;
5.P.Solberg +2'28"7; 6.Atkinson +3'32"1;
7.H.Solberg +3'07"1. 8.Aava+ 4'57"1...
J-WRC > 20.Ogier 2h47'30"1

SS15 Dhrontal 1 (22.22 km)
1.Duval 14'23"1; 2.Sordo +1"8;
3.Hirvonen +2"2; 4.Loeb +10"7;
5.P.Solberg +12"3; 6.Aava +22"4;
7.Gardemeister +28"4...
J-WRC > 22.Burkart 16'11"2

SS16 Moselwein 1 (18.08 km)
1.Duval 10'43"9; 2.Hirvonen +1"9
3.Loeb +3"0; 4.Sordo +8"4;
5.P.Solberg +10"01; 6.Latvala +14"4;
7.Aava +16"1; 8.Mikkelsen +17"8...
J-WRC > 21.Burkart 12'11"0

SS17 Dhrontal 2 (22.22 km)
1.Duval 14'15"7; 2.Hirvonen +3"7;
3.Loeb +7"0; 4.P.Solberg +10"1;
5.Sordo +13"4. 6.Latvala +14"6;
7.Aava +20"7; 8.Atkinson +23"4...
J-WRC > 24.Ogier 15'52"2

SS18 Moselwein 2 (18.08 km)
1.Duval 10'45"4; 2.Hirvonen +0"3;
3.P.Solberg +0"7; 4.Latvala +5"9;
5.Loeb +5"9; 6.Aava +8"0;
7.Sordo +9"1; 8.H.Solberg +11"8 ...
J-WRC > 21.Ogier 11'53"0

SS19 Circus Maximus Trier (4.37 km)
1.Loeb 3'22"4; 2.Mikkelsen +0"0;
3.P.Solberg +0"0; 4.Aava +0"1;
5.Atkinson +0"3; 6.Hirvonen +0"4;
7.Latvala +1"0; 8.Sordo +1"3...
J-WRC > 24.Abbring 3'37"7

Results

	Driver - Co-Driver	Car	Gr.	Time
1.	**Loeb - Elena**	**Citroën C4 WRC**	A8	**3h26'19"7**
2.	Sordo - Marti	Citroën C4 WRC 08	A8	+47"7
3.	Duval - Pivato	Ford Focus RS WRC 07	A8	+1'20"0
4.	Hirvonen - Lehtinen	Ford Focus RS WRC 08	A8	+1'30"1
5.	P. Solberg - Mills	Subaru Impreza WRC 2008	A8	+2'35"3
6.	Atkinson - Prévot	Subaru Impreza WRC 2008	A8	+4'45"9
7.	H. Solberg - Menkerud	Ford Focus RS WRC 07	A8	+5'36"2
8.	Aava - Sikk	Citroën C4 WRC	A8	+5'37"8
9.	Latvala - Anttila	Ford Focus RS WRC 08	A8	+6'17"2
10.	Gardmeister - Tuominen	Suzuki SX4 WRC	A8	+7'16"8
11.	Mikkelsen - Floene	Ford Focus RS WRC 06	A8	+8'30"8
19.	**Ogier - Ingrassia**	**Citroën C2 S1600**	A6/J	+21'16"3
22.	Burkart - Kölbach	Citroën C2 S1600	A6/J	+24'50"5
25.	Bettega - Scattolin	Renault Clio R3	A7/J	+26'30"7
27.	Gassner Jun. - Wüstenhagen	Mitsubishi Lancer Evo. IX	N4	+30'2"6

Leading Retirements (24)

Ctrl11	Schammel - Jamoul	Renault Clio R3	Engine
Ctrl9	Prokop - Tomanek	Citroën C2 S1600	Alternator
Ctrl5	Galli - Bernacchini	Ford Focus RS WRC 07	Off

Performers

	1	2	3	4	5	6	C6	Nb SS
Loeb	14	1	2	2	-	-	18	19
Duval	4	2	3	5	1	1	16	19
Sordo	1	9	3	2	1	-	16	19
P. Solberg	1	-	2	2	5	5	15	19
Mikkelsen	1	-	-	-	-	-	1	19
Hirvonen	-	6	7	4	-	1	18	19
Latvala	-	-	-	3	2	3	8	19
Aava	-	-	-	1	1	2	4	19
Atkinson	-	-	-	-	6	5	11	19
Galli	-	-	-	-	1	-	1	5
H. Solberg	-	-	-	-	-	1	1	19

Leaders

SS1 > SS24	Loeb

Sébastien Ogier

Previous Winners

2002	Loeb - Elena	2004	Loeb - Elena	2006	Loeb - Elena
	Citroën Xsara WRC		Citroën Xsara WRC		Citroën Xsara WRC
2003	Loeb - Elena	2005	Loeb - Elena	2007	Loeb - Elena
	Citroën Xsara WRC		Citroën Xsara WRC		Citroën C4 WRC

11 NEW ZEALAND

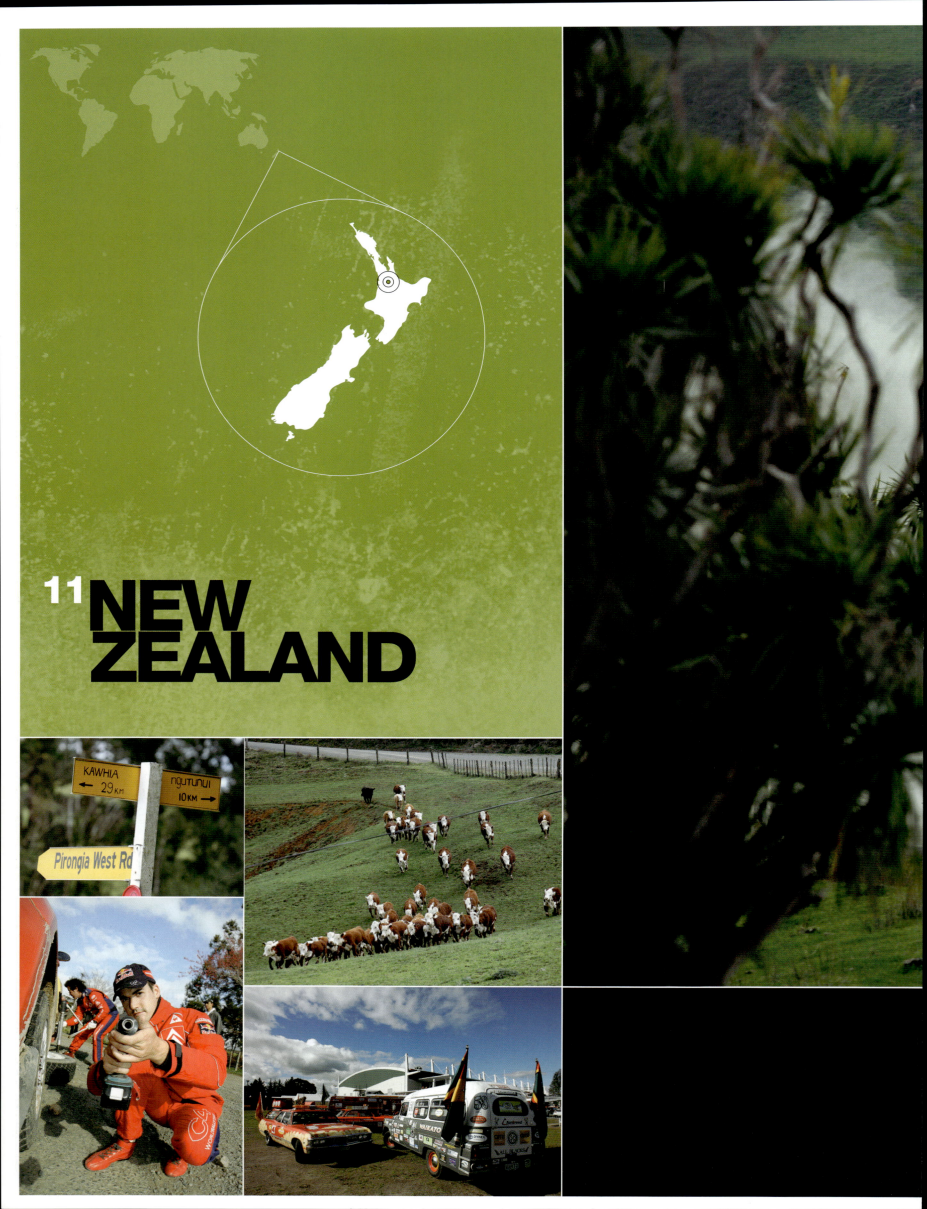

On a knife edge to the end
Citroën claimed their 50th World Championship victory – and what a way to do it! Loeb and Sordo's 1-2 finish was as amazing as it was unexpected, coming at Ford's expense when they had been within a whisker of a similar result themselves. All was decided in the unforgiving final few kilometres of the last stage of the Antipodean event, and in the end it tipped the scales the Chevron's way.

11 | New Zealand

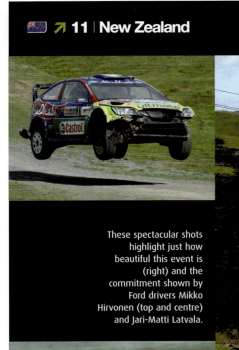

These spectacular shots highlight just how beautiful this event is (right) and the commitment shown by Ford drivers Mikko Hirvonen (top and centre) and Jari-Matti Latvala.

THE RALLY
Citroën all smiles, frustration for Ford

Dateline Sunday August 31, 2008: the start of SS15, Whaanga Coast 2 – 27.92 km, one of the World Rally Championship's iconic stages, winding its way from tropical forest to coast via a superb route overlooking the Tasman Sea.

After that timed section there was only one stage left on the rally, a superspecial at Mystery Creek to be specific. Not much to worry about there. So Ford could afford to smile, given the order at that point. Miko Hirvonen was in front, 9.8 clear of team-mate Jari-Matti Latvala, 12.8 ahead of Dani Sordo in the leading C4 WRC and with 15.3 seconds in hand over Sébastien Loeb. The Spaniard and the Frenchman both knew the game was up; unless mechanical trouble intervened, they couldn't hope for much better against the Blue Oval forces this time. Their chances had slipped away in the first two legs. To underline that fact, that very Sunday morning Loeb, trying to close the gap, had got it wrong in SS14, Te Hutewai 1, losing 10 seconds in the resultant spin. "It's not over yet, we're not giving up," he said soon after as he thought about maybe sneaking second. First was out of reach – Hirvonen had that in his masterful grasp and the Finn had a quietly confident air about him.

So where were we... yes, the start of SS15. Everyone was keeping a watchful eye on everyone else as Ford sniffed a 1-2, while Citroën were refusing to admit defeat even if they were no longer favourites for the win.

Suddenly the sky fell in on the Anglo-American team, and the first man to feel it was Latvala.
Just 3.5 kilometres in, the young Finn dropped yet another clanger. He got caught in the ruts on a left-hander, unbalanced the Focus and clouted a bank. The radiator was shattered, and Latvala was out. "I was coming up to a long left-hander where the last cars had made a narrow track first time through. I lost grip to the rear and the car started to slide. I stood on the accelerator to try and keep it straight but it kept turning and took me to the inside of the corner. I hit a bank, there was a rock embedded in the sand, and the impact broke the radiator and the cooling system. I knew straight away it was all over – the water and oil alarms went off at once. I'm extremely disappointed because I've let points slip away, both for me and for the team. I was going so well – I was so happy with the way I was driving on these roads I thought I could finish second."

Ford hadn't had time to swallow that bitter pill before it was Hirvonen's turn to let it all slip away, or very nearly all – the win, yes, the title, a little bit. This is how the man himself saw it: "When I saw Jari-Matti stopped by the roadside (Latvala was opening the road, so Hirvonen was second to go through) I realised straight away that all I had to do was finish and it was in the bag. But about nine kilometres after the start I also realised my car had a slow puncture on the right rear. I had no idea where it had happened, or when. Then, just a kilometre out, I had a sudden spin, the car touched the bank and it tore the front bumper off. It just wasn't to be... It's obviously one of my biggest disappointments as a driver, but that's how it is in sport. I was confident, I thought I could maintain the pace, finish that stage and win. Now it's going to be really hard to take the world title, but it's not impossible. I'm on the podium, and we have to take the positives out of that. And what doesn't kill you only makes you stronger."

Dani Sordo has come a long way on gravel and his performance helped Citroën to a welcome 1-2 finish.

Fifth place for Uumo Aava's privateer C4 WRC completed a triumphant weekend for Citroën.

Sébastien Loeb didn't give an inch to his Ford foes as he claimed an unexpected win.

refused to fire up for the start of SS6, the last significant one on the first leg. The Franco-Monegasque pairing were three minutes late and copped a 30-second penalty... though it suited him quite nicely, because even though he set another fastest time Loeb was now second overall and therefore didn't have to open the road next day. Was it tactics? Who knows...

Next day, though, it all became clear. Citroën had decided to go down the tactical route Ford had already taken on a previous event. By the end of SS10 Loeb was back in front overall, 4.2 seconds ahead of Hirvonen.

That, then, is how you lose an unloseable rally; how 18 points slipped through Ford's fingers, leaving them with just six; and how Hirvonen lost more ground to a durable, cool and opportunistic Loeb in the drivers' standings. And that's what makes great champions.

To say Blue Oval boss Malcolm Wilson was disappointed would be quite an understatement. "Seriously, I've seen it all in my career, both as a team manager and as a driver. But that's the biggest blow I've ever had to take. We were first and second, there was only one real special left and here we are on the third step of the podium. I'm really disappointed for Mikko, because he drove immaculately and showed he could beat Loeb." That was the way things ended, sadly, for Ford – and the triumphant outcome for Citroën, who obviously hadn't been expecting such a dramatic turn-around, especially after having been dominated up to that point, both on the road and in tactical terms. The proof of that fact lies in the first two legs.

On the opening day the World Champion was simply hanging on through the first few stages. No matter whether the route has had rain dumped on it in the weeks building up to an event, opening the road, as the man leading the drivers' standings has to do, is always a real handicap. In the first three stages the Ford boys made hay before Loeb clean-sheeted them all second time through. By the end of SS5 he was just seven-tenths down on Hirvonen. Unfortunately his C4's engine

Henning Solberg got an early one-minute penalty for being late at a starting-gate, had a lacklustre event and finished just outside the points in ninth.

11 | New Zealand

There was a first for Suzuki as the Japanese constructor got both cars into the points, Gardemeister (seen from the rear) 7th and P-G Andersson 6th.

And by the end of the leg, in the final stage, he took it nice and easy, leaving the way clear on the final leg for Finland's Latvala, not Hirvonen – Malcolm Wilson had left him free to run his own race.

Giving up those 14 seconds meant the Frenchman was in the ideal position, or so he thought, for the final leg, 13.3 behind Latvala and 9.3 down on Hirvonen. After condemning Ford for using similar tactics in the past, Citroën now found themselves having to be just as pragmatic.
" I let my rivals through reluctantly," the Alsace driver explained after the second leg. " That's not really my idea of rallying at all – it's a discipline where the idea is to go faster than everybody else, not get on the brakes. But there are rules and we have to make full use of them. Tomorrow will tell us if we did the right thing!"

The answer came soon enough, and it was a 'No'. As the third day got under way, the World Champion couldn't make up the gap they had given away to their opponents. He went for it, even had a spin, but it seemed there was nothing he could do – until that unbelievable turn of events on Whaanga Coast.

The New Zealand Rally always seems to throw up a dramatic climax. In 2007 the wheel of fortune swung the way of Marcus Grönholm and Ford by just three-tenths of a second, still the smallest winning margin between two drivers in rally history. Lady Luck probably wanted to even things out and give something back to the other side...

Sébastien Loeb, of course, was immaculate, never letting up for a minute, but we mustn't forget Dani Sordo either as we look back on the 2008 event. For the Spaniard, who excelled in his dual role of team-mate and gravel rally apprentice, it was a well-deserved and convincing second place. " I'm delighted with the way it felt out there over those three days," said the jubilant Spaniard. " I know I need more practice on this surface, but I can also see the progress I've made since last year. My touch at the wheel of the C4 is getting better and better, and

Jari-Matti Latvala can be relied upon to be spectacular, but once again he went too far, retiring after an off in the Whaanga Coast stage right at the end of the event.

Federico Villagra had an untroubled run as he took the point for eighth place.

Stobart's dynamic stand-in François Duval also had a late off.

I'm getting a lot closer to the best guys on gravel. So it's all looking very good." As it was for Citroën as well: not only did they have that 1-2 finish in the bag, but they also had Urmo Aava's fine fifth place in his privateer C4 WRC to enter in the 'plus' column.

There were other teams with something to smile about by the end of the event. Subaru for one, with Solberg's fourth place as the Japanese team celebrated the 15th anniversary of their first World Championship win with Colin McRae and the 200th World Championship start for an Impreza (on what was virtually a home event for him, Atkinson contrived to roll it on the first leg). Suzuki also kept their heads above water with both X4's in the points, Andersson in sixth place, one ahead of Gardemeister. ∎

In 2007 fortune favoured Grönholm and Ford in Kiwi-land. This time the luck was on Loeb's side.

So where were the front-runners in the title chase? A long way behind, that's where. Their ambitions were thwarted on the very first stage when Aigner got a puncture and Hänninen had an off. The Austrian was out altogether by SS10 after an off of his own, though the Finn did some useful damage limitation with fifth place. That left the two men separated by just four points, Aigner still in front. But with four drivers covered by just eight points as Ketomaa and Sandell threatened the top two, it looked like being pretty tense in the closing stages of the season. ∎

New Zealand has always been a happy hunting-ground for Subaru. Some 15 years after Colin McRae's historic win, Petter Solberg brought his Impreza home in fourth place.

PRODUCTION CARS
A first for Prokop

An Antipodean race of attrition saw Martin Prokop take his first win in the Production class. It promised to be a close fight on such wonderful terrain between Aigner and Hänninen, who had shared the five wins to that date between them (three to the Austrian, two to the Finn). And there were penty of others to play a telling part, such as Fumio Nutahara, whose Mitsubishi enjoyed theearly lead before being quickly overtaken by Mirco Baldacci, also in a Mitsubishi. Under severe pressure, he clung to his lead before going off into a ditch in SS10. That put Prokop into the lead. We all thought the brilliant Russian 17-year-old Evgeniy Novikov (Mitsubishi) might hang on to his fine second place, but gearbox trouble forced him out. So Patrik Sandell, in a Mitsubishi for this event rather than his Peugeot 207 S2000, took over that rather flattering position as Martin Rauam in third made it a Mitsubishi 1-2-3.

11 | New Zealand | Results

38th RALLY OF NEW ZEALAND

Organiser Details
PO Box 62021,
Mt Wellington 1641, Auckland,
New Zealand
Tel.: +6492 760882
Fax: +6492 760881

Rally of New Zealand

11th leg of FIA 2008 World Championship for constructors and drivers.
6th leg of FIA Production Car World Championship.

Date August 28 - 31, 2008

Route
1218.38 km divised in three legs.
16 special stages on dirt roads (354.58 km);
18 raced

Ceremonial Start
Thursday, August 28 (18:30),
Hood Street, Hamilton City
Leg 1
Friday, August 29 (09:18/17:03),
Hamilton > Hamilton, 430.40 km;
5 special stages (139.54 km); 7 raced
Leg 2
Saturday, August 30 (09:08/15:46),
Hamilton > Hamilton, 545.39 km;
6 special stages (130.00 km)
Leg 3
Sunday, August 31 (09:23/14:00),
Hamilton > Hamilton, 242.59 km;
5 special stages (85.04 km)

Entry List (64) - 57 starters

N°	Driver (Nat.)	Co-Driver (Nat.)	Team	Car	Group & FIA Priority
1	SEBASTIEN LOEB (F)	DANIEL ELENA (MC)	CITROEN TOTAL WORLD RALLY TEAM	CITROEN C4 WRC	A8 1
2	DANI SORDO (E)	MARC MARTI (E)	CITROEN TOTAL WORLD RALLY TEAM	CITROEN C4 WRC	A8 1
3	MIKKO HIRVONEN (FIN)	JARMO LEHTINEN (FIN)	BP FORD ABU DHABI WORLD RALLY TEAM	FORD FOCUS RS WRC 07	A8 1
4	JARI-MATTI LATVALA (FIN)	MIIKKA ANTTILA (FIN)	BP FORD ABU DHABI WORLD RALLY TEAM	FORD FOCUS RS WRC 07	A8 1
5	PETTER SOLBERG (N)	PHILIP MILLS (GB)	SUBARU WORLD RALLY TEAM	SUBARU IMPREZA WRC 2008	A8 1
6	CHRIS ATKINSON (AUS)	STEPHANE PREVOT (B)	SUBARU WORLD RALLY TEAM	SUBARU IMPREZA WRC 2008	A8 1
7	FRANCOIS DUVAL (B)	PATRICK PIVATO (F)	STOBART VK M-SPORT FORD RALLY TEAM	FORD FOCUS RS WRC 07	A8 1
8	MATTHEW WILSON (GB)	SCOTT MARTIN (GB)	STOBART VK M-SPORT FORD RALLY TEAM	FORD FOCUS RS WRC 07	A8 1
9	FEDERICO VILLAGRA (RA)	JORGE PEREZ COMPANC (RA)	MUNCHI'S FORD WORLD RALLY TEAM	FORD FOCUS RS WRC 07	A8 1
10	HENNING SOLBERG (N)	CATO MENKERUD (N)	MUNCHI'S FORD WORLD RALLY TEAM	FORD FOCUS RS WRC 07	A8 1
11	TONI GARDEMEISTER (FIN)	TOMI TUOMINEN (FIN)	SUZUKI WORLD RALLY TEAM	SUZUKI SX4 WRC	A8 1
12	PER-G. ANDERSSON (S)	JONAS ANDERSSON (S)	SUZUKI WORLD RALLY TEAM	SUZUKI SX4 WRC	A8 1
14	URMO AAVA (EE)	KULDAR SIKK (EE)	WORLD RALLY TEAM ESTONIA	CITROEN C4 WRC	A8 2
15	CONRAD RAUTENBACH (ZW)	DAVID SENIOR (GB)	CONRAD RAUTENBACH	CITROEN C4 WRC	A8 2
31	TOSHI ARAI (J)	GLENN MACNEALL (AUS)	SUBARU TEAM ARAI	SUBARU IMPREZA WRX STI	N4 3
32	MIRCO BALDACCI (RSM)	GIOVANNI AGNESE (I)	MIRCO BALDACCI	MITSUBISHI LANCER EVO IX	N4 3
33	MARTIN PROKOP (CZ)	JAN TOMÁNEK (CZ)	MARTIN PROKOP	MITSUBISHI LANCER EVO IX	N4 3
34	GIANLUCA LINARI (I)	FRANCO GIUSTI (I)	GIANLUCA LINARI	SUBARU IMPREZA WRX STI	N4 3
35	EVGENY NOVIKOV (RUS)	DALE MOSCATT (AUS)	EVGENY NOVIKOV	MITSUBISHI LANCER EVO IX	N4 3
37	SPYROS PAVLIDES (CY)	DENIS GIRAUDET (F)	AUTOTEK	SUBARU IMPREZA WRX STI	N4 3
38	STEWART TAYLOR (NZ)	WARWICK SEARLE (NZ)	ORION WORLD RALLY TEAM	MITSUBISHI LANCER EVO IX	N4 3
39	MISFER AL-MARRI (QA)	CHRIS PATTERSON (GB)	QMMF	SUBARU IMPREZA WRX STI	N4 3
41	ANDREAS AIGNER (A)	KLAUS WICHA (D)	RED BULL RALLYE TEAM	MITSUBISHI LANCER EVO IX	N4 3
42	BERNARDO SOUSA (P)	JORGE CARVALHO (P)	RED BULL RALLYE TEAM	MITSUBISHI LANCER EVO IX	N4 3
43	EVGENIY VERTUNOV (RUS)	GEORGY TROSHKIN (RUS)	SUBARU RALLY TEAM RUSSIA	SUBARU IMPREZA WRX STI	N4 3
44	CAO DONG LIU (CN)	ANTHONY MCLOUGHLIN (AUS)	GABOKO RALLY TEAM	SUBARU IMPREZA WRX STI	N4 3
46	JARI KETOMAA (FIN)	MIIKA TEISKONEN (FIN)	MOTORING CLUB 2	SUBARU IMPREZA WRX STI	N4 3
47	GIORGIO BACCO (I)	FABIO PIZZOL (I)	MOTORING CLUB 3	SUBARU IMPREZA WRX STI	N4 3
50	ARMINDO ARAUJO (P)	MIGUEL RAMALHO (P)	RALLIART ITALY	MITSUBISHI LANCER EVO IX	N4 3
51	SUBHAN AKSA (RI)	HENDRIK MBOI (RI)	INDONESIA RALLY TEAM	MITSUBISHI LANCER EVO IX	N4 3
52	JUHO HÄNNINEN (FIN)	MIKKO MARKKULA (FIN)	RALLIART NEW ZEALAND	MITSUBISHI LANCER EVO IX	N4 3
54	KEN BLOCK (USA)	ALEX GELSOMINO (USA)	SUBARU RALLY TEAM USA	SUBARU IMPREZA WRX STI	N4 3
55	PATRIK SANDELL (S)	EMIL AXELSSON (S)	PEUGEOT SPORT SWEDEN	MITSUBISHI LANCER EVO IX	N4 3
56	FUMIO NUTAHARA (J)	DANIEL BARRITT (GB)	ADVAN-PIAA RALLY TEAM	MITSUBISHI LANCER EVO IX	N4 3
57	MARTIN RAUAM (EE)	SILVER KÜTT (EE)	WORLD RALLY TEAM ESTONIA	MITSUBISHI LANCER EVO IX	N4 3
58	NAREN KUMAR (IND)	NICKY BEECH (GB)	TEAM SIDVIN INDIA	SUBARU IMPREZA WRX STI	N4 3
59	HAYDEN PADDON (NZ)	JOHN KENNARD (NZ)	PADDON DIRECT	MITSUBISHI LANCER EVO IX	N4 3
60	CHRIS WEST (NZ)	GARRY COWAN (NZ)	RALLIART NEW ZEALAND	MITSUBISHI LANCER EVO IX	N4 3
61	RICHARD MASON (NZ)	SARA MASON (NZ)	BNT MASON MOTORSPORT	SUBARU IMPREZA WRX STI	N4
64	CALLUM MCINNES (NZ)	DAVID CALDER (NZ)	MILKBAR RALLY TEAM	SUBARU IMPREZA WRX STI	N4
66	NATHAN THOMAS (NZ)	RICHARD KELLY (NZ)	WILFORD MOTORSPORT	MITSUBISHI LANCER EVO VII	N4
67	EMMA GILMOUR (NZ)	CLAIRE MOLE (GB)	EMMA GILMOUR	SUBARU IMPREZA WRX STI	N4
69	SLOAN COX (NZ)	TARRYN COX (NZ)	TASLO ENGINEERING	MITSUBISHI LANCER EVO VIII	N4
73	ANDRE MEIER (NZ)	JASON FARMER (NZ)	MEIER MOTORSPORT	SUBARU IMPREZA	N4
74	KIRSTY NELSON (NZ)	MICHELE BRUNT (NZ)	NELSON MOTORSPORT LTD	SUBARU IMPREZA	N4
75	TONY GREEN (NZ)	JOHN ALLEN (AUS)	AUTOTEK	SUBARU IMPREZA WRX STI	N4
76	BRUCE FULLERTON (AUS)	HUGH REARDON-SMITH (AUS)	PRESTIGE MOTORSPORTS AND PERFORMANCE	MITSUBISHI LANCER EVO VIII	N4
77	BRENT TAYLOR (NZ)	CHRIS RAMSAY (NZ)	CHRIS RAMSAY RALLYSPORT	MITSUBISHI LANCER EVO VIII	N4
78	MASAHIRO NAKAJIMA (J)	NAOKI KUROSAKI (J)	MASAHIRO NAKAJIMA	SUBARU IMPREZA WRX STI	N4
80	BRETT MARTIN (NZ)	GRANT MARRA (NZ)	RAY WILSON RALLYSPORT	MITSUBISHI LANCER EVO IX	N4
81	TREVOR TAYLOR (NZ)	JASON TIMMINS (NZ)	TAYLOR MOTORSPORT	MITSUBISHI LANCER EVO IX	N4
82	BRENDAN REEVES (AUS)	RHIANON SMYTH (AUS)	KAYNE BARRIE MOTORSPORT LTD	FORD FIESTA ST	N3
83	PATRICK MALLEY (NZ)	RAYMOND BENNETT (NZ)	M RALLY TEAM	FORD FIESTA ST	N3
84	BEN JAGGER (NZ)	BEN HAWKINS (NZ)	BEN JAGGER RALLYSPORT	FORD FIESTA ST	N3
85	TOMOKI OHASHI (J)	KAZUYOSHI FUNAKI (J)	TAKAYAMA COLLEGE	SUBARU IMPREZA WRX STI	N4
86	DERMOTT MALLEY (NZ)	LINZI MALLEY (NZ)	M RALLY TEAM	FORD FIESTA ST	N3
87	MOTOHARU KASEYA (J)	YUKO MITSUKURI (J)	MOTOHARU KASEYA	FORD FIESTA ST	N3

P. Sandell

M. Rauam

J. Hänninen

J. Ketomaa

A. Aigner

Championship Classifications

•R•: Rookie

FIA Drivers (11/15)			FIA Constructors (11/15)			FIA Production Car WRC (6/8)			FIA Junior WRC (5/7)		
1. Loeb	8🏆	86	1. Citroën Total World Rally Team	8🏆	141	1. Aigner	3🏆	30	1. Ogier	3🏆	34
2. Hirvonen	2🏆	78	2. BP-Ford Abu Dhabi World Rally Team	3🏆	121	2. Hänninen	2🏆	26	2. Gallagher		25
3. Sordo		51	3. Subaru World Rally Team		74	3. Ketomaa		23	3. Burkart		24
4. Atkinson		40	4. Stobart VK M-Sport Ford Rally Team		51	4. Sandell		22	4. Kosciusko	1🏆	22
5. Latvala	1🏆	34	5. Munchi's Ford World Rally Team		22	5. Prokop	1🏆	17	5. Bettega		14
6. P. Solberg		32	6. Suzuki World Rally Team		20	6. Rauam		15	6. Sandell		14
7. H. Solberg		22				7. Nutahara		14	7. Prokop	1🏆	12
8. Galli		17				8. Sousa		12	8. Mölder		8
9. Wilson		12				9. Araujo		12	9. Schammel		8
10. Duval		11				10. Beltrán		8	10. Albertini		7
11. Aava		11				11. Valimaki		8	11. Bertolotti		7
12. Villagra		9				12. M. Baldacci		6	12. Niegel •R•		6
13. Rautenbach		6				13. Aksakov		6	13. Abbring		6
14. Gardemeister		5				14. Vertunov		6	14. Cortinovis		4
15. Mikkelsen		4				15. Svedlund		5	15. Weijs Jr. •R•		2
16. Andersson		4				16. Paddon		5	16. Fanari •R•		1
17. Rantanen		2				17. Nittel		4	17. Komljenovic		1
18. Cuoq		2				18. Farrah		3	18. Pinomaki		0
19. Aigner		1				19. Tiippana		3			
20. Ogier		1				20. Arai		3	Rookie		
21. Hänninen		1				21. Campedelli		3	1. Fanari		44
22. Østberg,		0				22. Bacco		1	2. Weijs Jr.		20
K. Al-Qassimi,		0				23. L. Baldacci		1	3. Niegel		8
Beltrán, Mölder,		0				24. Taylor		1			
Ketomaa, Prokop,		0				24. Linari, Frisiero,		0			
Clark, Kosciuszko,		0				Dong, Pavlides,		0			
Sandell, Nutahara,		0				Aksa, Brynilsden,		0			
Rauam, Burkart,		0				Al-Attiyah, Kumar,		0			
Gallagher, Broccoli,		0				Manfrinato,		0			
Paddon, Farrah,		0				Athanassoulas,		0			
Schammel, Nittel		0				Errani, Pastrana,		0			
Baldacci, Valimaki,		0				Block, Jereb,		0			
Artru, Guerra,		0				Novikov, Flodin,		0			
Arai, A. Al-Qassimi,		0				Marrini		0			
Mercier											

Special Stages Times

SS1 Pirongia West 1 (24.22 km)
1.Latvala 17'08"1; 2.Hirvonen +1"2;
3.Loeb +5"9; 4.Sordo +8"5;
5.Atkinson +18"3; 6.Duval +23"5;
7.Aava +26"3; 8.Wilson +30"4...
P-WRC > 12.Nutahara 18'12"9

SS2 Waitomo 1 Part 1 (25.85 km)
1.Hirvonen 15'12"5; 2.Sordo +0"1;
3.Loeb +1"4; 4.Latvala +6"2;
5.Atkinson +6"4; 6.Duval +15"5;
7.Aava +21"7; 8.P.Solberg +21"8;
P-WRC > 12.Baldacci 16'01"2

SS3 Waitomo 1 Part 2 (17.36 km)
1.Hirvonen 14'13"5; 2.Latvala +0"3;
3.Sordo +3"5; 4.Loeb +4"1;
5.Andersson +4"2; 6.Aava +6"9;
7.Duval +7"5; 8.Wilson +11"1...
P-WRC > 13.Novikov 14'36"8

SS4 Pirongia West 2 (24.22 km)
1.Loeb 16'35"8; 2.Hirvonen +1"8;
3.Latvala +5"6; 4.Sordo +3"8;
5.Duval +14"5; 6.P.SOlberg +28"2;
7.Aava +33"8; 8.Wilson +34"0...
P-WRC > 14.Hänninen 17'42"0

SS5 Waitomo 2 Part 1 (25.85 km)
1.Loeb 14'39"6; 2.Hirvonen +6"9;
3.Sordo +12"2; 4.Latvala +13"1;
5.Duval +18"0; 6.P.Solberg +23"6;
7.Aava +29"3; 8.Gardemeister +39"8...
P-WRC > 12.Hänninen 15'40"2

SS6 Waitomo 2 Part 2 (17.36 km)
1.Loeb 13'37"8; 2.Hirvonen +3"3;
3.Sordo +9"2; 4.Aava +14"4;
5.Duval +16"7; 6.Latvala +17"4;
7.P.Solberg +20"6; 8.Andersson +23"3...
P-WRC > 11.Hänninen 14'06"8

SS7 Mystery Creek Super Special 1 (3.14 km)
1.Hirvonen 3'03"8; 2.Sordo +0"2;
3.Loeb +0"4; 4.Latvala +0"7;
5.Andersson +1"4; 6.Aava +2"1;
7.Gardemeister +2"6;
8.H.Solberg +2"8...
P-WRC > 11.Hänninen 3'08"1

Classification Leg 1
1.Hirvonen 1h34'44"3; 2.Loeb +27"8;
3.Sordo +30"0; 4.Latvala +30"1;
5.Duval +1'27"9; 6.Aava +2'01"3;
7.P.Solberg +2'25"8;
8.Andersson +2'50"5 ...
P-WRC > 13.Baldacci 1h40'27"2

SS8 Port Waikato (17.22 km)
1.H.Solberg 10'02"2; 2.Loeb +4"4;
3.Latvala +4"5; 4.Sordo +5"1;
5.Wilson +6"8; 6.P.Solberg +7"0;
7.Aava +7"8; 8.Duval +9"3...
P-WRC > 16.Hänninen 10'38"8

SS9 Possum (13.78 km)
1.Loeb 10'39"2; 2.Hirvonen +3"1;
3.Latvala +5"6; 4.H.Solberg +6"4;
5.Sordo +8"8; 6.Wilson +12"3;
7.P.Solberg +14"7; 8.Duval +17"2...
P-WRC > 14.Hänninen 3'08"1

SS10 Franklin (31.58 km)
1.Latvala 22'02"7; 2.Loeb +0"8;
3.Sordo +8"1; 4.Aava +10"4;
5.Wilson +10"7; 6.H.Solberg +11"1;
7.Hirvonen +11"2; 8.Duval +13"4...
P-WRC > 13.Prokop 11'53"1

SS11 Mystery Creek Super Special 2 (3.14 km)
1.H.Solberg 2'58"0; 2.Loeb +1"7;
3.Hirvonen +3"2; 4.Duval +3"6;
5.Sordo +9"9; 6.Latvala +4"0;
7.P.Solberg +4"0; 8.Aava +4"9...
P-WRC > 15.Hänninen 3'06"4

SS12 Te Akau South (31.92 km)
1.H.Solberg 18'37"0; 2.Sordo +6"5;
3.Loeb +8"0; 4.Latvala +8"3;
5.Atkinson +9"9; 6.Duval +14"3;
7.Hirvonen +17"5; 8.Aava +18"3...
P-WRC > 14.Hänninen 19'31"1

SS13 Te Akau North (32.36 km)
1.H.Solberg 17'29"7; 2.Latvala +3"4;
3.Atkinson +5"3; 4.P.Solberg +7"2;
5.Sordo +9"2; 6.Duval +11"1;
7.Aava +12"1; 8.Wilson +16"5...
P-WRC > 16.Hänninen 18'29"0

Classification Leg 2
1.Latvala 2h57'29"0; 2.Hirvonen +9"3;
3.Loeb +13"3; 4.Sordo +15"7;
5.Duval +1'40"9; 6.Aava +2'49"8;
7.P.Solberg +2'52"8;
8.Andersson +4'31"0...
P-WRC > 14.Prokop 3h07'17"8

SS14 Te Hutewai 1 (11.23 km)
1.H.Solberg 8'03"0; 2.Wilson +1"8;
3.Atkinson +1"8; 4.P.Solberg +6"3;
5.Sordo +7"0; 6.Aava +7"0;
7.Duval +10"0; 8.Gardemeister +17"8...
P-WRC > 14.Hänninen 8'20"4

SS15 Whaanga Coast 1 (29.72 km)
1.H.Solberg 21'26"4; 2.Hirvonen +8"6;
3.P.Solberg +10"2; 4.Sordo +10"5;
5.Loeb +11"7; 6.Wilson +16"3;
7.Latvala +18"9; 8.Aava +20"7...
P-WRC > 13.Hänninen 22'12"1

SS16 Te Hutewai 2 (11.23 km)
1.Loeb 7'47"5; 2.Hirvonnen +2"3;
3.H.Solberg +3"4; 4.Latvala +5"0;
5.Wilson +5"4; 6.P.Solberg +5"8;
7.Sordo +6"2; 8.Duval +8"1...
P-WRC 14.Hänninen 8'15"9

SS17 Whaanga Coast 2 (29.72 km)
1.Loeb 20'47"0; 2.H.Solberg +14"7;
3.P.Solberg +16"5; 4.Sordo +18"7;
5.Aava +24"2; 6.Wilson +31"9;
7.Gardemeister +49"1;
8.Hirvonen +57"1...
P-WRC > 10.Hänninen 22'19"3

SS18 Mystery Creek Super Special 3 (3.14 km)
1.H.Solberg 3'00"6; 2.P.Solberg +2"7;
3.Hirvonen +3"3; 4.Wilson +3"4;
5.Loeb +3"5; 6.Villagra +4"4;
7.Gardemeister +4"7; 8.Sordo +4"8...
P-WRC > 11.Araujo 3'10"0

Results

	Driver - Co-Driver	Car	Gr.	Time
1.	Loeb - Elena	Citroën CA WRC	A8	3h59'18"9
2.	Sordo - Marti	Citroën C4 WRC	A8	+17"5
3.	Hirvonen - Lehtinen	Ford Focus RS WRC 08	A8	+41"5
4.	P.Solberg - Mills	Subaru Impreza WRC 2008	A8	+2'48"9
5.	Aava - Sikk	Citroën C4 WRC	A8	+3'30"7
6.	Andersson - Andersson	Suzuki SX4 WRC	A8	+7'37"4
7.	Gardmeister - Tuominen	Suzuki SX4 WRC	A8	+7'54"9
8.	Villagra - PerezCompanc	Ford Focus RC WRC 07	A8	+8'35"0
9.	H. Solberg - Menkerud	Ford Focus RS WRC 07	A8	+9'15"2
10.	Prokop - Tomanek	Mitsubishi Lancer Evo. IX	N4/P	+13'49"0
11.	Sandell - Axelsson	Mitsubishi Lancer Evo. IX	N4/P	+14'25"2
12.	Rauam - Kutt	Mitsubishi Lancer Evo. IX	N4/P	+14'46"8

Leading Retirements (22)

Ctrl18	Rautenbach - Senior	Citroën C4 WRC		Accelerator
Ctrl17	Latvala - Antilla	Ford Focus RS WRC 07		Off
Ctrl17	Duval - Pivato	Ford Focus RS WRC 07		Off
Ctrl15	Atkinson - Prévot	Subaru Impreza WRC 2008		Radiator

Performers

	1	2	3	4	5	6	C6	Nb SS
H. Solberg	7	1	1	1	-	1	11	18
Loeb	6	3	4	1	2	-	16	18
Hirvonen	3	7	1	-	1	-	12	18
Latvala	2	2	4	5	-	2	15	16
Sordo	-	3	4	5	3	1	16	18
P. Solberg	-	1	2	2	-	4	9	18
Wilson	-	1	-	1	3	3	8	15
Atkinson	-	-	2	-	3	-	5	11
Aava	-	-	-	2	1	2	5	18
Duval	-	-	-	1	3	4	8	16
Villagra	-	-	-	-	-	1	1	18

Leaders

SS1	Latvala
SS2 > SS9	Hirvonen
SS10	Loeb
SS11 > SS12	Latvala
SS13 > SS14	Hirvonen
SS15 > SS16	Loeb

Martin Prokop

Previous Winners

1977	Bacchelli - Rosetti Fiat 131 Abarth	1988	Haider - Hinterleitner Opel Kadett GSI	1998	Sainz - Moya Toyota Corolla WRC
1978	Brookes - Porter Ford Escort RS	1989	Carlsson - Carlsson Mazda 323 Turbo	1999	Mäkinen - Mannisenmäki Mitsubishi Lancer Evo 6
1979	Mikkola - Hertz Ford Escort RS	1990	Sainz - Moya Toyota Celica GT-Four	2000	Grönholm - Rautiainen Peugeot 206 WRC
1980	Salonen - Harjanne Datsun 160J	1991	Sainz - Moya Toyota Celica GT-Four	2001	Grönholm - Rautiainen Peugeot 206 WRC
1982	Waldegaard - Thorzelius Toyota Celica GT	1992	Sainz - Moya Toyota Celica Turbo 4WD	2002	Grönholm - Rautiainen Peugeot 206 WRC
1983	Rohrl - Geistdorfer Opel Ascona 400	1993	McRae - Ringer Subaru Legacy RS	2003	Grönholm - Rautiainen Peugeot 206 WRC
1984	Blomqvist - Cederberg Audi Quattro A2	1994	McRae - Ringer Subaru Impreza	2004	Solberg - Mills Subaru Impreza WRC 2004
1985	Salonen - Harjanne Peugeot 205 T16	1995	McRae - Ringer Subaru Impreza	2005	Loeb - Elena Citroën Xsara WRC
1986	Kankkunen - Piironen Peugeot 205 T16	1996	Burns - Reid Mitsubishi Lancer Ev.3	2006	Grönholm - Rautiainen Ford Focus RS WRC 06
1987	Wittmann - Patermann Lancia Delta HF 4WD	1997	Eriksson - Parmander Subaru Impreza WRC	2007	Grönholm - Rautiainen Ford Focus RS WRC 07

12 Spain

🇪🇸 One and one make two

Sébastien Loeb and Dani Sordo were streets ahead of the rest as they claimed a third consecutive 1-2 finish to go along with those in Germany and New Zealand. François Duval was on top tarmac rally form for his return to a works team, Ford, but had to follow team boss Malcolm Wilson's orders and let Blue Oval number one Mikko Hirvonen through for third.

Spain

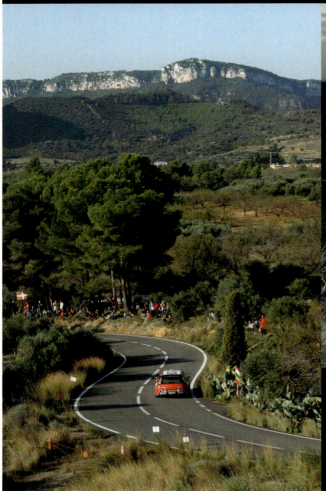

Another overwhelming tarmac win for Sébastien Loeb, the Citroën driver's ninth of the season and his fourth in a row in Catalunya.

After a sparkling start to the season, Chris Atkinson had fallen back into the pack. He was sixth in Germany, and here, on another tarmac rally, he slipped back one more spot in the standings.

THE RALLY
Duval deserved better

Two and a half years after his Australian win for Citroën, François Duval was back, this time in the colours of a works Ford driver, for this edition of the Rally of Catalunya. His showing in Germany had finally convinced Malcolm Wilson, who had turned his back on the Belgian when he turned down a long-term contract at the end of 2004 in order to join Citroën instead. But the boss man at M-Sport, the company that develops and runs the works Focuses in the World Championship, knew Ford's ongoing involvement in rallying hinged on a third successive constructors' title. He also knew Duval was a safer bet than Latvala on tarmac, so he sent the Finn back to find his feet with satellite outfit Stobart. More than anything, Wilson also knew that if the German scenario were to happen again, with Duval in front of Hirvonen, then he would be able to ask the Belgian to back off and help the Finn keep whatever chance he had left of taking the drivers' title.

And to the surprise of few, that same scenario did indeed unfold. Slow to get going, Hirvonen dropped back a length or so behind his new team-mate, then dropped the ball on the second leg, finishing it in fourth place overall, 13.2 seconds away from a podium the Belgian semed to have a firm grip on. It was on the penultimate test that Duval gave up his position, dropping around 20 seconds on orders from his team. "It's not much fun taking so many risks for three days only to have to slow down, but that's what happens when you're in my position. At least I don't have to go to the press conference!" Obelix joked with his national press. "I hope it'll be worth a day's testing in Britain, at least – or a little envelope from Mikko's manager!" Hirvonen wasn't saying too much. "I'd like to have got on the podium another way, so I really must thank François," he acknowledged. "He acted like a true team-mate and helped me score an extra Championship point. Taking the drivers' title will be very difficult, but I'll keep trying right to the end."

Given Loeb's dominance in Catalonia, it was hard to see how Hirvonen's extra point could turn things around. A 12-point deficit to the Frenchman seemed pretty insurmountable, with another tarmac rally to come. Duval knew that and found it hard to accept the sacrifice, his frustration perfectly understandable. Let's hope Malcolm Wilson gives him another crack in 2009.

< New livery for François Duval, drafted into the Ford works team in place of Jari-Matti Latvala and running in a creditable third place before backing off late in the day to let team leader Mikko Hirvonen through.

A number of drivers were sorry to see smaller crowds in the Catalan stages, but there was still plenty of support on hand, especially for local favourite Dani Sordo.

Things looked just as bleak for Ford on the constructors' front. One week out from the Tour of Corsica, Citroën made a show of strength on tarmac with their third 1-2 finish on the trot. The French team, nine points behind Ford after the Turkish event, were now 27 points ahead just four rallies later! "What really pleased me about this result was the way we did it," said a satisfied Citroën Psort director Olivier Quesnel. "Our two C4's were always one and two, they were astonishingly reliable and all the mechanics desrve great credit for immaculate work. Sébastien and Daniel drove the perfect race, getting into the lead then managing it from there, and behind them, it was a great effort from Dani and Marc. They used second place to control what was happening in third. It's been the perfect weekend for us in both Championships."

Everything, in fact, worked wonderfully for the Reds, starting with the two C4's of Loeb and Sordo, who took 12 stage wins between them (11 to Loeb) and relegated Hirvonen in the leading Ford to a minute behind by the finish. "It would have been hard to ask for a better result," said the four-time World Champion. "A win for me, a 1-2 for Citroën: what more could you ask for?

Tonight I'm 12 points ahead of Hirvonen in the Drivers'Championship, and that gives me a card up my sleeve at the best possible stage of the season – though I hope I won't have to use it. But don't go thinking it was a walk in the park: I gave it everything to clean-sheet so often on the opening day, building the gap second by second. I like it when rallies go like that: push hard on the first couple of days, build a big enough gap, no stress on the final day – and that's what happened here. The car was running perfectly and I felt great, really good."

Urmo Aava was in the running for fifth for quite a while before being caught out in the final leg and chalking up a third retirement in 10 starts.

A happy day too for Dani Sordo, who was asked by Citroën to back up Loeb and did it to perfection. "This is the third time in a row we've been second in Spain to help Citroën take a 1-2 finish.Of course I'd love to win here one day, but it's a good result for me," the Spaniard would have us believe. "Our rally went beautifully on roads where there weren't nearly as many apexes as usual. We fine-tuned the settings on Friday to get the best out of our tyres, so then I was able to get into a rhythm that was fast but safe enough to lock down our position. Our C4 was fantastic from start to finish, the reliability was excellent. Another step closer to the title for Citroën."

Over at Ford they were searching for grounds for optimism a week out from the Tour of Corsica. "The Citroëns were just too strong for us on this surface," admitted Duval. "The tarmac here is too smooth – no grip, too much understeer. But in the twistier, dirtier stages at the weekend we were closer, in front even, though I guess Loeb and Sordo weren't pushing as hard as they could have. I've always said I would go better in Corsica, because the roads are more abrasive and twisty down there. There's more driving to be done. This was good practice, and now I'm ready to go for the win."

12 | Spain

No miracles for Henning Solberg this time: after managing to nick some points in Germany, the Norwegian finished the Catalan event in a position more in keeping with his skills on tarmac – 11th.

With no anti-puncture foam to call on this year all the drivers had to be more than usually careful through the Catalan corners – all except Loeb, that is, who was as direct and precise as ever.

Coming out of Catalunya, it seemed the Belgian was indeed the only one capable of tickling up the C4's on the Beautiful Island. Petter Solberg finished fifth, over three minutes behind – a real slap in the face – after a dour struggle with Urmo Aava that cost the Finn his C4. Chris Atkinson, nowhere near as happy on tarmac as on gravel, was seventh – and there was a third Subaru in the top 10. For Catalunya and Corsica, France's Bruce Tirabassi was drafted into the Japanese team, but the 2003 Junior World Champion, only an occasional visitor to the rally scene after failing to find a works drive, struggled to find his bearings again. His 10th place came about when Conrad Rautenbach had to retire. It was a black Sunday for the privateer C4's!

Jari-Matti Latvala, meanwhile, was doing what good pupils do and going back to basics. Sixth in the end, the Finn was under the radar all weekend. But then that's what they had asked him to do – avoid bad publicity! His Stobart team-mate for the weekend, Matthew Wilson, had taken tarmac driving lessons in the UK and finished just outside the points. The one for eighth place eventually went to Andrea Mikkelsen, whose own driving instructor goes by the name of Marcus Grönholm. Maybe that was the difference between the two youngsters! The Norwegian hadn't been in the top eight since Sweden.

There were no-scores, on the other hand, for both Munchi's and Suzuki. Nominated by the third-tier Ford team, Henning Solberg and Federico Villagra could do no better than 11th and 12th. Gardemeister started well but was delayed by a puncture and eventually had his SX4 just behind the Argentine driver, while team-mate Per-Gunnar Anderson went off on Friday but played a joker called SupeRally to make it to the end in 32nd place. ∎

Uphill battle for François Duval. Drafted in as a reinforcement by Malcolm Wilson, the Belgian did the job beautifully but didn't get the reward of a podium finish.

After a somewhat laboured start, Petter Solberg moved up a gear to claim fifth place after an enjoyable fight with Aava's privateer Citroën C4.

Mikko Hirvonen had starred on previous Catalan Rallies and was hoping to make the sparks fly again this year, but in the end he needed team orders to help him take third place.

Andreas Mikkelsen might soon have people talking about more than just his angelic good looks. This was the first point on tarmac for Marcus Grönholm's protégé.

JUNIORS
Prokop owes Ogier one

Going into the Catalunya round, Sébastien Ogier had the title more or less sewn up after three wins in four events. Another win would have made him France's third Junior World Champion after Loeb and Tirabassi. Confident in what he could do, the Citroën man went out hard. Five wins in the six specials on the first-leg schedule gave him a nice 47-second cushion over Martin Prokop. 'I wanted to be quick right from the start," he said, "but even I was surprised at the gaps between all the drivers. Julien (co-driver Ingrassia) and I decided to ease up and not take any risks. Now we need to manage that gap and get the best result we can." Next day, though, the young crew had to swallow their first World Championship disappointment. They hadn't really eased up – they won four of the first five specials on the second leg. They were playing with fire, and they duly got burned. A minute and nine seconds in hand over Prokop, Ogier made a mistake in the day's final timed section. "It was on a quick left hander," the youngster from the Hauts-Alpes explained. "We took the apex to get the ideal line through the corner but as we came out the back of the car let go on a thick layer of dust and gravel. We spun, then we had a little tap back and front, and it cut a radiator hose. We did the remaining eight kilometres that way then tried to fix it on the road link. We tried everything but the engine was too badly damaged to keep going. We weren't supposed to make any mistakes on this event – the margin we built up in the first few stages meant we were leading comfortably, more than a minute ahead of Martin Prokop. Unfortunately we're not immune to mistakes and that's what happened. Naturally I'm very disappointed. Now we have to move on – we've got Corsica starting in just a few days, and that has to be our target now."

Ogier's blunder was meat and drink to Prokop and Burkart, the former picking up a second win of the season to go with the one in Finland. It soothed the Czech driver's wounds from a season he started as a title contender only for it all to go wrong. "It's very satisfying for the team and me," he exclaimed. "Coming on top of my win in Finland, this is a nice birthday present to myself. The points here mean I'm back in contention for a top-three finish overall, so it's been a very satisfying weekend all round." Alesandro Bettega claimed an outstanding second place in the Clio R3 and Burkart, who was third, still had an arithmetical chance of the title, as he was now just four behind Ogier. All to play for in Corsica. ∎

Go and stand in the corner, Latvala! The fiery Finn was sent back to school with Stobart for the last two tarmac events of the year. In the car Duval had in Germany, he finished sixth.

12 | Spain | Results

44th RALLY OF CATALUNYA

Organiser Details
RACC - Area Esportiva
Av. Diagonal 687
08028 Barcelona
Spain
Tel.: +3493 4955029
Fax: +3493 4482490

Rallye de Espana

12th leg of FIA 2008 World Championship for constructors and drivers.
6th leg of FIA WRC Junior Championship.

Date October 2 - 5, 2008

Route
1313.99 km divised in three legs.
18 special stages on tarmac (353.62 km)

Ceremonial Start
Thursday, October 2 (20:00),
Salou, Passeig Jaume

Leg 1
Friday, October 3 (08:16/16:29),
Port Aventura > Port Aventura, 511.52 km;
6 special stages (131.76 km)

Leg 2
Saturday, October 4 (08:44/15:31),
Port Aventura > Port Aventura, 437.58 km;
6 special stages (127.98 km)

Leg 3
Sunday, October 5 (08:05/13:58),
Port Aventura > Salou, 364.89 km;
6 special stages (93.88 km)

Entry List (79) - 69 starters

N°	Driver (Nat.)	Co-Driver (Nat.)	Team	Car	Group & FIA Priority
1	SÉBASTIEN LOEB (F)	DANIEL ELENA (MC)	CITROËN TOTAL WRT	CITROËN C4 WRC	A8 1
2	DANIEL SORDO (E)	MARC MARTÍ (E)	CITROËN TOTAL WRT	CITROËN C4 WRC	A8 1
3	MIKKO HIRVONEN (FIN)	JARMO LEHTINEN (FIN)	BP FORD ABU DHABI	FORD FOCUS RS WRC 08	A8 1
4	FRANÇOIS DUVAL (B)	PATRICK PIVATO (F)	BP FORD ABU DHABI	FORD FOCUS RS WRC 08	A8 1
5	PETTER SOLBERG (N)	PHILIP MILLS (GB)	SUBARU WRT	SUBARU IMPREZA WRC 08	A8 1
6	CHRIS ATKINSON (AUS)	STEPHANE PREVOT (B)	SUBARU WRT	SUBARU IMPREZA WRC 08	A8 1
7	MATTHEW WILSON (GB)	SCOTT MARTIN (GB)	STOBART VK M-SPORT	FORD FOCUS RS WRC 07	A8 1
8	JARI-MATTI LATVALA (FIN)	MIIKKA ANTTILA (FIN)	STOBART VK M-SPORT	FORD FOCUS RS WRC 07	A8 1
9	FEDERICO VILLAGRA (RA)	JORGE PEREZ COMPANC (RA)	MUNCHI'S FORD WRT	FORD FOCUS RS WRC 07	A8 1
10	HENNING SOLBERG (N)	CATO MENKERUD (N)	MUNCHI'S FORD WRT	FORD FOCUS RS WRC 07	A8 1
11	TONI GARDEMEISTER (FIN)	TOMI TUOMINEN (FIN)	SUZUKI WORLD RALLY TEAM	SUZUKI SX4	A8 1
12	PER-GUNNAR ANDERSSON (FIN)	JONAS ANDERSSON (FIN)	SUZUKI WORLD RALLY TEAM	SUZUKI SX4	A8 1
14	KHALID AL QASSIMI (UAE)	MICHAEL ORR (GB)	BP FORD ABU DHABI	FORD FOCUS RS WRC 07	A8 2
15	BRICE TIRABASSI (F)	FABRICE GORDON (F)	SUBARU WRT	SUBARU IMPREZA WRC 08	A8 2
16	URMO AAVA (EE)	KULDAR SIKK (EE)	WORLD RALLY TEAM ESTONIA	CITROËN C4	A8 2
17	CONRAD RAUTENBACH (ZW)	DAVID SENIOR (GB)	CONRAD RAUTENBACH	CITROËN C4	A8 2
18	ANDREAS MIKKELSEN (N)	OLA FLOENE (N)	RAMSPORT	FORD FOCUS WRC 07	A8 2
19	MADS OSTBERG (N)	OLE KRISTIAN UNNERUD (N)	ADAPTA WRT	SUBARU WRC S12B	A8 2
21	EAMONN BOLAND (IRL)	MJ MORRISSEY (IRL)	EAMONN BOLAND	SUBARU WRC S12B	A8 2
22	PETER VAN MERKSTEIJN (NL)	EDDY CHEVAILLIER (B)	VAN MERKSTEIJN MOTORSPORT	FORD FOCUS RS WRC 06	A8 2
23	GARETH JONES (GB)	CLIVE JENKINS (GB)	GARETH JONES	SUBARU WRC S12B	A8 2
24	PETER VAN MERKSTEIJN (NL)	ERWIN BERKHOF (NL)	VAN MERKSTEIJN MOTORSPORT	FORD FOCUS RS WRC 07	A8 2
31	MARTIN PROKOP (CZ)	JAN TOMÁNEK (CZ)	MARTIN PROKOP	CITROËN C2 S1600	A6 3
32	JAAN MÖLDER (EE)	FREDERIC MICLOTE (B)	JAAN MÖLDER	SUZUKI SWIFT S1600	A6 3
33	AARON NICOLAI BURKART (D)	MICHAEL KOELBACH (D)	AARON BURKART	CITROËN C2	A6 3
35	MICHAL KOSCIUSZKO (PL)	MACIEK SZCZEPANIAK (PL)	MICHAL KOSCIUSZKO	SUZUKI SWIFT S1600	A6 3
37	SIMONE BERTOLOTTI (I)	DANIELE VERNUCCIO (I)	SIMONE BERTOLOTTI	RENAULT CLIO SPORT CR R3	A7 3
38	FRANCESCO FANARI (I)	DANIELE BENEDETTI (I)	FRANCESCO FANARI	CITROËN C2 R2	A6 3
39	STEFANO ALBERTINI (I)	PIERCARLO CAPOLONGO (I)	STEFANO ALBERTINI	RENAULT CLIO	A7 3
40	KRIS MEEKE (GB)	CHRIS PATTERSON (GB)	INTERSPEED RACING TEAM	RENAULT CLIO R3	A7 3
41	PATRIK SANDELL (S)	EMIL AXELSSON (S)	INTERSPEED RACING TEAM	RENAULT CLIO R3	A7 3
42	SÉBASTIEN OGIER (F)	JULIEN INGRASSIA (F)	EQUIPE DE FRANCE	CITROËN C2 S1600	A6 3
43	FLORIAN NIEGEL (D)	ANDRÉ KACHEL (D)	SUZUKI RALLY JUNIOR TEAM GERMANY	SUZUKI SWIFT S1600	A6 3
44	HANS WEIJS JR. (NL)	HANS VAN GOOR (NL)	KNAF TALENT FIRST TEAM HOLLAND	CITROËN C2 R2 MAX	A6 3
45	KEVIN ABBRING (NL)	BJORN DEGANDT (B)	KNAF TALENT FIRST TEAM HOLLAND	RENAULT CLIO RS R3	A7 3
46	SHAUN GALLAGHER (IRL)	PAUL KIELY (IRL)	WRT IRELAND	CITROËN C2	A6 3
47	GILLES SCHAMMEL (L)	RENAUD JAMOUL (B)	JPS JUNIOR TEAM LUXEMBOURG	RENAULT CLIO R3	A7 3
48	ALESSANDRO BETTEGA (I)	SIMONE SCATTOLIN (I)	TRT SRL	RENAULT CLIO R3	A7 3
59	SERGIO PEREZ DONOSTI (E)	ORIOL JULIÁ (E)	SERGIO PEREZ DONOSTI	CITROËN C2 S1600	A6 3
61	JOAN OLLÉ (E)	NICOLAS DEL CORRAL (E)	ESCUDERIA MOTOR TERRASSA	SUBARU IMPREZA WRC	A8
62	ALBERT ORRIOLS (E)	LLUIS PUJOLAR (E)	ESCUDERIA OSONA	PEUGEOT 206 WRC	A8
64	JUHO HANNINEN (FIN)	MIKKO MARKKULA (FIN)	JUHO HANNINEN	MITSUBISHI EVO 9	N4
66	JASPER VAN DEN HEUVEL (NL)	MARTINE KOLMAN (NL)	JASPER VAN DEN HEUVEL	MITSUBISHI EVO 9	N4
67	EYVIND BRYNILDSEN (N)	DENIS GIRAUDET (F)	EYVIND BRYNILDSEN	MITSUBISHI EVO 9	N4
68	HENRI MARC VENTURINI (F)	FRÉDERIC DURET (F)	HENRI MARC VENTURINI	RENAULT CLIO R3	A7
69	LUCA GRIOTTI (I)	CORRADO BONATO (I)	LUCA GRIOTTI	RENAULT CLIO 2.0	A7
70	JOAN BALCELLS (E)	JOAN B. ANTICH (E)	ESCUDERIA MOTOR TERRASSA	RENAULT CLIO R3	A7
73	JAROMIR TOMASTIK (CZ)	JAROSLAV VRECKA (CZ)	JAROMIR TOMASTIK	SUBARU IMPREZA WRX STI	N4
75	JOAN FONT (E)	MANEL MUÑOZ (E)	JOAN FONT	MITSUBISHI EVO 9	N4
76	ALBERT LLOVERA (AND)	DIEGO VALLEJO (E)	ALBERT LLOVERA	FIAT GRANDE PUNTO	N4
77	MICHAEL ECKHAUS (NL)	EDUARD EERTINK (NL)	MICHAEL ECKHAUS	MITSUBISHI EVO 9	N4
78	DANIEL PEÑA (E)	PABLO GONZALEZ (E)	AUTOGOMAS CANTABRIA	CITROËN C2 R2 MAX	A6
79	MARTIN VAN IERSEL (NL)	SYLVIA BOS (NL)	SYLVIA BOS	MITSUBISHI EVO 9	N4
81	FABRIZIO FONTANA (I)	SIMONA SAVASTANO (I)	FABRIZIO FONTANA	MITSUBISHI EVO 9	N4
82	EGOI EDER VALDES (E)	ISAAC ZURBANO (E)	ESC. MENDI RACING	SUBARU IMPREZA WRX STI	N4
83	GERT VAN DEN HEUVEL (NL)	HARMEN SCHOLTALBERS (NL)	GERT VAN DEN HEUVEL	MITSUBISHI EVO 9	N4
84	AUGUST NAVARRO (E)	CARLES RESCLOSA (E)	AUGUST NAVARRO	SEAT LEON CUPRA R	N4
85	MANUEL CORDOBA (E)	CARLOS VEGA (E)	ESC. PENEDÈS COMPETICIÓ	SUBARU IMPREZA STI	N4
86	FERNADO BARCENA (E)	JOSE LUIS HERRERA (E)	AUTOGOMAS CANTABRIA	CITROËN C2 R2 MAX	A6
87	GERMAN AGREDA (E)	ENEKO ARTETXE (E)	ESCUDERIA EIBAR	CITROËN SAXO	A6
88	EMRE YURDAKUL (TR)	CAN ERKAL (TR)	CASTROL FORD TEAM TURKIYE	FORD FIESTA ST	N3
89	BURCU CETÍNKAYA (TR)	CICEK GUNEY (TR)	CASTROL FORD TEAM TURKIYE	FORD FIESTA ST	N3
90	KORAY MURATOGLU (TR)	CAGLAR SUREN (TR)	CASTROL FORD TEAM TURKIYE	FORD FIESTA ST	N3
91	JOAQUIM MÜLLER-WENDE (D)	ROGER BURKILL (GB)	JOACHIM MÜLLER-WENDE	FORD FIESTA ST	N3
93	RICHARD MOORE (GB)	ANDREW ROUGHEAD (GB)	RICHARD MOORE	FORD FIESTA ST	N3
94	DAMIANO FUMAGALI (I)	ROBERTO CRIVELLARO (I)	DAMIANO FUMAGALI	RENAULT CLIO RS	N3
95	MICHELE GIUNTA (I)	GIUSEPPE TRICOLI (I)	MICHELE GIUNTA	RENAULT CLIO RS	N3
96	ANTONI GIBERT (E)	EDUARD CODINA (E)	ESCUDERIA OSONA	RENAULT CLIO RS	N3
97	MIRAN JERMAN (SLO)	BORIS TONEJC (SLO)	AK OLIMPIJA	PEUGEOT 206 RC	N3

A. Bettega

A. N. Burkart

B. Tirabassi

P. Sandell

K. Al-Qassimi

Championship Classifications
·R·: Rookie

FIA Drivers (12/15)
1. Loeb 9⚑ 96
2. Hirvonen 2⚑ 84
3. Sordo 59
4. Atkinson 42
5. Latvala 1⚑ 37
6. P. Solberg 36
7. H. Solberg 22
8. Galli 17
9. Duval 16
10. Wilson 12
11. Aava 11
12. Villagra 9
13. Rautenbach 6
14. Mikkelsen 5
15. Gardemeister 5
16. Andersson 4
17. Rantanen 2
18. Cuoq 2
19. Aigner 1
20. Ogier 1
21. Hänninen 1
22. Østberg, 0
K. Al-Qassimi, 0
Beltrán, Mölder, 0
Ketomaa, Prokop, 0
Clark, Kosciuszko, 0
Sandell, Nutahara, 0
Rauam, Burkart, 0
Gallagher, Broccoli, 0
Paddon, Farrah, 0
Schammel, Nittel 0
Baldacci, Valimaki, 0
Artru, Guerra, 0
Arai, Boland, 0
A. Al-Qassimi, 0
Mercier 0

FIA Constructors (12/15)
1. Citroën Total World Rally Team 9⚑ 159
2. BP-Ford Abu Dhabi World Rally Team 3⚑ 132
3. Subaru World Rally Team 80
4. Stobart VK M-Sport Ford Rally Team 55
5. Munchi's Ford World Rally Team 22
6. Suzuki World Rally Team 20

FIA Production Car WRC (6/8)
1. Aigner 3⚑ 30
2. Hänninen 2⚑ 26
3. Ketomaa 23
4. Sandell 22
5. Prokop 1⚑ 17
6. Rauam 15
7. Nutahara 14
8. Sousa 12
9. Araujo 12
10. Beltrán 8
11. Valimaki 8
12. M. Baldacci 6
13. Aksakov 6
14. Vertunov 6
15. Svedlund 5
16. Paddon 5
17. Nittel 3
18. Farrah 3
19. Tiippana 3
20. Arai 3
21. Campedelli 3
22. Bacco 1
23. L. Baldacci 1
24. Taylor 1
24. Linari, Frisiero, 0
Dong, Pavlides, 0
Aksa, Brynildsen, 0
Al-Attiyah, Kumar, 0
Manfrinato, 0
Athanassoulas, 0
Errani, Pastrana, 0
Block, Jereb, 0
Novikov, Flodin, 0
Marrini 0

FIA Junior WRC (6/7)
1. Ogier 3⚑ 34
2. Burkart 30
3. Gallagher 30
4. Prokop 2⚑ 22
5. Kosciusko 1⚑ 22
6. Bettega 22
7. Sandell 18
8. Mölder 11
9. Albertini 9
10. Schammel 8
11. Bertolotti 8
12. Niegel ·R· 6
13. Abbring 6
14. Cortinovis 4
15. Weijs Jr. ·R· 2
16. Fanari ·R· 1
17. Komljenovic 1
18. Pinomaki 0
19. Meeke 0

Rookie
1. Fanari 44
2. Weijs Jr. 20
3. Niegel 8

Special Stages Times

www.rallyracc.com
www.wrc.com

SS1 La Mussara 1 (20.48 km)
1.Loeb 11'17"3; 2.Sordo +1"5;
3.Duval +7"0; 4.Hirvonen +7"2;
5.Mikkelsen +13"6; 6.Aava +17"6
7.Latvala +19"8; 8.P.Solberg + 23"3...
J-WRC > 21.Ogier 12'13"7

SS2 Querol 1 (21.26 km)
1.Loeb 11'13"2; 2.Sordo +5"9;
3.Hirvonen +7"2; 4.Duval +9"2;
5.P.Solberg +18"0; 6.Aava +23"4;
7.Mikkelsen +23"5; 8.Atkinson +26"8...
J-WRC > 20.Ogier 12'18"9

SS3 El Montmell 1 (24.14 km)
1.Loeb 12'39"0; 2.Sordo +0"1;
3.Duval +7"4; 4.Hirvonen +11"4;
5.P.Solberg +14"8; 6.Aava +21"1
7.Latvala +23"3; 8.Mikkelsen +30"1...
J-WRC > 19.Ogier 13'48"4

SS4 La Mussara 2 (20.48 km)
1.Loeb 11'14"0; 2.Sordo +1"3;
3.Hirvonen +3"5; 4.Duval +4"3;
5.Atkinson +11"1; 6.Latvala +15"2;
7.P.Solberg +16"5; 8.Mikkelsen +16"6...
J-WRC > 19.Ogier 12'09"1

SS5 Querol 2 (21.26 km)
1.Loeb 11'15"0; 2.Sordo +3"5;
3.Hirvonen +5"5; 4. Duval +6"7;
5.Atkinson +15"3; 6.P.Solberg +16"4;
7.Latvala +18"6; 8.Aava +19"3...
J-WRC > 20.Prokop 12'15"6

SS6 El Montmell 2 (24.14 km)
1.Loeb 12'33"0; 2.Sordo +3"5;
3.Duval +6"7; 4.Hirvonen +9"5;
5.Atkinson +17"7; 6.P.Solberg +18"7;
7.Latvala +20"4; 8.Aava +21"5...
J-WRC > 19.Ogier 13'42"1

Classification Leg 1
1.Loeb 1h10'11"5; 2.Sordo +15"8;
3.Duval +41"1; 4.Hirvonen +44"1;
5.P.Solberg +1'47"5; 6.Aava +2'01"2;
7.Latvala +2'04"4;
8.Atkinson +2'13"4...
J-WRC > 19.Ogier 1h16'30"4

SS7 El Priorat / La Ribera d'Ebre 1 (38.27 km)
1.Loeb 21'30"9; 2.Duval +1"4;
3.Sordo +2"4; 4.Hirvonen +6"5;
5.Atkinson +21"4; 6.P.Solberg +24"8;
7.Aava +25"0; 8.Latvala +30"5...
J-WRC > 20.Ogier 23'06"0

SS8 Les Garrigues 1 (8.60 km)
1.Loeb 5'02"7; 2.Sordo +2"6;
3.Duval +3"5; 4.Hirvonen +5"1;
5.Aava +6"1; 6.Atkinson +6"4;
7.P.Solberg +7"2; 8.Mikkelsen +7"6...
J-WRC > 21.Ogier 5'32"0

SS9 La Llena 1 (17.12 km)
1.Loeb 9'35"6; 2.Sordo +2"9;
3.Duval +4"2; 4.Hirvonen +5"9;
5.Aava +11"7; 6.P.Solberg +14"7;
7.Latvala +17"7; 8.Atkinson +20"6...
J-WRC > 24.Ogier 10'38"3

SS10 El Priorat / La Ribera d'Ebre 2 (38.27 km)
1.Hirvonen 21'39"3; 2.Loeb +0"2;
3.Sordo +1"5; 4.Duval +2"9;
5.Atkinson +14"9; 6.P.Solberg +16"1;
7.Aava +17"1; 8.Latvala +20"3...
J-WRC > 20.Prokop 23'07"6

SS11 Les Garrigues 2 (8.60 km)
1.Loeb 5'04"8; 2.Duval +0"9;
3.Hirvonen +1"1; 4.Sordo +2"6;
5.Aava +3"2; 6.P.Solberg +4"2;
7.Mikkelsen +5"0; 8.Atkinson +5"6...
J-WRC > 19.Ogier 5'31"7

SS12 La Llena 2 (17.12 km)
1.Duval 9'49"6; 2.Loeb +1"2;
3.Sordo +2"7; 4.Hirvonen +4"7;
5.Aava +6"8; 6.P.Solberg +15"2;
7.Rautenbach +17"1; 8.Latvala +19"8...
J-WRC > 21.Prokop 10'45"6

Classification Leg 2
1.Loeb 2h22'57"2; 2.Sordo +27"7;
3.Duval +51"4; 4.Hirvonen +1'04"6;
5.P.Solberg +3'06"9; 6.Aava +3'08"3;
7.Atkinson +3'42"7; 8.Latvala +3'49"1
J-WRC > 18. Prokop 2h36'27"7

SS13 Riudecanyes 1 (16.32 km)
1.Duval 10'32"8; 2.Sordo +2"3;
3.Loeb +3"7; 4.Mikkelsen +5"5;
5.Latvala +5"5; 6.Atkinson +6"4;
7.Hirvonen +6"9; 8.Aava +7"4...
J-WRC > 21.Burkart 11'24184

SS14 Santa Marina 1 (26.51 km)
1.Loeb 15'49"1; 2.Sordo +1"2;
3.Duval +3"2; 4.Hirvonen +5"0;
5.P.Solberg +10"8; 6.Aava +12"2;
7.Atkinson +13"0; 8.Latvala +13"4...
J-WRC > 19.Burkart 17'11"7

SS15 La Serra d'Almos 1 (4.11 km)
1.Sordo 2'37"3; 2.Hirvonen +0"5;
3.Aava +1"2; 4.Loeb +1"9;
5.Duval +2"3; 6.Atkinson +2"6;
7.P.Solberg +3"3; 8.Latvala +4"0...
J-WRC > 21.Kosciuszco 2'54"8

SS16 Riudecanyes 2 (16.32 km)
1.Hirvonen 10'32"7; 2.Latvala +1"4;
3.Sordo +2"2; 4.Loeb +5"1;
5.Aava +5"5; 6.Mikkelsen +5"7;
7.Atkinson +5"8; 8.Duval +8"1...
J-WRC > 21.Burkart 11'21"6

SS17 Santa Marina 2 (26.51 km)
1.Hirvonen 15'53"9; 2.Loeb +1"8;
3.P.Solberg +3"1; 4.Sordo 4"3;
5.Latvala +5"6; 6.Atkinson +8"4;
7.Mikkelsen +20"2; 8.Duval +20"2...
J-WRC > 18.Kosciuszco 17'17"8

SS18 La Serra d'Almos 2 (4.11 km)
1.Hirvonen 2'39"9; 2.Duval +0"1;
3.Atkinson +0"5; 4.P.Solberg +1"3;
5.Sordo +1"7; 6.Loeb +2"0;
7.Latvala +2"3; 8.H.Solberg +5"4...
J-WRC > 17.Mölder 2'54"0

Results

	Driver - Co-Driver	Car	Gr.	Time
1.	**Loeb - Elena**	**Citroën C4 WRC**	A8	3h21'17"4
2.	Sordo - Marti	Citroën C4 WRC	A8	+24"9
3.	Hirvonen - Lehtinen	Ford Focus RS WRC 08	A8	+1'02"5
4.	Duval - Pivato	Ford Focus RS WRC 08	A8	+1'10"8
5.	P. Solberg - Mills	Subaru Impreza WRC 2008	A8	+3'27"4
6.	Latvala - Antilla	Ford Focus RC WRC 07	A8	+4'03"8
7.	Atkinson - Prévot	Subaru Impreza WRC 2008	A8	+4'04"9
8.	Mikkelsen - Floene	Ford Focus RC WRC 07	A8	+5'19"6
9.	Wilson - Martin	Ford Focus RS WRC 07	A8	+7'43"2
10.	Tirabassi - Gordon	Subaru Impreza WRC 2008	A8	+9'05"0
16.	**Prokop - Tomanek**	**Citroën C2 S1600**	A6/J	+20'07"6
17.	Bettega - Scattolin	Renault Clio R3	A7/J	+20'32"2
20.	Burkart - Koelbach	Citroën C2 S1600	A6/J	+21'12"1

Leading Retirements (21)

Ctrl18A	Aava - Sikk	Citroën C4 WRC	Suspension
Ctrl13	Rautenbach - Senior	Citroën C4 WRC	Off
Ctrl12D	Ogier - Ingrassia	Citroën C2 S1600	Engine

Performers

	1	2	3	4	5	6	C6	Nb SS
Loeb	11	3	1	2	-	1	18	18
Hirvonen	4	1	4	8	-	-	17	18
Duval	2	3	6	4	1	-	16	18
Sordo	1	10	4	2	1	-	18	18
Latvala	-	1	-	1	1	1	4	18
P. Solberg	-	-	1	1	3	7	12	18
Atkinson	-	-	1	-	5	4	10	18
Aava	-	-	1	-	5	4	10	18
Mikkelsen	-	-	-	1	1	1	3	18

Leaders

SS1 > SS18	Loeb

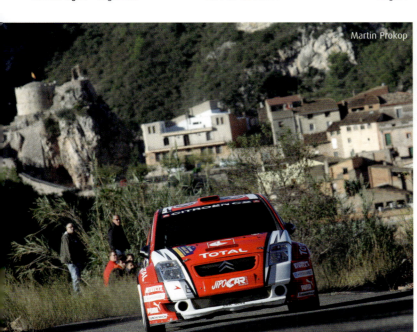

Martin Prokop

Previous Winners

1991	Schwarz - Hertz Toyota Celica GT-Four	1997	Mäkinen - Harjanne Mitsubishi Lancer Evo IV	2003	Panizzi - Panizzi Peugeot 206 WRC
1992	Sainz - Moya Toyota Celica Turbo 4WD	1998	Auriol - Giraudet Toyota Corolla WRC	2004	Märtin - Park Ford Focus RS WRC 04
1993	Delecour - Grataloup Ford Escort RS Cosworth	1999	Bugalski - Chiaroni Citroën Xsara Kit Car	2005	Loeb - Elena Citroën Xsara WRC
1994	Bertone - Chiapponi Toyota Celica Turbo 4WD	2000	C. McRae - Grist Ford Focus WRC	2006	Loeb - Elena Citroën Xsara WRC
1995	Sainz - Moya Subaru Impreza	2001	Auriol - Giraudet Peugeot 206 WRC	2007	Loeb - Elena Citroën C4 WRC
1996	McRae - Ringer Subaru Impreza	2002	Panizzi - Panizzi Peugeot 206 WRC		

13 FRANCE

🇫🇷 There's Loeb... and then there's the rest

Untouchable on tarmac, Sébastien Loeb claimed yet another victory, conceding just two fastest times to his opponents. Mikko Hirvonen kept his title hopes alive with the help of team tactics some judged out of place. Elsewhere, one of the chevron men took his own crown in Corsica as Sébastien Ogier won the World Junior title.

13 | France

Mikko Hirvonen had clearly progressed on tarmac, just not enough to be any danger to Loeb in normal circumstances.

But there was utter chaos in the Ford camp when it came to the final leg. Hirvonen shattered a rim when he hit a pothole in the first Sunday stage. The Finn stopped to change the wheel, which cost him two minutes and, of course, dropped him down the order, to fifth in fact behind Duval, Latvala and Solberg. In the next stage he got past the Norwegian when he sufered the same fate, but it wasn't enough to keep his title hopes alive, far from it. In fact Loeb might have been thinking the crown could well be his on his own home event.

Enter Malcolm Wilson. His Finnish driver might not have been asking to get a couple of places back with some scheme to slow down his Blue Oval buddies, but the man who runs M-Sport, the outfit that develops and runs the Focuses in the World Championship, wasn't about to settle for things the way they stood.

The new Subaru Impreza, seen here in the hands of Petter Solberg, hadn't been too good on gravel, and it wasn't exactly a weapon on tarmac either, even if it did manage fifth place on the Tour of Corsica.

For this running of the Tour of Corsica Jari-Matti Latvala was back in a Stobart Ford after handing over his normal Focus drive to François Duval.

THE RALLY
Loeb's Grand Tour

It may be cutting corners to say the Tour of Corsica is a formality for Loeb and Daniel Elena these days – but it's the simple truth. In fact the man himself could only shrug his shoulders after this latest one: was it his fault if none of the rest of them could get near him? "Of course it's better to win after a tough fight," he said, "but what can I do about it? I'm not the one you should be asking how to beat me here! Winning your home event, in front of your own home crowd, is always something special. We built this victory bit by bit, opening a gap slowly but surely then managing our lead at our own pace. Our C4 was quick and reliable and the settings we chose meant we got the maximum out of our tyres. We're unbeaten on tarmac, and we've increased our Championship lead: there have been worse weekends!" He was right: this hadn't been a particularly difficult one. The Franco-Monegasque pairing led from the end of the first special stage and were never threatened, dropping just two fastest times out of a possible 16: SS12, which went to François Duval, and the very last one to Mikko Hirvonen.

So, a 46th victory for the gritty Loeb, who's just unbeatable on tarmac. That put him just two short of the record for the Beautiful Island, six wins, shared by Bernard Darniche and Didier Auriol. While it was plain sailing for the 208 winners, there was controversy over second place.

It was ear-marked for Hirvonen to keep him in with a slim chance of the title after the French round. The Ford driver may not have what it takes to beat Loeb on tarmac, especially the Corsican variety, but he certainly was a candidate for second. That's where he was by the end of the first timed test and he stayed there despite the efforts of François Duval, who knows a thing or two about being second himself. As in Catalunya, the Belgian was in the second works Focus instead of Latvala, still a bit wet behind the ears on a surface like this.

The Finn candidly acknowledged Loeb's dominance after the first leg: "He's quicker than me all over the place and if he keeps up this pace he'll be unbeatable. I just can't push any harder without taking huge risks."

Same thing on next day's second leg. They all stayed where they were: Loeb in front, then Hirvonen, Duval and Latvala – clearly making progress on tarmac. Next came the Subarus of Solberg and Atkinson, Aava's Citroën and the last of the Imprezas, entered for Frenchman Bruce Tirabassi.

Ever the pragmatist, a man to whom the result matters rather than the way you got it, Wilson brought the righteous wrath of Citroën down upon his head by asking Duval and Latvala to take a penalty each. "Rallying's a complex business," said the British boss. "And the situation we found ourselves in was far from ideal. We have to do all we can to give Mikko the best possible chance and win the constructors' title for the third year running." Subject closed. Like it or not, at least it was clear. All of a sudden, there was Duval ahead of himself for the start of the final stage – two-minute penalty – while Latvala got there late and got 90 seconds. The double manoeuvre put Hirvonen back in second place behind Loeb. Somewhat embarrassed by having his sportsmanship compromised, the Finn could only thank his two pals. "I really appreciate what Jari-Matti and François did in the context of my title bid," he said. "It means I still have a chance of the crown and I'll be doing all I can in the last two rallies of the year." No qualms for either Duval or Latvala: they'd done their job, which is what Ford pays them for. "My role is to help the team," insisted the Belgian, "and that being the case, what happened was perfectly logical. And for my part I'm delighted: I didn't make any mistakes, and a podium is still a super result."

Scenes from rallying life: Loeb and Elena rotate their tyres under the watchful gaze of passer-by François Duval.

Solberg, Atkinson, Aava and Wilson were in the points as well, but Subaru's tarmac wild card Tirabassi wasn't so lucky. On Sunday's second stage he had engine failure on his Impreza WRC and had to retire. There was one other notable retirement, this one on the first leg, and that was Dani Sordo. He made a mistake in the third stage and the impact with a banking destroyed his C4 WRC so comprehensively that the stewards would not allow him to start next day under SupeRally either. The roll cage was damaged in the area around the driver's legs, so the crew's safety couldn't be guaranteed. The Spaniard had been on a charge to get back second place, over-cooked it and his was a costly loss for his employer. A fourth straight 1-2 finish had been on the cards, but now, instead of leaving Corsica with 177 points, Citroën had just 169, 23 more than Ford in the Constructors' Championship. With two rallies left in season 2008 that title was much more wide open than the drivers'. As well as Loeb's win and Ogier's world title (see below), the French team could have really broken clear... ∎

Job done for François Duval – he was there to help Ford and had no hesitation when the time came to hand over second place to Mikko Hirvonen.

Dani Sordo makes a big mistake: impatience caught the Spaniard out early in the event and wiped out Citroën's chances of a 1-2 finish.

The Beautiful Island at its best: it's made for rallying, so watching Chris Atkinson go through seems absolutely natural.

JUNIORS
Triumph for Ogier and Citroën

You learn by your experience. That's probably what Sébastien Ogier was telling himself as he lined up for the start of the Tour of Corsica following the bitter disappointment of his off in Catalunya. On the Spanish round the young Frenchman would have been crowned champion if he hadn't ovedone things. A driving error, maybe a young man's mistake: off he went, handing victory to Czech driver Martin Prokop and giving Germany's Burkart, both in C2's like Ogier, another chance to fight for the title, since there were just four points between the two front-runners. Until his explosive performance in France.

Thre was no question of repeating his Spanish gaffe, so Ogier and co-driver Julien Ingrassia let Prokop go, along with the quick and promising Corsican driver Pierre Campana – in only his 15th rally ever. In fact the latter, in his Clio R3, was in the lead after the opening leg, though he was helped when the Czech's Citroën picked up a puncture. Prokop took back what was rightfully his next day and held on to the lead for his third win of the season. He must have been regretting his poor start to the 2008 campaign... Campana eventually took second, Ogier third after a canny

Young Norwegian Andreas Mikkelsen was having his first go at a tarmac rally – and did more damage to his Focus than he did on the time-sheets.

Handy if you're a spectator: Matthew Wilson always seems to take longer getting through than the other drivers do...

> Although in a car known for its abilities on tarmac, Uumo Aava showed he still had a way to go on this surface.

Keen to avoid any repetition of his mistake in Spain, Sébastien Ogier (top) took it very carefully on the Tour of Corsica – and it paid off as he won the Junior world title.

Showtime for Ogier and Julien Ingrassia on a happy podium as they accept the congratulations of their elders Loeb and Elena and team boss Olivier Quesnel and celebrate with their pals. These two are real champions.

run that duly brought him the title, as Burkart was invisible all weekend and finished down in fifth. It was seven years since another Seb had been crowned champion in Corsica, one by the name of Loeb. The comparison may be a flattering one, but it's not as silly as it may sound – 'old Seb' himself is keeping a close watch on the younger man's career and already there are some who see this young man in a hurry as the Alsace driver's successor. "A perfect day in the perfect place!" said the new top dog among the Juniors. "All my family are here, and a lot of my friends have made the trip specially to watch me. It was a tough week after what happened in Spain. I led the Championship all the way, and I knew all I had to do here was concentrate on keeping in front of Burkart. I hope to take part in the Rally of GB, though I don't know what car I'll be in." The answer came a few days later: it would be a WRC, a handsome reward from Citroën. Aaron Burkart's second place overall owed more to consistency than class. He didn't win a single 2008 event, his best result a second place on his home round in Germany. Third was Martin Prokop, winner of three events like Ogier, but the victim of early-season bad luck. "Given the problems we've had, we're fairly happy with this placing," he reflected.

"It was satisfying to have three wins, but we paid heavily for our mistakes. We were as quick as Sébastien and Julien and we had a few good fights with them."

Satisfaction all round, then, for Citroën, with one Champion, the top four in the standings (Ogier, Burkart, Prokop and Ireland's Gallagher) and six wins from seven events. The one that got away went to Polish driver Kosciuszko, fifth overall, whose Suzuki Swift took the win in Sardinia. The quick, reliable C2 Super 1600 is the benchmark in class. Add a good driver and you've got an unbeatable combination. ∎

This was Brice Tirabassi's second outing in a works Subaru, but an engine failure meant the Frenchman didn't make it to the finish.

13 | France | Results

52nd RALLY OF FRANCE

Organiser Details
FFSA,
17-21 Avenue du Général Mangin,
F-75781 Parix Cedex 16,
France
Tel.: +3349 5236143
Fax: +3349 5236155

Rallye de France - Tour de Corse

13th leg of FIA 2008 World Championship for constructors and drivers.
7th and last leg of FIA WRC Junior Championship.

Date October 10 - 12, 2008

Route
1094.36 km divised in three legs.
16 special stages on tarmac (359.02 km)

Ceremonial Start
Thursday, October 9 (18:00),
Ajaccio, Place Foch
Leg 1
Friday, October 10 (09:18/16:28),
Ajaccio > Ajaccio, 442.68 km;
6 special stages (119.92 km)
Leg 2
Saturday, October 11 (08:48/16:33),
Ajaccio > Ajaccio, 406.54 km;
6 special stages (122.84 km)
Leg 3
Sunday, October 12 (08:43/13:07),
Ajaccio > Ajaccio, 245.14 km;
4 special stages (116.26 km)

Entry List (80) - 71 starters

N°	Driver (Nat.)	Co-Driver (Nat.)	Team	Car	Group & FIA Priority
1	SEBASTIEN LOEB (F)	DANIEL ELENA (MC)	CITROEN TOTAL WRT	CITROËN C4	A8 1
2	DANI SORDO (E)	MARC MARTI (E)	CITROEN TOTAL WRT	CITROËN C4	A8 1
3	MIKKO HIRVONEN (FIN)	JARMO LEHTINEN (FIN)	WORLD RALLY TEAM BP FORD ABU DHABI	FORD FOCUS RS WRC	A8 1
4	FRANÇOIS DUVAL (B)	PATRICK PIVATO (F)	WORLD RALLY TEAM BP FORD ABU DHABI	FORD FOCUS RS WRC	A8 1
5	PETTER SOLBERG (N)	PHILIP MILLS (GB)	SUBARU WORLD RALLY TEAM	SUBARU IMPREZA WRC	A8 1
6	CHRIS ATKINSON (AUS)	STÉPHANE PREVOT (B)	SUBARU WORLD RALLY TEAM	SUBARU IMPREZA WRC	A8 1
7	MATTHEW WILSON (GB)	SCOTT MARTIN (GB)	FORD RALLY TEAM STOBART VK M-SPORT	FORD FOCUS RS WRC	A8 1
8	JARI MATTI LATVALA (FIN)	MIIKKA ANTTILA (FIN)	FORD RALLY TEAM STOBART VK M-SPORT	FORD FOCUS RS WRC	A8 1
10	TONI GARDEMEISTER (FIN)	TOMI TUOMINEN (FIN)	SUZUKI WORLD RALLY TEAM	SUZUKI SX4	A8 1
12	PER GUNNAR ANDERSSON (S)	JONAS ANDERSSON (S)	SUZUKI WORLD RALLY TEAM	SUZUKI SX4	A8 1
14	BRICE TIRABASSI (F)	FABRICE GORDON (F)	SUBARU WORLD RALLY TEAM	SUBARU IMPREZA WRC	A8 1
15	BARRY CLARK (GB)	PAUL NAGLE (F)	FORD RALLY TEAM STOBART VK M-SPORT	FORD FOCUS RS WRC	A8 2
16	HENNING SOLBERG (N)	CATO MENKERUD (N)	FORD RALLY TEAM STOBART VK M-SPORT	FORD FOCUS RS WRC	A8 2
17	KALID AL QASSIMI (UAE)	MICHAEL ORR (GB)	WORLD RALLY TEAM BP FORD ABU DHABI	FORD FOCUS RS WRC	A8 2
21	MADS OSTBERG (N)	OLE KRISTIAN UNNERUD (N)	ADAPTA WRT	SUBARU IMPREZA WRC	A8 2
22	GARETH JONES (GB)	CLIVE JENKINS (GB)	GARETH JONES	SUBARU IMPREZA WRC	A8 2
23	ANDREAS MIKKELSEN (N)	OLA FLOENE (N)	RAMSPORT	FORD FOCUS WRC	A8 2
24	CONRAD RAUTENBACH (ZIM)	DAVID SENIOR (GB)	CONRAD RAUTENBACH	CITROËN C4 WRC	A8 2
25	URMO AAVA (EE)	KULDAR SIKK (EE)	WORLD RALLY TEAM ESTONIA	CITROËN C4 WRC	A8 2
31	MARTIN PROKOP (CZ)	JAN TOMANEK (CZ)	MARTIN PROKOP	CITROËN C2 S1600	A6 3
32	JAAN MOLDER (EE)	FREDERIC MICLOTTE (B)	JAAN MOLDER	SUZUKI SWIFT S1600	A6 3
33	AARON BURKART (D)	MICHAEL KOELBACH (D)	AARON BURKART	CITROËN C2	A6 3
35	MICHAL KOSCIUSZKO (PL)	MACIEK SZCZEPANIAK (PL)	MICHAL KOSCIUSZKO	SUZUKI SWIFT S1600	A6 3
37	SIMONE BERTOLOTTI (I)	DANIELE VERNUCCIO (I)	SIMONE BERTOLOTTI	RENAULT CLIO R3	A7 3
39	STEFANO ALBERTINI (I)	PIERCARLO CAPOLONGO (I)	STEFANO ALBERTINI	RENAULT CLIO R3	A7 3
40	ARNAUD AUGOYARD (F)	NICOLAS BAUDIN (F)	INTERSPEED RACING TEAM	RENAULT CLIO R3	A7 3
41	PATRICK SANDELL (S)	EMIL AXELSSON (S)	INTERSPEED RACING TEAM	RENAULT CLIO R3	A7 3
42	SEBASTIEN OGIER (F)	JULIEN INGRASSIA (F)	EQUIPE DE FRANCE FFSA	CITROËN C2 S1600	A6 3
43	FLORIAN NIEGEL (D)	ANDRÉ KACHEL (D)	TEAM GERMANY SUZUKI RALLYE JUNIOR	SUZUKI SWIFT SUPER 1600	A6 3
44	HANS WEIJS JR (NL)	HANS VAN GOOR (NL)	TEAM HOLLAND KNAF TALENT FIRST	CITROËN C2 R2	A6 3
45	KEVIN ABBRING (NL)	ERWIN MOMBAERTS (B)	TEAM HOLLAND KNAF TALENT FIRST	RENAULT CLIO R3	A7 3
47	GILLES SCHAMMEL (LUX)	RENAUD JAMOUL (B)	TEMA LUXEMBOURG JPS JUNIOR	RENAULT CLIO R3	A7 3
48	ALESSANDRO BETTEGA (I)	SIMONE SCATTOLIN (I)	TRT SRL	RENAULT CLIO R3	A7 3
59	PIERRE CAMPANA (F)	SAMUEL TEISSIER (F)	PIERRE CAMPANA	RENAULT CLIO R3	A7 3
60	PIERRE MARCHE (F)	JULIEN GIROUX (F)	SUZUKI FRANCE	SUZUKI SWIFT S1600	A6 3
61	ALAIN VAUTHIER (F)	GAETAN HOUSSIN (F)	ALAIN VAUTHIER	PEUGEOT 206 WRC	A8
63	FRANCOIS PADRONA (F)	JEAN FRANCOIS MANCINI (F)	FRANCOIS PADRONA	SUBARU IMPREZA WRC	A8
64	ARMANDO PEREIRA (F)	ANTOINE PAQUE (F)	ARMANDO PEREIRA	PEUGEOT 307 WRC	A8
65	GEORGES GUEBEY (F)	NADEGE PASSAQUIN (F)	GEORGES GUEBEY	PEUGEOT 206 WRC	A8
66	JOSÉ MICHELI (F)	VIRGINIE DEJOYE (F)	JOSÉ MICHELI	PEUGEOT 307 WRC	A8
68	JUHO HANNINEN (FIN)	MIKKO MARKKULA (FIN)	JUHO HANNINEN	MITSUBISHI LANCER EVO 9	N4
70	JEAN-DOMINIQUE MATTEI (F)	UGO GREGORJ (F)	JEAN-DOMINIQUE MATTEI	PEUGEOT 207 S2000	N4
71	PIERRE NATALI (F)	GILBERT FRANCOIS DINI (F)	PIERRE NATALI	MITSUBISHI EVO 9	N4
72	MICHEL BRANCA (F)	GERALD FORNS (F)	MICHEL BRANCA	MITSUBISHI LANCER EVO 7	N4
73	JAROMIR TOMASTIK (CZ)	JAROSLAV VRECKA (CZ)	JAROMIR TOMASTIK	SUBARU WRX STI	N4
75	THOMAS BARRAL (F)	JULIEN REBUT (F)	THOMAS BARRAL	RENAULT CLIO R3	A7
76	PIERRE ANTOINE GUGLIELMI (F)	GILLES CLER (F)	PIERRE ANTOINE GUGLIELMI	RENAULT CLIO R3	A7
77	MATHIEU BIASION (F)	CLAUDE BLANC RAFINI (F)	MATHIEU BIASION	RENAULT CLIO R3	A7
78	PIERRE QUILICI (F)	JULIEN PASTORINO (F)	PIERRE QUILICI	RENAULT CLIO R3	A7
80	JACQUES FABREGAT (F)	DOMINIQUE PASQUIER (F)	JACQUES FABREGAT	RENAULT CLIO R3	A7
81	RIZZIERO ZIGLIANI (I)	LUDWIG ZIGLIANI (I)	RIZZIERO ZIGLIANI	RENAULT CLIO R3	A7
83	GUY FIORI (F)	JEAN-JACQUES FERRERO (F)	GUY FIORI	RENAULT CLIO S1600	A6
84	CHARLES ZUCCARELLI (F)	PIERRE ANTOINE BONIFET (F)	CHARLES ZUCCARELLI	RENAULT CLIO S1600	A6
85	PAOLO ALDEGHI (F)	FEDERICO TEDIOLI (I)	PAOLO ALDEGHI	RENAULT CLIO S1600	A6
86	ANTONIN TLUSTAK (CZ)	JAN SKALOUD (CZ)	ANTONIN TLUSTAK	CITROËN C2 S1600	A6
88	JEAN-PHILIPPE MUSELLI (F)	DOMINIQUE FOLACCI (F)	JEAN-PHILIPPE MUSELLI	RENAULT CLIO RAGNOTTI	N3
89	PHILIPPE GIOVANNI (F)	XAVIER NANNI (F)	PHILIPPE GIOVANNI	RENAULT CLIO	N3
90	LILIAN VIALLE (F)	PATRICE ROISSAC (F)	LILIAN VIALLE	RENAULT CLIO	N3
91	BASTIEN MURACCIOLI (F)	FLORENT ELIGERT (F)	BASTIEN MURACCIOLI	RENAULT CLIO RAGNOTTI	N3
92	CLAUDE BENSIMON (F)	BERNARD GRANGIER BIANCAMARIA (F)	CLAUDE BENSIMON	PEUGEOT 206 RC	N3
93	JEAN MATTEO ANTONINI (F)	JEAN GERARD LEONETTI (F)	JEAN MATTEO ANTONINI	RENAULT CLIO	N3
94	JEAN-MARC POISSON (F)	OLIVIER LESIGNE (F)	JEAN-MARC POISSON	HONDA CIVIC TYPE R	N3
95	JEAN PASCAL GOBERT (F)	MARC LABYDOIRE (F)	JEAN PASCAL GOBERT	CITROËN C2	A6
96	ERIC LAFONT (F)	NADINE LAFONT (F)	ERIC LAFONT	CITROËN C2 R2	A6
97	PHILIPPE ROVINA (F)	ALEXANDRE MUZI (F)	PHILIPPE ROVINA	PEUGEOT 206 XS	A6
99	SABRINA DE CASTELLI (F)	ANNE BRAHY (F)	SABRINA DE CASTELLI	CITROËN C2 R2	A6
100	PATRICK COLLEIE (F)	FRÉDÉRIC POISSON (F)	PATRICK COLLEIE	CITROËN SAXO VTS	A6
101	JEREMY BOULEGE (F)	JEROME BOISNARD (F)	JEREMY BOULEGE	PEUGEOT 206 XS	A6
102	SYLVIE CANCELLIERI (F)	JEANNE DOMINIQUE CANCELLIERI (F)	SYLVIE CANCELLIERI	PEUGEOT 206 XS	A6
103	PIERRE KEMP (F)	JEAN MARC KEMP (F)	PIERRE KEMP	PEUGEOT 206 XS	A6
104	FRANCOIS MAESTRACCI (F)	OLIVIER POGGI (F)	FRANCOIS MAESTRACCI	SKODA FABIA	N1

S. Ogier

P. Campana

P. Marche

B. Clark

H. Solberg

Championship Classifications

·R·: Rookie

FIA Drivers (13/15)
1. Loeb 10🏆 106
2. Hirvonen 2🏆 92
3. Sordo 59
4. Atkinson 45
5. Latvala 1🏆 42
6. P. Solberg 40
7. Duval 22
8. H. Solberg 22
9. Galli 17
10. Wilson 13
11. Aava 13
12. Villagra 9
13. Rautenbach 6
14. Mikkelsen 5
15. Gardemeister 5
16. Andersson 4
17. Rantanen 2
18. Cuoq 2
19. Aigner 1
20. Ogier 1
21. Hänninen 1
22. Østberg, 0
K. Al-Qassimi, 0
Beltrán, Mölder, 0
Ketomaa, Prokop, 0
Clark, Kosciuszko, 0
Tirabassi, Sandell, 0
Nutahara, Rauam, 0
Burkart, Gallagher, 0
Broccoli, Paddon, 0
Farrah, Schammel, 0
Nittel, Baldacci, 0
Valimaki, Artru, 0
Guerra, Arai, Boland, 0
A. Al-Qassimi, 0
Mercier 0

FIA Constructors (13/15)
1. Citroën Total World Rally Team 10🏆 169
2. BP-Ford Abu Dhabi World Rally Team 3🏆 146
3. Subaru World Rally Team 87
4. Stobart VK M-Sport Ford Rally Team 62
5. Munchi's Ford World Rally Team 22
6. Suzuki World Rally Team 21

FIA Production Car WRC (6/8)
1. Aigner 3🏆 30
2. Hänninen 2🏆 26
3. Ketomaa 23
4. Sandell 22
5. Prokop 1🏆 17
6. Rauam 15
7. Nutahara 14
8. Sousa 12
9. Araujo 12
10. Beltrán 8
11. Valimaki 8
12. M. Baldacci 6
13. Aksakov 6
14. Vertunov 6
15. Svedlund 5
16. Paddon 5
17. Nittel 4
18. Farrah 3
19. Tiippana 3
20. Arai 3
21. Campedelli 3
22. Bacco 1
23. L. Baldacci 1
24. Taylor 1
24. Linari, Frisiero, 0
Dong, Pavlides, 0
Aksa, Brynildsen, 0
Al-Attiyah, Kumar, 0
Manfrinato, 0
Athanassoulas, 0
Errani, Pastrana, 0
Block, Jereb, 0
Novikov, Flodin, 0
Marrini 0

FIA Junior WRC (7/7)
1. Ogier 🏆 3🏆 42
2. Burkart 34
3. Prokop 3🏆 32
4. Gallagher 30
5. Kosciusko 1🏆 22
6. Bettega 22
7. Sandell 21
8. Mölder 11
9. Albertini 9
10. Schammel 8
11. Niegel ·R· 8
12. Bertolotti 8
13. Abbring 7
14. Campana 6
15. Marche 5
16. Cortinovis 4
17. Weijs Jr. ·R· 2
18. Fanari ·R· 1
19. Komljenovic 1
20. Pinomaki 0
21. Meeke 0

Rookie
1. Fanari 44
2. Weijs Jr. 30
3. Niegel 8

Special Stages Times

www.rallyedefrance.com
www.wrc.com

SS1 Acqua Doria - Serra Di Ferro 1 (15.92 km)
1.Loeb 9'27"4. 2.Hirvonen +4"0;
3.Sordo +4"5. 4.Duval +7"3;
5.Latvala +10"6; 6.Atkinson +12"6;
7.P.Solberg +14"4; 8.Aava +18"3....
J-WRC > 21.Prokop 10'29"2

SS2 Portigliolo - Bocca Albitrina 1 (16.62 km)
1.Loeb 9'21"9; 2.Sordo +2"7;
3.Duval +5"4; 4.Hirvonen +6"4;
5.Latvala +10"6; 6.P.Solberg +11"0;
7.Atkinson +11"8; 8.Mikkelsen +18"8...
J-WRC > 22.Prokop 10'22"4

SS3 Arbellara - Aullenne 1 (27.42 km)
1.Loeb 15'51"4; 2.Duval +3"9;
3.Hirvonen +4"0; 4.P.Solberg +10"9;
5.Atkinson +14"2; 6.Latvala +15"8;
7.Mikkelsen +23"4; 8.Aava +38"0...
J-WRC > 20.Prokop 17'18"3

SS4 Acqua Doria - Serra Di Ferro 2 (15.92 km)
1.Loeb 9'32"2; 2.Hirvonen +6"1;
3.Duval +6"8; 4.Atkinson +11"3;
5.Latvala +12"8; 6.Mikkelsen +16"6;
7.P.Solberg +17"2; 8.Aava +18"7...
J-WRC > 20.Campana 10'30"3

SS5 Portigliolo - Bocca Albitrina 2 (16.62 km)
1.Loeb 9'22"5; 2.Hirvonen +5"2;
3.Duval +5"3; 4.P.Solberg +10"4;
5.Atkinson +11"4; 6.Latvala +12"0;
7.Aava +14"9; 8.Mikkelsen +16"6...
J-WRC > 20.Bettega 10'21"6

SS6 Arbellara - Aullenne 2 (27.42 km)
1.Loeb 15'48"9; 2.Duval +5"3;
3.Hirvonen +6"6; 4.P.Solberg +7"6;
5.Latvala +11"5; 6.Atkinson +14"1;
7.Aava +18"2; 8.Mikkelsen +20"5...
J-WRC > 18.Campana 17'12"1

Classification Leg 1
1.Loeb 1h09'24"3; 2.Hirvonen +32"5;
3.Duval +34"1; 4.P.Solberg +1'11"5;
5.Latvala +1'12"7; 6.Atkinson +1'15"4;
7.Gardemeister +3'16"1;
8.Mikkelsen +3'18"5...
J-WRC > 19.Campana 1h16'23"7

SS7 Carbuccia - Scalella 1 (21.88 km)
1.Loeb 14'26"3; 2.Duval +2"9;
3.Hirvonen +5"0; 4.P.Solberg +0"6;
5.Atkinson +13"1; 6.Latvala +14"3;
7.Aava +17"5; 8.Tirabassi +29"4...
J-WRC > 20.Prokop 15'50"8

SS8 Calcatoggio -Plage du Liamone 1 (25.17 km)
1.Loeb 17'09"2; 2.Hirvonen +1"2;
3.Duval +5"6; 4.Latvala +8"5;
5.P.Solberg +12"7; 6.Atkinson +13"3;
7.Mikkelsen +19"3; 8.Aava +26"1...
J-WRC > 21.Prokop 18'30"8

SS9 Appricciani - Coggia 1 (14.37 km)
1.Loeb 9'23"9; 2.Duval +1"8;
3.Hirvonen +3"2; 4.Latvala +5"3;
5.P.Solberg +8"6; 6.Mikkelsen +9"2;
7.Aava +20"6; 8.Gardemeister +26"3...
J-WRC > 17.Prokop 10'20"4

SS10 Carbuccia - Scalella 2 (21.88 km)
1.Loeb 14'33"6; 2.Hirvonen +3"3;
3.Latvala +3"7; 4.Duval +5"0;
5.P.Solberg +7"2; 6.Aava +15"2;
7.Mikkelsen 16"2; 8.Atkinson +17"3...
J-WRC > 21.Prokop 15'53"8

SS11 Calcatoggio -Plage du Liamone 2 (25.17 km)
1.Loeb 17'08"0; 2.Latvala +5"8;
3.Hirvonen +7"4; 4.Duval +8"6;
5.P.Solberg +15"6; 6.Atkinson +21"9;
7.Aava +33"7; 8.Ostberg +39"7...
J-WRC > 13.Prokop 18'21"9

SS12 Appricciani - Coggia 2 (14.37 km)
1.Loeb 9'21"3; 2.Loeb +1"3;
3.Hirvonen +1"3; 4.Latvala +1"6;
5.P.Solberg +8"0; 6.Mikkelsen +16"2;
7.H.Solberg +21"1; 8.Atkinson +21"7...
J-WRC > 19.Ogier 10'20"3

Classification Leg 2
1.Loeb 2h31'27"9; 2.Hirvonen +52"4;
3.Duval +56"1; 4.Latvala +1'50"6;
5.P.Solberg +2'13"0;
6.Atkinson +4'06"2; 7.Aava +5'49"9;
8.Tirabassi +7'04"8...
J-WRC > 18.Prokop 2h45'55"3

SS13 Agosta - Pont de Calzola 1 (31.81 km)
1.Loeb 19'10"0; 2.Latvala +6"1;
3.Duval +10"2; 4.P.Solberg +14"8;
5.Wilson +28"4; 6.Aava +29"4;
7.Mikkelsen +30"0; 8.Tirabassi +31"4...
J-WRC > 19.Bettega 20'46"1

SS14 Pietro Rossa - Verghia 1 (26.32 km)
1.Loeb 16'25"6; 2.Hirvonen +0"6;
3.Latvala +1"4; 4.Mikkelsen +14"7;
5.Aava +16"4; 6.Duval +17"1;
7.H.Solberg +25"6; 8.Wilson +29"6...
J-WRC > 21.Ogier 17'58"2

SS15 Agosta - Pont de Calzola 2 (31.81 km)
1.Latvala/Loeb 19'22"0;
3.Duval +1"4; 4.Hirvonen +2"3;
5.P.Solberg +2"9; 6.Mikkelsen +10"0;
7.H.Solberg +22"0; 8.Aava + 25'0...
J-WRC > 19.Marche 20'57"5

SS16 Pietro Rossa - Verghia 2 (26.32 km)
1.Hirvonen 16'27"4; 2.Loeb +4"9;
3.Duval +11"1; 4.Mikkelsen +11"2;
5.Latvala +14"0; 6.H.Solberg +23"1;
7.Ostberg +26"6; 8.Rautenbach +26"8...
J-WRC > 20.Ogier 18'02"0

Results

	Driver - Co-Driver	Car	Gr.	Time
1.	**Loeb - Elena**	**Citroën C4 WRC**	A8	3h42'58"0
2.	Hirvonen - Lehtinen	Ford Focus RS WRC 08	A8	+3'24"7
3.	Duval - Pivato	Ford Focus RS WRC 08	A8	+3'31"6
4.	Latvala - Antilla	Ford Focus RS WRC 07	A8	+3'37"5
5.	P. Solberg - Mills	Subaru Impreza WRC 2008	A8	+5'35"4
6.	Atkinson - Prévot	Subaru Impreza WRC 2008	A8	+6'10"4
7.	Aava - Sikk	Citroën C4 WRC	A8	+7'25"2
8.	Wilson - Martin	Ford Focus RS WRC 07	A8	+9'02"2
9.	Ostberg -Unnerud	Subaru Impreza WRC	A8	+9'13"3
10.	Clark -Nagle	Ford Focus RS WRC	A8	+13'38"3
19.	Prokop -Tomanek	Citroën C2 S1600	A6/J	+21'45"9
20.	Ogier - Ingrassia	Citroën C2 S1600	A6/J	+22'03"6
21.	Campana - Teissier	Renault Clio R3	A7/J	+22'39"2

Leading Retirements (17)

Ctrl15	Bettega - Scattolin	Renault Clio R3	Off
Ctrl14	Tirabassi - Gordon	Subaru Impreza S14	Electronics
Ctrl3	Sordo - Marti	Citroën C4 WRC	Off
Ctrl1	Kosciuszko - Szczepaniak	Suzuki Swift S1600	Off

Performers

	1	2	3	4	5	6	C6	Nb SS
Loeb	14	2	-	-	-	-	16	16
Hirvonen	1	7	5	2	-	-	15	16
Duval	1	4	7	3	-	1	16	16
Latvala	1	2	2	3	5	3	16	16
Sordo	-	1	1	-	-	-	2	3
P. Solberg	-	-	-	5	6	1	12	16
Mikkelsen	-	-	-	2	-	3	5	16
Atkinson	-	-	-	1	3	5	9	16
Aava	-	-	-	-	1	2	3	16
Wilson	-	-	-	-	1	-	1	16
H. Solberg	-	-	-	-	-	1	1	16

Leaders

SS1 > SS16	Loeb

Previous Winners

1973	Nicolas - Vial Alpine Renault A 110	1985	Ragnotti - Andrié Renault 5 Turbo	1997	McRae - Grist Subaru Impreza WRC
1974	Andruet - "Biche" Lancia Stratos	1986	Saby - Fauchille Peugeot 205 T16	1998	McRae - Grist Subaru Impreza WRC
1975	Darniche - Mahé Lancia Stratos	1987	Béguin - Lenne BMW M3	1999	Bugalski - Chiaroni Citroën Xsara Kit Car
1976	Munari - Maiga Lancia Stratos	1988	Auriol - Occelli Ford Sierra RS Cosworth	2000	Bugalski - Chiaroni Peugeot 206 WRC
1977	Darniche - Mahé Fiat 131 Abarth	1989	Auriol - Occelli Lancia Delta Integrale	2001	Puras - Marti Citroën Xsara WRC
1978	Darniche Mahé Fiat 131 Abarth	1990	Auriol - Occelli Lancia Delta Integrale	2002	Panizzi - Panizzi Peugeot 206 WRC
1979	Darniche - Mahé Lancia Stratos	1991	Sainz - Moya Toyota Celica GT-Four	2003	Solberg - Mills Subaru Impreza WRC 2003
1980	Thérier - Vial Porsche 911SC	1992	Auriol - Occelli Lancia Delta HF Integrale	2004	Märtin - Park Ford Focus RS WRC 04
1981	Darniche - Mahé Lancia Stratos	1993	Delecour - Grataloup Ford Escort RS Cosworth	2005	Loeb - Elena Citroën Xsara WRC
1982	Ragnotti - Andrié Renault 5 Turbo	1994	Auriol - Occelli Toyota Celica Turbo 4WD	2006	Loeb - Elena Citroën Xsara WRC
1983	Alen - Kivimaki Lancia Rally 037	1995	Auriol - Giraudet Toyota Celica GT-Four	2007	Loeb - Elena Citroën C4 WRC
1984	Alen - Kivimaki Lancia Rally 037	1996	Bugalski - Chiaroni Renault Maxi Megane		

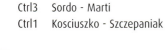

Martin Prokop

14 JAPAN

And one more makes five
Third place was enough to give Sébastien Loeb and Daniel Elena their fifth consecutive world titles for drivers and co-drivers respectively. Mission accomplished, then, after a tricky event dominated by Ford, who still had a chance of the constructors' title as they left Sapporo thanks to another 1-2 finish from Hirvonen and Latvala.

Japan

Mikko Hirvonen produced a flawless drive in Japan, but it wasn't enough to help his title chase.

Dani Sordo's event was cut short by a turbo failure.

One clean sheet, one off: Henning Solberg didn't make it to the finish of the rally.

THE RALLY
Hirvonen's last throw of the dice

The stakes were pretty clear as the 14th round of the World Rally Championship approached. If Loeb wanted to clinch the title after this event and before the final round in Great Britain, he needed to finish at least third should Hirvonen win it. If he finished in front of the Finn, no matter where they were in the final results, he had it in the bag. For the Ford driver to retain any chance of usurping the Frenchman's throne, his job was to win – and then worry about where Loeb was.

As the first leg got under way, Hirvonen would have been thinking he had every chance of coming out on top. He likes the Rally of Japan – he won it in 2007. OK, mistakes from Loeb and Grönholm helped as the two of them got caught up in their title duel, but it's a rally he had always enjoyed.

And it showed as he took the lead through the early kilometers. His Ford Focus WRC quite at home in the muddy stretches – and there were plenty of those in the Japanese autumn – he took control of proceedings right from the end of the opening stage. All right, it was just a super-special, but he went on to set fastest times in all bar one of the stages on a first leg foreshortened by three because of snow in Isepo 1 and 2 and the delay caused by François Duval's accident in Pipao 2. The one he didn't win was Pipao 1, which went to Loeb. So the Ford man had cause for satisfaction at the end of the opening day: "It was a great day on soft tracks, they were narrow and twisty," he said once back in Sapporo, new epicentre of the Nipponese event. "But I felt at home right away, so I was able to keep pushing, pushing all the time. It was cold and muddy this morning – so cold I had a hard job getting temperature into the tyres. I really wasn't expecting quite so much snow!"

He was out in front, 26.2 seconds clear of team-mate Jari-Matti Latvala, the latter playing his subordinate role to perfection as he positioned himself between his team leader and Loeb. "I didn't make a single mistake," he said. "But it was a day of ups and downs – I'm not 100 per cent happy with my driving. I couldn't get into a rhythm."

So much so that he was briefly overtaken by François Duval. Ford's wild card had been drafted into the Stobart team to back up Hirvonen and stop Loeb garnering too many points, and he did a very competent job of it early in the rally. And of course the Belgian is one of the few men in the world without a regular WRC drive you can count on to get among the front-runners right from the off. Sadly, not for long... By the end of the fifth stage Obelix was second behind Hirvonen. But in the sixth he had an enormous accident that left his co-driver Patrick Pivato seriously injured (see below).

For Loeb and Citroën, then, it hadn't been a good start: a solitary fastest time on that opening leg, and that's nothing to a man of the World Champion's calibre. "I really took things very carefully," the French driver admitted. "Too carefully, maybe: there was snow about and I was worried about hitting ice. In those conditions it was no easy matter to strike a balance between pushing and being careful, it wasn't easy to get into the right tempo. Second time through I tried to stay focused but I was watching the splits to try and keep up the pressure on our opponents. So, one day down, and that's good. I hate driving defensively."

The entry of the gladiators, Sébastien Loeb leading Jari-Matti Latvala into the arena.

P.-G. Andersson's fifth place gave Suzuki the chance to shine on their home event.

At least he hadn't thrown it all away. More than could be said for team-mate Dani Sordo, for once again the Spaniard was the cause of any trouble that came the Chevron's way. "It was all going great," he said at the end of that first day. "We'd found our rhythm, we were quick but we weren't taking risks. I was happy with where I was (fifth, 33S behind Hirvonen), then the engine lost power in SS6 (the turbo was broken). We had to stop."

The first leg behind them, the Ford men had done what they needed to do; Loeb was doing only what he had to do; and the Subaru duo, with Atkinson ahead of Solberg, hadn't starred but had kept their manufacturer in the top five on home soil. But the awful accident to Duval and Pivato had cast a dark shadow over the whole event.

Nothing in the second leg altered the course of events: Ford still in front, Loeb in their wake. Hirvonen saw Latvala close the gap between them but there was no danger, and Loeb was once again not quite his usual brilliant self. He was after the title, not the win.

"I do prefer it when I can drive to win," he acknowledged that Saturday. "But we had to keep ourselves in check. The forest roads south of Sapporo were just as narrow, but they were a lot faster, so you had a bigger chance of getting it wrong. When I felt it was all getting a bit too much, I had no hesitation in getting on the brakes earlier. I didn't want to risk throwing it all away. We're focused on one target: consolidating third place."

Hirvonen had no reason to be unhappy with himself either. In fact the title contenders were cancelling each other out. "I came to Japan to win," said the Finn, happy enough with his position if a bit low-key. "But even if I do it tomorrow, it looks as if it won't be enough to help me where the title's concerned."

If it was a race you were looking for, you needed to go further back behind the leading trio to find it. Gardemeister in the Suzuki had no end of technical problems (diff, overheating engine and so on). Henning Solberg, who'd had a little tap in SS17, couldn't make the most of the Fords' excellent handling on this terrain and stopped for good at the end of that stage. The same fate befell his World Champion brother Petter in the next one as he ripped a wheel off his Subaru against a rock – not the thing to do in your employers' backyard when they're already unhappy with the performance of their Prodrive-prepared cars.

As was to be expected, the third leg was a non-event as they all stayed right where they were. Ford claimed the 1-2, Hirvonen the victory and Loeb/Elena a richly-deserved fifth title. Mind you, the Franco-Monegasque duo gave themselves a little fright two corners from the end of the very last serious test when they spun, a harmless little electrical problem causing understandable concern among the Citroën personnel, but it turned out all right in the end and the team greeted their hero, all wearing Samurai-style headbands with a big '5' in the middle.

The Rally of Japan was an important event for Subaru on their home ground, and Chris Atkinson took a fine fourth place for them.

14 | Japan

Seventh place earned Matthew Wilson two points.

Latvala deserved to have won this event, but rather than trying to beat Hirvonen he backed off late in the day to safeguard the points he already had.

So there you had it – the best driver in rallying history: better than Juha Kankkunen with his four titles, or Tommi Mäkinen and the four he won on the trot, unlike Mr K. Now there's Alsace's own Sébastien Loeb... and then there's the rest. He hung around in the press conference for ages afterwards. "It's a great joy," he said delightedly. "Obviously it's what Daniel and I were after – I really wanted to get it done and dusted in Japan so that we could go to Britain with our minds at ease. I don't know if this one's better than the other four – the first will always be a bit special, just because it was the first. I'm not saying it's something you get used to, but it's not the same feeling. One thing that doesn't change is the pleasure of sharing it with the whole team – this is their title as well." Elena, a five-time champion co-driver in his own right, was just as happy: "It was a long time coming, but it's so nice. It's our fifth and every one makes you feel just as happy. I don't look at the stats, I just remember how much fun we have in the car, the atmosphere in the team and the way Seb and I work together."

Rally winner Hirvonen sportingly offered his own congratulations to the man who came out on top. "We did

It's not all fun on the Rally of Japan, it can be pretty hard on the cars – just ask Toni Gardemeister.

everything we could to stop Sébastien winning this title," he said, "but in the end he really deserves it and I want to congratulate him warmly."

'See you in 2009' was the message from a man who may have come up short but had really grown in stature and experience – and that will make him an even bigger threat to our new five-time king of the rallying world. ■.

THE ACCIDENT
Miraculous escape for Pivato

S S6, Yuparo 2: François Duval has been brought in by Ford and installed in a Stobart Focus WRC to try and insinuate himself between Hirvonen and Loeb to delay the Frenchman's coronation. And he's holding his own. Eighth to go, second overall, he has been convincing in the early stages of the rally. But with Obelix genius and gaffes go hand-in-hand. Five kilometres after the start, his car comes to a tarmac-covered left-hander at around 100 km/h. The surface is slippier than the driver expected and he can't keep control. As it starts to get sideways he yanks on the handbrake, but it's too late: the Focus spears into the iron posts with cables strung between them that pass for safety barriers hereabouts. A 50-centimetre piece of metal pierces the cockpit, literally cutting through the car: it hits Duval's co-driver Patrick Pivato. Despite the searing pain he doesn't lose consciousness. The rally is neutralised straight away, the emergency services alerted. Pivato is comforted by his friend Denis Giraudet and by Japanese drivers Toshi Araï and Fumio Nutahara among others, then finally extracted after 40 difficult minutes. Taken to Sapporo's Higashi Tokushukai hospital, he is diagnosed with fractures of the pelvis and the right tibia. But in fact he is far more seriously injured and soon suffers severe internal bleeding. Put in an induced coma, he endures a desperate first night: his blood group, A-, is rare in Japan and that's a problem – he needs blood, and lots of it. Giraudet and his friends put out the rallying cry – literally – among the

Petter Solberg was out to win this event but it all went wrong, yet again, for the unlucky Norwegian. He was quick, but an off in the second leg saw him finish well down the order.

And one more makes five! Loeb and Elena fought their way to another title – hats off to the champions.

event's entourage; no fewer than nine people – team members, journalists, organizers – offer their blood. Thanks to this magnificent show of support, and the skill of the Japanese medical team, his condition is stabilized. Giraudet, who had left his driver in the lurch on Friday while they were leading the Production class, got back into the action – the other drivers asked the stewards not to penalize Norwegian Eyvind Brynildsen and his French co-driver.

The Japanese fans had a big smile for François Duval and Patrick Pivato.

With Hirvonen and Latvala on the podium after a 1-2 finish, Ford didn't forget Patrick Pivato as he lay in his hospital bed.

A five-time World Champion at work: Loeb is on another planet...

With his rally mates and his wife around him, Patrick Pivato eventually made a reasonably quick recovery. He was able to be repatriated to France two weeks after the accident, but faced more operations and a long spell of convalescence. (*)

For 15 years or so co-drivers have been the ones who have suffered most in any accidents – the tragic death of Michael Park on the 2005 Rally of Great Britain being the starkest example. But we have also seen Risto Männisenmäki, Tommi Mäkinen's sidekick, Daniel Grataloup, Jean-Paul Chiaroni... and, sadly, far too many others suffer severe injury. We can always pontificate about these things, put it down to driver reflexes helping them protect themselves when they see an off coming, or the 'working conditions' that mean their right-hand men don't necessarily get to see it coming at all. But that's the way it is. Rallying is a dangerous sport, as Patrick Pivato has found out to his cost. Happily he is still with us. That's not the end of the story, though. Denis Giraudet, ever the gentleman, offered to slip in alongside Duval for the Rally of Great Britain as a mark of friendship for Pivato. We take our hats off to you, Mr Giraudet. ∎

(*) As a way of acknowledging the countless messages of support and keeping everyone up to date, Patrick Pivato's people set up a website where you can follow his progress: http://www.pivato.fr

14 | Japan | Results

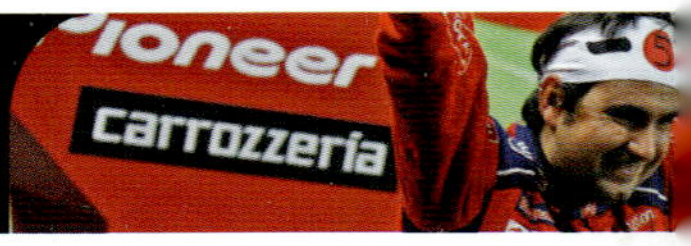

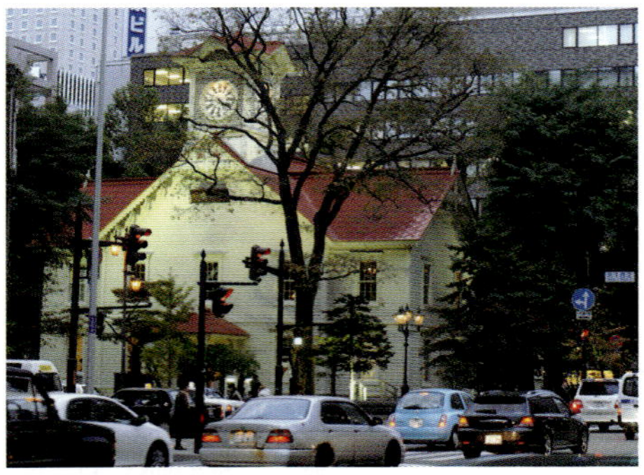

5th RALLY OF JAPAN

Organiser Details
Event Competition Secretariat
Homei Bldg 4-9 Nangodori19,
Shiroishi-ku, Sapporo
Hokkaiod, Japan 003-0022
Tel.: +8111 8642003
Fax: +8111 8641192

Pioneer Carrozzeria Rally Japan

14th leg of FIA 2008 World Championship for constructors and drivers.
7th leg of FIA Production Car World Championship.

Date October 30 - November 2, 2008

Route
1316.28 km divised in three legs.
29 special stages on dirt roads (343.69 km);
26 raced

Ceremonial Start
Thursday, October 30,
Sapporo Dome
Leg 1
Friday, October 31 (09:11/18:24),
Sapporo > Sapporo, 498.01 km;
10 special stages (90.48 km); 7 raced
Leg 2
Saturday, November 1 (08:28/18:19),
Sapporo > Sapporo, 470.31 km;
10 special stages (156.78 km)
Leg 3
Sunday, November 2 (07:07/13:44),
Sapporo > Sapporo, 347.96 km;
9 special stages (96.43 km)

Entry List (90) - 86 starters

N°	Driver (Nat.)	Co-Driver (Nat.)	Team	Car	Group & FIA Priority
1	SEBASTIEN LOEB (F)	DANIEL ELENA (MC)	CITROEN TOTAL WRT	CITROEN C4 WRC	A8 1
2	DANI SORDO (E)	MARC MARTI (E)	CITROEN TOTAL WRT	CITROEN C4 WRC	A8 1
3	MIKKO HIRVONEN (FIN)	JARMO LEHTINEN (FIN)	BP FORD ABU DHABI WORLD RALLY TEAM	FORD FOCUS RS WRC 08	A8 1
4	JARI-MATTI LATVALA (FIN)	MIIKKA ANTTILA (FIN)	BP FORD ABU DHABI WORLD RALLY TEAM	FORD FOCUS RS WRC 08	A8 1
5	PETTER SOLBERG (N)	PHILIP MILLS (GB)	SUBARU WORLD RALLY TEAM	SUBARU IMPREZA WRC 2008	A8 1
6	CHRIS ATKINSON (AUS)	STEPHANE PREVOT (B)	SUBARU WORLD RALLY TEAM	SUBARU IMPREZA WRC 2008	A8 1
7	FRANCOIS DUVAL (B)	PATRICK PIVATO (F)	STOBART VK M-SPORT FORD RALLY TEAM	FORD FOCUS RS WRC 07	A8 1
8	MATTHEW WILSON (GB)	SCOTT MARTIN (GB)	STOBART VK M-SPORT FORD RALLY TEAM	FORD FOCUS RS WRC 07	A8 1
9	FEDERICO VILLAGRA (RA)	JORGE PEREZ COMPANC (RA)	MUNCHI'S FORD WORLD RALLY TEAM	FORD FOCUS RS WRC 07	A8 1
10	HENNING SOLBERG (N)	CATO MENKERUD (N)	MUNCHI'S FORD WORLD RALLY TEAM	FORD FOCUS RS WRC 07	A8 1
11	TONI GARDEMEISTER (FIN)	TOMI TUOMINEN (FIN)	SUZUKI WORLD RALLY TEAM	SUZUKI SX4	A8 1
12	PER-GUNNAR ANDERSSON (S)	JONAS ANDERSSON (S)	SUZUKI WORLD RALLY TEAM	SUZUKI SX4	A8 1
14	CONRAD RAUTENBACH (ZW)	DAVID SENIOR (GB)	CONRAD RAUTENBACH	CITROEN C4	A8 2
31	TOSHI ARAI (J)	GLENN MACNEALL (AUS)	SUBARU TEAM ARAI	SUBARU IMPREZA WRX STI	N4 3
32	MIRCO BALDACCI (RSM)	GIOVANNI AGNESE (I)	MIRCO BALDACCI	MITSUBISHI LANCER EVO IX	N4 3
34	GIANLUCA LINARI (I)	MATTEO BRAGA (I)	GIANLUCA LINARI	SUBARU IMPREZA WRX STI	N4 3
35	EVGENY NOVIKOV (RUS)	DALE MOSCATT (AUS)	NOVIKOV EVGENY	MITSUBISHI LANCER EVO IX	N4 3
36	EYVIND BRYNILDSEN (N)	DENIS GIRAUDET (F)	EYVIND BRYNILDSEN	MITSUBISHI LANCER EVO IX	N4 3
37	YASUNORI HAGIWARA (J)	KOICHI KATO (J)	AUTOTEK	SUBARU IMPREZA	N4 3
40	STEFANO MARRINI (I)	TIZANIA SANDRONI (I)	ERRANI TEAM GROUP	MITSUBISHI LANCER EVO IX	N4 3
43	EVGENIY VERTUNOV (RUS)	GEORGY TROSHKIN (RUS)	SUBARU RALLY TEAM RUSSIA	SUBARU IMPREZA WRX STI	N4 3
50	ARMINDO ARAUJO (P)	MIGUEL RAMALHO (P)	RALLIART ITALY	MITSUBISHI LANCER EVO IX	N4 3
51	SUBHAN AKSA (RI)	HENDRIK MBOI (RI)	INDONESIA RALLY TEAM	MITSUBISHI LANCER EVO IX	N4 3
52	JUHO HANNINEN (FIN)	MIKKO MARKKULA (FIN)	RALLIART NEW ZEALAND	MITSUBISHI LANCER EVO IX	N4 3
54	HIROSHI YANAGISAWA (J)	OSAMU YODA (J)	SUBARU RALLY TEAM USA	SUBARU IMPREZA WRX STI	N4 3
56	FUMIO NUTAHARA (J)	HAKARU ICHINO (J)	ADVAN-PIAA RALLY TEAM	MITSUBISHI LANCER EVO X	N4 3
57	MARTIN RAUAM (EE)	SILVER KUTT (EE)	WORLD RALLY TEAM ESTONIA	MITSUBISHI LANCER EVO IX	N4 3
58	NAREN KUMAR (IND)	NICKY BEECH (GB)	TEAM SIDVIN INDIA	SUBARU IMPREZA N14	N4 3
59	KATSUHIKO TAGUCHI (J)	MARK STACEY (AUS)	MITSUBISHI MOTORS DEALER TEAM	MITSUBISHI LANCER EVO X	N4 3
60	TAKUMA KAMADA (J)	NAOKI KASE (J)	TERAOKA AUTO DOOR	SUBARU IMPREZA WRX STI	N4 3
61	JARI KETOMAA (FIN)	MIKA STENBERG (FIN)	SUBARU RALLY TEAM JAPAN	SUBARU IMPREZA WRX STI	N4
62	NORIHIKO KATSUTA (J)	TAKAHIRO YASUI (J)	SUBARU RALLY TEAM JAPAN	SUBARU IMPREZA WRX STI	N4
63	KAZUHIRO KITAMURA (J)	NORIKO TAKESHITA (J)	AHRESTY RALLY TEAM	SUBARU IMPREZA WRX STI	N4
64	ATSUSHI MASUMURA (J)	KOJI WATANABE (J)	SUPER ALEX TROOP	MITSUBISHI LANCER EVO IX	N4
65	EIICHI IWASHITA (J)	AKIHIKO TAKAHASHI (J)	TEAM OKUYAMA	MITSUBISHI LANCER EVO IX	N4
66	OSAMU FUKUNAGA (J)	HISATSUGU OKUMURA (J)	HASEPRO RALLY TEAM	MITSUBISHI LANCER EVO IX	N4
67	HARUO OSHIMA (J)	TATSUYA IDEUE (J)	KASE E RACING	MITSUBISHI LANCER EVO IX	N4
68	HIROSHI HOSHINO (J)	SHIGEKI SATO (J)	HIROSHI HOSHINO	MITSUBISHI LANCER EVO X	N4
69	YOZO WATANABE (J)	SHIGERU IKEDA (J)	YOZO WATANABE	MITSUBISHI LANCER EVO IX	N4
70	SEIICHIRO TAGUCHI (J)	YASUYUKI ATSUCHI (J)	SEIICHIRO TAGUCHI	MITSUBISHI LANCER EVO IX	N4
71	KYOSUKE KAMATA (J)	CHIEKO KAMATA (J)	KYOSUKE KAMATA	MITSUBISHI LANCER EVO IX	N4
72	MITSUGU NAKAMURA (J)	YOSHITAKA FUJISHIMA (J)	MITSUGU NAKAMURA	MITSUBISHI LANCER EVO VIII	N4
73	YOSHIKAZU MITANI (J)	MASAKAZU ARAI (J)	YOSHIKAZU MITANI	MITSUBISHI LANCER EVO VII	N4
75	KOJI BABA (J)	MITSUHIRO ONAYA (J)	KOJI BABA	MITSUBISHI LANCER EVO IX	N4
76	FUYUHIKO TAKAHASHI (J)	MITSUO NAKAMURA (J)	AHRESTY RALLY TEAM	SUBARU IMPREZA WRX STI	N4
77	MITSUHIRO AOKI (J)	FUMIKA AOKI (J)	MITSUHIRO AOKI	MITSUBISHI LANCER EVO IX	N4
78	TATSURU SAITO (J)	AKIRA ENDO (J)	TATSURU SAITO	MITSUBISHI LANCER EVO X	N4
79	SATORU ITO (J)	AKIKO NAKAGAWA (J)	SATORU ITO	MITSUBISHI LANCER EVO IX	N4
80	TAKAHIRO YOSHII (J)	MASAHIKO NABEKURA (J)	STREETLIFE WORLD RALLY TEAM	MITSUBISHI LANCER EVO VII	N4
81	SHIGEO KOBAYASHI (J)	JYUNICHI IIDA (J)	SHIGEO KOBAYASHI	MITSUBISHI LANCER EVO VIII	N4
82	TAKASHI NISHI (J)	TSUYOSHI KAJIYAMA (J)	TAKASHI NISHI	SUBARU IMPREZA WRX STI	N4
83	YU MATSUI (J)	AKIHIRO TAMAKI (J)	SUPER ALEX TROOP	MITSUBISHI LANCER EVO X	N4
84	HIROAKI TOMIZAWA (J)	KAZUYUKI FUNATSU (J)	HIROAKI TOMIZAWA	SUBARU IMPREZA WRX STI	N4
85	HIDEAKI NAMBA (J)	TAKASHI KAMEMORI (J)	HIDEAKI NAMBA	SUBARU IMPREZA WRX STI	N4
86	MASAMICHI FUKUMOTO (J)	TERUAKI YASUE (J)	MASAMICHI FUKUMOTO	MITSUBISHI LANCER EVO VI	N4
87	YUICHI NAKAMURA (J)	TOSHIYUKI KAYAHARA (J)	YUICHI NAKAMURA	MITSUBISHI LANCER EVO VII	N4
88	TAKESHI ISHIGURO (J)	TADAYOSHI SATO (J)	TAKESHI ISHIGURO	MITSUBISHI LANCER EVO IX	N4
89	YUICHI YAMADA (J)	MUNENORI KITAHARA (J)	YUICHI YAMADA	MITSUBISHI LANCER EVO VII	N4
90	KAZUTOMO KUSAMA (J)	HIROKAZU MATSUI (J)	MITSUBISHI RALLY TEAM GUNMA	MITSUBISHI LANCER EVO IX	N4
91	TETSURO SUGIMURA (J)	KAZUKO MATSUI (J)	TETSURO SUGIMURA	MITSUBISHI LANCER EVO IX	N4
92	AJI KIM (ROK)	MORITOSHI NAKASATO (J)	TEAM RALLYTECH WORKS	MITSUBISHI LANCER EVO VIII MR	N4
93	KOJI MIYAMOTO (J)	NAOKI KUROSAKI (J)	KOJI MIYAMOTO	SUBARU IMPREZA WRX SEDAN 2.0 4WD TURBO	N4
94	KUNIYUKI KANBE (J)	TAKAHIRO YONEDA (J)	KUNIYUKI KANBE	MITSUBISHI LANCER EVO VIII	N4
95	MITSUHIRO KUNISAWA (J)	MASAHIKO KIHARA (J)	KUNISAWA MITSUHIRO	SUBARU IMPREZA WRX STI	N4
96	KOJI KAWANO (J)	MIKIO OOTANI (J)	KOJI KAWANO	SUBARU IMPREZA 555 GC8	N4
97	JUNICHI HASEGAWA (J)	KOICHI SAWADA (J)	JUNICHI HASEGAWA	SUBARU IMPREZA 555 GC8	N4
98	NOBUAKI MIYANO (J)	ATSUSHI ISHII (J)	NOBUAKI MIYANO	MITSUBISHI LANCER EVO VIII	N4
99	HISATOSHI YOSHITANI (J)	SHINJI TAKATA (J)	HISATOSHI YOSHITANI	MITSUBISHI LANCER EVO VIII	N4
101	TOMOHIDE HASEGAWA (J)	NOBUYOSHI HARA (J)	HASEPRO RALLY TEAM	MITSUBISHI LANCER EVO VIII	N4
102	MASAMI SUGIYAMA (J)	MIKI ITOH (J)	MASAMI SUGIYAMA	TOYOTA ZZE123	A7
103	HIROSHI SUDOH (J)	SEIICHIRO YAYANAGI (J)	HIROSHI SUDOH	HONDA CIVIC TYPE R	A7
104	HIDEKI KAGAWA (J)	SAYAKA ADACHI (J)	SAYAKA ADACHI	HONDA INTEGRA TYPE R	A7
105	TADAHIRO HIRATSUKA (J)	HIROSHI SUZUKI (J)	TEAM DCCS	DAIHATSU SIRION/BOON	A5
106	KIYOYUKI ONODERA (J)	YOUYA OIKAWA (J)	TEAM DCCS	DAIHATSU SIRION/BOON	A5
107	TAKASHI IRINATSU (J)	HIROSHI HAENUKI (J)	TEAM-ASE	HONDA CIVIC	A6
108	YASUSHI HARA (J)	SATOKO HARA (J)	YASUSHI HARA	DAIHATSU SIRION/BOON	N1
109	MASATO NAKANISHI (J)	AYUMI URUSHIDO (J)	MASATO NAKANISHI	DAIHATSU SIRION/BOON	N1
110	MASUHIRO ITO (J)	JUN CHIGAMI (J)	MASUHIRO ITOH	DAIHATSU SIRION/BOON	N1
111	MASATOSHI OGURA (J)	MARI HIRAYAMA (J)	MASATOSHI OGURA	DAIHATSU SIRION/BOON	N1
112	KIMITO KONDO (J)	TAKAHIRO WAKI (J)	KIMITO KONDO	DAIHATSU SIRION/STORIA	N1
113	SHOW AIKAWA (J)	SADATOSHI ANDO (J)	SHOW AIKAWA	FORD FIESTA ST	N3
114	KUMIKO KOIDE (J)	TADAYUKI AKIMA (J)	KUMIKO KOIDE	DAIHATSU SIRION/STORIA	A5
115	YOSHIAKI YAMAOKA (J)	TAKAAKI NAKANISHI (J)	TAKAAKI NAKANISHI	DAIHATSU SIRION/STORIA	N1
116	TAKANOBU KAWAMURA (J)	MASATO NAKAMURA (J)	TAKANOBU KAWAMURA	DAIHATSU SIRION/STORIA	N1
117	TOMOYUKI AMANO (J)	YUKIKO INOUE (J)	TOMOYUKI AMANO	TOYOTA YARIS	A5
118	YOKO FUKUZAWA (J)	TAKAYUKI TANAKA (J)	YOKO FUKUZAWA	MITSUBISHI LANCER EVO VIII	N4

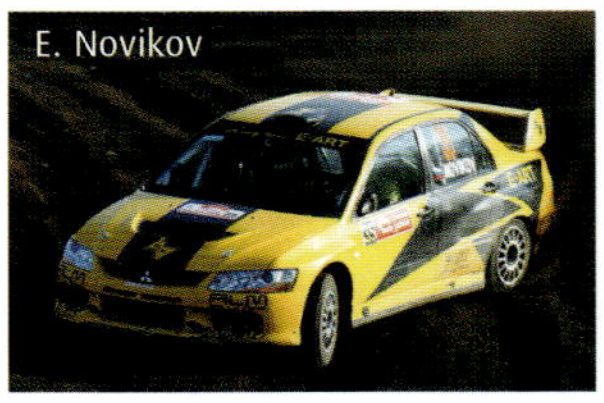
E. Novikov

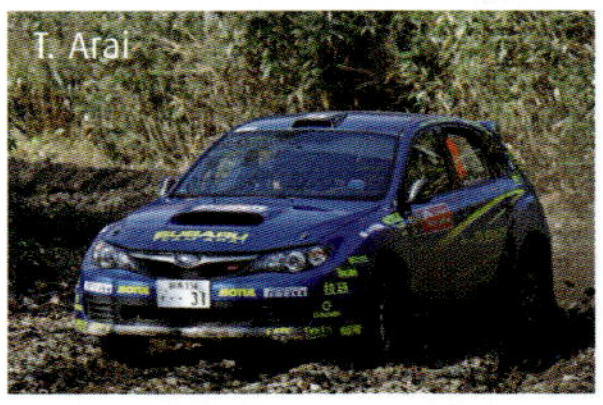
T. Arai

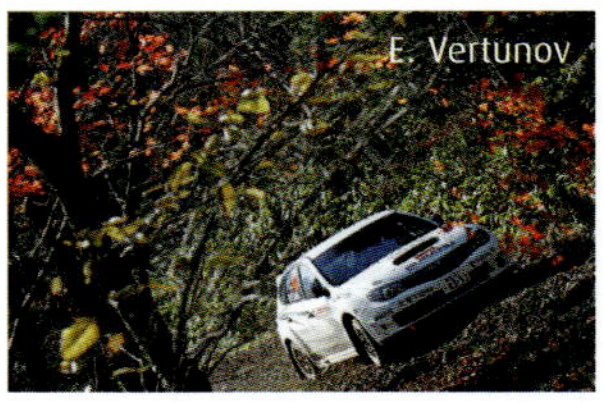
E. Vertunov

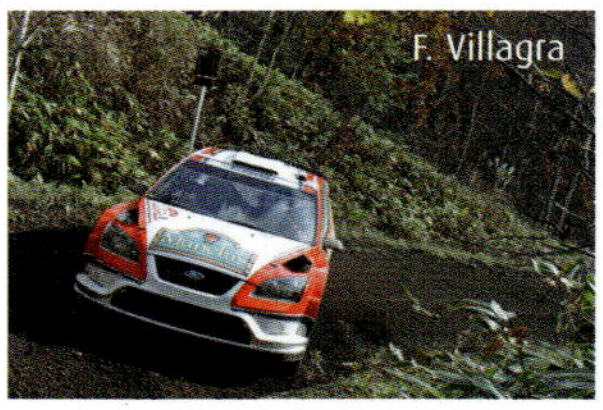
F. Villagra

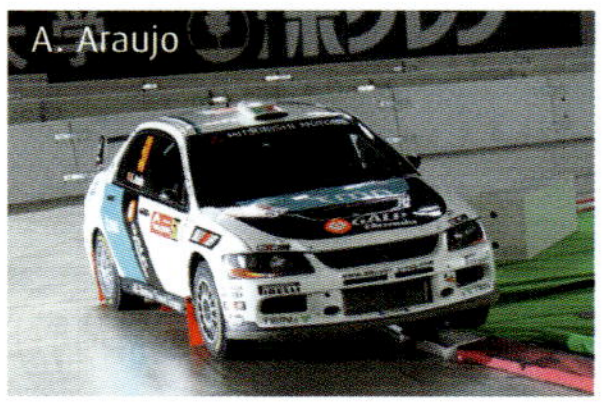
A. Araujo

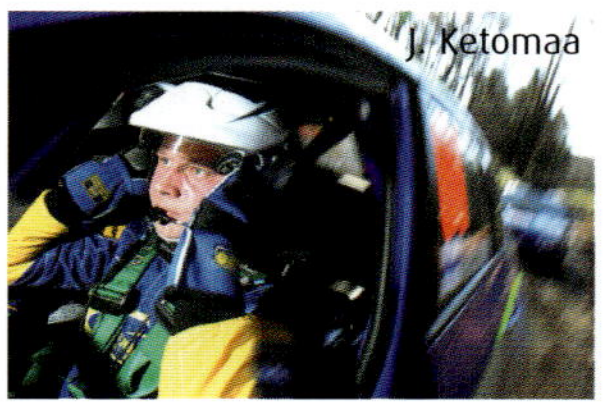
J. Ketomaa

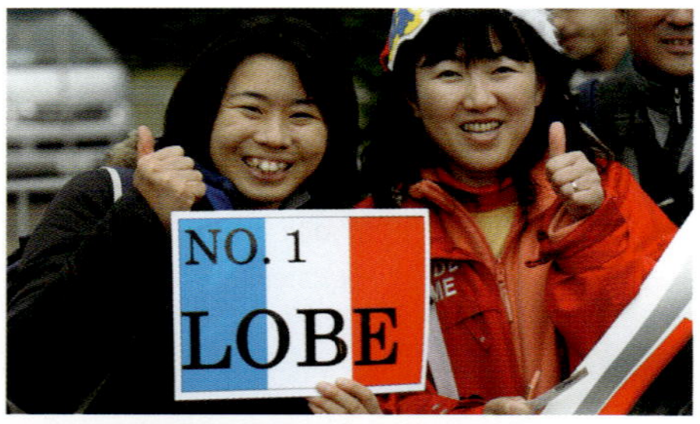

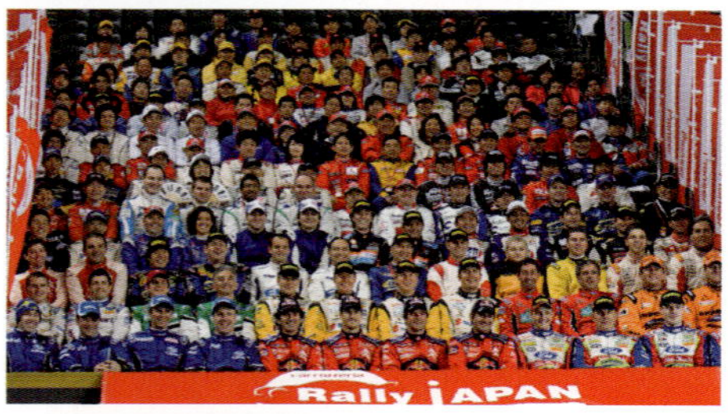

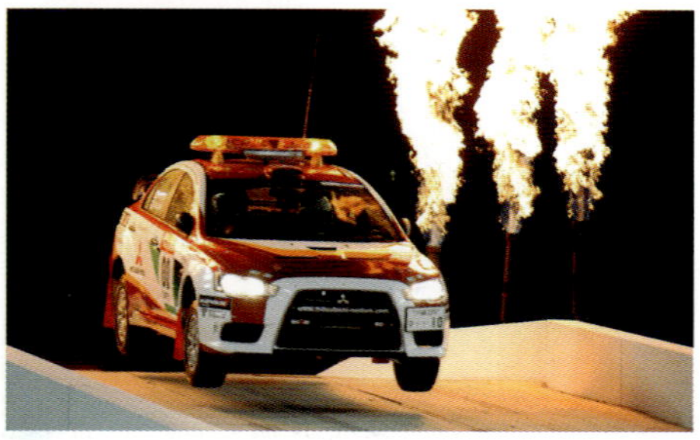

Championship Classifications

•R•: Rookie

FIA Drivers (14/15)

1.	**Loeb**	10🏆	112
2.	Hirvonen	3🏆	102
3.	Sordo		59
4.	Latvala	1🏆	50
5.	Atkinson		50
6.	P. Solberg		41
7.	Duval		22
8.	H. Solberg		22
9.	Galli		17
10.	Wilson		15
11.	Aava		13
12.	Villagra		9
13.	Andersson		8
14.	Gardemeister		8
15.	Rautenbach		6
16.	Mikkelsen		5
17.	Rantanen		2
18.	Cuoq		2
19.	Hänninen		1
20.	Aigner		1
21.	Ogier		1
22.	Østberg, K. Al-Qassimi, Mölder, Beltrán, Clark, Ketomaa, Prokop, Kosciuszko, Tirabassi, Sandell, Nutahara, Novikov, Rauam, Burkart, Gallagher, Broccoli, Brynildsen, Paddon, Farrah, Schammel, Nittel, Baldacci, Valimaki, Kamada, Artru, Guerra, Mercier, Arai, Boland, A. Al-Qassimi,		0

FIA Constructors (14/15)

1.	Citroën Total World Rally Team	10🏆	175
2.	BP-Ford Abu Dhabi World Rally Team	4🏆	164
3.	Subaru World Rally Team		93
4.	Stobart VK M-Sport Ford Rally Team		64
5.	Suzuki World Rally Team		28
6.	Munchi's Ford World Rally Team		22

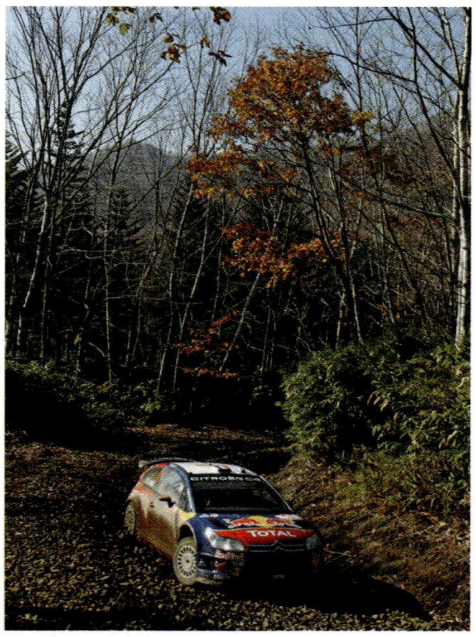

FIA Production Car WRC (7/8)

1.	Hänninen	3🏆	36
2.	Aigner	3🏆	30
3.	Ketomaa		23
4.	Sandell		22
5.	Prokop	1🏆	17
6.	Rauam		15
7.	Nutahara		15
8.	Sousa		12
9.	Araujo		12
10.	M. Baldacci		9
11.	Arai		9
12.	Novikov		8
13.	Beltrán		8
14.	Valimaki		8
15.	Aksakov		6
16.	Vertunov		6
17.	Brynildsen		5
18.	Svedlund		5
19.	Paddon		5
20.	Nittel		4
21.	Kamada		4
22.	Farrah		3
23.	Tiippana		3
24.	Campedelli		3
25.	Taguci		2
26.	Bacco		1
27.	L. Baldacci		1
28.	Taylor		1
29.	Linari, Frisiero, Dong, Aksa, Pavlides, Marrini, Al-Attiyah, Kumar, Manfrinato, Athanassoulas, Errani, Hagiwara, Pastrana, Block, Jereb, Flodin,		0

FIA Junior WRC (7/7)

1.	**Ogier**	3🏆	42
2.	Burkart		34
3.	Prokop	3🏆	32
4.	Gallagher		30
5.	Kosciusko	1🏆	22
6.	Bettega		22
7.	Sandell		21
8.	Mölder		11
9.	Albertini		9
10.	Schammel		8
11.	Niegel •R•		8
12.	Bertolotti		8
13.	Abbring		7
14.	Campana		6
15.	Marche		5
16.	Cortinovis		4
17.	Weijs Jr. •R•		2
18.	Fanari •R•		1
19.	Komljenovic		1
20.	Pinomaki		0
21.	Meeke		0

Rookie

1.	Fanari	44
2.	Weijs Jr.	30
3.	Niegel	8

Special Stages Times

www.rallyjapan.jp
www.wrc.com

SS1 Heper 1 (13.24 km)
1.Hirvonen 9'57"9. 2.Latvala +3"8;
3.Duval +7"0. 4.Sordo +11"1;
5.Wilson +13"0; 6.P.Solberg +13"3;
7.Loeb +13"5; 6.Wilson +8"0;
P-WRC > 14.Brynildsen 10'43"1

SS2 Yuparo 1 (11.10 km)
1.Hirvonen 8'24"2; 2.Loeb +2"1;
3.Duval +3"3; 4.Latvala +4"1;
5.Sordo +4"7; 6.Wilson +8"0;
7.Andersson +8"3; 8.Atkinson +10"0...
P-WRC > 13.Novikov 8'56"6

SS3 Isepo1 (13.67km)
Cancelled - (Snow)

SS4 Pipao 1 (5.74 km)
1.Loeb 3'17"3; 2.Latvala +1"3;
3.Hirvonen +2"3; 4.Duval +2"6;
5.Atkinson +3"6; 6.P.Solberg +3"7;
7.Sordo +4"0; 8.Andersson +4"9...
P-WRC > 13.Arai 3'36"5

SS5 Heper 2 (13.24 km)
1.Hirvonen 9'35"6; 2.Duval +1"3;
3.Loeb +7"3; 4.Latvala +8"6;
5.Atkinson +13"3; 6.Sordo +16"0;
7.P.Solberg +16"7; 8.Andersson +17"8...
P-WRC > 13.Novikov 10'31"2

SS6 Yuparo 2 (11.10 km)
1.Hirvonen 8'02"5; 2.Latvala +6"6;
3.Loeb +6"9; 4.Wilson +8"7;
5.Andersson +8"7; 6.Atkinson +11"2;
7.P.Solberg +12"4; 8.Tomizawa +16"7...
P-WRC > 40.Marrini 8'19"2

SS7 Isepo 2 (13.67 km)
Cancelled - (Snow)

SS8 Pipao 2 (5.74 km)
Cancelled -
(Duval - Pivato accident in the SS6)

SS9 Sapporo 1 (1.49 km)
1.Hirvonen 1'39"4; 2.Loeb +0"1;
3.Latvala +2"0; 4.Atkinson +2"9;
5.H.Solberg +3"3; 6.P.Solberg +3"4;
7.Villagra +5"5; 8.Grademeister +5"5...
P-WRC > 10.Hänninen 1'46"6

SS10 Sapporo 2 (1.49 km)
1.Hirvonen 1'41"6; 2.Atkinson +1"3;
3.Latvala +2"1; 4.Gardemeister +2"9;
5.Loeb +3"9; 6.Villagra +4"2;
7.P.Solberg +4"2; 8.Wilson + 4"2....
P-WRC > 9.Hänninen 1'45"9

Classification Leg 1
1.Hirvonen 42'40"8; 2.Latvala +26"2;
3.Loeb +30"6; 4.Atkinson +1'00"3;
5.P.Solberg +1'02"0; 6.Wilson +1'03"2;
7.Andersson +1'03"6;
8.Gardemeister +1'36"8...
P-WRC > 11.Novikov 45'49"6

SS11 Imeru 1 (2.57 km)
1.Sordo 1'42"5; 2.Andersson +1"5;
3.H.Solberg +1"6; 4.Wilson +1"9;
5.Atkinson +1"9; 6.Loeb +2"5;
7.Latvala +2"6; 8.Hirvonen +3"2...
P-WRC > 12.Hänninen 1'50"8

SS12 Nikara1 (31.12 km)
1.P.Solberg 18'37"0; 2.Hirvonen +1"8;
3.Sordo +1"8; 4.Latvala +4"4;
5.Loeb +7"7; 6.H.Solberg +13"1;
7.Atkinson +17"2; 8.Andersson +19"4...
P-WRC > 13.Hänninen 19'51"1

SS13 Kamuycep 1 (33.66 km)
1.Latvala 21'58"1; 2.Sordo +4"7;
3.Loeb +8"5; 4.Hirvonen +10"9;
5.P.Solberg +16"5; 6.Atkinson +23"5;
7.Andersson +30"2; 8.H.Solberg +35"9...
P-WRC > 14.Hänninen 23'37"2

SS14 Kina 1 (9.55 km)
1.H.Solberg 5'54"6; 2.Sordo +0"7;
3.Latvala +1"2; 4.Hirvonen +1"6;
5.Loeb +1"8; 6.P.Solberg +5"4;
7.Atkinson +6"2; 8.Andersson +8"5...
P-WRC > 12.Hänninen 6'22"8

SS15 Imeru 2 (2.57 km)
1.Loeb 1'42"5; 2.H.Solberg +0"3;
3.Sordo +0"3; 4.Hirvonen +0"7;
5.P.Solberg +0"8; 6.Wilson +1"0;
7.Atkinson +1"5; 8.Latvala +1"7...
P-WRC > 13.Araujo 1'51"4

SS16 Nikara 2 (31.12 km)
1.Latvala 18'22"8; 2.Hirvonen +1"2;
3.Loeb +1"3; 4.P.Solberg +2"0;
5.Atkinson +4"9; 6.Sordo +18"5;
7.H.Solberg +19"7;
8.Gardemeister +48"5...
P-WRC > 12.Novikov 20'16"3

SS17 Kamuycep 2 (33.66 km)
1.Hirvonen 21'22"7; 2.Latvala +3"2;
3.H.Solberg +7"5; 4.Sordo +16"1;
5.Atkinson +21"1; 6.Loeb +21"6;
7.Andersson +30"1;
8.Gardemeister +50"7...
P-WRC > 13.Arai 23'33"1

SS18 Kina 2 (9.55 km)
1.Hirvonen 5'54"3; 2.Sordo +0"8;
3.Latvala +1"1; 4.Loeb +2"3;
5.Andersson +7"7; 6.Wilson +13"3;
7.Gardemeister 13"6;
8.Rautenbach +23"0...
P-WRC > 11.Arai 6'33"7

SS19 Sapporo 3 (1.49 km)
1.Grademeister 1'25"4; 2.Sordo +0"0;
3.Latvala +2"0; 4.Andersson +2"4;
5.Villagra +2"6;
P-WRC > 6.Hänninen +3"2 (1'28"6);
7.Wilsson +3"6; 8.Loeb +3"6...

SS20 Sapporo 4 (1.49 km)
1.Sordo 1'23"2; 2.Gardemeister +0"4;
3.Latvala +1"0; 4.Hirvonen +1"5;
5.Loeb +1"5; 6.Wilson +1"7;
7.Atkinson +1"8; 8.Villagra + 1"9....
P-WRC > 10.Hänninen 1'28"3

Classification Leg 2
1.Hirvonen 2h21'31"8; 2.Latvala +15"5;
3.Loeb +53"5; 4.Atkinson +2'26"0;
5.Wilson +4"31"6;
6.Gardemeister +4'38"5;
7.Andersson +5'11"8;
8.Villagra +9'59"6...
P-WRC > 10.Novikov 2h34'01"3

SS21 Koyka 1 (3.57 km)
1.P.Solberg 2'00"2; 2.Hirvonen +0"4;
3.Andersson +1"2; 4.H.Solberg +1"9;
5.Loeb +2"5; 6.Sordo +2"9;
7.Latvala +3"3; 8.Gardemeister +3"6...
P-WRC > 13.Novikov 2'12"1

SS22 Iwanke 1 (13.57 km)
1.Hirvonen 8'13"0; 2.Latvala +1"8;
3.P.Solberg +6"2; 4.Andersson +7"5;
5.Gardemeister +11"2; 6.Wilson +12"1;
7.Loeb +13"8; 8.Atkinson +14"5...
P-WRC > 12.Hänninen 9'10"7

SS23 Sikot 1 (27.76 km)
1.Latvala 17'49"5; 2.Andersson +12"3;
3.Hirvonen +13"8; 4.P.Solberg +26"5;
5.Gardemeister +33"7; 6.Wilson +42"7;
7.Atkinson + 44"9. 8.Loeb +47"2...
P-WRC > 10.Novikov 19'29"2

SS24 Imeru 3 (2.57 km)
1.Latvala 1'57"3; 2.Hirvonen +0"2;
3.P.Solberg +0"6; 4.Atkinson +2"0;
5.Loeb +4"6; 6.Andersson +5"4;
7.Gardemeister +6"6; 8.Sordo +7"9...
P-WRC > 11.Arai 2'10"9

SS25 Sapporo 5 (1.49 km)
1.Kim 1'45"7; 2.Atkinson +0"1;
3.Kitamura +0"8; 4.Gardemeister +1"0;
P-WRC > 5.Taguchi +1"2 (1'46"9);
6.Brynildsen +1"2;
7.Latvala +1"4; 8.Araujo + 1"6....

SS26 Koyka 2 (3.57 km)
1.Hirvonen 2'08"6; 2.P.Solberg +0"9;
3.Latvala +4"6; 4.Andersson +4"6;
5.Sordo +4"8; 6.Atkinson +5"9;
7.Gardemeister +6"6; 8.Wilson +10"5...
P-WRC > 11.Arai 2'28"0

SS27 Iwanke 2 (13.57 km)
1.Hirvonen 8'39"9; 2.Andersson +0"6;
3.P.Solberg +2"6; 4.Latvala +14"1;
5.Sordo +15"3; 6.Loeb +15"5;
7.Gardemeister +24"3;
8.Atkinson +30"0...
P-WRC > 10.Arai 9'24"9

SS28 Sikot 2 (27.76 km)
1.P.Solberg 10'00"2;
2.Andersson +16"3;
3.Sordo +16"9; 4.Atkinson +24"1;
5.Hirvonen +30"6; 6.Loeb +41"4;
7.Latvala + 41"5;
8.Gardemeister +52"2...
P-WRC > 10.Hänninen 19'22"1

SS29 Imeru 4 (2.57 km)
1.P.Solberg 2'03"8; 2.Sordo +0"5;
3.Latvala +2"1; 4.Atkinson +2"4;
5.Andersson +4"0;
6.Gardemeister +4"7;
7.Hirvonen +5"3; 8.Wilson +5"8...
P-WRC > 11.Kamada 2'16"4

Results

	Driver - Co-Driver	Car	Gr.	Time
1.	Hirvonen - Lehtinen	Ford Focus RS WRC 08	A8	3h25'03"0
2.	Latvala - Antilla	Ford Focus RS WRC 08	A8	+31"1
3.	Loeb - Elena	Citroën C4 WRC	A8	+2'30"6
4.	Atkinson - Prévot	Subaru Impreza WRC 2008	A8	+3'42"4
5.	Andersson - Andersson	Suzuki SX4 WRC	A8	+5'12"9
6.	Gardemeister - Tuominen	Suzuki SX4 WRC	A8	+6'09"4
7.	Wilson - Martin	Ford Focus RS WRC 07	A8	+7'05"3
8.	P. Solberg - Mills	Subaru Impreza WRC 2008	A8	+13'19"9
9.	Villagra - Perez Companc	Ford Focus RS WRC 07	A8	+15'40"8
10.	**Hänninen - Markkula**	**Mitsubishi Lancer Evo. IX**	**N4/P**	**+18'27"4**
11.	Novikov - Moscatt	Mitsubishi Lancer Evo. IX	N4/P	+18'33"7
12.	Arai - MacNeall	Subaru Impreza WRx STi	N4/P	+18'36"6

Leading Retirements (29)

Ctrl29C	Sordo - Marti	Citroën C4 WRC	Withdraw
Ctrl23	H. Solberg - Menkerud	Ford Focus RS WRC 07	Off
Ctrl6	Duval - Pivato	Ford Focus RS WRC 07	Off

Performers

	1	2	3	4	5	6	C6	Nb SS
Hirvonen	11	4	2	3	5	-	22	26
Latvala	5	4	9	4	-	-	22	26
Sordo	5	2	3	2	4	3	19	23
P. Solberg	4	1	4	2	3	4	18	24
Loeb	2	2	3	2	5	5	19	26
Gardemeister	2	1	-	1	2	1	7	26
Atkinson	1	1	-	6	4	2	14	26
H. Solberg	1	1	1	1	1	1	6	23
Duval	-	1	3	1	-	-	5	5
Villagra	-	-	-	1	1	-	2	26
Wilson	-	-	-	-	2	6	8	26
Hänninen	-	-	-	-	-	1	1	26

Leaders

SS1 > SS29   Hirvonen

Previous Winners

2004	Solberg - Mills Subaru Impreza WRC 2004
2005	Grönholm - Rautiainen Peugeot 307 WRC
2006	Loeb - Elena Citroën Xsara WRC
2007	Hirvonen - Lehtinen Ford Focus RS WRC 07

Juho Hänninen

15 GREAT BRITAIN

🇬🇧 A finale to savour

Notable for Ogier's first WRC appearance and a sensational duel between Loeb and Latvala, the season's final round saw the Frenchman claim a record 11th win of the year, and with it the constructors' title for Citroën –a useful contribution coming from Sordo in third place.

15 | Great Britain

First rally, first stage... first clean sheet for Sébastien Ogier! The Junior World Champion made a grand entry onto the WRC stage, but then put his C4 on its roof at the start of the second leg. He'll be back at the wheel of a C4 in Ireland next January – and he'll be one to keep an eye on.

Fourth was Petter Solberg's best result since New Zealand. On difficult going, Subaru's Norseman showed plenty of commitment but not much sparkle – much like the rest of his season, really.

Toni Gardemeister had the satisfaction of bringing his SX4 home in the points for the fifth time this season. Seventh is a good effort: the only problem for the Finn was that team-mate Andersson did a lot better, not only here but over the whole year.

THE RALLY
Loeb still hungry for more

There was still plenty at stake going into this 64th Rally of Great Britain, with Juho Hanninen and Anreas Aigner fighting out the PWRC title and Ford and Citroën going for the constructors' crown. This is how things stood: 11 points behind, Hirvonen and Latvala really needed to take a 1-2 finish, whereas Loeb and Sordo could afford to go for a place. There were, too, three newcomers on hand to enliven the last round of the Championship year. At just 17 and 18 days Tom Cave, in a Ford Fiesta, was the youngest man ever to contest a World Championship event. As for MotoGP's own Loeb, Valentino Rossi, he was back on the WRC scene in a Ford Focus, two years after a low-key appearance in a Subaru Impreza in New Zealand and six years after debuting in the category in a Peugeot 206, also in Great Britain. Last but not least, Citroën were giving Junior World Champion Sébastien Ogier his first outing among the big boys in a C4.

The young Frenchman's debut came on an event that lived up to its own reputation, with a revised itinerary around Builth Wells, a spot the rally hadn't visited for eight years, and weather that was simply hellish. Even Loeb got caught out by the snow and ice on the recce, ending up on his roof! The organisers were forced to shorten most of the first-leg stages as Pirelli's gravel tyres just weren't up to the conditions – the first test was actually cancelled altogether.

Ogier struck the first blow in the second stage, cleansheeting for an unheard-of rally lead in his first-ever World Championship stage. Fifth-fastest through SS3, the young prodigy hung on to that lead right into the midday service park. "It's like a dream," he said at the end of SS3. "I'm really surprised – even with the advantage of seeing the lines and braking-points the cars ahead of me used, the conditions were still just unbelieveable!"

In fact it was the beginners who were in control early in the day: Mads Ostberg n the privateer Subaru and P.-G. Andersson's Suzuki had also made good use of their

starting positions to upset the applecart and be up there in the top four. By day's end Ogier was the only one of the threesome not to be near the top of the timesheets. He had gone straight on in SS6, costing himself 44 seconds and seven places. Ninth at the end of the opening leg, the Citroën prospect ruined that fine showing next day by going off the road. Ostberg and Andersson, meanwhile, were still in solid front-running spots, the former fourth on Friday evening, ahead of Petter Solbergs works Subaru, while the second of the 2009 Imprezas had been destroyed in a major off for Chris Atkinson. The Swede, for his part, was in a podium position by the time the first leg ended, somethng the SX4 had never previously managed. "I'm pretty proud," said Andersson, "it was a really good first day. It's the first time it's happened to either Suzuki or me! It shows that the huge amount of work we've put in all season is starting to bear fruit. I've never seen anything like these conditions – it was treacherous even on the road links! But it was a lot of fun." Life was about to get a bit more complicated for the two youngsters: an engine failure forced Ostberg out on Saturday morning, while Andersson gradually lost touch with the leaders but still managed to take fifth place by the finish, as he had in Japan.

So where were the big names while all this was going on? The 2007 winner Mikko Hirvonen was first to be caught out by the apocalyptic conditions. After rolling it in SS5 he dropped nearly four minutes in the ditch – and with them went Ford's hopes of taking their third title in

François Duval was sixth on return from that horrible off in Japan – a more than creditable comeback for the Belgian after that tragic incident, and with a new co-driver in the shape of France's Denis Giraudet.
v

a row. "I knew my car would get sideways through that lying water near the end," said Hirvonen, "but not as badly as it did. The car hit a bank and rolled. The spectators weren't allowed to come to our assistance and we lost four minutes before we got going again." Latvala had done what was required of him – he led after the first leg. "If I'd had the right tyres for the job I'd certainly have enjoyed myself," he said, "but you really couldn't do that stretch on the gravel tyres the rules require us to use. The conditions were quite extreme – snow, ice, heavy rain... It would be fantastic to win here, but Loeb will be pushing hard tomorrow." In fact since Latvala couldn't score the 18 points Ford needed all by himself, the constructors' pressure was off Loeb and he could do his own thing in the bid to win this, one of the few rallies missing from his record. After a cautious start, and with the handicap of having to open the road, the Frenchman ended the first leg 12.9 seconds down on Latvala, while in sixth place team-mate Dani Sordo was in a good position to back up for the title should anything untoward happen to his team leader.

But contrary to what Latvala expected, it was in fact the Spaniard who was to provide the threat on the second leg. Winning two of the three morning stages, Sordo was up to third behind Loeb and Latvala, whose high-flying duel saw them separated by just 7.3 seconds at day's end. "In the first few stages I had no chance of being quicker than the cars that started behind me," said Latvala, "because the road was absolutely frozen. The ground was as hard as stone and as soon as I touched the throttle I got wheelspin and had to lift off. Whenever I could I was going right over on to the verges to try and pick up some grip, and that meant the rest were able to close in." The Finn actually had quite a moment late in the day on the way to the super-special in Cardiff's Millenium Stadium. "There was a lot of traffic in the city," he explained, "and we were crawling along, so I was having to use the clutch a lot. It started smoking, and I got worried – we shut everything down and pushed it for the 400 metres! It was quite stressful. Then I struggled to get going in the stage and dropped over three seconds."

The final leg of the 2008 Championship boiled down to a fierce battle between Latvala and Loeb. Winning both morning stages, the Frenchman was back within 1.4 seconds of the Finn. When he crossed the finish line in the penultimate stage, Loeb was back in front, thanks to a demon time – only to be told that he had jumped the start and had been given a 10-second penalty! So there were just 2.2 seconds between the Ford and the Citroën going into the last 20 kilometres

This is how Ford lost their last chance of retaining the constructors' title. After an off in the first leg, Hirvonen was eighth, the first driver in history to score at least one point in every round of a Championship year.

This time Jari-Matti Latvala kept a tight rein on himself and his Ford Focus for the whole weekend, despite unrelenting pressure from Loeb. A pity for his sake that it didn't happen more often this year.

Six years earlier his first crack at the WRC ended up in a Welsh ditch. Valentino Rossi did rather better this time – he made it to the finish. But the Italian missed out on his target of a top-10 place, finishing only 12th.
v

of the season. Both men gave it their all. Loeb clean-sheeted again, beating Latvala, who was now 4.9 seconds down. The Frenchman was on top – and saw that 10-second penalty wiped out after on-board footage had been reviewed. "That was a good one," said Loeb of his 47th win, his 11th of the season. "I really didn't enjoy this event, it was just too tricky, dangerous in fact, to go all-out on those hidden patches of ice when no-one was opening the road. But it was a full-on fight with Jari-Matti today, I was flat-out through the last one." His will to win showed that rallying was still Loeb's priority, and what he did best, even if he had been off seeking new thrills in a Red Bull F1 car and a Peugeot prototype in recent weeks.

"I did what I could, I gave it everything I had, but it wasn't enough," lamented Latvala, who had done a Grönholm all weekend at the end of an inconsistent season. "Going first didn't suit me, and I'm really disappointed." Third overall, Sordo claimed a fifth podium of the season in a major contribution to a constructors' title that had been Ford property for the last two years. Once again Petter Solberg, in fourth, had done what he could with what he had. Despite the pressure of recent weeks since it was rumoured that Grönholm would be with Subaru in 2009, the Norwegian didn't crack, he had a flawless weekend. "It wasn't much fun out there," he said at the finish. "Whenever there was a bit of grip we were right in it, but as soon as it got slippery there was nothing we could do. Now we need to work hard through the winter and roll up our sleeves to come back stronger next year."

Suzuki finished the year on a high with fifth and seventh for Andersson and Gardemeister, building on a successful Japanese round. François Duval was back after his dreadful Sapporo accident and right back on the pace with Patrick Pivato's friend Denis Giraudet in the co-driver's seat. The Franco-Belgian pairing took advantage of Henning Solberg's suspension failure late in the day to come home sixth, a very creditable result in the circumstances. Fighting back for eighth, Mikko Hirvonen was the first driver in history ever to go through an entire season finishing in the points in every round. As for Valentino Rossi, he fell short of his target, which was to be in the top 10, finishing 12th, beaten by the first Group N car but quicker than Rautenbach and Al-Qasimi. The two-wheeled ace was happy not to have got caught out – and to have had a lot of fun in the process. Last but not least, the youngest man in the field, Tom Cave, impressed with 30th place and a comfortable win in the Ford Fiesta ST round. ■

By finishing third Dani Sordo did what had to be done to make Citroën World Champion Constructors once more, something the French marque had missed out on for the past two seasons to Ford's advantage.

<
Mads Ostberg has a guaranteed drive in a privateer Subaru for 2009, but he wasn't about to wait until then to get himself noticed. He was fourth on the opening leg but sadly his engine let him down next day.

P.-G. Andersson closed out his season in magnificent style. Suzuki's Swedish driver finished fifth, as he had done in Japan – the Japanese manufacturer's best result. At the end of the first leg he was actually in a podium place!

PRODUCTION CARS
Aigner scoops the pool

Going into the final meeting of the season Juho Hanninen looked likeliest to succeed Toshihiro Araï: with a six-point lead over Andreas Aigner, fourth place would be good enough for the Finn. But he threw it all away early in the piece, when transmission failure on his Mitsubishi Lancer cost him two minutes straight off while Aigner was getting into a podium position behind Wilks and Flodin. "Nearly all morning I was in an ordinary car instead of a four-wheel-drive," he raged. That wasn't the end of his woes either. Going through a ford he drowned the Mitsi's engine and it refused to start again. That was the end of his race: Aigner had only to finish on the podium for the title to be his. The Austrian took it steadily, let his title rivals go and was relieved to see other big names like Novikov and Prokop retire. First-leg leader Guy Wilks was slowed by a turbo failure, which left Sweden's Flodin (Subaru Impreza) and Sandell (Peugeot 207 Super 2000) to fight it out for the win. Sandell had closed to within 11 seconds of Flodin before the last stage, where he tried everything he knew before being forced out by an engine failure, handing Flodin his first Group win and Aigner the second place that also meant the title. It was a nice way for the 24-year-old Red Bull protégé to get back at his critics after an unconvincing 2006 in the works Skoda Fabia WRC. ■

A fifth world title might have been enough for Sébastien Loeb, but he gave everything he had to grab his 11th win of the season and his first on the Rally of Great Britain – at the sixth attempt.

15 | Great Britain | Results

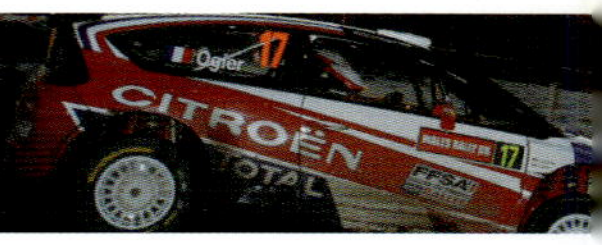

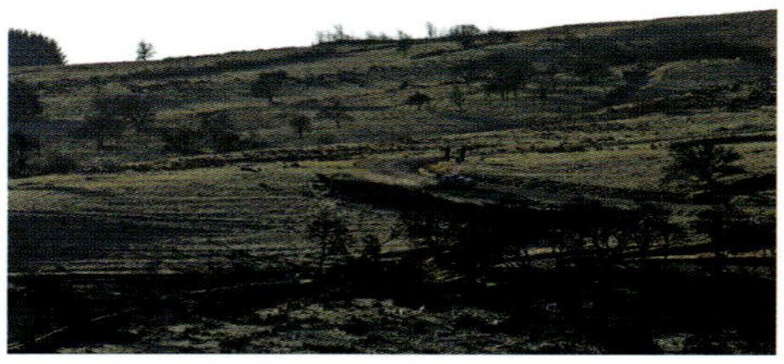

64th RALLY OF GREAT BRITAIN

Organiser Details
International Motor Sports Ltd,
Motor Sports House, Riverside Park,
Colnbrook, Slough, SL3 0HG,
Great Britain
Tel.: +44 1753 765 100
Fax: +44 1753 765 106

Wales Rally GB

15th and last leg of FIA 2008 World Championship for constructors and drivers.
8th and last leg of FIA Production Car World Championship.

Date December 5 - 7, 2008

Route
1428,44 km divised in three legs.
19 special stages on dirt roads (348.99 km);
17 raced

Ceremonial Start
Thursday, December 4 (18:00),
Cardiff
Leg 1
Friday, December 5 (09:08/17:17),
Swansea > Swansea, 561.54 km;
8 special stages (123.68 km); 6 raced
Leg 2
Saturday, December 6 (08:18/18:15),
Swansea > Swansea, 547.26 km;
7 special stages (129.21 km)
Leg 3
Sunday, december 7 (07:55/12:18),
Swansea > Swansea > Cardiff, 319.64 km;
4 special stages (96.10 km)

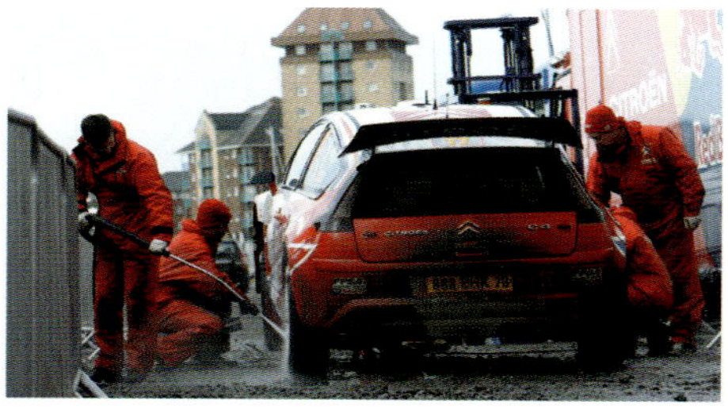

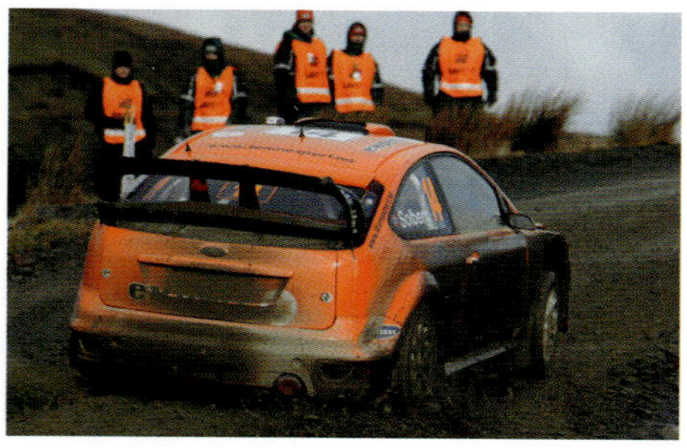

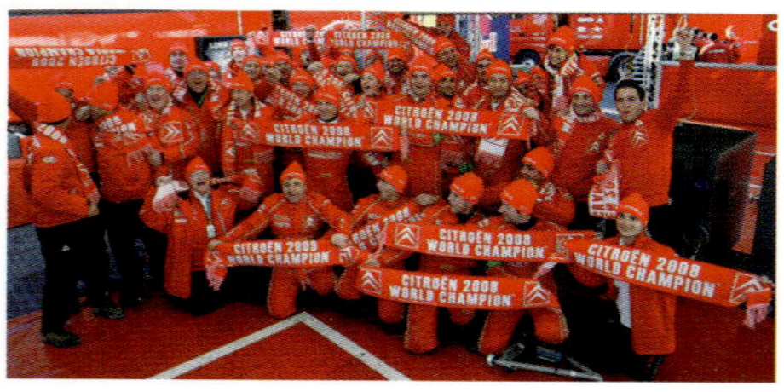

Entry List (80) - 79 starters

N°	Driver (Nat.)	Co-Driver (Nat.)	Team	Car	Group & FIA Priority
1	SÉBASTIEN LOEB (F)	DANIEL ELENA (MC)	CITROËN TOTAL WRT	CITROËN C4	A8 1
2	DANI SORDO (E)	MARC MARTI (E)	CITROËN TOTAL WRT	CITROËN C4	A8 1
3	MIKKO HIRVONEN (FIN)	JARMO LEHTINEN (FIN)	BP FORD ABU DHABI WORLD RALLY TEAM	FORD FOCUS RS WRC 07	A8 1
4	JARI-MATTI LATVALA (FIN)	MIIKKA ANTTILA (FIN)	BP FORD ABU DHABI WORLD RALLY TEAM	FORD FOCUS RS WRC 07	A8 1
5	PETTER SOLBERG (N)	PHILIP MILLS (GB)	SUBARU WORLD RALLY TEAM	SUBARU IMPREZA WRC 2008	A8 1
6	CHRIS ATKINSON (AUS)	STEPHANE PREVOT (B)	SUBARU WORLD RALLY TEAM	SUBARU IMPREZA WRC 2008	A8 1
7	FRANÇOIS DUVAL (B)	DENIS GIRAUDET (F)	STOBART VK M-SPORT FORD RALLY TEAM	FORD FOCUS RS WRC 07	A8 1
8	MATTHEW WILSON (GB)	SCOTT MARTIN (GB)	STOBART VK M-SPORT FORD RALLY TEAM	FORD FOCUS RS WRC 07	A8 1
11	TONI GARDEMEISTER (FIN)	TOMI TUOMINEN (FIN)	SUZUKI WORLD RALLY TEAM	SUZUKI SX4	A8 1
12	PER-GUNNAR ANDERSSON (S)	JONAS ANDERSSON (S)	SUZUKI WORLD RALLY TEAM	SUZUKI SX4	A8 1
14	HENNING SOLBERG (N)	CATO MENKARUD (N)	STOBART VK M-SPORT FORD RALLY TEAM	FORD FOCUS RS WRC 07	A8 2
16	CONRAD RAUTENBACH (ZW)	DAVID SENIOR (GB)	CONRAD RAUTENBACH	CITROËN C4 WRC	A8 2
17	SÉBASTIEN OGIER (F)	JULIEN INGRASSIA (F)	EQUIPE DE FRANCE FFSA	CITROËN C4 WRC	A8 2
18	MADS ØSTBERG (N)	OLE KRISTIAN UNNERUD (N)	ADAPTA AS	SUBARU IMPREZA WRC	A8 2
19	KHALID AL QASSIMI (UAE)	MICHAEL ORR (GB)	BP FORD ABU DHABI WORLD RALLY TEAM	FORD FOCUS RS WRC 07	A8 2
20	BARRY CLARK (GB)	PAUL NAGLE (IRL)	STOBART VK M-SPORT FORD RALLY TEAM	FORD FOCUS RS WRC 07	A8 2
21	EAMONN BOLAND (IRL)	DAMIEN MORRISSEY (IRL)	EAMONN BOLAND	SUBARU IMPREZA WRC	A8 2
22	GARETH JONES (GB)	CLIVE JENKINS (GB)	GARETH JONES	SUBARU IMPREZA WRC	A8 2
23	STEVE PEREZ (GB)	PAUL SPOONER (GB)	STOBART VK M-SPORT FORD RALLY TEAM	FORD FOCUS	A8 2
24	DAVE WESTON (GB)	ALED DAVIES (GB)	STOBART VK M-SPORT FORD RALLY TEAM	FORD FOCUS RS WRC 05	A8 2
32	MIRCO BALDACCI (RSM)	GIOVANNI AGNESE (I)	MIRCO BALDACCI	MITSUBISHI LANCER EVOLUTION IX	N4 3
33	MARTIN PROKOP (CZ)	JAM TOMÁNEK (CZ)	MARTIN PROKOP	MITSUBISHI LANCER EVOLUTION IX	N4 3
35	EVGENY NOVIKOV (RU)	DALE MOSCATT (AUS)	EVGENY NOVIKOV	MITSUBISHI LANCER EVOLUTION IX	N4 3
36	EYVIND BRYNILDSEN (N)	GLENN MACNEALL (AUS)	EYVIND BRYNILDSEN	MITSUBISHI LANCER EVOLUTION IX	N4 3
37	SPYROS PAVLIDES (CY)	()	AUTOTEK	SUBARU IMPREZA WRX STI	N4 3
39	NASSER AL-ATTIYAH (Q)	CHRIS PATTERSON (GB)	QMMF	SUBARU IMPREZA	N4 3
40	LORIS BALDACCI (RSM)	RUDY POLLET (I)	ERRANI TEAM GROUP	MITSUBISHI LANCER EVOLUTION IX	N4 3
41	ANDREAS AIGNER (A)	KLAUS WICHA (D)	RED BULL RALLYE TEAM	MITSUBISHI LANCER EVOLUTION IX	N4 3
42	BERNARDO SOUSA (P)	JORGE CARVALHO (P)	RED BULL RALLYE TEAM	MITSUBISHI LANCER EVOLUTION IX	N4 3
44	PATRIK FLODIN (S)	GÖRAN BERGSTEN (S)	GABOKO RALLY TEAM	SUBARU IMPREZA WRX STI	N4 3
45	TEEMU ARMINEN (FIN)	TUOMO NIKKOLA (FIN)	MOTORING CLUB	SUBARU IMPREZA N14	N4 3
46	VALENTINO ROSSI (I)	CARLO CASSINA (I)	VALENTINO ROSSI	FORD FOCUS RS WRC 07	A8 2
47	JAROMIR TARABUS (CZ)	DANIEL TRUNKET (CZ)	MOTORING CLUB	FIAT GRANDE PUNTO S2000	N4 3
48	EVGENY AKSAKOV (RU)	ALEKSANDER KORNILOV (EE)	RED WINGS - MOSCOW REGION RALLY TEAM	MITSUBISHI LANCER EVOLUTION IX	N4 3
49	SIMONE CAMPEDELLI (I)	DANILO FAPPANI (I)	SCUDERIA RUBICONE CORSE	MITSUBISHI LANCER EVOLUTION IX	N4 3
50	ARMINDO ARAÚJO (P)	MIGUEL RAMALHO (P)	RALLIART ITALY	MITSUBISHI LANCER EVOLUTION IX	N4 3
52	JUHO HÄNNINEN (FIN)	MIKKO MARKKULA (FIN)	RALLIART NEW ZEALAND	MITSUBISHI LANCER EVOLUTION IX	N4 3
53	GIOVANNI MANFRINATO (I)	CARLO PISANO (I)	PRO RACE RALLY	MITSUBISHI LANCER EVOLUTION IX	N4 3
54	MARK HIGGINS (GB)	RORY KENNEDY (IRL)	SUBARU RALLY TEAM USA	SUBARU IMPREZA WRX STI	N4 3
55	PATRIK SANDELL (S)	EMIL AXELSSON (S)	PEUGEOT SPORT SWEDEN	PEUGEOT 207 S2000	N4 3
56	FUMIO NUTAHARA (J)	DANIEL BARRITT (GB)	ADVAN-PIAA RALLY TEAM	MITSUBISHI LANCER EVOLUTION IX	N4 3
57	MARTIN RAUAM (EE)	SILVER KUTT (EE)	WORLD RALLY TEAM ESTONIA	MITSUBISHI LANCER EVOLUTION IX	N4 3
58	NAREN KUMAR (IND)	NICKY BEECH (GB)	TEAM SIDVIN INDIA	SUBARU IMPREZA WRX STI	N4 3
59	DAVID HIGGINS (GB)	IEUAN THOMAS (GB)	DAVID HIGGINS	SUBARU IMPREZA WRX STI	N4 3
60	GUY WILKS (GB)	PHIL PUGH (GB)	MITSUBISHI MOTORS UK	MITSUBISHI LANCER EVOLUTION IX	N4 3
61	GWYNDAF EVANS (GB)	GARETH ROBERTS (GB)	MITSUBISHI MOTORS UK	MITSUBISHI LANCER EVOLUTION IX	N4
62	MATTIAS THERMAN (FIN)	JANNE PERÄLÄ (FIN)	MATTIAS THERMAN	MITSUBISHI LANCER EVOLUTION IX	N4
64	ARI LAIVOLA (FIN)	KARI MUSTALAHTI (FIN)	ARI LAIVOLA	MITSUBISHI LANCER EVOLUTION IX	N4
65	BRIAN O MAHONY (IRL)	JOHN HIGGINS (IRL)	BRIAN O MAHONY	RENAULT CLIO S1600	A6
66	TOMMI LUOSTARINEN (FIN)	S SUHONEN (FIN)	S SUHONEN	MITSUBISHI LANCER EVOLUTION IX	N4
67	HERMANN GASSNER JUNIOR (D)	KATHERINA WUESTENHAGEN (D)	HERMANN GASSNER JUNIOR	MITSUBISHI LANCER EVOLUTION IX	N4
68	HUGH EVANS (GB)	IESTYN WILLIAMS (GB)	HUGH EVANS	SUBARU IMPREZA WRX STI	N4
69	DANIEL UNGUR (RO)	SEBASTIAN ITU (RO)	DANIEL UNGUR	SUBARU IMPREZA WRX STI	N4
70	MARCO TEMPESTINI (I)	DORIN PULPEA (RO)	MARCO TEMPESTINI	SUBARU IMPREZA WRX STI	N4
71	OLEKSII TAMRAZOV (UA)	OLEKSANDR SKOCHYK (UA)	OLEKSII TAMRAZOV	SUBARU IMPREZA WRX STI	N4
72	ROB GILL (GB)	ANDERS HOWARD (GB)	ROB GILL	MITSUBISHI LANCER EVOLUTION IX	N4
74	TOM WALSTER (GB)	TIM STURLA (GB)	TOM WALSTER	FORD FIESTA ST	N3
75	PETER STEPHENSON (GB)	()	PETER STEPHENSON	MG ZR S2000	N4
76	JASON PRITCHARD (GB)	GEORGE GWYNN (GB)	JASON PRITCHARD	CITROËN C2R2	A6
77	JAMES SMITH (GB)	SIMON WALLIS (GB)	JAMES SMITH	SUBARU IMPREZA	N4
78	MATT COTTON (GB)	ANTHONY GODDEN (GB)	MATT COTTON	CITROËN C2R2	A6
79	ANDREW HOCKRIDGE (GB)	RICH MILLS (GB)	ANDREW HOCKRIDGE	CITROËN C2R2	A6
80	STEVEN HOLDER (GB)	STEVE MCPHEE (GB)	STEVEN HOLDER	SUBARU IMPREZA WRX STI	N4
81	EMRE YURDAKUL (TR)	CAN ERKAL (TR)	CASTROL FORD TEAM TURKIYE	FORD FIESTA ST	N3
83	LUCA GRIOTTI (I)	CORRADO BONATO (I)	LUCA GRIOTTI	RENAULT CLIO	A7
84	BURCU CETINKAYA (TR)	CICEK GUNEY (TR)	CASTROL FORD TEAM TURKIYE	FORD FIESTA ST	N3
85	NATHAN O'CONNOR (GB)	JESSICA ROGAN (GB)	NATHAN O'CONNOR	CITROËN C2R2	A6
86	KORAY MURATOGLU (TR)	CAGLAR SUREN (TR)	CASTROL FORD TEAM TURKIYE	FORD FIESTA ST	N3
87	TONY JARDINE (GB)	DAVID SMITH (GB)	TONY JARDINE	FORD FIESTA ST150	N3
88	DEIVIDAS JOCIUS (LT)	MINDAUGAS VARZA (LT)	DEIVIDAS JOCIUS	MITSUBISHI LANCER EVOLUTION IX	N4
89	GORDON NICHOL (GB)	EMMA MORRISON (GB)	GORDON NICHOL	SUZUKI SWIFT	N2
91	DAVID MATTHEWS (GB)	IAN HARRAWAY (GB)	DAVID MATTHEWS	SUBARU IMPREZA	N4
92	MARKO JERAM (SLO)	SIMON LAPAJNE (SLO)	MARKO JERAM	FORD FIESTA ST	N3
93	DENIS GRODETSKIY (RU)	SAFONIY LOTKO (RU)	CUEKS RACING	FORD FIESTA ST	N3
94	THOMAS CAVE (GB)	GEMMA PRICE (GB)	THOMAS CAVE	FORD FIESTA ST	N3
95	NEVILLE JONES (GB)	IAN CAPEWELL (GB)	NEVILLE JONES	SUBARU IMPREZA WRX STI	N4
96	SUPRADIP DEY ROY (GB)	BOB STOKOE (GB)	SUPRADIP DEY ROY	MG ZR 160	N3
97	DAVID HARRISON (GB)	GLYN THOMAS (GB)	DAVID HARRISON	MG ZR 105	N1
98	DARREN JONES (GB)	PAUL BURLEY (GB)	DARREN JONES	SKODA FELICIA	A5
146	JARI KETOMAA (FIN)	MIIKA TEISKONEN (FIN)	MOTORING CLUB	SUBARU IMPREZA WRX STI	N4 3

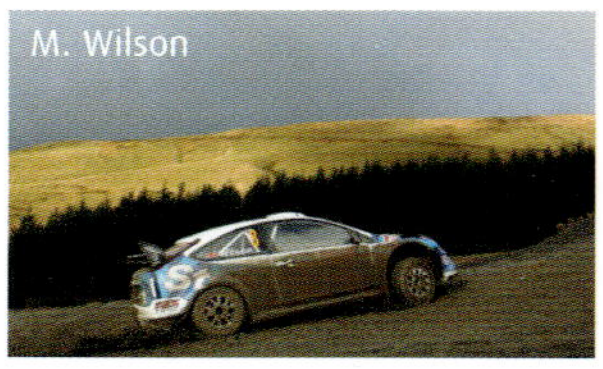
M. Wilson

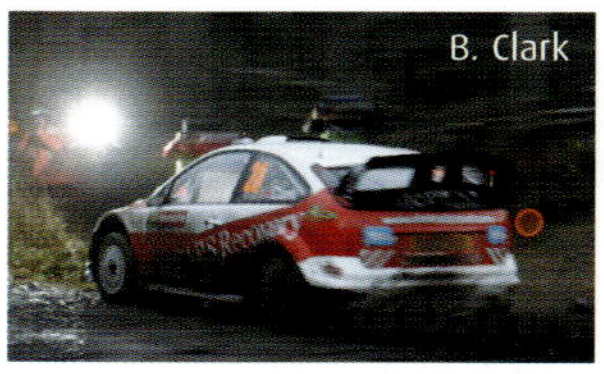
B. Clark

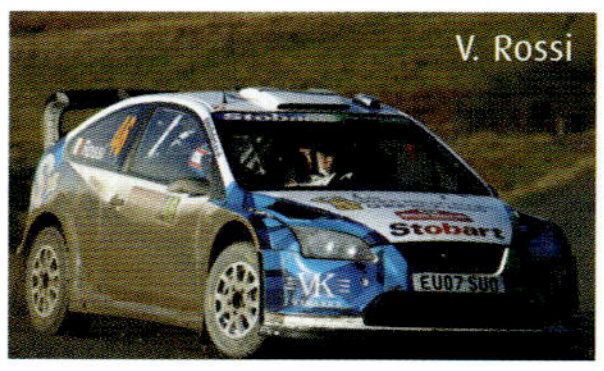
V. Rossi

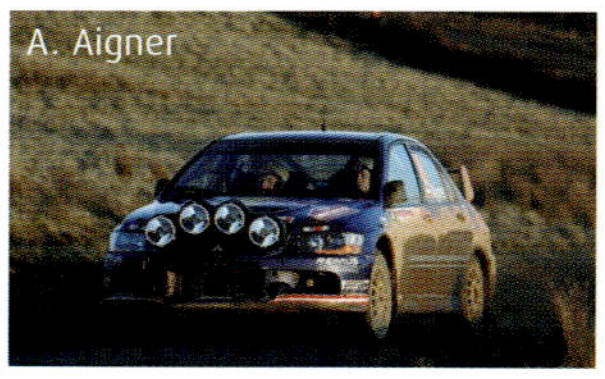
A. Aigner

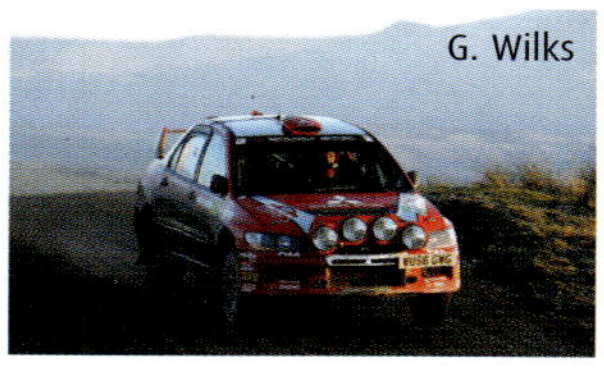
G. Wilks

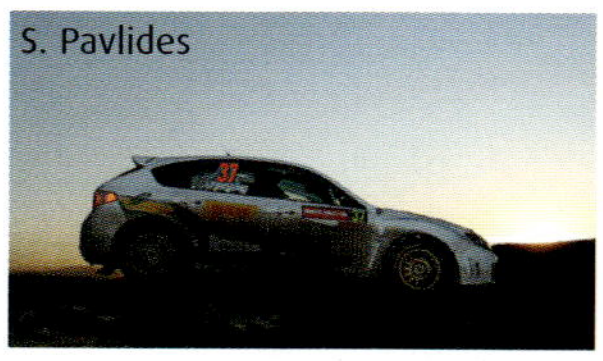
S. Pavlides

Championship Classifications

•R•: Rookie

FIA Drivers (15/15)

1. **Loeb** 11🏆 122
2. Hirvonen 3🏆 103
3. Sordo 65
4. Latvala 1🏆 58
5. Atkinson 50
6. P. Solberg 46
7. Duval 25
8. H. Solberg 22
9. Galli 17
10. Wilson 15
11. Aava 13
12. Andersson 12
13. Gardemeister 10
14. Villagra 9
15. Rautenbach 6
16. Mikkelsen 5
17. Rantanen 2
18. Cuoq 2
19. Hänninen 1
20. Aigner 1
21. Ogier 1
22. Østberg, K. Al-Qassimi, 0
Mölder, Beltrán, Clark, 0
Ketomaa, Prokop, 0
Kosciuszko, Tirabassi, 0
Sandell, Nutahara, Novikov, 0
Flodin, Rauam, Burkart, 0
Rossi, Gallagher, Broccoli, 0
Brynildsen, Paddon, Farrah, 0
Schammel, Nittel, Baldacci, 0
Valimaki, Kamada, Artru, 0
Wilks, Guerra, Mercier, Arai, 0
Boland, A. Al-Qassimi, 0

FIA Constructors (15/15)

1. **Citroën Total World Rally Team** 11🏆 191
2. BP-Ford Abu Dhabi World Rally Team 4🏆 173
3. Subaru World Rally Team 98
4. Stobart VK M-Sport Ford Rally Team 67
5. Suzuki World Rally Team 34
6. Munchi's Ford World Rally Team 22

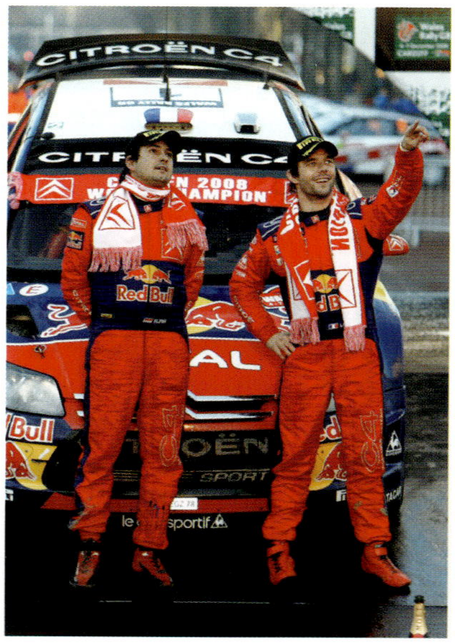

FIA Production Car WRC (8/8)

1. **Aigner** 3🏆 38
2. Hänninen 3🏆 36
3. Ketomaa 28
4. Sandell 22
5. Prokop 1🏆 17
6. Rauam 15
7. Nutahara 15
8. Araujo 14
9. Sousa 12
10. Flodin 1🏆 10
11. M. Baldacci 9
12. Arai 9
13. Novikov 8
14. Beltrán 8
15. Valimaki 8
16. Wilks 6
17. Aksakov 6
18. Vertunov 6
19. Brynildsen 5
20. Svedlund 5
21. Paddon 5
22. Nittel 4
23. Kamada 4
24. Tarabus 4
25. Farrah 3
26. Pavlides 3
27. Tiippana 3
28. Campedelli 3
29. Taguci 2
30. Bacco 1
31. Higgins 1
32. L. Baldacci 1
33. Taylor 1
34. Linari, Frisiero, Dong, 0
Aksa, Marrini, Al-Attiyah, 0
Kumar, Manfrinato, 0
Athanassoulas, Errani, 0
Hagiwara, Pastrana, Block, 0
Jereb 0

FIA Junior WRC (7/7)

1. **Ogier** 3🏆 42
2. Burkart 34
3. Prokop 3🏆 32
4. Gallagher 30
5. Kosciusko 1🏆 22
6. Bettega 22
7. Sandell 21
8. Mölder 11
9. Albertini 9
10. Schammel 8
11. Niegel •R• 8
12. Bertolotti 8
13. Abbring 7
14. Campana 6
15. Marche 5
16. Cortinovis 4
17. Weijs Jr. •R• 2
18. Fanari •R• 1
19. Komljenovic 1
20. Pinomaki 0
21. Meeke 0

Rookie
1. Fanari 44
2. Weijs Jr. 30
3. Niegel 8

Special Stages Times

www.walesrallygb.com
www.wrc.com

SS1 Hafren 1 (19.10 km) (3.67 km)
Cancelled

SS2 Sweet Lamb 1 (5.11 km)
1.Ogier 2'48"6; 2.Duval +5"1;
3.P.Solberg +5"4; 4.Andersson +5"9;
5.Østberg +7"5; 6.Atkinson +8"3;
7.Gardemeister +9"3; 8.Loeb +10"5...
P-WRC > 17.Higgins 3'06"6

SS3 Myherin 1 (35.34 km) (18.28 km)
1.Latvala 10'59"2; 2.Østberg +2"0;
3.Loeb +4"8; 4.Sordo +6"7;
5.Ogier +7"2; 6.Andersson +8"0;
7.Atkinson +9"4.
8.Gardemeister +10"7...
P-WRC > 15.Wilks 11'41"5

SS4 Hafren 2 (19.10 km) (3.67 km)
Cancelled

SS5 Sweet Lamb 2 (5.11 km)
1.Loeb 2'50"4; 2.Duval +1"8;
3.Østberg +2"0; 4.P.Solberg +2"0;
5.H.Solberg +2"4; 6.Ogier +4"0;
7.Latvala +4"3; 8.Gardemeister +4"8...
P-WRC > 14.Wilks 3'01"9

SS6 Myherin 2 (35.34 km) (18.28 km)
1.Latvala 10'56"5; 2.Loeb +11"5;
3.Andersson +12"8; 4.Sordo +13"3;
5.Atkinson +16"9; 6.H.Solberg +18"1;
7.P.Solberg +20"1; 8.Østberg +23"0...
P-WRC > 14.Wilks 11'56"0

SS7 Walters Arena 1 (2.29 km)
1.Latvala 1'44"5; 2.Loeb +2"4;
3.P.Solberg +2"6; 4.Sordo +2"8;
5.Østberg +3"1; 6.Andersson +4"0;
7.H.Solberg +5"2; 8.Duval +5"2...
P-WRC > 9.Wilks 1'51"1

SS8 Walters Arena 2 (2.29 km)
1.Loeb 1'45"0; 2.Andersson +0"7;
3.Sordo +0"8; 4.P.Solberg +0"8;
5.Latvala +0"9; 6.Duval +1"9;
7.Østberg +2"7;
P-WRC > 8.Al-Attiyah +4"1 (1'49"1)...

Classification Leg 1
1.Latvala 31'20"5; 2.Loeb +12"9;
3.Andersson +22"5; 4.Østberg +24"0;
5.P.Solberg +27"4; 6.Sordo +32"2;
7.Duval +52"0; 8.H.Solberg +54"7...
P-WRC > 13.Wilks 33'26"9

SS9 Resolfen 1 (30.68 km)
1.Sordo 17'12"5; 2.Hirvonen +18"0;
3.Loeb +23"5; 4.P.Solberg +26"1;
5.Gardemeister +28"9; 6.Latvala +31"4;
7.Østberg +38"8; 8.Duval +39"8...
P-WRC > 12.Flodin 18'19"1

SS10 Halfway 1 (18.57 km)
1.Latvala 11'24"3; 2.Loeb +5"0;
3.Hirvonen +16"2; 4.Sordo +21"0;
5.P.Solberg +21"3; 6.Andersson +24"1;
7.Østberg +26"7; 8.Duval +27"4...
P-WRC > 13.Sandell 12'17"0

SS11 Crychan 1 (14.86 km)
1.Sordo 9'25"1; 2.Hirvonen +1"8;
3.Loeb +3"1; 4.Latvala +4"2;
5.H.Solberg +4"6; 6.P.Solberg +7"1;
7.Østberg +8"9; 8.Andersson +10"7...
P-WRC > 12.Sandell 9'50"6

SS12 Resolfen 2 (30.68 km)
1.Hirvonen 16'19"9; 2.Loeb +15"5;
3.P.Solberg +15"7; 4.Latvala +16"0;
5.H.Solberg +19"1; 6.Sordo +19"8;
7.Duval +34"8; 8.Østberg +42"1...
P-WRC > 14.Flodin 17'44"7

SS13 Halfway 2 (18.57 km)
1.Loeb 11'11"9; 2.Hirvonen +5"0;
3.Latvala +6"0; 4.Sordo +7"2;
5.P.Solberg +8"9; 6.H.Solberg +13"4;
7.Andersson +16"8; 8.Østberg +20"4...
P-WRC > 14.Sandell 12'08"0

SS14 Crychan 2 (14.86 km)
1.Latvala 9'00"6; 2.Hirvonen +3"1;
3.P.Solberg +6"7; 4.Sordo +7"4;
5.Loeb +8"4; 6.H.Solberg +10"9;
7.Andersson +15"2;
8.Gardemeister +20"4...
P-WRC > 13.Sandell 9'48"5

SS15 Cardiff (0.99 km)
1.Loeb 56"5; 2.P.Solberg +0"4;
3.Duval +0"6; 4.Hirvonen +1"3;
5.Sordo +1"4; 6.H.Solberg +2"0;
7.Gardemeister +2'06"1;
8.Wilson +2"1...
P-WRC > 10.Araujo 58"9

Classification Leg 2
1.Latvala 1h47'52"4; 2.Loeb +7"3;
3.Sordo +27"9; 4.P.Solberg +52"5;
5.Andersson +2'06"1;
6.H.Solberg +2'09"3; 7.Duval +2'29"6;
8.Gardemeister +3'33"0...
P-WRC > 12.Flodin 1h55'43"8

SS16 Rheola 1 (27.96 km)
1.Loeb 16'15"0; 2.Latvala +5"1;
3.Sordo +10"3; 4.P.Solberg +19"2;
5.Hirvonen +27"7; 6.Andersson +33"1;
7.Gardemeister +35"4;
8.H.Solberg +47"5...
P-WRC > 14.Flodin 17'50"0

SS17 Port Talbot 1 (20.09 km)
1.Loeb 11'17"9; 2.Latvala +0"8;
3.Sordo +10"6; 4.Hirvonen +14"9;
5.H.Solberg +18"0; 6.P.Solberg +23"5;
7.Andersson +24"2;
8.Gardemeister +25"8...
P-WRC > 15.Sandell 12'17"5

SS18 Rheola 2 (27.96 km)
1.Loeb 16'25"0; 2.Hirvonen +8"7;
3.Latvala +9"2; 4.P.Solberg +15"7;
5.Sordo +24"5; 6.Ogier +25"5;
7.Andersson +34"0;
8.Gardemeister +34"0...
P-WRC > 14.Flodin 17'27"5

SS19 Port Talbot 2 (20.09 km)
1.Loeb 11'12"0; 2.Latvala +4"9;
3.Hirvonen +10"3; 4.Sordo +14"6;
5.P.Solberg +16"0;
6.Gardemeister +24"1; 7.Ogier +27"8;
8.Andersson +34"0...
P-WRC > 13.Flodin 12'10"8

Results

	Driver - Co-Driver	Car	Gr.	Time
1.	Loeb - Elena	Citroën C4 WRC	A8	2h43'09"6
2.	Latvala - Anttila	Ford Focus RS WRC 08	A8	+12"7
3.	Sordo - Marti	Citroën C4 WRC	A8	+1'20"6
4.	P. Solberg - Mills	Subaru Impreza WRC 2008	A8	+1'59"6
5.	Andersson - Andersson	Suzuki SX4 WRC	A8	+4'04"1
6.	Duval - Giraudet	Ford Focus RS WRC 07	A8	+5'07"8
7.	Gardemeister - Tuominen	Suzuki SX4 WRC	A8	+5'25"0
8.	Hirvonen - Lehtinen	Ford Focus RS WRC 08	A8	+5'38"8
9.	Wilson - Martin	Ford Focus RS WRC 07	A8	+8'13"9
10.	Clark - Nagle	Ford Focus RS WRC 07	A8	+9'53"1
11.	Flodin - Bergsten	Subaru Impreza WRX Sti	N4/P	+12'51"7
12.	Rossi - Cassina	Ford Focus RS WRC 07	A8	+13'20"4
13.	Aigner - Wicha	Mitsubishi Lancer Evo. IX	N4/P	+14'33"8
14.	Wilks - Pugh	Mitsubishi Lancer Evo. IX	N4/P	+14'59"4

Leading Retirements (32)

Ctrl18	H. Solberg - Menkerud	Ford Focus RS WRC 07	Suspension
Ctrl15E	Østberg - Unnerud	Subaru Impreza WRC	Off
Ctrl7	Atkinson - Prévot	Subaru Impreza WRC 2008	Off
Ctrl6	Hänninen - Markkula	Mitsubishi Lancer Evo. IX	Engine

Performers

	1	2	3	4	5	6	C6	Nb SS
Loeb	8	4	3	-	1	-	16	17
Latvala	5	3	2	2	1	1	14	17
Sordo	2	-	3	7	2	1	16	17
Hirvonen	1	5	2	2	1	-	11	17
Ogier	1	-	-	-	1	2	4	17
Duval	-	2	1	-	-	1	4	17
P. Solberg	-	1	4	5	3	2	15	17
Andersson	-	1	1	1	-	4	7	17
Østberg	-	1	1	-	2	-	4	15
H. Solberg	-	-	-	-	4	4	8	16
Gardemeister	-	-	-	-	1	1	2	17
Atkinson	-	-	-	-	1	1	2	7

Leaders

SS1	(Cancelled)
SS2 > SS5	Ogier
SS6 > SS17	Latvala
SS18 > SS19	Loeb

Patrik Flodin

Previous Winners

1974	Mäkinen - Liddon Ford Escort RS 1600
1975	Mäkinen - Liddon Ford Escort RS
1976	Clark - Pegg Ford Escort RS
1977	Waldegaard - Thorszelius Ford Escort RS
1978	Mikkola - Hertz Ford Escort RS
1979	Mikkola - Hertz Ford Escort RS
1980	Toivonen - White Talbot Sunbeam Lotus
1981	Mikkola - Hertz Audi Quattro
1982	Mikkola - Hertz Audi Quattro
1983	Blomqvist - Cederberg Audi Quattro
1984	Vatanen - Harryman Peugeot 205 T16
1985	Toivonen - Wilson Lancia Delta S4
1986	Salonen - Harjanne Peugeot 205 T16
1987	Kankkunen - Piironen Lancia Delta HF
1988	Alen - Kivimaki Lancia Delta Integrale
1989	Airikkala - McNamee Mitsubishi Galant VR4
1990	Sainz - Moya Toyota Celica GT-Four
1991	Kankkunen - Piironen Lancia Delta Integrale
1992	Sainz - Moya Toyota Celica Turbo 4WD
1993	Kankkunen - Piironen Toyota Celica Turbo 4WD
1994	McRae - Ringer Subaru Impreza
1995	McRae - Ringer Subaru Impreza
1996	Schwarz - Giraudet Toyota Celica GT-Four
1997	McRae - Grist Subaru Impreza WRC
1998	Burns - Reid Mitsubishi Carisma GT
1999	Burns - Reid Subaru Impreza WRC
2000	Burns - Reid Subaru Impreza WRC 2000
2001	Gronholm - Rautiainen Peugeot 206 WRC
2002	P. Solberg - Mills Subaru Impreza WRC 2002
2003	P. Solberg - Mills Subaru Impreza WRC 2003
2004	P. Solberg - Mills Subaru Impreza WRC 2004
2005	P. Solberg - Mills Subaru Impreza WRC 2005
2006	Grönholm - Rautiainen Ford Focus RS WRC 06
2007	Hirvonen - Lehtinen Ford Focus RS WRC 07

2008 FIA World Rally Championship / Drivers

21 DRIVERS / 54	Nationalities	1. Monte-Carlo	2. Sweden	3. Mexico	4. Argentina	5. Jordan	6. Italy	7. Greece	8. Turkey	9. Finland	10. Germany	11. New Zealand	12. Spain	13. France	14. Japan	15. Great Britain	TOTAL
1. Sébastien Loeb	(F)	10	-	10	10	0	10	10	6	10	10	10	10	10	6	10	122
2. Mikko Hirvonen	(FIN)	8	8	5	4	10	8	6	10	8	5	6	6	8	10	1	103
3. Daniel Sordo	(E)	0	3	0	6	8	4	4	5	5	8	8	8	-	-	6	65
4. Jari-Matti Latvala	(FIN)	0	10	6	0	2	6	2	8	0	0	-	3	5	8	8	58
5. Chris Atkinson	(AUS)	6	0	8	8	6	3	-	0	6	3	-	2	3	5	-	50
6. Petter Solberg	(N)	4	5	0	-	-	0	8	3	3	4	5	4	4	1	5	46
7. François Duval	(B)	5									6		5	6		3	25
8. Henning Solberg	(N)	0	0	4	-	5	2	1	4	4	2	0	0	0	-	-	22
9. Gigi Galli	(I)	3	6	-	2	1	5	-	-	-	-						17
10. Matthew Wilson	(GB)	0	-	3	-	4	0	3	2	0	0	0	0	1	2	0	15
11. Urmo Aava	(EE)		0			1	5		0	1	4	0	2				13
12. Per-Gunnar Andersson	(S)	1	-	-	0	-	0	0	-	0	3	0	0	4	4		12
13. Toni Gardemeister	(FIN)	-	2	-	-	-	-	0	-	1	0	2	0	0	3	2	10
14. Federico Villagra	(RA)		2	3	3	0	0	0	-		1	0		0			9
15. Conrad Rautenbach	(ZW)	-	0	0	5	0	0	1	0	0	-	-	-	0	-	0	6
16. Andreas Mikkelsen	(N)		4						0	0	0		1	0			5
17. Matti Rantanen	(FIN)									2							2
18. Jean-Marie Cuoq	(F)	2															2
19. Juho Hänninen	(FIN)		1					0		0		0	0		0	-	1
20. Andreas Aigner	(A)		0		1		0	0	-		-				0		1
21. Sébastien Ogier	(F)			1		0	0			0	0		-	0		0	1

22. Mads Østberg (N), Khalid Al-Qassimi (UAE), Jaan Mölder (EE), Sebastián Beltrán (RA), Barry Clark (GB), Jari Ketomaa (FIN), Martin Prokop (CZ), Michal Kosciuszko (PL), 0
30. Brice Tirabassi (F), Patrik Sandell (S), Fumio Nutahara (J), Evgeny Novikov (RUS), Patrik Flodin (S), Martin Rauam (EE), Aaron Burkart (D), Valentino Rossi (I), 0
38. Shaun Gallagher (IRL), Alessandro Broccoli (RSM), Eyvind Brynildsen (N), Hayden Paddon (NZ), Amjad Farrah (JOR), Gilles Schammel (LUX), Uwe Nittel (D), Mirco Baldacci (I), 0
46. Jussi Valimaki (FIN), Takuma Kamada (J), Patrick Artru (F), Guy Wilks (GB), Benito Guerra (MEX), Eddie Mercier (F), Toshihiro Arai (J), Eamonn Boland (IRL), Abdullah Al-Qassimi (UAE) 0

2008 FIA World Rally Championship / Manufacturers

MANUFACTURERS	1. Monte-Carlo	2. Sweden	3. Mexico	4. Argentina	5. Jordan	6. Italy	7. Greece	8. Turkey	9. Finland	10. Germany	11. New Zealand	12. Spain	13. France	14. Japan	15. Great Britain	TOTAL
1. Citroën Total World Rally Team	11	4	10	16	9	14	15	11	15	18	18	18	10	6	16	191
2. BP Ford Abu Dhabi World Rally Team	8	18	11	7	13	14	10	18	9	7	6	11	14	18	9	173
3. Subaru World Rally Team	10	6	9	8	6	3	8	3	9	7	5	6	7	6	5	98
4. Stobart VK M-Sport Ford Rally Team	8	8	3	3	7	5	3	4	4	6	0	4	7	2	3	67
5. Suzuki World Rally Team	2	3	0	1	0	1	3	0	2	1	7	0	1	7	6	34
6. Munchi's Ford World Rally Team			6	4	4	2	0	3	0		3	0		0		22

REGULATIONS: DRIVERS' CHAMPIONSHIP : All result count. 1st - 10 points, 2nd - 8 points, 3rd - 6 points, 4th - 5 points, 5th - 4 points, 6th - 3 points, 7th - 2 points, 8th - 1 point.
MANUFACTURERS' CHAMPIONSHIP: To be eligible, the constructors who have registered with FIA, must take part in all the events with a minimum of two cars. The first two cars score the points according to their finishing position. All results are taken into consideration. Points scale is the same as for the drivers.

World Championship for Manufacturers

1973	Alpine-Renault	1982	Audi	1991	Lancia	2000	Peugeot
1974	Lancia	1983	Lancia	1992	Lancia	2001	Peugeot
1975	Lancia	1984	Audi	1993	Toyota	2002	Peugeot
1976	Lancia	1985	Peugeot	1994	Toyota	2003	Citroën
1977	Fiat	1986	Peugeot	1995	Subaru	2004	Citroën
1978	Fiat	1987	Lancia	1996	Subaru	2005	Citroën
1979	Ford	1988	Lancia	1997	Subaru	2006	Ford
1980	Fiat	1989	Lancia	1998	Mitsubishi	2007	Ford
1981	Talbot	1990	Lancia	1999	Toyota	2008	Citroën

World Championship for Drivers

1977	Sandro Munari (I)	1988	Miki Biasion (I)	1999	Tommi Makinen (SF)
1978	Markku Alen (SF)	1989	Miki Biasion (I)	2000	Marcus Grönholm (SF)
1979	Bjorn Waldegaard (S)	1990	Carlos Sainz (E)	2001	Richard Burns (GB)
1980	Walter Rohrl (D)	1991	Juha Kankkunen (SF)	2002	Marcus Grönholm (SF)
1981	Ari Vatanen (SF)	1992	Carlos Sainz (E)	2003	Petter Solberg (N)
1982	Walter Rohrl (D)	1993	Juha Kankkunen (SF)	2004	Sébastien Loeb (F)
1983	Hannu Mikkola (SF)	1994	Didier Auriol (F)	2005	Sébastien Loeb (F)
1984	Stig Blomqvist (S)	1995	Colin McRae (GB)	2006	Sébastien Loeb (F)
1985	Timo Salonen (SF)	1996	Tommi Makinen (SF)	2007	Sébastien Loeb (F)
1986	Juha Kankkunen (SF)	1997	Tommi Makinen (SF)	2008	Sébastien Loeb (F)
1987	Juha Kankkunen (SF)	1998	Tommi Makinen (SF)		

1977-1978: FIA Cup for drivers

2008 FIA Production Car World Rally Championship (for drivers)

	DRIVERS	Nationalities	1. Sweden	2. Argentina	3. Greece	4. Turkey	5. Finland	6. New Zealand	7. Japan	8. Great Britain	TOTAL
1.	Andreas Aigner	(A)	0	10	10	10	-			8	38
2.	Juho Hänninen	(FIN)	10		2		10	4	10	-	36
3.	Jari Ketomaa	(FIN)	8	6	-		6	3		5	28
4.	Patrik Sandell	(S)	6	-	-	8		8			22
5.	Martin Prokop	(CZ)	5	2	0	Exc.		10		-	17
6.	Martin Rauam	(EE)			4	Exc.	5		6	-	15
7.	Fumio Nutahara	(J)		5	5		4	-	1	-	15
8.	Armindo Araujo	(P)	2		6	4		0	0	2	14
9.	Bernardo Sousa	(P)	1	1	8	0		2		0	12
10.	Patrik Flodin	(S)	0				Exc.			10	10
11.	Mirco Baldacci	(I)		-	-	6		-	3	-	9
12.	Toshihiro Arai	(J)	3	-	-	-		-	6		9
13.	Evgeny Novikov	(RUS)		-	0	-		-	8	-	8
14.	Sebastián Beltrán	(RA)		8							8
15.	Jussi Valimaki	(FIN)					8				8
16.	Guy Wilks	(GB)								6	6
17.	Evgeny Aksakov	(RUS)	0	0	4	-	2			-	6
18.	Evgeny Vertunov	(RUS)	-		3	3	-	-			6
19.	Eyvind Brynildsen	(N)	0		-	-	0		5		5
20.	Oscar Svedlund	(S)	-				5				5
21.	Hayden Paddon	(NZ)						5			5
22.	Uwe Nittel	(D)	4	-	-	-					4
23.	Takuma Kamada	(J)							4		4
24.	Jaromir Tarabus	(CZ)								4	4
25.	Amjad Farrah	(JOR)		3	0	-					3
26.	Spyros Pavlides	(CY)		0	-			0		3	3
27.	Jussi Tiippana	(FIN)	0				3				3
28.	Simone Campedelli	(I)	0	0	-	2	1			0	3
29.	Katsuhiko Taguci	(J)							2		2
30.	Giorgio Bacco	(I)		0		1		-			1
31.	David Higgins	(GB)								1	1
32.	Loris Baldacci	(I)		1					-		1
33.	Stewart Taylor	(NZ)						1			1
34.	Gianluca Linari (I), Fabio Frisiero (I), Liu Cao Dong (C), Subhan Aksa (IND), Stefano Marrini (I),										0
39.	Nasser Al-Attiyah (Q), Naren Kumar (IND), Giovanni Manfrinato (I), Lambos Athanassoulas (GR),										0
43.	Riccardo Errani (I), Yasunori Hagiwara (J), Travis Pastrana (US), Ken Block (US), Andrej Jereb (SLO)										0

Production Car Championship (Gr. N)

- 1987 Alex Fiorio (I)
- 1988 Pascal Gaban (B)
- 1989 Alain Oreille (F)
- 1990 Alain Oreille (F)
- 1991 Grégoire de Mevius (B)
- 1992 Grégoire de Mevius (B)
- 1993 Alex Fassina (I)
- 1994 Jesus Puras (E)
- 1995 Rui Madeira (PT)
- 1996 Gustavo Trelles (RO)
- 1997 Gustavo Trelles (RO)
- 1998 Gustavo Trelles (RO)
- 1999 Gustavo Trelles (RO)
- 2000 Manfred Stohl (D)
- 2001 Gabriel Pozzo (RA)
- 2002 Karamjit Singh (MAL)
- 2003 Martin Rowe (GB)
- 2004 Niall McShea (GB)
- 2005 Toshihiro Arai (J)
- 2006 Nasser Al-Attiyah (Q)
- 2007 Toshihiro Arai (J)
- 2008 Andreas Aigner (A)

2008 FIA Junior World Rally Championship (for drivers)

	DRIVERS	Nationalities	1. Mexico	2. Jordan	3. Italy	4. Finland	5. Germany	6. Spain	7. France	TOTAL
1.	Sébastien Ogier	(F)	10	10	4		10	-	8	42
2.	Aaron Burkart	(D)	5		6	5	8	6	4	34
3.	Martin Prokop	(CZ)	2		0	10	-	10	10	32
4.	Shaun Gallagher	(IRL)	3	8	5	4	5	5		30
5.	Michal Kosciuszko	(PL)	6	-	10	6		0	-	22
6.	Alessandro Bettega	(I)		-	8	-	6	8	-	22
7.	Patrik Sandell	(S)	4	-	2	8		4	3	21
8.	Jaan Mölder	(EE)	8	-	0	-		3	0	11
9.	Stefano Albertini	(I)		4	3	0	0	2	0	9
10.	Gilles Schammel	(LUX)	6		2	-	-		0	8
11.	Florian Niegel	(D)	5	-		0	1	0	2	8
12.	Simone Bertolotti	(I)	3	-		0	4	1	-	8
13.	Kevin Abbring	(NL)	-			3	3	0	1	7
14.	Pierre Campana	(F)						6		6
15.	Pierre Marche	(F)						5		5
16.	Andrea Cortinovis	(I)		2	0		2			4
17.	Hans Weijs Jr.	(NL)		-	1	1	-		0	2
18.	Francesco Fanari	(I)	1	0	0	0	0			1
19.	Milos Komljenovic	(SER)	-	1		0				1
20.	Kalle Pinomaki	(FIN)				-				0
21.	Kris Meeke	(GB)						-		0

World Junior Championship

- 2001 Sébastien Loeb (F)
- 2002 Daniel Solà (E)
- 2003 Brice Tirabassi (F)
- 2004 Per-Gunnar Andersson (S)
- 2005 Daniel Sordo (E)
- 2006 Patrik Sandell (S)
- 2007 Per-Gunnar Andersson (S)
- 2008 Sébastien Ogier (F)

DRIVERS WHO HAVE WON WORLD CHAMPIONSHIP RALLIES FROM 1973 TO 2008

DRIVERS	NATIONALITIES	Nbr. of VICTORIES	RALLIES
Andrea Aghini	(I)	1	**1992** I
Pentti Airikkala	(FIN)	1	**1989** GB
Markku Alen	(FIN)	20	**1975** P · **1976** FIN · **1977** P · **1978** P, FIN, I · **1979** FIN · **1980** FIN · **1981** P · **1983** F, I · **1984** F · **1986** I, USA · **1987** P, GR, FIN · **1988** S, FIN, GB
Alain Ambrosino	(F)	1	**1988** CI
Ove Andersson	(S)	1	**1975** EAK
Jean-Claude Andruet	(F)	3	**1973** MC · **1974** F · **1977** I
Didier Auriol	(F)	20	**1988** F · **1989** F · **1990** MC, F, I · **1991** I · **1992** MC, F, GR, RA, FIN, AUS · **1993** MC · **1994** F, RA, I · **1995** F · **1998** E · **1999** C · **2001** E
Fulvio Bacchelli	(I)	1	**1977** NZ
Bernard Beguin	(F)	1	**1987** F
Miki Biasion	(I)	17	**1986** RA · **1987** MC, RA, I · **1988** P, EAK, GR, USA, I · **1989** MC, P, EAK, GR, I · **1990** P, RA · **1993** GR
Stig Blomqvist	(S)	11	**1973** S · **1977** S · **1979** S · **1982** S, I · **1983** GB · **1984** S, GR, NZ, RA, CI
Walter Boyce	(CDN)	1	**1973** USA
Philippe Bugalski	(F)	2	**1999** E, F
Richard Burns	(GB)	9	**1998** EAK · **1999** GR, AUS, GB · **2000** EAK, P, RA, GB · **2001** NZ
Ingvar Carlsson	(S)	2	**1989** S, NZ
Roger Clark	(GB)	1	**1976** GB
Gianfranco Cunico	(I)	1	**1993** I
Bernard Darniche	(F)	7	**1973** MA · **1975** F · **1977** F · **1978** F · **1979** MC, F · **1981** F
François Delecour	(F)	4	**1993** P, F, E · **1994** MC
Ian Duncan	(EAK)	1	**1994** EAK
François Duval	(B)	1	**2005** AUS
Per Eklund	(S)	1	**1976** S
Mikael Ericsson	(S)	2	**1989** RA, FIN
Kenneth Eriksson	(S)	6	**1987** CI · **1991** S · **1995** S, AUS · **1997** S, NZ
Tony Fassina	(I)	1	**1979** I
Guy Frequelin	(F)	1	**1981** RA
Marcus Grönholm	(FIN)	30	**2000** S, NZ, F, AUS · **2001** FIN, AUS, GB · **2002** S, CY, FIN, NZ, AUS · **2003** S, NZ, RA · **2004** FIN · **2005** FIN, J · **2006** MC, S, GR, FIN, TR, NZ, GB · **2007** S, I, GR, FIN, NZ
Sepp Haider	(A)	1	**1988** NZ
Kyosti Hamalainen	(FIN)	1	**1977** FIN
Mikko Hirvonen	(FIN)	7	**2006** AUS · **2007** N, J, GB · **2008** JOR, TR, J
Mats Jonsson	(S)	2	**1992** S · **1993** S
Harry Kallstom	(S)	1	**1976** GR
Juha Kankkunen	(FIN)	23	**1985** EAK, CI · **1986** S, GR, NZ · **1987** USA, GB · **1989** AUS · **1990** AUS · **1991** EAK, GR, FIN, AUS, GB · **1992** P · **1993** EAK, RA, FIN, AUS, GB · **1994** P · **1999** RA, FIN
Anders Kullang	(S)	1	**1980** S
Jari-Matti Latvala	(FIN)	1	**2008** S
Piero Liatti	(I)	1	**1997** MC
Sébastien Loeb	(F)	47	**2002** D · **2003** MC, D, I · **2004** MC, S, CY, TR, D, AUS · **2005** MC, NZ, I, CY, TR, GR, RA, D, F, E · **2006** MEX, E, F, RA, I, D, J, CY · **2007** MC, MEX, P, RA, D, E, F, IRL · **2008** MC, MEX, RA, I, GR, FIN, D, NZ, E, F, GB
Colin McRae	(GB)	25	**1993** NZ · **1994** NZ, GB · **1995** NZ, GB · **1996** GR, I, E · **1997** EAK, F, I, AUS, GB · **1998** P, F, GR · **1999** EAK, P · **2000** E, GR · **2001** ARG, CY, GR · **2002** GR, EAK
Timo Makinen	(FIN)	4	**1973** FIN, GB · **1974** GB · **1975** GB
Tommi Mäkinen	(FIN)	24	**1994** FIN · **1996** S, EAK, RA, FIN, AUS · **1997** P, E, RA, FIN · **1998** S, RA, NZ, FIN, I, AUS · **1999** Mc, S, NZ, I · **2000** MC · **2001** MC, POR, EAK · **2002** MC
Markko Märtin	(EE)	5	**2003** GR, FIN · **2004** MEX, F, E
Shekhar Mehta	(EAK)	5	**1973** EAK · **1979** EAK · **1980** EAK · **1981** EAK · **1982** EAK
Hannu Mikkola	(FIN)	18	**1974** FIN · **1975** MA, FIN · **1978** GB · **1979** P, NZ, GB, CI · **1981** S, GB · **1982** FIN, GB · **1983** S, P, RA, FIN · **1984** P · **1987** EAK
Joaquim Moutinho	(P)	1	**1986** P
Michèle Mouton	(F)	4	**1981** I · **1982** P, GR, BR
Sandro Munari	(I)	7	**1974** I, CDN · **1975** MC · **1976** MC, P, F · **1977** MC
Jean-Pierre Nicolas	(F)	5	**1973** F · **1976** MA · **1978** MC, EAK, CI
Alain Oreille	(F)	1	**1989** CI
Jesus Puras	(E)	1	**2001** FR
Gilles Panizzi	(F)	6	**2000** F, I · **2001** IT · **2002** F, E, I · **2003** E
Rafaelle Pinto	(P)	1	**1974** P
Jean Ragnotti	(F)	3	**1981** MC · **1982** F · **1985** F
Jorge Recalde	(RA)	1	**1988** RA
Walter Röhrl	(D)	14	**1975** GR · **1978** GR, CDN · **1980** MC, P, RA, I · **1982** MC, CI · **1983** MC, GR, NZ · **1984** MC · **1985** I
Harri Rovanperä	(FIN)	1	**2001** S
Bruno Saby	(F)	2	**1986** F · **1988** MC
Carlos Sainz	(E)	26	**1990** GR, NZ, FIN, GB · **1991** MC, P, F, NZ, RA · **1992** EAK, N, E, GB · **1994** GR · **1995** MC, P, E · **1996** RI · **1997** GR, RI · **1998** MC, NZ · **2000** CY · **2002** RA · **2003** TR · **2004** RA
Timo Salonen	(FIN)	11	**1977** CDN · **1980** NZ · **1981** CI · **1985** P, GR, NZ, RA, FIN · **1986** FIN, GB · **1987** S
Armin Schwarz	(D)	1	**1991** E
Kenjiro Shinozuka	(J)	2	**1991** CI · **1992** CI
Joginder Singh	(EAK)	2	**1974** EAK · **1976** EAK
Petter Solberg	(N)	13	**2002** GB · **2003** CY, AUS, F, GB · **2004** NZ, GR, J, GB, I · **2005** S, MEX, GB
Patrick Tauziac	(F)	1	**1990** CI
Jean-Luc Thèrier	(F)	5	**1973** P, GR, I · **1974** USA · **1980** F
Henri Toivonen	(FIN)	3	**1980** GB · **1985** GB · **1986** MC
Ari Vatanen	(FIN)	10	**1980** GR · **1981** GR, BR, FIN · **1983** EAK · **1984** FIN, I, GB · **1985** MC, S
Bjorn Waldegaard	(S)	16	**1975** S, I · **1976** I · **1977** EAK, GR, GB · **1978** S · **1979** GR, CDN · **1980** CI · **1982** NZ · **1983** CI · **1984** EAK · **1986** EAK, CI · **1990** EAK
Achim Warmbold	(D)	2	**1973** PL, A
Franz Wittmann	(A)	1	**1987** NZ

A: Austria, AUS: Australia, B: Belgium, BG: Bulgaria, BR: Brazil, C: China, CDN: Canada, CI: Ivory Coast, CY: Cyprus, CZ: Czech Republic, D: Germany, E: Spain, EAK: Kenya, EE: Estonia, F: France, FIN: Finland, GB: Great Britain, GR: Greece, H: Hungary, I: Italy, IRL: Ireland, J: Japan, JOR: Jordan, LT: Lithuania, MA: Marocco, MAL: Malaysia, MX: Mexico, MC: Monte-Carlo, N: Norway, NZ: New Zealand, PE: Peru, PL: Poland, PT: Portugal, PY: Paraguay, QAT: Qatar, RA: Argentina, RI: Indonesia, RL: Leganon, RO: Romania, ROK: Republic of Korea, RSM: San Marino, RUS: Russia, S: Sweden, SK: Slovakia, SLO: Slovenia, TR: Turkey, UAE: United Arab Emirates, USA : United States of America, ZW: Zimbabwe.